Young Shakespeare's Young Hamlet

History of Text Technologies, developed in conjunction with an interdisciplinary research program at Florida State University, is dedicated to new scholarship and theory in the history of books and, more generally, the transformation of sign systems into engineered objects. This exciting new series moves from the analysis of texts as material objects to the analysis of texts as material agents. It is committed to the recognition that texts cannot be separated from the various and changing technologies through which they are created. Included are analytic bibliography, paleography and epigraphy, history of authorship, history of reading, study of manuscript and print culture, and history of media. Rather than being solely a historical overview, this series seeks out scholarship that provides a frame for understanding the consequences of both globalism and technology in the circulation of texts, ideas, and human culture. For more on the series, see the History of Text Technologies website at http://hott.fsu.edu.

Series Editors

Gary Taylor is George Matthew Edgar Professor of English and the founding director of the History of Text Technologies program at Florida State University.

A.E.B. Coldiron is Professor of English, and Courtesy Professor of French, at Florida State University.

Francois Dupuigrenet Desroussilles is Professor of Religion at Florida State University.

Published Volumes in Series

Mapping Ethnography in Early Modern Germany: New Worlds in Print Culture
Stephanie Leitch

Literary Folios and Ideas of the Book in Early Modern England
Francis X. Connor

Shakespeare and the Imprints of Performance
J. Gavin Paul

Young Shakespeare's Young Hamlet: Print, Piracy, and Performance
Terri Bourus

Young Shakespeare's Young Hamlet

Print, Piracy, and Performance

Terri Bourus

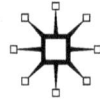

YOUNG SHAKESPEARE'S YOUNG HAMLET
Copyright © Terri Bourus, 2014.

All rights reserved.

First published in 2014 by
PALGRAVE MACMILLAN®
in the United States—a division of St. Martin's Press LLC,
175 Fifth Avenue, New York, NY 10010.

Where this book is distributed in the UK, Europe and the rest of the world, this is by Palgrave Macmillan, a division of Macmillan Publishers Limited, registered in England, company number 785998, of Houndmills, Basingstoke, Hampshire RG21 6XS.

Palgrave Macmillan is the global academic imprint of the above companies and has companies and representatives throughout the world.

Palgrave® and Macmillan® are registered trademarks in the United States, the United Kingdom, Europe and other countries.

ISBN: 978–1–137–46561–0

Library of Congress Cataloging-in-Publication Data is available from the Library of Congress.

A catalogue record of the book is available from the British Library.

Design by Newgen Knowledge Works (P) Ltd., Chennai, India.

First edition: October 2014
10 9 8 7 6 5 4 3 2 1

For Rocky, who never stops fighting for me

Contents

List of Illustrations	ix
The History of Text Technologies: General Editor's Preface	xi
Acknowledgments	xv
Prologue: Questions	1
1 Piratical Publishers?	11
2 Piratical Actors?	35
3 Piratical Reporters?	69
4 How Old Is Young?	101
5 Young Shakespeare?	137
6 Revising *Hamlet*?	181
Epilogue: Conclusions and Rebeginnings	209
Notes	213
Works Cited	265
Index	281

Illustrations

Figures

4.1 A 30-something Gertrude (Imogen Stubbs) tries to pacify a sulky, adolescent Hamlet (Ben Whishaw) in the second scene of *Hamlet*, dir. Trevor Nunn (Old Vic, 2004). Photo by Alastair Muir ... 118

4.2 The Queen (Terri Bourus) kneels and swears to conspire with her son Hamlet, still dressed in the threateningly offensive teenage combination of Marine Corps jacket and swastika armband (Thomas Cardwell) in *Young Hamlet*, dir. Terri Bourus (Hoosier Bard, 2011). Photo by John Gentry ... 125

4.3 An out-of-control teenage Hamlet (Ben Whishaw) in the "Mousetrap" scene in *Hamlet*, dir. Trevor Nunn (Old Vic, 2004). Photo by Alastair Muir ... 126

4.4 A teenage Hamlet (Joshua McGuire) comforted by Ophelia (Jade Anouka) in a touring production of *Hamlet*, dir. Dominic Dromgoole (Shakespeare's Globe, 2011). Photo by Fiona Moorhead ... 127

4.5 A teenage Hamlet (Thomas Cardwell) berates a grandfatherly Corambis (Stephen Scull) in *Young Hamlet*, dir. Terri Bourus (Hoosier Bard, 2011). Photo by John Gentry ... 129

4.6 Hamlet (Thomas Cardwell) in the "Mousetrap" scene in *Young Hamlet*, dir. Terri Bourus (Hoosier Bard, 2011). Photo by John Gentry ... 130

Tables

2.1 Possible "actors' additions" ... 47
2.2 Irace's list of "actors' additions" in the 1603 edition ... 50

The History of Text Technologies: General Editor's Preface

Texts and images are not just isolated, inert material objects; they are also material agents, made by material agents, catalyzing other material agents. As D. F. McKenzie's phrase "sociology of texts" implies, the relationship of one text to others entails relationships to human makers and human users. Texts cannot be separated from the various, overlapping, and restless human technologies through which those texts are created and then do the cultural work that texts do. To recognize that texts depend upon technologies does not imply any simplistic technological determinism. But that recognition does encourage us to focus on change rather than stability: changes in technology, changes in culture, and the changing relationship between the two.

Text/image technologies have historically been irresistibly invasive and transformative. Unlike most areas of humanities research, the history of text technologies is not limited to a particular nationality, language, or geographical area. "The technologizing of the word," as Walter Ong called it, is best understood as the multimillennial evolution and dispersal of increasingly complicated, comprehensive, and multisensory artificial memory systems that have driven human cultural evolution. Those memory machines, because they are prosthetic, are proximity engines, recording some part of a culture in a portable form that can then be transmitted and translated into another culture. Travelers like Marco Polo and John Smith could record their own transnational experience in text-packages, which then traveled even more extensively than they had. Texts are travelers, pioneers, immigrants, and founding fathers. The text that has influenced European and American cultures more than any other, "The Book," the Bible, migrated from Hebrew and Greek into Latin and then into every European and most native American vernaculars. Texts are time-traveling technologies, too, what Joseph Roach calls "time portals": they can connect two cultures separated by time as well as space. Through texts, Dante could feel a profound personal relationship to Virgil, who had been dead for more than a thousand years, and Montaigne could write one of the most powerful expressions of his own individuality through an essay, "On Some Verses of Virgil." The study of text technologies thus is the ideal engine of interdisciplinary transformation and integration in the humanities, because those technologies for textualizing words and images cross the boundaries that separate nations, ethnicities, and religions. Against the fragmenting of the humanities into ever-smaller identity categories, this series studies the mechanisms by which inherited identities are connected and transformed.

Those mechanisms are not only material, economic, and political but also aesthetic. As they enable, exploit, extend, transform, or resist certain artistic possibilities, text technologies are inevitably also aesthetic technologies. They create media platforms that shape, and are shaped by, evolving and contested generic categories and ideals. The collector's interest in the medieval illuminated manuscript, the Dürer print, or the seventeenth-century French folio as an *objet d'art* in its own right mirrors the bibliographer's interest in artisanal routines and material products of the book trade. The history of the forms of texts is also a history of human culture in its largest sense, a history that speaks to how we use texts and images to establish ways of thinking, means of knowing, practices of living, assemblings of identity, and definitions of "the beautiful."

Such histories do not simply turn toward the past as an escape from the present. They frame and shape our understanding of possible transnationalisms, possible synesthesias, possible genres of humanness. These histories are explorations of incarnate becomings. And we hope that they will come to be a part of every reader's own becoming.

Certainly, *Young Shakespeare's Young Hamlet* has been a part of my own becoming. It is a study of the changes between the three early texts of *Hamlet*, and of how those English texts change a French Renaissance novella about medieval Denmark. In tracing the relationship between textual change and textual stability, Terri Bourus challenges the paradigms that have governed our assumptions about early modern publishers, piracy, memorial transmission, the relationship between the media of manuscript and performance, the changing technologies of note-taking and the rise of professional reporters. I edited *Hamlet* thirty years ago for the Oxford University Press edition of *Shakespeare's Complete Works*. Bourus has convinced me that I was wrong about the early texts of *Hamlet*, wrong about the 1589 reference to *Hamlet*, wrong about the date(s) of Hamlet, wrong about Shakespeare's changing relationship to the play. Even readers who disagree with this original and transformative book will need new evidence to answer the questions that Bourus raises: this book will change our research agendas, and our understanding of the most famous play in English.

GARY TAYLOR

Acknowledgments

This book has been a long time coming and so I've not only accumulated a lot of debts along the way, but also owe a lot of accumulated interest to people who believed in me enough to invest in my work. The first among them is my longtime teacher, mentor, and friend, William Proctor Williams. Through him I first became fascinated with the early modern book trade and he has continued to contribute to my research in the years since, providing invaluable feedback on many drafts of this book. I can never thank him enough.

Two scholars from Indiana University (IU) guided me through the morass of grant-writing and the other research needs of a new tenure-track teacher-scholar: the late Albert Wertheim and the late Peter Lindenbaum. Would that they were here to see this work come to fruition. John G. Rudy led by example and taught me to listen to my heart and to remain steadfast in my belief in the life of the mind—no matter what. Rare book curators, John Goldfinch and the staff at the British Library, and Stephen Tabor and the staff of the Huntington Library, gave me indispensable time and personal assistance. An NEH grant allowed me valuable sustained research time in Antwerp, Oxford, and London, as did several New Frontiers' Grants from IU. Ralph M. Cohen at the American Shakespeare Center first offered me the opportunity to combine performance and scholarship. Two research theatres—Blackfriars in Staunton, Virginia, and Shakespeare's New Globe in London—have been essential to the development of this project, and more generally to my attempts to negotiate the relationship between my career as a professional theatre practitioner and my career as a professional scholar. Dean William Blomquist, at the IU School of Liberal Arts at Indiana University Purdue University Indianapolis, has consistently and generously supported my scholarship and my theatre work, and understood the importance of that combination; so too has IU president Michael McRobbie.

I could not have finished this book without the support of my colleagues and my many wonderful students, past and present; the generosity and professionalism of our department administrative assistant, Wanda Colwell; or the tech-savvy assistance of my former student and current administrative assistant for the New Oxford Shakespeare (NOS) project, Chad Andrews. Finally, Gary Taylor invited me to collaborate on NOS precisely because he believed in the importance of uniting the practicalities of performance with the practicalities of book production and scholarly editing. He also helped me to create Hoosier Bard Productions, and to test my theories about a young Hamlet in performance. All the cast and crew of that 2011 Hoosier Bard production have left their mark on this book, especially our own young Hamlet, Thomas Cardwell.

George Walton Williams, Jay Halio, and Thomas L. Berger read the earliest incarnations of what would become this book and encouraged and advised me. Most recently, Andrew Gurr, Gabriel Egan, John Jowett, MacDonald P. Jackson, and Gary Taylor read and commented on a late draft; Mark Bland, David Gants, Farah Karim-Cooper, and Laurie Maguire read individual chapters. They each, in their own ways, saved me from many mistakes and inspired me to many new thoughts.

Finally, *Hamlet* is a play about family and I am lucky in the one that surrounds me. I owe to my grandmother, the late Catherine Margaret Welch Jackson, and to my mother, the late Elizabeth Anne Jackson Bourus, my lifelong fascination with music, dance, and the love of a good story. To my nine sisters and brothers, my sense of humor and wonder, and of the possible. And especially to my children, Mary and Katharine, Amy and Albert: you are always at the center of my heart and are, therefore, central to this and all of my work.

Prologue: Questions

"I'll call thee Hamlet!"

Between 1603 and 1623, three radically different versions of a play called *Hamlet*, all attributed to Shakespeare, were printed in London. Why?

The first two versions were published by one publishing house, and the third by its successor. Why?

Between 11 June 1594, and 24 January 1637, a play called *Hamlet* was repeatedly performed in and around London, always by the same acting company. Why?

The first of the three printed versions makes Hamlet much younger than the other two. Why?

Our collective failure to provide a satisfactory answer to the first question is due, in part at least, to our failure to remember the second, third, and fourth. More generally, the failure to solve all four problems results from a collective misremembering that began in 1825.

* * *

The relationship between the three early printed versions of *Hamlet* is the most complicated and important textual problem in the study of Shakespeare. But it is not just an editorial or bibliographical technicality. All three versions reproduce many of the same sentences and stage directions, but each of the three preserves some dialogue and action that is not present in the other two, and each of the three contains unique errors. The three tell the story in different ways, and those differences affect our sense of the play's meaning, sometimes locally, sometimes globally. Moreover, references to a tragedy about Hamlet stretch for the entire length of Shakespeare's career, from 1589 to the posthumous publication of his *Comedies, Histories, and Tragedies* in 1623. More than any other of his plays, *Hamlet* has remained constantly in the theatrical repertoire; but it was also the first of his plays to be canonized by a university scholar as appropriate reading for "the wiser sort," and the first to be printed in a way that called attention to its literary quotability. It has never lost that elect status among connoisseurs of literature. The problem of the three texts matters to anyone interested in one of our culture's most celebrated achievements, but it also matters to anyone interested in the relationships between theatre and print, spectators and readers, ephemeral voices and the seemingly fixed authority of ink. It matters to anyone curious about Shakespeare's development as one of the world's most influential artists. It matters to anyone trying to teach a 400-year-old play to high school and college students.

This multifaceted problem cannot be solved by the application of any single method. But because Shakespeare has become such a vast international enterprise, scholars who wish to make a contribution to our understanding of his work almost inevitably are forced to become specialists in a single method. Thus, Paul Menzer, himself a playwright with much personal theatrical experience at the American Shakespeare Center, has given us several original insights into issues related to the staging of the early texts of *Hamlet*.[1] But Menzer is not a bibliographer or an historian of print culture. Neither is Brian Walsh, who has illuminated Shakespeare's theatrical evolution from the very different perspective of sixteenth-century theatre history and contemporary performance theory.[2] On the other hand, Patrick Cheney explores Shakespeare's "counter-laureate authorship" and *Hamlet*'s "literary eternal" through a sophisticated readerly analysis of the texts, but he pays no attention to the practicalities of early modern performance or early modern book production.[3] Andrew Murphy does pay attention to the long archival history of Shakespeare as a printed text, a text read in specific editions by many different kinds of readers,[4] and Zachary Lesser has situated early printed editions in the social and political context of the individuals who published them.[5] But neither Murphy nor Lesser is a performer, a theatre historian, or a biographer. Hugh Craig has used computers and statistics to clarify or solve many authorship problems in early modern drama—but he is not a bibliographer or a performance scholar.[6]

The people who are supposed to combine all these talents—bibliography, the history of the book, biography, chronology, authorship, theatre history, performance, the history of critical readings—are editors. Indeed, most editors do juggle these methodologies to a greater or lesser degree. But the nature of their task as editors is to prioritize the confined space of a printed book, to prioritize one text over another, and to accept the priorities set by a publisher. I am an editor myself; indeed, I have edited *Hamlet*.⁷ But the publisher allowed me to print only a single version of the play—and my publisher was not unusual in that respect. The 1986 Oxford University Press edition of Shakespeare's *Complete Works*, revised in 2005, is famous for printing two versions of *King Lear*, instead of just one;⁸ the Norton edition of Shakespeare's *Works*, based on that Oxford text, actually printed three versions of *King Lear*. But both those publishers prioritized *King Lear* over *Hamlet*, giving us multiple *Lear*'s but only a single *Prince of Denmark*. The twenty-first-century Arden Shakespeare ("Arden 3") published all three versions of *Hamlet*—but two of them were lumped together in a more expensive and less accessible separate volume, treated as mere appendices to the diamond in the crown, the 1604 version.⁹ And the most recent edition of Shakespeare's *Complete Works*, the so-called RSC Shakespeare, flaunts its theatrical credentials, but prints only a single version of *Hamlet*.¹⁰ Since the nineteenth century, the single version of *Hamlet* contained in most editions of Shakespeare, including textbooks, combines elements from all three of the original seventeenth-century texts, thereby producing a fourth text that was probably never performed or read in Shakespeare's lifetime, but which is for most people "the" *Hamlet*.

But editors are not the only people forced to choose a single text. Theatres must do the same. Has any theatre ever produced all three versions of *Hamlet,* and run them in repertory? Teachers, too, face the same problem. Very few undergraduate Shakespeare courses survey all of his works; even if we include *Hamlet* in the syllabus of our "Introduction to Shakespeare," the constraints of time compel us to teach, as best we can, only one version of it. Those theatrical and pedagogical limits in turn loop back to publishers, who want to print the book most likely to sell the largest number of copies. What publishers publish and teachers teach inevitably affects what audiences expect, and therefore what theatres feel pressured to supply. The historical reality of three different early printed versions is overwhelmed by the self-reinforcing spiral created by the interactions of publishing, performing, and teaching. All those institutions share a benign desire for simplicity; they want a single text to serve as a shared reference point for different constituencies (students, teachers, scholars, actors, and directors). Together, those institutions create a powerful present-tense pressure for us all to replace the real historical diversity with a single, familiar, magical object. One text to rule them all.

By invoking these institutional pressures, I do not question the intellectual integrity of any individual scholar, theatre-maker, publisher, or teacher. But we are all influenced by what we have been taught; we are all "schooled" to interpret Shakespeare only in some ways but not others. Research monographs about Shakespeare's early texts do not usually consider pedagogy alongside print-shops and theatres, but I think they should. The history of reading is a crucial component of the history of print, and reading begins in schools. As teachers, Liam E. Semler reminds us, "we are engaged in practices that shape and limit the ways students will perceive the world and we ourselves are shaped and limited by the disciplines enveloping us." On a daily basis, we are shepherded, frustrated, and deformed by the "micro-managerial business models" of "educational institutions... increasingly driven by formal procedures that coercively standardize, itemize and instrumentalize teaching and learning," which "tell us what is important and what is nonsense" and "fuel our automatic eruptions of scorn towards 'manifestly' absurd or wrongheaded notions."[11] One of those "manifestly" absurd notions is that Shakespeare wrote the first play about Hamlet. Another is that the first play about Hamlet is preserved in the first printed edition of *Hamlet*.

To entertain such heterodox ideas, to unlearn assumptions that we don't even realize that we are making, we have to resist the institutional spirals that pressure us to be satisfied with a single, standardized text of *Hamlet*. Since those pressures depend upon interacting and interlocking disciplines, our resistance must also harness the engines of all those disciplines. We cannot set print against performance, or authors against readers, or history against biography, or pedagogy against research. Instead of these static binaries, I propose to emphasize the double helix of what I like to call "dramatic intersections."[12] Within the global community of people interested in Shakespeare's work, we need more interaction between book historians and theatre practitioners. Every author, after all, was first a reader, and never ceases to be one. Before he wrote a line of *Hamlet*, Shakespeare read the story of "Amleth" in François de Belleforest's *Les Histoires Tragiques*: a French version of a Latin version of a Danish tale. Shakespeare was also an actor; by 1595 certainly, and probably by mid-1594, he was a sharer in a joint-stock acting company; in 1599 he became part-owner of a theatre. His texts were transmitted by stationers *and* actors, received by readers *and* spectators, and Shakespeare's own writing was stimulated not only by his reading but also by his watching and hearing other plays. When Shakespeare, at the beginning of the seventeenth century, wrote the version of *Hamlet* most familiar to us, he had probably already acted, personally, in an earlier version of *Hamlet*, and he had certainly watched the reactions of audiences to performances of that earlier version of *Hamlet* by his own acting company. We cannot trust any model of Shakespeare's practice as a writer, any method of Shakespearian interpretation, that limits itself to one element of this double helix of creative interaction.

Dramatic intersections, in fact, happen throughout the process of creating, adapting, performing, reading, remembering, teaching, and directing a play. They are the points of reaction that structure the very nature of the experiment, for every performance is an experiment, every book and every theatre and every classroom a kind of laboratory, and at any given point there is a dependency on both memory and anticipation, the leap of an electric spark across the juncture of before and after.[13] Rather like racers in a tag team where one runner strains hard and fast to get to the next, they intersect for one brief moment—long enough to pass the baton—but it is upon those intersections that the success of the race is based. Certainly, Shakespeare's historical success as a global cultural agent depends upon the circulation and preservation of his work in the forms of books, of performances, and of lesson-plans.

Imagine the motion of a text—let's call it *"Hamlet"*—in the four-dimensional space-time of our culture. From a Writer comes the script, created in response to that individual's own reading of books and own experience of the theatre, whether as practitioner or consumer or both. The Writer hands off that script to the next point of the triangle, the Transmitter, a category which envelops the financier-producer, the actors, the physical space and mechanics of the theatre, but also the publisher, the compositors and booksellers, the mechanics of printing, and the physical location of the bookshop. But these two tracks of transmission also interact: actors are readers, publishers and booksellers may be playgoers, people who publish plays certainly have an interest in their marketability, which will initially be based in large part upon their success in the theatre. But their success in bookshops also will have the effect of advertising the vicarious experience for sale in nearby theatres, and their theatrical success will encourage spectators leaving a performance to buy an unbound, cheap, printed copy of the play being peddled to them as they exit.[14] So the success of a play in one transmission-track increases its prospects for success in the other. Books are not the same as performances, theatres are not the same as bookshops, but they intersect and interact.

The Transmitters hand it off to the Receivers, who may be audiences or readers. But those two categories also adjoin and interact. Two of the men who printed early texts of *Hamlet* also owned (at different times) the monopoly on printing playbills, which advertised daily performances in the London theatres; those two printers interacted with theatre companies on a daily basis, year after year. Moreover, many people who go to the theatre also read books, and people who read plays may also watch and listen to them being performed—or may know playgoers, who have recommended a particular title. The intersections and interactions continue. The writer responds to readers and spectators of his work (and other writers' work), but a play-writer also responds, indeed first responds, to the actors who read, memorize, embody, and perform his words. The actors, in turn, respond not only to the writer's catalytic text but also to the members of the audience, the watchers and listeners, who energize and reward (or not) and in any case always affect an actor's moment-by-moment, live, physical interpretation of the script. The audience's responses will determine, at the most basic level, whether the play is given another performance at all. Likewise, the booksellers respond to readers who are also customers, sometimes regular customers, whose reading choices determine the financial viability of a bookshop.

The creative double spirals of book and theatre, object and performance, are continually moving and interacting. While the play-writer is alive, the responses of actor-readers, the responses of the reader-market and audience-market, will restimulate and redirect his own creativity, leading in some cases to revisions of the original script, in other cases to the creation of entirely new plays, incorporating the lessons he has learned from his earlier ones. The writer's death, or retirement, ends his own participation in the spirals, but the end of his own race simply passes the baton on to other writer-interpreters, from Thomas Middleton to Tom Stoppard and on into a writerly future we cannot imagine. Long after the first writer dies, his words are remembered, and actor-readers, writer-adapters, teacher-students, keep reading and reinterpreting them. The intersections and the spirals continue, as long as the memory of the play survives, either in the hardware of a material text or the webware of a human memory.

But there are holes in this model. I have been imagining the category "Transmitter" as containing both actors and publishers; I have been imagining the category "Receiver" as containing both audiences and readers. But what if the actor, or the reader, switches categories? What if the categories intersect? If you've gone to a cinema in England in the last 20 years, you will have seen, before the movie started, a short plea by Federation against Copyright Theft (FACT), warning about the legal and economic consequences of pirating a movie. In the darkness of a cinema, a spectator can now record an entire film on an iPhone or other portable video camera.[15] In the same period, the global music industry has been devastated, and reshaped, by the fact that any customer with an internet connection can now download songs without paying for them. As historian Adrian Johns has demonstrated, debates about piracy and intellectual property, about "the nature of the relationship we want to uphold between creativity, communication and commerce," began with the invention of the printing press.[16] In the twentieth century, one of the most influential textual theories about the early printing of Shakespeare's plays claimed that some of them were the work of "pirates," and the twenty-first-century Arden edition of *Hamlet* considers that the 1603 edition may be a "bootlegged" text; indeed, Johns cites that "unauthorized quarto of Shakespeare's play" as one of the famous episodes of piracy "cited repeatedly" in our own debates about "the definitive transgression of the information age."[17] As readers, or performers, how can we distinguish between the pirate and the writer?

This is only one of the problems with the category "Writer." Shakespeare was an actor, but also a reader, so he belonged to all three categories; they intersected, daily, in his life, his body, his neurons. But in this he was not unique. Publishers are also, often, writers, and they are certainly, always, readers. Other playwrights have also been actors or directors, other writers have been printers, most writers have inscribed and copied their own works, thereby transmitting them to other people. Some readers and spectators write down their responses to what they have read or seen; indeed, our knowledge of early performances of *Hamlet* depends on such memories, sometimes preserved in manuscript, sometimes in print. Individuals can move between different categories, just as texts do.

I look at the early texts of *Hamlet* in terms of these dramatic intersections, creative spirals, and suspected piracies. I have focused upon the first edition, printed in 1603, because it raises most of the problems that have defeated or confused previous scholarship. Also, because it is less familiar, that text opens up relatively unexplored territory. For centuries, editions of the later, canonical version of *Hamlet* have been printed in thousands of editions and translations, in uncounted millions of copies, each corrected by editors and updated with modernized spelling, punctuation, and typography, all designed to make the play more immediately accessible to actors, students, and readers. The 1603 edition, by contrast, was invisible for centuries, and when rediscovered was most often reproduced in unedited, uncorrected transcripts, and in the unfamiliar, alienating costume of old spelling, old punctuation, old conventions of printing and performance. The canonical *Hamlet* has been treated as a poem and a play; the first edition has been treated as a document. Consequently, although I have worked for many years with the original documents (and am myself preparing a digital transcript and a new scholarly edition of those documents), in this book I quote the 1603 version in the same way that scholars, critics, and actors routinely quote the later versions: in an edited text with modern spelling and punctuation. For the same reason, I have generally ignored differences in the spelling of the characters' names (Ofelia/Ophelia, Leartes/Laertes), which are of dubious authority and no significance.

As my title already makes clear, this book argues that the 1603 text represents Shakespeare's earliest version of the play, a version written in the late 1580s, a version that imagines Hamlet as a volatile teenager, in the turmoil of his first love affair, and in rebellion against his mother, his stepfather, and the adult world generally. All six chapters of the book can be read independently, and each chapter will interest some readers more than others: Chapter 1, for instance, will appeal most to historians of the book trade, and chapter 4 will be most engaging to readers interested in performance practices. But my conclusion depends upon the cumulative interaction of all six chapters. In chapter 1, I trace the intersections between printers and publishers who transformed two manuscript versions of *Hamlet* into Nicholas Ling's printed editions of 1603 and 1604. This examination establishes the legitimacy of both publications as reading texts in their own time. In chapter 2, I turn from the book trade to the commercial theatre, and reconsider the relationship between the 1603 edition and early modern actors. This chapter demonstrates that theories of "memorial reconstruction" by an actor-thief cannot account for the 1603 text. In chapter 3, I turn from actors to audiences. This chapter argues that the 1603 text cannot be dismissed as the work of spectators, surreptitiously taking notes during a performance of the play in order to sell their bootlegged text to an unscrupulous printer. These first three chapters all focus upon the history of communication through the media of performance, manuscript, and print; all three consider, and reject, anachronistic claims about piracy. But the claims about piracy are also bolstered by the rejection of authorial revision. For the rest of the book I challenge the piracy narrative by focusing on the alternative theory: that the 1603 text represents an early version of Shakespeare's play. Chapter 4 supports that theory by returning to the play's French source, reconsidering the age of the protagonist, then tracing the related ages of three male characters (Laertes, Fortinbras, Osric) and two female characters (Ophelia and the Queen). Age has political consequences, particularly in a royal family. I relate those issues of age, gender, and politics to the often-demonstrated actability of the 1603 text, and in particular to the women's roles in that version. In chapter 5, I turn from the age of the characters to the age of the text itself. I connect the dots between various pieces of evidence about the intersections between a play called *Hamlet* (which was being performed in London and elsewhere for at least 14 years before it reached print) and an actor-playwright called Shakespeare (who was active on the London stage during those same years). This chapter connects the theatrical world of the late 1580s to the text printed in 1603, and challenges the traditional assumption that Shakespeare did not begin writing plays until 1591. In chapter 6, I return to the intersections between the three printed texts, and explore the implications of the theory of revision on our assumptions about the date and meaning of the canonical, expanded play that we almost always read, teach, and perform. I conclude that *Hamlet*, the most important of his works in terms of the subsequent history of his reputation, was also the play most important to Shakespeare himself, and that it began, in 1602, the run of great tragedies that are his most conspicuous contribution to world culture.

This study, like every account of intersections, is all about relationships. The relationship of one playwright to other writers, living and dead, and to his readers, living and unborn. Shakespeare's relationship to his son, his father, and a young woman named Katherine Hamlett. Shakespeare's relationship to other actors, and the relationship of actors to a script. The relationship of a play, interpreted through the actors, to the audience. The relationship of the early modern stage to the early modern printing house. The interactive relationships between the businessmen who manufactured and sold the printed texts and the readers engaging with words on those printed pages. All these dramatic intersections reflect back to the writer who first took up pen, ink, and paper and created (and recreated) *Hamlet*, a play about the intersection of "the fell incensed points of mighty opposites."

But *Hamlet* is also, of course, a play about memory, in particular a play about the memory of the dead. I imagine the intersections of Writers, Transmitters, and Receivers as a double helix, an image that invokes the biochemical memory-mechanism by which our species reproduces itself. Actors have to memorize their lines. Compositors have to remember words and phrases for long enough to set them into type. Readers have to remember what they have already read (in this text, and other texts) in order to make sense of what they are reading; audiences have to remember what they have already seen (in this play, and other plays) in order to make sense of what they are seeing and hearing. As anyone knows who has witnessed someone they love descending into the oblivion of Alzheimer's disease, all relationships depend upon memory. Shakespeare has been dead for almost four centuries, and our relationship to him, in the library or the classroom or the theatre, depends upon continual renewal of the memory of his texts. The texts of *Hamlet* printed in the early seventeenth century preserve for us, in a material form, the memory of what a dead writer wrote, what dead performers performed, what dead readers read. Those original printed texts, those embodied memories of the dead, are the ghosts that beckon us, that force us, like Hamlet himself, to ask "What may this mean?"

CHAPTER 1

Piratical Publishers?

"What do you read, my lord?"

Tom Stoppard's *Rosencrantz and Guildenstern Are Dead* premiered at the Edinburgh Festival on 24 August 1966. A version of the play then transferred to the National Theatre at the Old Vic, where it opened on 11 April 1967. A version of the text was published by Faber and Faber that year, and the play also opened on Broadway. Asked outside the theatre what the play was about, Stoppard answered (notoriously), "it's about to make me rich." As the copyright holder, he received royalties for performances, book sales, and translations. It has been often reprinted and anthologized. Stoppard revised the first edition, and also directed the 1990 film, further transforming playscript into screenplay.[1] Stoppard retained ownership of the texts of all these incarnations.

Shakespeare, by contrast, could not have retained ownership of the play that inspired Stoppard's. Almost everything we know about Shakespeare's *Hamlet* comes from editions printed between 1603 and 1623. But those machined texts did not belong to Shakespeare, and he would have received no percentage of the profit from book sales. Copyright, in the modern sense, was not created until the eighteenth century. The profits would have gone, instead, to a stationer: a printer or bookseller or publisher who belonged to the Stationers' Company.[2] To understand the early texts of *Hamlet* we must therefore understand the early modern book trade. Unfortunately, "book-trade fallacies have flourished" in textual and literary studies, especially in studies of Shakespeare.[3]

The Worshipful Company of Stationers, granted its royal charter by Queen Mary on 4 May 1557, controlled almost everything to do with the book business. It printed the books; it sold the books; it regulated the conduct of printers and booksellers. However, since the Stationers' Company was also an association of craftsmen and shopkeepers (much like the Butchers, Goldsmiths, Merchant Taylors, Cordwainers, and other London companies), it combined commercial with fraternal aspirations. Members of the Company of Stationers feasted on cakes and ale on Ash Wednesday, feasted at the election of Company officers, feasted for the annual replacement of the paper windows of print shops, and the like.[4] The social aspect of Company life was no doubt enhanced by the fact that (with the exception of the small university towns of Oxford and Cambridge) the Company's charter confined printing in the kingdom to the old medieval walled and incorporated City of London. Consequently, in Shakespeare's lifetime, nearly the whole book trade was crammed in and around St. Paul's Cathedral and its environs.[5] Thus, we must not imagine the business in the sixteenth and early seventeenth centuries in terms of modern large multinational corporations. Think of it, instead, in terms of cottage industries, like a modern dental office, or a local independent bookstore—or, even more precisely, a twenty-first-century microbrewery (an artisanal manufacturing business that often owns its own retail outlet but also seeks wholesale customers). Few printers had more than one press, and even a large operation such as the Jaggards' in the 1620s seems to have engaged fewer than 15 people, including apprentices.[6]

Into this fraternal business environment came the fraternal texts of a play called *Hamlet*. It made its first appearance in print in 1603, no earlier than the end of May. We know its date so precisely because the title page declares that the play had been "acted by his Highnesse servants." The male pronoun "his" refers to King James I, and the word "servants" specifies a company of actors that included William Shakespeare and Richard Burbage, which was rechristened (and upgraded) from the Lord Chamberlain's Men to the King's Men on 19 May 1603.[7] Modern scholars typically refer to this textual object as "Q1 *Hamlet*."[8] Seventeenth-century readers would have recognized it as a "quarto playbook."[9] As Lukas Erne observes, that phrase "encapsulates genre (play), medium (book), and format (quarto) to designate a product with a distinct cultural valence that differs from both the prestigious folio and the smaller-format poetry book."[10] Like most other quarto playbooks, the 1603 edition of *Hamlet* could almost certainly have been purchased for six pence, retail, and most copies were probably sold without a hard binding. Another, longer edition with the same title, author, and publisher—which scholars now call "Q2 *Hamlet*"—was published near the end of 1604.[11] We know its date so precisely because some copies of the title page are dated "1604," and others are dated "1605." This double dating is not unusual.[12] It indicates that printing was completed late in 1604, and that some copies were printed with the later date so that they would still seem "new" throughout the following year. The older a book, the harder it was to sell at full price.[13]

The dates of these two editions are clear enough, but they continue to be misunderstood. The 1603 edition is a Jacobean book, and therefore it could not "have been read during the uneasy final months of Elizabeth's reign," as one Shakespeare scholar claimed in 2012.[14] More importantly, the dates indicate that *Hamlet* sold quickly. A second edition by the same publisher appeared within, at the most, 18 months of the first, or perhaps as few as 12 or 13 months.[15] In the wider context of Shakespeare in the early London book trade, this is not surprising. *Venus and Adonis* was published in four editions in four successive years, then twice in 1599; *Richard II* had three editions in 1597–98; *1 Henry IV*, three editions in 1598–99; *Lucrece* was published twice in 1600; *Richard III* and *Love's Labour's Lost* were each published twice in 1597–98.[16] As a book, *The Tragical History of Hamlet, Prince of Denmark* was Shakespeare's first Jacobean bestseller, and it did much better in bookshops than *King Lear*, *Troilus and Cressida*, or the *Sonnets*.[17] There is absolutely no evidence for the recent conjecture that the second edition of *Hamlet* was "very probably" printed and distributed when "unsold copies" of the first edition remained in stock, which the publisher "still wanted to unload," perhaps "even at a discount."[18] Since the publisher owned what we would now call the copyright, he did not need to finance a second edition until he had unloaded the first. A new edition could be printed quickly enough, once he had exhausted his stock. Even if he acquired another or better manuscript, he had no incentive to rush it into print. No one else could infringe his exclusive right to print that title, so why should he? In any case, why would he want to finance another edition if the first had sold poorly? Moreover, the conjecture assumes that only the publisher had an investment in "unsold copies" that he might have to "sell off" at a discount. Although the publisher certainly retained a fraction of the print-run to sell in his own retail bookshop (perhaps 10%), most of the copies of the first edition would have been sold or traded, at wholesale prices, to other booksellers.[19] Those other booksellers had also invested their meager capital in copies of the first edition. With unsold stock on their hands, they would be most unlikely to purchase from him any copies of the new edition.[20] They would also probably, understandably, be annoyed if he published a premature and expanded second edition, thereby undercutting their chances of selling their own unsold copies of the first. Such behavior would undermine a retailer's faith in the wholesaler, and therefore threaten the publisher's ability to sell other books in future. In the small world of the London book trade, a publisher would have known, personally, the booksellers who were his most important customers. His reputation with those customers was the foundation of his business.

The "his" to whom the last sentence refers was Nicholas Ling. The 1603 edition also named "John Trundle" as copublisher, and the 1604 edition named "James Roberts" as the printer. The printer of the 1603 edition was not named, but we know that the type used to print it belonged to Valentine Simmes.[21] But although Trundle, Roberts, and Simmes played important supporting roles in the story of *Hamlet* as a printed book, Ling was the protagonist. Only two living individuals were identified on both title pages of the first two editions of *Hamlet*: the author "William Shakespeare" and the publisher "N. L."[22] We know that "N.L." was Nicholas Ling, because he normally used his initials on title pages and, in the small world of London stationers at the time, no one else had the same initials. Moreover, each title page conspicuously displayed Ling's large device—what we might call his "logo": a honeysuckle (an anagram for the name "Nicholas") wrapped around a North Atlantic fish (called a "ling"). That logo also contained his initials, which were thus published twice on each title page, and supplemented by a visual pun.[23] Like most Elizabethan writers, Ling apparently loved puns. Together, these three printed incarnations of the stationer's name take up more space on the page than the author's. As commodities in the book trade, both editions belonged to Ling.

They belonged to Ling until his death. On 9 April 1607, he was buried in the parish church of St. Dunstan's-in-the-West.[24] On 19 November of the same year, Ling's intellectual property rights to *Hamlet* and 15 other texts (what we would call his copyrights) were officially transferred to another stationer, John Smethwicke.[25] Smethwicke, like Ling, was working from a bookshop on the north side of Fleet Street, a short walk west of St. Paul's, in the churchyard of St. Dunstan's parish.[26] Ling had occupied a bookshop there since 1598, and from 1602 Ling and Smethwicke were close neighbors in that small churchyard (much smaller than the churchyard of St. Paul's).[27] Both *Hamlet* quartos were sold out of Ling's St. Dunstan's shop, and from St. Dunstan's Smethwicke published *Hamlet* in another "quarto playbook" in 1611. In November 1623, Smethwick was named as one of the four members of the syndicate that published the "Folio" edition of *Mr. William*

Shakespeare His Comedies, Histories, & Tragedies.[28] Most scholars believe that Smethwicke was included in that syndicate because he owned the copyrights to *Hamlet* and three other Shakespeare plays (all acquired from Ling).[29] He reprinted *Hamlet,* again as a stand-alone quarto, in 1625.[30] He was also a member of the syndicate that published the second Folio, in 1632. In 1637, Smethwicke published another reprint of the quarto, the last edition of *Hamlet* before the closing of the theatres in 1642. Thus, the intellectual property rights owned initially by Ling, and then acquired by Smethwicke, underlay all the early editions of *Hamlet,* from 1603 to 1637.

Four different stationers were involved in the publication of the first two editions of *Hamlet,* and soon after a fifth stationer acquired the rights. Consequently, any account of the early printings of *Hamlet* must be a description of "the dynamics of economic, political, and personal association that constitute a key vector of the trade in books."[31] Any theory that focuses on only a single stationer is bound to be misleading. We need to examine, instead, a network. The larger structure of that network was determined by the royal charter of 1557, by links between the Worshipful Company of Stationers and the government of church and state, by the Company's connection to the incorporated City of London and its many other chartered companies (large and small), and by the institutionalized governance of the Stationers' Company itself. These structures have been well described by historians of the trade. But particular nodes in the network were created by one-to-one relationships between individual stationers. In the case of *Hamlet,* the man at the center of that node was Nicholas Ling, who was personally and professionally linked to the four other stationers involved in the publication of *Hamlet* from 1603 to 1637.[32] Those editions were all published and sold by Ling, or in the shadow of his grave in the churchyard of St. Dunstan's-in-the-West.

Ling belongs to the charter generation described by Richard Helgerson: men like Shakespeare, Edmund Spenser, Michael Drayton, William Camden, Edward Coke, Richard Hakluyt, and Richard Hooker, all born between 1551 and 1564, who, in their different ways, made "the writing of England" a "concerted generational project."[33] Of this list of other, more famous men, Nicholas Ling perhaps resembles most closely not Shakespeare but the legal theorist and Parliamentarian Edward Coke; the two men were born within a year of one another and both received their early education in the politically and ecclesiastically important town of Norwich. Ling, who promoted "the writing of England" by editing and publishing it, was born there in 1553. His father, John Lyng, was a freeman rich enough to own several rental properties there by 1570, including two that housed 22 members of eight different families.[34] John was a parchment maker (and his son Robert followed in the family business).[35] Parchment was a traditional luxury commodity important to sixteenth-century textual culture but only peripherally related to the early modern printed-book business.[36] And parchment making was not the only trade that predated print: scriveners also remained a significant occupational group throughout the sixteenth century.[37] The town had a family of binders by the late fourteenth century, and in the Tudor and Stuart period printed books supplied from London would have been transported unbound, to lower shipping costs.[38] Norwich was not a printing center, but in 1568–71 an immigrant Dutchman did print occasionally, as a sideline to his more profitable occupation importing Rhenish wine.[39] Between 1562 and 1568, six Dutch immigrants, part of the large influx of Protestant refugees, were identified as booksellers there.[40] A seventh Norwich bookseller, Robert Scott, received stock on average every two weeks from London: thousands of ballads, and "many hundreds of other small books. including almanacs, primers, horn books, plays and jest books."[41] And Norwich did have ten schoolmasters, and (since 1547) one of King Edward VI's free grammar schools. Given his father's connections and his own future career, it is likely that Nicholas attended it, receiving there the same kind of humanist education that grounded the work of so many of the writers he would go on to publish.[42]

Certainly, when Nicholas was 17, he went to London, where on 29 September 1570 he was bound in an eight-year apprenticeship. His master, Henry Bynneman, was a prominent printer-publisher. But Ling never became a printer, so during those years he presumably worked in the bookselling side of Bynneman's business, waiting on customers, discovering what he liked to read himself, learning what customers liked, and how they could be persuaded to spend more than they anticipated, or to read something unexpected.[43] He also must have learned how to do the bookkeeping, to account for cash flow, costs and profits. Ling was made a freeman of the Stationers' Company (meaning that his apprenticeship had been successfully completed) on 19 January 1579. The next year, with Bynneman's help, Ling published his first title, and soon set up shop in two successive properties in the St. Paul's retail hub, both apparently leased to him by his former master, and containing a significant number of Bynneman's own books.[44]

But Bynneman died in April 1583, and Ling reappeared in Norwich in mid-1585. We can only guess at the reasons for Ling's move, but "by the middle years of the sixteenth century Norwich had become increasingly attractive as the capital city of its region—in effect, a lesser London," according to historian John Pound; "on a reduced scale the city had much the same advantages as the metropolis...and the great fairs, held at regular intervals throughout the year, brought in a vast concourse of people." At least one bookseller's shop seems to have been situated on the street facing the Norwich market, the biggest in East Anglia, held twice a week, and at least one Norwich bookseller died in 1603 with a significant estate.[45] By the mid-1580s, Norwich was experiencing a boom in demand for household goods and other elective or luxury commodities (such as books and ballads).[46] Ling was the first Norwich freeman who registered himself as a "stationer."[47] He probably made his living in the late 1580s as a bookseller there, perhaps converting one of the family rental properties into a shop. Like at least one other Elizabethan stationer, Ling might eventually have run two shops: one in London, and another in his provincial hometown, each supporting the other.[48] I suspect that he might have begun doing so in the second half of the 1580s, moving back and forth between the two locations.[49] Certainly, Ling's hometown remained important to his business (as it remained important to the career of Edward Coke). In 1606, Ling published two books by the Puritan preacher William Burton, who, in his "lucid and homely style," fondly remembered his "five years" in Norwich in the late 1580s, a period of "heavenly harmony" when the city fathers attended sermons "every day" and the common people gave "due obedience" to their spiritual leaders; Burton dedicated one to "the Maior, Shiriffes and Aldermen...in that religious and famous Citie of Norwich."[50] Likewise, although scholars now read Will Kemp's *Nine Days' Wonder* because Kemp had been the leading clown for the Chamberlain's Men in the 1590s, when Ling published it (in the spring of 1600) Kemp's association with Shakespeare's company had ended, and Ling was presumably interested in the little pamphlet because it described, as the title page declares, Kemp's "daunce from London to Norwich." Indeed, when Ling registered his copyright, he ignored London and simply called the book "Kemps *morris to Norwiche*," and it describes at length the celebrity's elaborate welcome by the town's mayor, aldermen, town musicians, social elite and, seemingly, the entire population.[51]

John Lyng died in 1590, and his will demonstrates that Nicholas, although a third son, acquired a substantial inheritance.[52] Unsurprisingly, Nicholas was then able to return to London and expand the business he had begun a decade earlier. Publishing requires a significant capital investment weeks or months or even years before there is a financial return, and the scale of Ling's publishing notably increased between the early 1580s and the early 1590s.[53] Ling's financial resources, combined with his long association with Bynneman, would have assured him an important place in London's book-trade community. He soon owned shares in what would become the English Stock (a lucrative set of shared monopolies, which provided a steady, risk-free income for those who could afford the initial investment). In 1598, he was elected to the livery of the Stationers' Company, and in 1603 became Renter Warden. Ling was 50 years old when he published the first edition of *Hamlet*: a well-established, respected elder statesman in the trade, with strong connections to literary London.

As Zachary Lesser has insisted, publishers "are themselves actual readers," and we can discern something about their reading, their cultural investments and agendas, by examining what they published.[54] Most of Ling's earliest publications were religious works, but there is nothing especially remarkable about his Protestantism or his politics.[55] More interesting, from our perspective, is his "commitment to the developing category of English 'literature.'"[56] He began his career by publishing, in 1580, a moralistic work by Thomas Churchyard and Richard Tarlton. Churchyard had served and learned from the poet Henry Howard, Earl of Surrey, been included in Tottel's influential poetry miscellany, defended the English plain style of Chaucer and Langland, composed pageants for the progresses of Queen Elizabeth, written broadside ballads, and contributed to *The Mirror for Magistrates*.[57] By 1580, he was about 60 years old, and in 1592 Thomas Nashe would acknowledge Churchyard's "aged Muse" as "grand-mother to our grand-eloquentest Poets at this present."[58] A warning poem by Tarlton, the greatest comedian of the period, is appended to Churchyard's account of the 1580 London earthquake; it, too, indicates Ling's interest in contemporary culture, combined with his attachment to the vernacular plain style. The same conservative taste is evident in Ling's second book, Anthony Munday's account of life among recusant Catholic Englishmen in Rome; *The English Romayne Lyfe* could be considered a religious work, but in place of theological subtlety it offers a scandalous travel narrative, written in the digestible, moralistic, middlebrow style that kept Munday employed as a writer for five decades.

When Ling restarted his London career in 1590, he published the first edition of Robert Greene's *Never Too Late*, which he would reprint again in 1599, 1602, and early 1607; he later published reprints of Greene's *Menaphon* (with a preface by Thomas Nashe) in 1599 and 1605, and of

Greene's *Ciceronis Amor* in 1601 and 1605. Greene was, like Ling, from Norwich, born there in 1558.[59] Greene's first book had been entered in the Stationers' Register in 1580, the year that Ling began publishing, and in the next two decades Greene became "the most successful Elizabethan print author."[60] Before Ling published *Hamlet* in 1603, Shakespeare's poetry and plays had been published in an impressive 42 editions, but Greene easily outstripped him with 74. Ling's eight editions of Greene reflect mainstream Elizabethan literary taste.[61] In 1590, Ling also declared another significant literary allegiance when he registered his copyright in Thomas Lodge's new romance, *Rosalynde* (now most famous as the source of Shakespeare's *As You Like It*, but in the sixteenth and seventeenth centuries much more successful as a printed commodity than Shakespeare's comedy).[62] In 1591, Ling published Lodge's *Robert, Duke of Normandy*, and in 1592 registered Lodge's *Euphues Shadow*; over the course of Ling's career he would publish five editions of work by Lodge.

After the severe plague of 1592–3, Ling broadened his literary list. In addition to the anonymous lyric sequence *Zepheria*,[63] he published in 1594 Thomas Kyd's translation of *Cornelia*. But neither of those books was a commercial success. More important, commercially and culturally, was the beginning of Ling's long association with Michael Drayton. *Matilda* and *Idea's Mirror* were the first of 17 Drayton books that Ling would eventually produce; he was clearly Drayton's "chosen publisher."[64] In the second half of the 1590s, Ling added prose by Thomas Nashe and Robert Southwell, alongside poetry by Sir John Davies (the admired philosophical poem *Orchestra*) and, at the other end of the verse spectrum, "the most popular contemporary poet" in England, Nicholas Breton.[65] By the end of his career, Ling had also published George Peele, Thomas Dekker, and Ben Jonson, alongside minor poets like Gervase Markham (translating Ariosto), Christopher Middleton, Edward Guilpin, and John Weever.[66] Finally, Ling was a successful editor and anthologist, who belonged to a circle of middle-class Londoners with an interest in legitimating vernacular literature.[67]

Ling's two editions of *Hamlet* obviously belong to this larger agenda. But what must strike us, from a twenty-first-century perspective, is that everyone now reads *Hamlet*, and almost no one reads any of the other literary works that Ling published. In terms of the scale or quality of his aesthetic investments, Ling shrinks and shrivels by comparison to William Ponsonby, the Elizabethan publisher of Sidney and Spenser, or Ponsonby's apprentice Edward Blount, the London-born and cosmopolitan seventeenth-century publisher of Montaigne, Cervantes, and the Shakespeare Folio, "the greatest literary critic of his generation."[68]

Even among scholars specializing in early modern English literature, most of Ling's titles are obscure, and some are ultra-obscure. Lukas Erne correctly observes that "Ling specialized in literary titles," but Erne does not acknowledge that Ling clearly preferred Drayton, Greene, and Lodge over Shakespeare.[69] Indeed, Ling also put Shakespeare lower on his scale than the "silver-tongued" preacher of the 1580s, Henry Smith, whom Thomas Nashe compared to Ovid, whose death the muses mourned.[70] Smith's sermons were as literary as those of John Donne or Lancelot Andrewes, but Smith's style was Elizabethan, not Jacobean.[71] Smith was also much more popular in print, and much more profitable for Ling, than Shakespeare.[72] *England's Helicon* (1600), which Ling apparently edited, anthologizes only one passage from Shakespeare— putting him behind Peele and Spenser (3 each), Drayton and Munday and Watson (5 each), Greene (7), Breton (8), and even farther behind Lodge (14) and Sidney (15).[73]

Insofar as Ling appreciated Shakespeare at all, he valued him as a poet, not a playwright.[74] Ling first published Shakespeare in excerpts in the important anthology *England's Parnassus* (1600), edited by Robert Allott; but in that collection the two narrative poems *Venus and Adonis* and *Lucrece* provide more than twice as many quotations as all Shakespeare's plays, from the 1590s, put together.[75] Defending his account of Shakespeare as a "literary dramatist," Erne summarizes Ling's credentials as a publisher of literary prose, verse, "and a few playbooks."[76] But even "a few" overestimates Ling's interest in the theatre. He published the first edition of only two play-books: Kyd's *Cornelia* (1594) and Shakespeare's *Hamlet* (1603). *Cornelia* is a translation of Robert Garnier's neoclassical French tragedy of 1574; there is no evidence that the closet drama was ever performed in England, but it was praised by readers (including the wife of the Mayor of London) and excerpted by anthologists.[77] That leaves *Hamlet* (1603) as Ling's one-and-only first edition of a play from the commercial theatres. Ling did publish the third edition of Jonson's *Every Man Out of his Humour*, but reprints are always less risky, and in this case particularly safe, given the speed with which the first and second editions sold out. Moreover, *Every Man Out* explicitly distanced itself from the commercial theatres. The title page of all its early quartos (including Ling's) does not mention any theatre or acting company, offering instead a Latin epigraph and the text *"As it was first composed by the author B.I. Containing more than hath been publikely spoken or acted. With the seuerall character of euery person."* Those quartos end with a defense of the comedy's ending, addressed to the "solide reader."

Ling's reprint of *Every Man Out of his Humour* is as untheatrical as his first edition of Kyd's *Cornelia*. Ling's close associate and first regular "partner," John Busby, started publishing commercial plays in 1599, but Ling did not join him in any of those ventures. Ling's favorite poet, Michael Drayton, wrote all or part of more than 20 commercial plays between 1597 and 1604, but Ling did not publish a single one of them. Nor did Ling publish any of the many commercial plays of other writers on his list (Greene, Lodge, Peele, Nashe, or Kyd). Ling's *Hamlet* thus comes from a publisher, and a business, that had long fostered a clientele primarily interested in nondramatic literature. Zachary Lesser and Peter Stallybrass call the 1603 edition "the First Literary *Hamlet*." Certainly, it was the first Shakespeare play to signpost quotable passages—as did *Cornelia* and *Every Man Out of his Humour*.[78] We have no way of determining whether that signposting was present in the manuscript that Ling acquired, or was added by Ling himself before he sent that manuscript to a printer. But we can say that the 1603 edition contains no actors' names and no duplicated stage directions (the two characteristics that, according to Paul Werstine, are the strongest indications that a text had been used in the playhouse).[79] It contains few music cues (another regular feature of commercial playbooks, as opposed to closet drama). The first edition of *Hamlet* looks like a literary text, not a theatrical one.

But, in saying this, we must also say that Ling's literary taste was old-fashioned, middle-class, and provincial. Ling was never "hip" or "cutting edge" or "groundbreaking." He published successful writers from the 1580s—Churchyard, Tarlton, Kemp, Munday, Greene, Lodge, Smith, Nashe, Peele, and Kyd—before he finally, belatedly published his first Shakespeare title, ten years after Shakespeare began conspicuously making his mark in print. Ling's first Shakespeare title, moreover, was the 1603 edition of *Hamlet*, which has more often than not been despised by literary critics. Consider Hamlet's first speech in that edition :

> My lord, 'tis not the sable suit I wear,
> No, nor the tears that still stand in my eyes,
> Nor the distracted 'havior of the visage,
> Nor all together, mixed with outward semblance,
> Is equal to the sorrow of my heart.
> Him have I lost, I must of force forgo;
> These but the ornaments and suits of woe.

From the perspective of Shakespeare's great Jacobean tragedies (*Othello, King Lear, Macbeth, Antony and Cleopatra, Coriolanus*), this speech, and

Ling's first edition of *Hamlet* generally, does look weak. But perhaps we would better appreciate its literary merits if we compared it to the old-fashioned poetry and old-fashioned prose that Ling admired. Judged by the standards of the 1580s and early 1590s, the first edition of *Hamlet* is a remarkable literary achievement.

Ling's literary investments were cautious. So were his business practices generally, and specifically in relation to the first editions of *Hamlet*. Although this conservatism may simply have been part of his personality, a string of traumatic events early in his bookselling career would have encouraged it. A few months after he ended his apprenticeship, in 1579, Norwich endured the worst outbreak of plague of any English town in the sixteenth or seventeenth century; more than a third of the population perished.[80] London's much less severe plague outbreak was concentrated in the previous year, 1578;[81] but then, in 1580, London was affected by an earthquake (the subject of Ling's first book). These incidents might have encouraged Ling to diversify his business geographically, in the hope that one location would prosper even if the other was devastated by unpredictable and uncontrollable events. Unlike most other stationers, Ling owned rental and/or retail property in Norwich, as well as a bookselling business in London (which for some years at least operated out of two shops, one in St. Paul's churchyard, the other in Fleet Street).

The death of Ling's master and mentor in 1583 might have encouraged a different kind of diversification. Bynneman died deeply in debt, financially overextended by the costs of a huge dictionary project that he did not live to complete. Ling was directly affected by his master's failure, because the dispute over the dead man's estate included valuation of hundreds of Bynneman's books in Ling's own bookshop.[82] Bynneman, like the English book trade more generally throughout the sixteenth century, was badly undercapitalized. Ling did not print the books he published, and so he never heavily invested in printing presses or movable type. As a bookseller, he favored, throughout his career, smaller books, which required a smaller initial investment, and therefore a smaller risk.[83] He never published large, ambitious Folio volumes like some of Bynneman's, which would have tied up too much of his capital in a single speculative project.

Bynneman's printing equipment was acquired by four stationers, who together created the so-called Eliot's Court Press, which prospered for 90 years.[84] Ling never established such a long-lived, formal, legal partnership, but he did adopt a similar business strategy of shared investment and shared risk. Kemp's description of his dance "to Norwich" and Burton's book dedicated to "that religious and famous Citie of Norwich" were two of the few first editions that Ling registered alone and published alone.[85] Most of his books were originally registered with or by someone else, or originally published with or by someone else.[86] The first quarto *Hamlet* belongs to this career-long pattern: the title page announces that Ling copublished it with John Trundle.

Trundle has often been ignored or dismissed by Shakespearians, probably because Q1 *Hamlet* was his only link to Shakespeare.[87] Even in that marginalized book, Trundle played a marginal role: Ling's name was listed first in 1603, and Ling monopolized the copyright after 1603. Unlike Ling, Trundle was just beginning his career.[88] *Hamlet* might even have been his first publication, and consequently we cannot comfortably or confidently situate it within the precedents set by decades of previous work. His only other surviving titles, in that inaugural year (or the next), were two single-sheet plague broadsides. Those broadsides would be characteristic of his subsequent publishing: he specialized in short, inexpensive texts belonging to various genres of ephemera. None of his later books had any cultural prestige at the time, and few of them have acquired such prestige in subsequent centuries (another reason that he has tended to be ignored by literary critics). The fact that he published only broadsheets, pamphlets, and short books demonstrates that his business was even more severely undercapitalized than most. The name of his bookshop was "Nobody," surely an ironic indication of his own status (and that of the customers he was most likely to attract). It was not in the most upscale retail location, and it may also have been a small shop.[89]

Nevertheless, Trundle matters. His subsequent publication of five other plays from the commercial theatres makes his involvement with *Hamlet* unsurprising, and tends to confirm the association of plays with pamphlets.[90] Trundle was a rule-conscious, law-abiding stationer, and those other plays were all apparently acquired from legitimate sources—which means that we have no *prima facie* reason to believe that there was anything suspicious about his involvement with *Hamlet*. Trundle's limited financial resources explain why he collaborated with another bookseller on almost all his titles, including *Hamlet*. Ling, too, often copublished. But Ling had more resources than Trundle, and both stationers sometimes *did* publish texts on their own. If either had been absolutely confident that the entire print-run of a first edition of *Hamlet* would quickly sell out, one or the other would have monopolized the initial investment and the subsequent profit.

The decision to copublish indicates that both Ling and Trundle regarded *Hamlet* as a commercially risky book. This may seem surprising to modern critics. Alan B. Farmer and Zachary Lesser have shown that playbooks were sometimes a profitable printed commodity in the early modern period, and Lukas Erne has argued that Shakespeare, in particular, "occupied a significant place within the London book trade" and "had a commanding bibliographical presence among the dramatists of his time."[91] A string of successful Shakespeare titles had indeed been printed between 1593 and 1599: ten first editions, with 19 reprints by 1600.[92] In those years not a single Shakespeare title had failed to be reprinted at least once. But Peter Blayney's evidence that printed playbooks were not the most profitable or popular investments in the trade remains generally valid. Monopolies and reprints had larger and safer profit margins; religion had a much, much larger market share.[93] And Shakespeare plays became dodgier investments at the beginning of the seventeenth century. Of the five Shakespeare titles first published in 1600 (*2 Henry IV*, *Henry V*, *The Merchant of Venice*, *A Midsummer Night's Dream*, and *Much Ado about Nothing*), only one had been reprinted by 1603 (*Henry V* in 1602). No new Shakespeare plays were published in 1601, and the lone 1602 title (*The Merry Wives of Windsor*) would not be reprinted until 1619, so it obviously did not sell quickly. *Thomas Lord Cromwell* was also printed in 1602, and attributed on its title page to "W.S."; like *Merry Wives*, it was not reprinted until 1619, and cannot have sold quickly. Any bookseller considering publication of a new Shakespeare play in 1603 would have looked back at the last three years and calculated that there was only one chance in seven that the new title would sell well enough to quickly reward the initial investment, turn a profit, and warrant a more profitable reprint. Moreover, in 1603 neither Ling nor Trundle had published anything by Shakespeare, and (as far as we know) neither had published a first edition of a commercial play, either.[94] They were both venturing into new territory, at a time when that territory did not look especially promising. Finally, by the time they published *Hamlet*, London was suffering from the worst plague outbreak in 40 years. Dead people don't buy books; people afraid of catching the plague leave town, or venture out of their houses as little as possible. Plague closed the theatres, too, which meant that playbills and performances would not be providing regular advertisements for a *Hamlet* in bookshops. In these circumstances, it makes perfect economic sense for Ling and Trundle to share the credit, and the risk, for publishing the first edition of *Hamlet*.

Although Ling had not worked with Trundle before their joint investment in the 1603 *Hamlet*, Ling's other collaborator on that edition was an old friend. Indeed, it's virtually certain that Ling, not Trundle, chose

Valentine Simmes to print the edition. Ling and Simmes had both been apprentices in Bynneman's shop, and probably overlapped there.[95] Ling was the older of the two, and also further along in his apprenticeship, and he was always the dominant partner in their relationship. From 1594 to his death in 1607, Ling was Simmes's most regular contractor. Ling employed Simmes for 27 titles. Like his master and mentor Bynneman, Simmes was a skilled and careful craftsman, particularly sensitive to the visual appearance of his books.

> With a good eye for detail and layout, he generally used good paper and careful inking to avoid the show-through that makes many books of the period unreadable. He was thus a printer whose work was certainly at or above the standard of the day.[96]

He had experience printing plays, including five by Shakespeare. Between the years 1597 and 1611, he printed no fewer than 27 quarto editions of plays.[97] There is nothing at all unusual about Simmes being hired to print a playbook, and nothing unusual about Simmes being hired by Ling to print *any* book. From the perspective of the careers of Ling and Simmes, the 1603 quarto of *Hamlet* represents business as usual.

The 1604 quarto of *Hamlet*, too, looks like business as usual. James Roberts replaced Simmes as printer. It was not at all odd for a new edition to be manufactured by a different printer. Indeed, Ling elsewhere repeatedly switched back and forth between his two favorite printers, Roberts and Simmes, on editions of the same title.[98] Finally, although the 1603 edition lists both Ling and Trundle as publishers, in the 1604 edition Trundle has disappeared. But again, this is not at all surprising. Ling is often listed as the sole publisher of a reprint, when the original was copublished, and Trundle often published a first edition but then sold the reprint rights to someone else.[99]

The title page of the 1604 edition announces that the book is "Newly imprinted and enlarged to almost as much againe as it was, according to the true and perfect Coppie." On the basis of this innocuous advertisement, Lesser and Stallybrass reiterate previous claims that "Ling himself could be seen as the first critic to label Q1 a bad text."[100] But none of the phrases of that title page support their interpretation. "Newly imprinted" occurs elsewhere without any suggestion that it is replacing something bad.[101] Indeed, "newly corrected," or "newly amended," or even "newly corrected and amended" is the usual phrase to indicate something seriously deficient in previous editions.[102] From the larger perspective of the book trade, Ling's choice of "newly imprinted" just means that he was emphasizing the freshness of this edition, rather than the corruption of a preceding one. The same explanation accounts for "the true and perfect copy." John Webster's *The Devil's Law Case* was first published, in 1623, in an edition that declared itself to be "The true and perfect copie from the originall. As it was approouedly well acted by her Maiesties Seruants. Written by Iohn Webster." Here, "true and perfect" does not distinguish the book from anything that preceded it, but simply assures readers of its reliability, and perhaps in particular of its completeness.[103] It does not even, in Webster's case, necessarily or unambiguously distinguish an authorial text from a theatrical one. Nor is this surprising: "true and perfect" are all-purpose adjectives, frequently used to persuade readers of the reliability of all sorts of printed matter, without any contrast to other editions.[104] Likewise, the dozens of title page claims that a book has been printed "according to the... copy" have little in common beyond the effort to establish some kind of authority.[105] The most prominent printed texts using "according to the" in combination with "true copy" in 1604 would have been the weekly broadsheets reporting plague mortalities.[106] *A briefe and true declaration of the sicknesse, last wordes, and death of the King of Spaine Philip the second* was, we are promised, "Written from Madri[d] in a Spanish letter, and translated into English according to the true copie" before being "Printed at London."[107] The "true copie" here is presumably the Spanish text of a letter reporting what Philip II said on his deathbed; the printer is selling us an English translation of a Spanish memorial report of spoken words. The stationer is presumably being honest here, but his honesty would not satisfy a modern textual skeptic, or anyone who believes that plays were printed from memorial reconstructions of performances. Anyone who doubts Ling's honesty in relation to his first edition of *Hamlet* should not be persuaded by the title page of his second; conversely, those who accept his credibility and integrity in the second edition have no reason to doubt it in the first.

"Perfect" (in the sense "complete") complements Ling's claim that the second edition is "enlarged." Another word routinely used by early publishers without any implied criticism of previous editions, "enlarged" occurs three times elsewhere in printed playbooks. The obvious precedent for Ling's use in the 1604 edition of *Hamlet* was the 1602 title page of Thomas Kyd's *The Spanish Tragedy*: "Newly corrected, amended, and enlarged with new additions of the Painters part, and others" (a claim repeated in a 1603 reprint). That edition did contain new material, apparently written for a revival, years after Kyd's own death; indeed, the latest scholarship on those additions argues that they were written by

Shakespeare for the Chamberlain's Men.[108] Edward Blount's 1607 edition of William Alexander's *Monarchic Tragedies* also advertises itself, correctly, as "Newly enlarged" by Alexander himself. Ling had used the word in his 1598 edition of Drayton's *England's Heroical Epistles: Newly enlarged* (STC 7194); given Ling's relationship to Drayton, he certainly did not mean to suggest anything irregular about the previous edition.[109] Nor do the many uses of "enlarged" on title pages by other stationers cast doubt on the legitimacy of their unenlarged predecessors.[110]

The second edition of *Hamlet* contains 175 percent as many words as the first edition. But the importance of "enlarged" in the 1604 *Hamlet* (and most other early books) is not its promise of additional lines of deathless poetry or prose. "Enlarged" announces that this book required more ink and more hours to manufacture. The second quarto also contains more paper than its predecessor. For printing an early modern book, paper was "by far the largest" expense.[111] The text of *Hamlet* printed in 1603 occupied eight sheets of paper (64 pages); the text of *Hamlet* printed in 1604 occupied 13 sheets (104 pages).[112] That means the 1604 edition required five additional sheets for every copy printed, or 162 percent of the paper supply than had been used for every copy of the 1603 edition. Ling wanted—indeed, *needed*—to alert customers to how much bigger this book was: hence the unique specificity of "enlarged *to almost as much againe as it was*." This is a pardonable exaggeration (much virtue in "almost"), but if there were no more copies of the 1603 edition in the shop, customers could not check the math. We know from a variety of contemporary evidence that quarto playbooks normally sold for sixpence.[113] But we have no specific evidence for the retail price of the 1604 *Hamlet*. The Stationers' Company regulated retail pricing, allowing a half pence for every sheet in pica quarto unbound; this means that the 1604 edition would have been priced at six and a half pence, unbound. It could have been more: the 1604 quarto crams 39 lines onto a page, instead of 37; if it had been set to 37, it would have been six pages longer (another three quarters of a sheet). The second quarto is a less elegant piece of workmanship, less visually attractive, than the first one, because Ling did not want to push the retail price up to seven pence.

In order to make a profit on this exceptionally long text, Ling (and Smethwicke after him) needed to emphasize that it was *not* a normal playbook. Perhaps for that reason, the 1604 title page also omits any reference to theatrical performance. That omission complements the addition of "enlarged to almost as much againe as it was." It implies "this is not an ephemeral commercial play" (for which a standard price can be expected) but a quarto book, priced according to Stationers' Company rules, which were based on the number of sheets of paper it contained. This book was, according to its title page, almost double the size of what customers were used to getting for sixpence. The wording of the title page to the "enlarged" text (repeated in Smethwicke's 1611, 1625, and 1639 reprints) made it possible to charge an extra halfpence for this book. The title page explains why *Hamlet* is now more expensive "than it was." To the modern reader, an extra halfpence may not sound like much money, because 400 years of economic history stand between us and Ling: by one measurement, the "economic power" of half a pence for Ling would have been over 61 pounds for an English bookseller in 2004, for every copy of the book sold.[114] Multiplied by a print-run of 500 copies, that's over thirty thousand pounds sterling. But there's an easier way to evaluate that half penny, which doesn't involve complicated historical calculations or speculation about which criteria to use. That half penny would have been an extra 16.7 percent of retail income, per book. In speculative investments with small profit margins, 16.7 percent is the difference between profit and loss. For a small business like an independent bookshop, 16.7 percent can make the difference between survival and bankruptcy. Ling *had* to convince customers to pay that extra half pence for the 1604 quarto. The unusually specific "enlarged to almost as much again as it was" on the title page was his best effort to convince them. And it worked, for him and for Smethwicke.

Examined from the perspective of Nicholas Ling and the early-seventeenth-century book trade, these two quarto editions both make perfect sense, individually and in relationship to one another. Ling cautiously copublished one edition of *Hamlet* in 1603; this investment quickly paid off, and a year later he published an "enlarged" edition, manufactured by a different printer, repackaged so that he could charge a higher retail and wholesale price.

* * *

Why then have modern scholars, from 1909 to 2013, so often condemned the 1603 quarto as a "pirated" text? They have been confused not by the quartos themselves, but by two documents that never name Ling or his editions of *Hamlet*. The first, and historically most important, is the preface "To the Great Variety of Readers" in the 1623 collection of Shakespeare's *Comedies, Histories, and Tragedies*. After urging all readers, "Whatever you do, buy," the expensive Folio volume assured potential purchasers that "where, before, you were abused with divers stolen and surreptitious copies, maimed and deformed by the frauds and stealths of injurious imposters, even those are now offered to your view cured and perfect of their limbs." Unlike the 1604 title page, this self-serving advertisement *does* explicitly condemn previous editions. But which "imposters" does it target? In 1909, an influential bibliographer at the British Museum, Alfred W. Pollard, reinterpreted this passage, taking it not as a blanket rejection of all the pre-1623 quartos, but as a specific criticism of only a few: *Romeo and Juliet* (1597), *Henry V* (1600), *Merry Wives of Windsor* (1602), *Hamlet* (1603), and *Pericles* (1609). These "bad quartos," Pollard decided, were "pirated" editions, printed by unscrupulous publishers.[115] Pollard's essential distinction between good quartos (which the Folio reprints with few changes) and "bad" ones (which the Folio explicitly condemns, and does not reprint) seems convincing, but which quartos belong among the "imposters" remains a matter of scholarly debate. The most immediate and obvious referent, in 1623, would have been a series of linked "Shakespeare" quartos, published by Thomas Pavier in 1619, which deliberately falsified dates and falsely attributed to Shakespeare plays he did not write.

Pavier reprinted the quartos of *Henry V* and *Merry Wives*, but did not include any text of *Hamlet*. Why would anyone think that the 1623 preface referred to a quarto two decades old? The most recent edition of *Hamlet* was Smethwicke's of 1611, and Smethwicke belonged to the small syndicate that published the 1623 Folio. He would not have wanted that Folio to discredit his *Hamlet* copyright (which derived from the 1603 edition). No reader of the 1623 collection is likely to have thought that it indicted one of its own publishers. Moreover, the 1623 text of *Hamlet* is actually shorter than the 1604 edition, so in this instance the Folio could hardly brag about being more "perfect" (or complete) than the quarto of the same play that customers were most likely to find in a London bookshop.

The other document is more specific. On 26 July 1602, the Stationers' Company's official register recorded that James Roberts had "Entred for his Copie...A booke called the Revenge of Hamlett Prince Denmarke as yt was latelie Acted by the Lo: Chamberleyne his servantes".[116] That is, Roberts paid a fee of six pence to secure what we would now call his copyright. This manuscript raises two obvious questions: why did Ling and Trundle publish a text that belonged to Roberts? Is there any significance to the difference between the title recorded in 1602 and the title page printed in 1603?

Pollard answered the first question by speculating that Ling and Trundle had illegally and unscrupulously "pirated" a text that belonged to Roberts. This seems wildly unlikely. Pollard misunderstood the purpose of the Stationers' Register, as other major scholars (E. K. Chambers, F. P. Wilson, Leo Kirschbaum, Gerald D. Johnson, and Peter W. M. Blayney) have repeatedly demonstrated.[117] Stationers routinely made business arrangements with one another, including transfers of copyright, that are not recorded in the registers. Neither Roberts, nor anyone else, ever contested Ling's right to publish *Hamlet,* which was acknowledged in the official registers when Ling's copyrights were transferred to Smethwicke.

Nevertheless, some scholars continue to repeat the discredited claim that Ling and Trundle pirated intellectual property that belonged to Roberts. Kirk Melnikoff, in an important book on *Shakespeare's Stationers* published in 2012, gives two explanations for the change of copyright. Melnikoff summarizes the contradictory alternatives, but does not arbitrate between them. The first explanation is that in 1603 "Ling violated Roberts's copyright in publishing the manuscript originally acquired by Trundle. Ling then reaches some 'private agreement' with Roberts whereby he would act as publisher of Q2."[118] This hypothesis (subsequently endorsed by Tiffany Stern) acknowledges that Roberts and Ling reached a private agreement, by which Ling acquired the copyright. But this scenario then speculates, on the basis of no evidence whatsoever, that their agreement was reached only *after* Ling "violated" the copyright held by Roberts. Given the long-standing, mutually profitable business relationship between Ling and Roberts, *why* would Ling do that? *Why* would he risk that relationship for the sake of a small book that was, itself, a risky investment? *Why* would he do that in order to publish, for the first time, a first edition of a commercial play? In 1602, Roberts printed for Ling *England's Heroical Epistles: Newly corrected* (STC 7197); in 1603, Roberts printed for Ling Drayton's extensively revised *Barons' Wars* and *Idea*, which were then bound together with the *Epistles* (STC 7189). These are much larger books than *Hamlet*, by an author much more important to Ling as a publisher.

The implausible speculation that Ling "violated" the copyright also depends on the unsubstantiated speculation that Ling published a manuscript brought to him by another allegedly unscrupulous stationer, Trundle. Let's ignore for the moment the fact that in his long career Trundle never had any connection to the Chamberlain/King's Men; let's ignore the fact that Trundle was a "law-abiding" stationer whose other published plays all seem to be authentic. The most implausible feature of this conjecture is that Ling had no relationship with his alleged source, Trundle; the 1603 *Hamlet* was their first and only collaboration.

By contrast, Ling had known Roberts for at least two decades.[119] *Why* then would Ling trust Trundle enough to embark with him on such a dubious venture? And *why* would Ling publish his only first edition of a commercial play without consulting Roberts, who had the monopoly on printing playbills?[120] In fact, it was Roberts, not Ling, who had a working relationship with Trundle. Roberts and Trundle were neighbors. They both had shops in the Barbican; they were physically much closer to each other than either was to Ling. Roberts printed Trundle's only other publication in 1603, and also printed his next publication (a play, in 1606).[121] The person most likely to have introduced Ling to Trundle was Roberts himself. The person most likely to have persuaded both Ling and Trundle that this particular commercial play was a safe investment was Roberts, who as the printer of all playbills knew better than any other stationer which plays had been most often performed since 1593 (when he acquired the monopoly).

Roberts, and Roberts alone, could also reassure them that the play would not get them in trouble with the authorities. After all, this is a play about the murder of two kings—a very dangerous topic in Elizabethan England, where the Pope had denied the legitimacy of their monarch, and where Catholics were repeatedly accused of conspiracies to assassinate her. The topic became, if anything, even more dangerous in March 1603, when England, for the first time in half a century, had a "king". But when Roberts entered the play in the Stationers' Register, it was officially approved by the state censor, Zachariah Pasfield.[122] To license the play, Pasfield must have read it, which means that Roberts did have a manuscript—the only manuscript that we *know* was circulating among London's stationers before late 1604. If Ling published Q1 from a different manuscript, then he would have been risking not only his money and his relationship with Roberts, but also his relationship to the censors.

Thus, the first explanation offered by Melnikoff is unsatisfactory and implausible in every way. The second explanation is that

> Q1 was likely printed from the copy that Roberts entered in 1602. Having neither the time nor the resources to finance an edition of the text, he rented the copy to Ling and Trundle, who promptly contracted Valentine Simmes to print Q1. The manuscript for Q2 was acquired at a later date by either Ling or by Roberts.

This hypothesis is based on more recent scholarship.[123] But Melnikoff's wording here is misleading: there is no evidence that Roberts ever "rented" the copy, and "rented" presupposes an ability to predict future reprints. Ling is much more likely than Trundle to have contacted and contracted Simmes. Moreover, this phrasing implies that Roberts wanted to publish *Hamlet*, but could not. It would be more accurate to say that Roberts had other priorities, and that he *chose* not to spend the time or the money on this text. Again, this may seem counterintuitive to modern Shakespearians. However, as Lukas Erne has pointed out, Roberts printed all sorts of material, but he preferred to *publish* religious texts. Although he entered three Shakespeare plays in the Stationers' Register, "he published none of them." Roberts printed 11 playbooks between 1594 and 1606, "but he never published a single one."[124]

On the evidence of his practice elsewhere, Roberts probably never intended to publish *Hamlet*. Why then did he enter it in the Stationers' Register? Roberts registered only five commercial plays, and all were from the repertoire of the Chamberlain's Men.[125] So it's entirely possible that Shakespeare's company offered the manuscript to Roberts. After all, he was the stationer they knew best, having worked with him several times a week for years; their own financial health depended on the sheets that he printed, advertising whichever play they were performing that day.[126] Having bought the manuscript (from the Chamberlain's Men, or someone else), Roberts would have wanted to secure his rights to it, knowing that he might not be able to find a publisher immediately. He may have expected to print it, but he registered the copyright for other titles that he neither printed nor published, and whose publication and printing by other stationers he never challenged.[127] Demonstrably, for whatever reasons, this is something that Roberts did. In any case, when he did sell the manuscript and the copyright to another publisher he also surrendered control over the printing and the timetable of publication.[128]

We have no way of knowing exactly when Roberts sold the copyright to Ling (or Ling and Trundle). But, given the slow sales of new Shakespeare plays from 1600 to 1603, a buyer may have been harder to find than he had initially anticipated. One way or another, it seems likely that Roberts was still involved with the text in May 1603. Roberts is more likely than either of the others to have learned, from someone in the acting company, about performances of the play in Oxford and Cambridge as well as London. He is also more likely than the others to have known about the company's transformation from the Lord Chamberlain's Men to the King's Men on 19 May. By the time that happened, plague had already engulfed London, closed down the theatres, and depressed the retail environment.[129] Roberts was thus probably responsible for the changes of wording between his 1602 entry in the Stationers' Register and the 1603 title page; those changes might even have helped him sell the manuscript to another stationer. Once Ling and Trundle owned the copyright, *they* would have decided when to publish, because *they* were the ones whose investment was now at risk. If Roberts was too busy when they wanted it printed, it would have made sense, from everyone's point of view, to pass the printing to Simmes. After all, Roberts's long-term relationship to Ling, and potential future relationship with his new neighbor Trundle, mattered more to him than the small sum he would get for printing the 1603 *Hamlet*.

Thus, from the perspective of the English book trade in the years just before and after the death of Elizabeth I, there is nothing irregular, suspicious, or piratical about Ling's 1603 edition of *Hamlet*. It was a perfectly legitimate book, the product of legal, logical, ethical, well-understood social, business, and political relationships. Shakespeare never used the words "pirate" or "piracy" in relation to his or anyone else's intellectual property, and, as Adrian Johns demonstrates, the words did not acquire that meaning until the middle of the seventeenth century.[130] But the term emerged in English before any other European language, and the tensions that eventually erupted in debates about piracy were already implicit in the sixteenth-century practices of licensing and registering printed texts. Nicholas Ling undoubtedly owned the right to print *Hamlet,* and there is no reason to suspect that he acquired that right by immoral means. But who sold him the two different manuscripts of the play that he published? James Roberts probably sold him one of them, but who sold it to Roberts? Shakespeare? The Chamberlain's Men? Someone else? Elizabethan England would have recognized the proprietary rights of a playwright to sell to an acting company a manuscript he had written, and the proprietary rights of an acting company to perform a play they had purchased from a playwright and paid to have licensed; either the playwright or the acting company could, then, claim a legal right to sell a manuscript of that play to a stationer. But what if some third party, by some other means, acquired or produced a manuscript of the play that had been written by Shakespeare and performed by the Chamberlain's Men? Ling would be the rightful owner of that manuscript, but had he unwittingly purchased stolen property? Phrased in this way, the question of piracy forces us to move from a printed text to the manuscript that lies behind it.

CHAPTER 2

Piratical Actors?

"Remember me"

In the history of Shakespeare scholarship and criticism, the text printed in 1603 has always been misremembered. It has suffered from being lost, then found and claimed, then unclaimed, then sort of claimed again—making its relationship with Shakespeare troublesome indeed—an unwanted little bastard striving to gain approval from the rest of the family. For 200 years, it was simply forgotten. It was unknown to the critics, poets, playwrights, scholars, and editors who institutionalized and canonized Shakespeare in the century and a half after the Restoration. Dryden, Rowe, Pope, Theobald, Warburton, Johnson, Capell, Steevens, and Malone never saw it. Neither did the great English actors from Betterton to Garrick, Kemble, and Kean, famous for their very different performances of Hamlet. Neither did the early Romantic poets and critics, German and English, who idolized Shakespeare the poet and Hamlet the character.

Although copies of the quarto survived in private hands, there are no public references to its contents until 1825. That disappearance is not in itself surprising. The first quarto of *1 Henry IV* survives in only a single fragment, as does the first quarto of *The Passionate Pilgrim*; we possess only a single copy of the first printings of *Richard Duke of York* (i.e., *3 Henry VI*), *Titus Andronicus*, and *Venus and Adonis*. All those first editions disappeared for centuries, and were rediscovered late in the history of Shakespeare criticism. The "1597" first edition of *Loves Labours Lost* has not survived at all.[1] A printed edition of *Loves Labours Won*, which has not survived, was listed alongside other plays in the inventory of an English bookseller in August 1603, about the time when Ling was publishing his first edition of *Hamlet*.[2] In Elizabethan and Jacobean England, printed plays were not particularly valuable objects, and Shakespeare had not yet become a cultural icon. Most quarto playbooks, like other pamphlets, were sold unbound, the papers simply stitched together. Such texts are disproportionately subject to the vagaries of destruction and loss.[3]

The first edition of a quarto playbook was always a speculative investment, and so the print-runs of such editions were not large. As I showed in chapter 1, Ling and Trundle had strong reasons to be particularly cautious about publishing *Hamlet* in 1603, and that caution would almost certainly have translated into a small print-run. When a first edition had sold out, a publisher could be more confident of demand for a second edition, and even more confident about a third, and consequently reprints might have larger print-runs. It's not surprising that, in general, the first quartos of Shakespeare's plays and poems survive in fewer copies; in particular, it's not surprising that each new quarto of *Hamlet*, from 1604 to 1637, survives in more copies than the one that preceded it.[4]

In 1821, the accomplished quartermaster and antiquarian Sir Henry Edward Bunbury inherited, along with his title as baronet, several estates, and in 1823 he found in a closet of one of them (Barton Hall near Bury St. Edmunds in Suffolk) a volume acquired at an unknown date by one of his ancestors: an imperfect copy of the 1603 quarto, missing the last two pages of the text, and therefore ending with the stage direction "*Hamlet dies.*"[5] That copy was acquired in 1914 by the American millionaire Henry Huntington, and today it resides in the great library he founded in San Marino, California. But Bunbury's rediscovery radiated outward into the wider world long before the original object reached its final resting place in the Los Angeles basin. In 1825, the 1603 text that Bunbury had found was reprinted for the first time in a little book published by the London firm of Payne and Foss (to whom Bunbury had sold it).[6] The unsigned preface to *The First Edition of the Tragedy of Hamlet, by William Shakespeare*, described it as "an accurate reprint from the only known copy of this Tragedy as originally written by Shakespeare, which he afterwards altered and enlarged," and noted that it contained "several lines of great beauty subsequently omitted."[7]

In 1856, another copy of the 1603 edition surfaced in Dublin (said to have been brought there from Nottinghamshire). It was purchased by the antiquarian and scholar James Orchard Halliwell, who sold it to the British Museum in 1858. This copy lacks the title page, but contains the ending of the play, missing from the Bunbury/Huntington copy. As a result, by 1858 Shakespeare editors and scholars had, for the first time, access to the entire text printed 255 years before. A lithographic facsimile was published that same year, the first of many such documentary reprints.

But even before the British Museum acquired its copy of the 1603 quarto, the German classical philologist Tycho Mommsen had dismissed its text as an unauthorized mess, produced by "an actor, who put down, from memory, a sketch of the original play, as it was acted, and who wrote illegibly." So began the theory of "memorial reconstruction" that attributes most of the unique features of the first edition to a single actor and his inadequate recollection of performances. The first thing to notice about this theory is that, even in its initial incarnation, the actor and his memory were not enough. Mommsen also presupposed bad handwriting. Perhaps he considered actors particularly prone to illegibility, but I have known highly educated professionals who scribble more indecipherably than actors of my acquaintance. Bad handwriting could come from many sources, and Mommsen does indeed presuppose two other baleful influences on the manuscript from which the first quarto was printed: "a bad poet, most probably 'a bookseller's hack.'"[8] The actor's inadequate memory has been supplemented by the inadequate writing of a "hack," and as always an unethical bookseller is imagined, lurking in the background. In chapter 1, I have tried to exorcise the ghost of the evil bookseller, and his appearance in Mommsen's theory is demonstrably anachronistic. The word "hack" derives from "hackney," and it did not acquire the sense of "a literary drudge" until the eighteenth-century rise of Grub Street journalism. In fact, Mommsen quoted (and placed in quotation marks) the earliest recorded use of the word in that sense.[9]

> Here lies Poor Ned Purdon, from misery freed,
> Who long was a bookseller's hack;
> He led such a damnable life in this world,
> I don't think he'll wish to come back.

Oliver Goldsmith's "Epitaph on Edward Purdon" memorialized the life of an Irish-born "scribbler in the newspapers," educated at Trinity College, Dublin, who died in London in 1767.[10] The theory of memorial reconstruction was ushered into the world by an anachronistic assumption about the book trade.

Nevertheless, Mommsen's theory, and its complications, were soon taken up by others. Its most influential champion was W. W. Greg, who lent "memorial reconstruction" the formidable "scientific" authority of the New Bibliography. In 1910—the year after his friend Pollard published his fanciful story about "bad quartos"—Greg published an analysis of the 1602 quarto edition of *The Merry Wives of Windsor*. Greg concluded that the text had been printed from a manuscript compiled by memory, probably by a "playhouse thief," specifically the actor who played the Host.¹¹ Greg's argument was taken, for most of the twentieth century, as scholarly proof of the theory of "memorial reconstruction," a theory eventually applied to ten early texts in the Shakespeare canon (including *Hamlet*) and to 32 other early modern dramatic texts.

But Greg's theory always had problems, and Greg himself was uneasy about its application to *Hamlet*. For one thing, memorial reconstruction was immediately linked to Pollard's conjecture about piratical stationers, which (as chapter 1 demonstrated) is not sustainable. But even as a freestanding hypothesis, it was subject to many logical and historical objections, objections that were raised even during Greg's lifetime.[12] Evelyn May Albright, one of the first women to make a major contribution to the field of early modern bibliography and textual theory, laid out its weaknesses and self-contradictions as early as 1927.[13] Although the theory continued to dominate Shakespeare editing throughout the twentieth century, criticism accumulated and intensified in its closing decades. Such diverse scholars as Randall McLeod, Steven Urkowitz, Leah Marcus, Paul Werstine, and Lucas Erne, who perhaps agreed about nothing else, joined in challenging the credibility of earlier claims about bad quartos and memorial reconstruction. The most devastating skeptical critique remains Laurie E. Maguire's 1996 book-length analysis of the theory. Rather than focus on a single text, Maguire provided a comprehensive account of all the different kinds of arguments and evidence that had been used, since the middle of the nineteenth century, to discredit early play texts as the product of radically unreliable memories. She surveyed historical and empirical studies of memory, and cases where reporting indisputably took place in England and elsewhere in Europe; on the basis of these examples, she systematically analyzed all the various criteria used by scholars to substantiate their claims about memorial reconstruction. Of the 18 categories of such "evidence," only two proved to be reliable, with a third occasionally useful. Of the 42 texts condemned by Greg and/or other proponents of the theory, Maguire did not find a single example that was "unquestionably" a memorial reconstruction, and only four for which "a strong case can be made." The 1603 *Hamlet* was not among them.[14]

Nevertheless, reputable scholars continue to dismiss the 1603 text as a memorial reconstruction. In 2008, Paul Menzer, in a book-length examination of the three *Hamlet* texts, urges scholars to "rehabilitate" the theory of memorial reconstruction: he then proceeds to argue that the 1603 edition *and the 1623 edition* both depend on the textual transmission of actors' memories of performances.[15] Menzer leans heavily on Ann Thompson and Neil Taylor's 2006 Arden edition of the play. Thompson and Taylor print edited texts of all three versions, but this apparently even-handed approach is belied by their relegation of the 1603 and 1623 texts to a subsidiary volume, and by their conclusion that the manuscript used by the printer of the 1603 quarto "was based on a reconstruction of a performance based on the text behind" the 1623 Folio.[16] Although this summary omits the telltale word "memorial," to all intents and purposes Thompson and Taylor simply reiterate the hypothesis defended in the 1982 Arden *Hamlet*, the conflated traditional text edited by Harold Jenkins. Moreover, their commentary on the 1603 text repeatedly cites the claims of scholars like Jenkins and G. I. Duthie, whose methods had been thoroughly discredited by Maguire. Looking at twenty-first-century scholarship, one could easily get the impression that Maguire's damning critique of the theory of memorial reconstruction had never been written.

To some extent, Maguire herself is responsible for this sidelining of her work. Her book concludes with a series of "Tables" that conveniently summarize the evidence for the 42 texts accused of being memorial reconstructions (pp. 227–322), and those tables themselves are then further summarized and abbreviated in another, concluding Table (pp. 324–5). This arrangement makes it much easier for scholars to jump to the summaries without having to read the actual analysis in Maguire's first 200-plus pages. The summary table of the evidence for the 1603 *Hamlet* concludes with the verdict "Possibly [memorial reconstruction], but if so, a very good one" (256). This is the most frequently cited phrase from her 427-page book. Much virtue in "if"—and much virtue in "possibly." Having quoted Maguire's conclusion, scholars can then proceed to ignore it, and in particular to ignore the caveat "a very good one." If the 1603 edition is a "very good" memorial reconstruction, how can it be that it contains only 591 unaltered verse lines of its original? How can it misremember the names of the characters, invent an entirely new scene, give speeches and cues to the wrong actors, and reduce the text from 27,602 words (in the Folio) to a mere 15,983? Is a memory that forgets more than 42 percent of the text "a very good one"? Is a memory that changes most of the 42 percent that it retains "a very good one"?

And why, in the first place, did Maguire conclude that the 1603 edition was "possibly" a memorial reconstruction? According to her own summary, it does not contain a single example of the three most reliable categories of evidence for memorial contamination (external echoes, internal repetitions, and formulae).[17] She characterizes the style of the 1603 text as "pedestrian" and "uneven," and on that basis "suggests the presence of two hands," of which the second "seems to have a moral agenda" (255). But Maguire herself had earlier concluded that "while stylistic unevenness can be attributable to memorial reconstruction, there are too many other complicating factors for it to function as a symptom of memory. It is at best a symptom of some hiccup in textual transmission" (204). So the one piece of evidence that might justify her "possibly" is, by her own account, even "at best" not a reliable symptom of memorial transmission. Nowhere in her book does she provide evidence that "a moral agenda" distinguishes pirates from authors, or one author from another. Are actors more likely to have a moral agenda than playwrights? Are "pirates" stealing and corrupting a text more likely to have a moral agenda than the author of the original? Thousands of ordinary readers and extraordinary scholars have assumed, indeed celebrated, Shakespeare's own "moral agendas."

Maguire seems to have suffered, here, uncharacteristically, from a failure of nerve. After all, she was dealing, in this instance, with the most famous of English plays, edited by the most prestigious of Shakespeare's editors.[18] Although major editions of the play published by Oxford, Cambridge, and Arden in the 1980s disagreed vehemently about the 1623 Folio, they had formed an impressive chorus, singing in perfect harmony that the 1603 quarto was a memorial reconstruction. In such company, what young scholar wants to be singing off-key? Facing this daunting professorial unanimity, Maguire may also have quailed at the prospect of being associated with the opinions of the notorious amateur gadfly, Eric Sams. Maguire's bibliography lists four articles by Sams, including his critique of theories of memorial reconstruction in *Hamlet,* but her text concedes him only a single three-word sentence ("Sams challenged everyone").[19] She could be forgiven for not wanting to be targeted by Brian Vickers, who in the *Times Literary Supplement* had ferociously defended the traditional view, labeling the 1603 edition "Hamlet by Dogberry."[20]

Whatever its causes, Maguire's caution about *Hamlet* unfortunately was flanked (and outflanked) by the work of other scholars who showed no such reticence. In the 1980s, Stanley Wells, Gary Taylor, and John Jowett championed the then-heretical idea that Shakespeare was an actor-playwright who revised his own scripts; their new theory was most influentially expressed in *The Division of the Kingdoms,* a book that systematically criticized G. I. Duthie's argument that the first quarto of *King Lear* was a memorial reconstruction.[21] But in their Oxford edition of Shakespeare's *Complete Works,* and its *Textual Companion,* Taylor accepted that the first quarto of *Hamlet* was a memorial reconstruction—thus endorsing the same kind of arguments, made by the same scholar (G. I. Duthie), that he had rejected in the case of *Lear.*[22] Taylor's support for memorial reconstruction in *Hamlet* also ignored his own statistical analysis of function words, which showed that the first quarto of *Hamlet* was indistinguishable from other undisputed Shakespeare texts.[23] This self-contradiction meant that the Oxford Shakespeare, in other respects the embodiment of textual revisionism, in the case of *Hamlet* became the guardian of orthodoxy. In 1997—a year after Maguire's monograph—the Oxford Shakespeare became the textual basis of the Norton Shakespeare, edited by Stephen Greenblatt, and Norton also reprinted for the first time, in paperback, the Oxford *Textual Companion*. Given Norton's dominance of the American college textbook market, and the status of Greenblatt as godfather of the New Historicism, these events guaranteed that, in undergraduate and graduate classrooms, and in critical books and articles written by the scholars who taught those classes, Taylor's contradictory position was reinforced and perpetuated. In 2000, John Jowett's edition of *Richard III*, in the Oxford World Classics series, refuted and abandoned the old theory that the first quarto of that play was a memorial reconstruction.[24] The theory that Jowett rejected had been endorsed by Taylor in their 1986 *Complete Works*, so Taylor's position on *Hamlet* was now contradicted by his own work on *Lear* and by Jowett's on *Richard III*. Nevertheless, revised editions of the Oxford *Complete Works* in 2005, and of the Oxford-based Norton *Shakespeare* in 2006, left Taylor's anomalous *Hamlet* intact, promising up-to-date scholarship but ignoring Maguire's challenge to his assumptions about memorial reconstruction.

As a result of this publishing history, Taylor's position in the mid-1980s can seem, or be made to seem, more up-to-date than Maguire's in the mid-1990s. The 2006 Arden edition, for example, *first* acknowledges that Maguire "is not entirely convinced" that the first quarto was a memorial reconstruction, *then* immediately records that "Gary Taylor, however, is convinced."[25] The historical present tense, and the sequence of these sentences, gives the impression, to unwary readers, that Taylor had read and rejected Maguire's arguments. In fact, Maguire had read and rejected his, and Taylor's older view about *Hamlet* was simply being perpetuated and repackaged by publishers for 20 years, while he was away editing Middleton (and changing his mind about Shakespeare's texts).

The other scholar whose work flanked and obscured Maguire's was Kathleen O. Irace. In 1994, Irace published a study of the "bad" quartos which put "bad" in titular quotation marks but then systematically relegitimated the damning adjective. The heart of her argument was a "computer-based" study of verbal variation in the "bad" quartos of six plays by Shakespeare: *2 Henry VI, 3 Henry VI, Romeo and Juliet, Henry V, Merry Wives of Windsor*, and *Hamlet*. Like Maguire, Irace looked at more than one text, apparently providing a new global foundation for analysis of individual plays. Irace concluded that none of these quartos represented an early Shakespearian version of the play; instead, all six "must have been" printed from manuscripts "reconstructed and adapted by actors." The heart of her argument was a "statistical" demonstration that "the role of one character is remarkably similar" to the longer text, and that "lines spoken by others when the likely reporters are on stage also match in a surprisingly high proportion of cases."[26] These results are graphically displayed in an appendix of "Charts Indicating Likely Reporters" (180–85). In the case of *Hamlet*, Irace's method identified the actor who played Marcellus (and who doubled the smaller roles of Voltemand, Lucianus, and the Prologue to "The Mousetrap") as the reporter (118–19). In fact, the analysis of *Hamlet* in her 1994 book had been anticipated, and more fully defended, in her contribution to a 1992 collection of essays on the 1603 quarto.[27] Visually, that earlier article is even more impressive than the book: a mere 32 pages display seven tables of variants, combined with seven charts, pie-graphs, and diagrams. The result is a compellingly scientific picture of memorial reconstruction by a single actor; this formidable "computer-assisted" quantitative rhetoric comfortingly confirms an old orthodoxy.[28]

As a result of her two studies, Irace was commissioned to produce a modern-spelling critical edition of the 1603 *Hamlet* as a volume in the series of "The Early Quartos" produced in conjunction with, and as appendices to, The New Cambridge Shakespeare. Published in 1998, Irace's edition canonized her claims about the text's memorial reconstruction, adding to her earlier evidence an appendix of "Possible 'actors' additions" in Q1 only.[29] With three publications between 1992 and 1998—one in the only anthology of critical essays on Q1, one a global reconsideration of the theory of memorial reconstruction, and one a scholarly edition by a prestigious academic press—Irace re-consigned the first edition of *Hamlet* to the dustbin of texts produced by radically unreliable pirate-actors. Thanks to Irace, by 2001 James P. Bednarz could declare that "after a rigorous testing in recent Revisionist scholarship, the theory that the First Quarto of *Hamlet* is a memorial reconstruction, probably concocted by the actor who played Marcellus (and perhaps doubled as Voltemand, Lucianus, and the Prologue to 'The Mousetrap') is more compelling than ever."[30]

In fact, Irace did not provide any new evidence for the theory of memorial reconstruction. She simply reorganized, and redisplayed, the old evidence and the old arguments. Her use of computers was merely rhetorical. She made her parallel texts by hand, and collated them by eye; her UCLA computer just displayed the results in graphic forms routinely used by scientists. But unlike the real scientists, Irace subjected her data to no sophisticated statistical evaluation. Her most complicated mathematical operation was to turn fractions into percentages. Professors of English are notoriously bad at math, but you don't need to be Einstein to realize that Irace's mathematical analysis is naïve. Respected early modern attribution scholars like MacDonald P. Jackson had shown, as early as 1979, that word-counts have to be evaluated in terms of "degrees of freedom" and precise calculations of "probability."[31] Irace's attribution of the first quarto of *Hamlet* to the pirate-actor playing Marcellus used the language of certainty but never even applied the technologies of probability.

The circularity of Irace's reasoning was diagnosed by Maguire in 1996; Irace "assumes the text under examination to be a report, identifies the reporter, and thereby confirms that the text is reported. Methods of detecting memorially reconstructed texts have not changed significantly" in more than a century (12). This logical weakness was compounded by specific empirical problems. For one thing, in order to account for the pattern of variation between Q1 and the later texts, Irace had to assume a particular pattern of doubling in the Elizabethan performances of the play. But Thompson and Taylor point out that "while such an actor would have been quite busy in the early scenes, he would thereafter have been offstage for the bulk of the play...As it stands, then, the memorial reconstruction theory seems uneconomical, and does not fit with the assumption that doubling arose out of a need to save on man- and boy-power."[32] Even before Irace published her work, Ralph Berry (in 1986) had surveyed doubling patterns in more than 100 productions of *Hamlet*; not one of them used the pattern presumed by Irace and her predecessors in the Marcellus blame-game.[33]

That pattern of doubling is possible only if one presumes that the 1603 quarto misrepresents the very roles played by the very actor who allegedly reported the text. In that quarto, the putative actor-pirate Marcellus speaks the last two lines of the play's first scene; no exit direction for Marcellus, Barnardo, and Horatio is provided, but all three must apparently exit (as they are ordered to do in the later quartos and Folios). Having failed to record the alleged pirate's own exit, the 1603 quarto does nevertheless specify that *the two ambassadors* (including Voltemar) enter in the opening stage direction of scene two. In Q1 as it stands, Voltemar must enter just as Marcellus is exiting, which means that the two roles *could not possibly be doubled*. Proponents of memorial reconstruction must also assume that the actor playing Marcellus misremembered the name of the second character he was playing—and also forgot his cue for the entrance of that second character. Would any actor forget his own cues, his own exits, his own entrances, his own costume-changes, and the name of his character? I have met one or two incompetent amateur actors in my lifetime in the theatre, but I have never encountered any creature who matches this cartoon profile.

Supporters of memorial reconstruction routinely assert that this incompetent actor was a "hired man," who left the company voluntarily, or was fired, and might therefore be willing to betray them by selling a debased text of the play to a bookseller.[34] But jobbing professional actors, in my experience, are not incompetent (or they would never get any jobs). Moreover, this assumption about the acting profession is as anachronistic as Mommsen's about booksellers. Marcellus is the eighth largest role in the play.[35] If the actor who played Marcellus also doubled Voltemand, Lucianus, and the Prologue, his role would be even larger. Roles that large would normally have been played by one of the leading actors in the Chamberlain's Men. As "sharers," those actors were shareholders and co-owners of the company; they were not, like most actors after the Restoration, mere employees of a theatrical manager. For an actor, the distinction between "sharers" and "hired men" matters as much as the difference, in twenty-first-century American universities, between "tenured full professor" and "adjunct." No shareholder had a motive to betray the company for something as petty as the money he could make by selling a text of *Hamlet* to a bookseller. No shareholder would have needed to reconstruct a text from memory, because he had access to the company's manuscripts. No shareholder left the Chamberlain's Men between Shakespeare's composition of the long text of *Hamlet* and Ling's publication of the first edition.[36] No shareholder in London's most successful acting company could have been as incompetent as the presumed actor-reporter.

The treatment of cues is another weakness of Irace's work, and of memorial reconstruction theories more generally. Irace focused on, and separately charted, two patterns of verbal variation: differences in the words *spoken* by an actor, and differences in the words *heard* by an actor when he was onstage. She rightly insisted that any actor would remember his own lines better than the lines he overheard. However, her analysis of lines overheard lumped together two significantly different categories: the cues that prompted the actor's own speeches, and everything else spoken on stage. But, in any historical period, an actor's own cues are much more important to him (or her) than anything else heard on stage. More specifically, as Simon Palfrey and Tiffany Stern have reminded us, Elizabethan actors were not given manuscript copies of an entire play. Instead, each actor was given only his own "part," a manuscript that included the words he needed to speak, some relevant stage directions, and the two-to-five-word cues he needed to listen for and respond to.[37] Paul Menzer, in what has been called "a startling and important contribution to our study of the text" of *Hamlet*, has taken this fact as the starting point for a reexamination of the three early texts.[38] Menzer demonstrates that, from the perspective of the cues he gives and the cues he receives, the character most perfectly represented by the quarto of 1603 was not Marcellus, Voltemar, or any role either of them could double, but Corambis (the character better known as Polonius, the name he is given in the 1604 quarto and the Folio). As Menzer notes, "proponents of 'memorial reconstruction'" will need to explain why "Corambis's Q1 cues (both given and received) should accord with those of Polonius in Q2/F at a rate nearly double that of other roles."[39] But, of course, neither Irace nor anyone else can provide such an explanation, because the Corambis cues-evidence directly contradicts the speeches-evidence used to support the Marcellus hypothesis. In fact, as Menzer concludes, the part of Corambis "looks nothing like a 'memorial reconstruction' of Q2 or F...but rather an autonomous part that a later playwright rewrote in Q2" (120). Corambis, in other words, suggests that Ling's 1603 edition represents, at least in part, an earlier version of the play than Ling's 1604 edition. James J. Marino takes this argument even further, focusing not on cues but on the use of the name in spoken dialogue (rather than speech prefixes or stage directions). In Q1 the name is spoken only by the Queen; in Q2 and F, it is spoken only by the King.

> The switch has been accomplished by removing the earlier name from one actor's lines and adding the newer name, which scans differently, to another actor's part.... This revision of the old man's name is too exactingly specific, and indeed too odd, to be the result of memorial reconstruction...The supposed reconstructor would have no reason to reproduce that limitation; that he would reproduce it in the wrong actor's part, with the wrong name, entirely by chance, is improbable.... Whatever led the Chamberlain's Men to alter the old man's name, the alteration is bound up with other changes in the text, seemingly irrelevant to the issue of the name itself.[40]

The theory of memorial reconstruction alleges that the first quarto of *Hamlet* derives from an actor's memories of Elizabethan performance. But the theory repeatedly conflicts with the material realities of early modern performance practice (doubling, cues, actors' parts). Another crucial performance practice has been recently described by Matthew Vadnais: what he calls "speech burden," the number of speeches and cues that an actor had to remember in a particular play, scene, or subscene. Like Maguire, Vadnais does not concentrate on individual texts, but instead analyzes larger patterns. He demonstrates that Shakespeare carefully constructed his plays with an attention to managing and distributing the speech burden among a company of actors in a repertory system based on rapid turnover. This pattern is as visible in the "bad quartos" as in the "good quartos." In particular, all three texts of *Hamlet* are equally "performance texts," because all three carefully organize the succession of speeches and scenes in order to minimize the speech burden on actors, make it easier for them to remember their cues, and make it easier for them to recover the narrative if another actor forgets a speech or a cue. Vadnais finds it very unlikely that a radically corrupt reconstruction would preserve such patterns, and he concludes that "Shakespeare's variant play texts were written short and made longer."[41]

Irace's entire speculative edifice collapses when Marino's study of the change of names from Corambis to Polonius *is combined with* Menzer's study of cues, Thompson and Taylor's history of doubling, and Vadnais's analysis of speech burden. Nevertheless, twenty-first-century scholars still cling to the nineteenth-century raft of memorial reconstruction. Thompson and Taylor, for instance, do acknowledge that it is "plausible" that the first quarto might represent "Shakespeare's early draft" of *Hamlet* (as I am arguing in this book). But they immediately conclude that it is "slightly more probable that Q1 is a reconstruction...of a performed text." They give two pieces of evidence for this claim. One is the presence in Q1 of details in two stage directions that do not appear in the later editions: the Ghost's final entrance "*in his night gown*" (11.57) and Ophelia's mad entrance "*playing on a lute, and her hair down*" (13.14).[42] But stage directions in more than 30 other plays from the period specify a character's appearance in a nightgown; a lute is specified in 26 stage directions in other plays; hair is even more widely mentioned in stage directions, "most commonly when a female figure enters with *her hair loose, disheveled,* or *about her ears* to convey that she is distraught with madness, shame, rage, extreme grief."[43] These facts were available in a scholarly reference work published seven years earlier, which Thompson and Taylor cite elsewhere in their edition. No one believes that all those other stage directions in all those other plays result from "reconstruction" of a performance.

Their second piece of evidence comes from Irace: her argument that the 1603 quarto contains "interpolations" by actors (table 2.1). Appendix I of Irace's edition (pp. 115–16), which lists those alleged interpolations, is rhetorically effective, because the added words—interjections,

Table 2.1 Possible "actors' additions"

1. Not so *much*, my lord, I am too much i'th' "son" [extrametrical anticipation]
2. List, *list,* O list [repetition]
3. *By the mass,* I was about to say something! [superfluous oath]
4. *Come,* go with me [superfluous interjection, which awkwardly contradicts "go"]
5. *Come* [superfluous extrametrical interjection, after a scene-ending couplet]
6. except my life, *except* my life, *except my life* [repetition]
7. It is not *very* strange [superfluous intensifier]
8. give twenty, forty, *fifty,* a hundred ducats apiece for his picture
9. *'Sblood,* there is something in this more than natural if philosophy could find it out [superfluous strong oath, one of several in this text alone] [47]
10. Your hands, come, *then*!
11. O old friend, *why,* thy face is valenced since I saw thee last!
12. I'll have thee speak out the rest *of this* soon
13. You could for need study a speech of some dozen *lines*, or sixteen lines [anticipation]
14. About my brains! / *Hum,* I have heard / That guilty creatures sitting at a play
15. To hear of it. They are *here* about the Court [extrametrical]
16. O, 'tis *too* true
17. Will be some danger—which *for* to prevent
18. If once *I be* a widow, ever I be *a* wife [extrametrical anticipation and repetition]
19. The story is extant and written in *very* choice Italian. [Compare no. 7 above.]
20. Or rather, *as* you say, my mother
21. But is there no sequel at the heels of this mother's admiration? *Impart*
22. Ay, *sir,* but while the grass grows—the proverb is something musty [repetition from vocative in character's previous speech]
23. O, the recorders! Let me see *one*
24. What's near it with it; *or* it is a massy wheel [extrametrical]
25. Who was in life a *most* foolish prating knave [extrametrical]
26. *But soft,* what noise?
27. But if indeed you find him not *within* this month you shall nose him as you go up the stairs into the lobby
28. *O ho!* [superfluous interjection, inappropriate for Ophelia]
29. Larded *all* with sweet flowers [extrametrical]
30. *He answers* [extrametrical]
31. All from her father's death, *and now behold,* O Gertrude, Gertrude [extrametrical]
32. Pray *you,* love, remember
33. His beard *was* as white as snow [extrametrical]
34. Finding ourselves too slow of sail, we put on a compelled valour, *and* in the grapple I boarded them
35. As by your safety, *greatness,* wisdom, all things else [extrametrical]
36. 'Twill not be seen in him *there,* there the men are as mad as he [repetition]
37. The King, sir, hath laid, *sir,* that in a dozen passes... [repeated vocative: compare no. 22 above]

vocatives, connectives, commonplace modifiers, mundane phrases—are all unremarkable from a literary point of view. Indeed, in some cases they ruin famous lines from the play (see numbers 1 and 25, below), and in general they "vulgarize" the language, often in ways that most critics consider inappropriate to the characters or the setting. Irace specifically cites and endorses Harold Jenkins's analysis of actors' interpolations in the Folio text of *Hamlet*, and the items in her list resemble the items in his.[44] They epitomize what nonactors expect actors to do: fill pauses with ill-considered verbiage, or dilute the precision and formal polish of Shakespeare's language. Collected together, the passages listed below seem to endorse Maguire's description of the style of Q1 as "pedestrian." For the convenience of readers, my list above (table 2.1) modifies Irace's list (appended to her own edition) by giving the full modern-spelling context of the lines that contain the suspect words (which I italicize). In each case, the italicized words do not appear in either of the other early texts of the play. All the italicized words and phrases are superfluous; I provide additional comments, in square brackets, where appropriate.

The foregoing list demonstrates, comprehensively and in detail, the kind of evidence that has convinced so many scholars that the 1603 quarto contains actors' interpolations. But unfortunately for the theory, the 37 "Possible Actors' Additions" I list above are all *unique to Q2*, rather than Q1.[45] Which is to say: the criteria that Irace applies can just as easily identify "evidence of memorial reconstruction" in variants unique to the 1604 quarto as it does in variants unique to the 1603 quarto.

Let me begin again, and this time actually examine the evidence cited by Irace in her appendix. But before I do so, I need to establish two kinds of context, which Irace and other scholars systematically ignore. First, every hypothesis about a memorial reconstruction or "bad" quarto cites, as evidence, cases where the indicted text produces an "extrametrical" or "unmetrical" line. But these claims are based on the assumption that Shakespeare's verse was always perfectly regular iambic pentameter. It was not. The sanest and most comprehensive discussion of "Shakespeare's Metrical Art" remains the 1988 book on that subject by the respected scholar-poet George T. Wright. Wright is not a partisan, pushing a particular agenda about the 1603 edition of *Hamlet*. He simply describes, and illustrates, Shakespeare's repeated use of long lines, short lines, and lines with omitted or additional syllables (particularly at the beginning of the line, or on either side of the midline caesura).[46] My comments on metrical issues (table 2.2) are not special pleading: they simply put a few local variants in the global context of Shakespeare's own metrical practice.

Piratical Actors? • 49

Second, the 1603 edition was manufactured by hand, and as such it was prone to human error. Quarto playbooks were cheap commodities, and like other low-cost low-prestige products they were not subjected to the rigorous quality controls demanded for scholarly books or Bibles. Hand-press printing requires a skilled workman (the compositor) to look back and forth between the manuscript and his "composing stick." He reads a line or phrase or sentence in the manuscript, then re-creates that string of words by picking up individual metal types from his type-case and placing each corresponding letter, space, and punctuation mark in the stick. This is harder than it may sound: like Ginger Rogers (who famously mirrored the dancing of Fred Astaire, but "in high heels and backwards"), the compositor mirrors the text he has just read, but upside down or backward. Like any repetitive-motion task, this deliberate and artificial dyslexia requires a constant battle against the inattention created by boredom. Moreover, this task depends upon short-term memory: the compositor reads the text, then carries it in his head for as long as it takes to re-create it on the stick. So even a text handprinted from an author's manuscript will sometimes contain errors that result from short-term memory failure, including repetition and anticipation. What I am describing here is not just "a theory" about compositorial error: it has been confirmed by experiments on short-term memory, and observation of countless errors in reprints (and in other printed texts that we can compare with their manuscript sources). We would not expect compositors in the printing house to mix up their memories of the line they just looked at with another line three acts later, but they can certainly mix up memories within a single line or sentence, or mix up the line they are setting now with a line they just set. We know that, in the course of being manufactured, every printed text passed through the short-term memory of a compositor; very few, if any, of those printed texts passed through the long-term memory of an actor. If observed facts about routine compositorial error can explain a particular textual variant, we do not need to resort to the extraordinary and abnormal hypothesis of memorial reconstruction by a pirate-actor.

In table 2.2 I have preserved the sequence and substance of Irace's evidence, but I have displayed it somewhat differently. Line numbers refer not to Irace's edition (for Q1) or to the conflated text of the old Riverside edition (as she did), but to Thompson and Taylor's Arden editions of the Q1, Q2, and F versions. Normally, I follow Irace in giving only the added word(s), but in some cases (no. 9, 15, 16, etc.), in order to clarify the nature of the alleged addition, I have given part of the context, and italicized the additional word or words.

Table 2.2 Irace's list of "actors' additions" in the 1603 edition

	Q1	Q2	F
*1. O	1.2	1.1.4	1.1.4
[Like other asterisked items in this list, this is a stressed extra monosyllable at the beginning of a verse line. Although this is technically a departure from regular iambic pentameter, it is a metrical license common in Shakespeare's plays, as editors have long recognized.]			
2. By heaven	1.40	1.1.50	1.1.50
[In Q1, this produces a metrically regular line, in contrast to Q2 and F, where the line is irregular]			
3. Marry	1.68	1.1.78	1.1.78
[This variant produces in Q1 a line of six feet, instead of the five in a normal pentameter. Hexameters can be found in all Shakespeare's plays, as James Boswell noted as early as 1821.]			
4. to me	1.93	1.1.134	1.1.116
[With or without these two words, this is an isolated part-line in all three versions.]			
5. speak	1.97	1.1.138	1.1.120
[We learn later that "It was about to speak when the cock crew" (1.104), and immediately after this part-line Horatio says "Stop it, Marcellus" (1.99). Clearly, between this part-line and the following line there is significant stage action: the Ghost indicating in some way that it is about to speak, the offstage crowing of the cock, the Ghost's move to depart. In these circumstances there is nothing unusual, undramatic or un-Shakespearian about Q1's isolated part-line.]			
*6. O	1.99	1.1.142	1.1.124
*7. Lords	2.1	1.2.27	1.2.27
[Q1's lineation differs here from Irace's emended lineation. In Q1, which the Arden edition retains, this line does not have too many syllables; instead, it is short one unstressed initial syllable.]			
8. (H) Sir	2.88	1.2.172	1.2.170
[Q1 produces an additional stressed syllable after the caesura. Like other examples in this list prefixed with the letter "H," this is spoken by Hamlet.]			
9. My *good* lord	2.90	1.2.175	1.2.173
*10. (H) O	2.91	1.2.176	1.2.174
*11. (H) O my father	2.98	1.2.183	1.2.181

[This additional phrase is extrametrical, but in Q2 both this line and the following line are metrically irregular.]

12. (H) Why	2.99	1.2.184	1.2.182

[Q1 is here more regular than Q2.]

13. (H) Aha!...kee you?	2.105	1.2.190	1.2.188

[This is an isolated part-line in both Q2 and F.]

14. (H) it	2.109	1.2.194	1.2.192

[This word in Q1 gives the iambic pentameter line a "feminine ending"—which is far and away the most common metrical license in Shakespeare's blank verse, and more common in Q2 and F than in Q1.]

15. my *good* lord	2.139	1.2.225	1.2.223
16. my *good* lord	2.140	1.2.226	1.2.224

[The second example of this phrase is much less metrical than the first, but in this context the repetition, if it is an error, could clearly be a mistake by a compositor; there's nothing specifically actorly about it.]

*17. (H) Why	2.141	1.2.227	1.2.225

[An isolated part-line in all three texts.]

18. (H) Yea	2.149	1.2.234	1.2.233

[This is metrically regular in Q1.]

*19. O	2.151	1.2.237	1.2.235

[An irregular part-line in all three texts.]

*20. (H) O your loves	2.165	1.2.252	1.2.251

[The line in Q2 and F is a foot short.]

21. (H) *Well,* all's not well	2.166	1.2.253	1.2.252

[This phrase is metrical in Q1. The other texts have "All is not well." The alleged addition is thus related to an adjacent variant. Moreover, the addition produces a possible play on the word "well."]

*22. (H) O	4.6	1.4.8	1.4.8
23. here	4.10	1.4.12	1.4.12

[Q2 here has a feminine ending; Q1 has an hexameter.]

24. (H) in	4.13	1.4.16	1.4.16

[Q1's additional word is the second use of the preposition in the line "More honoured in the breach than *in* the observance." The addition could be a compositorial error, but the line—like a number of lines elsewhere in Q1, Q2, and F—would be metrically regular if the penultimate *the* were elided to *th'* before the following vowel: "th'observance." Stressing the repeated preposition makes better sense than stressing the article "the," which the Q2/F variant here seems to require.]

25. my lord	4.38	1.4.62	1.4.41

[In Q1 this produces an hexameter, made up of two part-lines with different speakers, each with three feet. Shakespeare often creates such symmetries, and Q1 produces a more symmetrical exchange than the other texts.]

26. My lord	4.52	1.4.81	1.4.56

[This vocative is actually present in both Q2 and F, which expand Q1's single speech into two speeches. Q1 reads "*My lord*, be ruled, you shall not go," where the other texts have "*You shall not go, my lord*" (1.4.80) and then "Be ruled, *you shall not go*" (1.4.81), both addressed to Hamlet. The later texts are actually more repetitive here than Q1.]

27. Nay	5.7	1.5.5	1.5.5

[This is metrical in Q1.]

28. (H) my uncle	5.35	1.5.41	1.5.41

[The context is metrically irregular in all three texts.]

29. (H) So, 'tis enough	5.85	1.5.112	1.5.112

[This is part of a full line in Q1. By contrast Q2 and F have an isolated part-line here.]

30. (H) wonderful, *wonderful*	5.89	1.5.117	1.5.117

[Metrical irregularity in all three texts. The repetition could be compositorial.]

31. (H) not I	5.90	1.5.118	1.5.118

[Metrical irregularity in all three texts.]

32. (H) Nay	5.126	1.5.156	1.5.156

[The Q1 lineation of this speech actually produces more metrical regularity than Q2's lineation. The additional word in Q1 is at the caesura.]

*33. (H) (P) O	7.162	3.1.116	3.1.117

[Like other examples marked with "P," this is in prose, so meter cannot help us to determine the authenticity of variants.]

34. (H) (P) For God's sake	7.175	3.1.131	3.1.132
35. (H) (P) to you	7.288	2.2.323	2.2.384
36. (P) Why	7.302	2.2.341	2.2.404
37. (H) (P) sir	7.322	2.2.365	2.2.426

[Middleton's two holograph manuscripts of the last two scenes of *A Game at Chess* demonstrate that a playwright—even a playwright who was not a professional actor—often added, omitted, or transposed this vocative.[48]]

38. (H) (P)—*No*, 'tis not so, it begins with "Pyrrhus." *O, I have it*—	7.341	2.2.389	2.2.448

[In Q2 and F this is verse. But in Q1 it is clearly prose, like Hamlet's words before and after his recitation of parts of the speech by Aeneas to Dido. Q1 continues the formal distinction between Hamlet's speech and the inset play-speech. That formal distinction is lost in the later texts. Thus, although Q1 is locally more "irregular" (because it's prose), in its dramatic context Q1's prose actually produces greater formal regularity than Q2 or F.]

39. but all	7.357	2.2.410	2.2.468

[Metrical in Q1 context.]

40. (P) Enough, my friend	7.360	2.2.436	2.2.494
41. (H) (P) I can tell you	7.382	2.2.463	2.2.521
42. (H) (P) not	7.391	2.2.474	2.2.533

[In all three texts Hamlet's following request to the players is expressed negatively, like this one here. Q1 thus produces more grammatical regularity than Q2 and F.]

43. (P) Yes, *very easily*, my *good* lord	7.397	2.2.479	2.2.538

[In Q2 and F the two consecutive speeches here replying to Hamlet are identical: "Ay, my lord" (2.2.475) and "Ay, my lord" (2.2.479). In Q1 the second is more expansive than the first. For proponents of memorial reconstruction, the variant in the later texts could "very easily" be dismissed as memorial repetition.]

44. (H) (P) I thank you	7.398	2.2.480	2.2.539
45. (H) Why	7.406	2.2.494	2.2.553

[Again, the additional word in Q1 coincides with a change in the immediate context, from Q1's "Why what is" to Q2/F's "What's." In F the line is a hexameter (preceded by an isolated part-line). In Q2 the line itself is irregular, but preceded by an isolated part-line—and emended by most editors. In all three texts there is metrical irregularity.]

46. (P) My lord	9.72	3.2.99	3.2.101
47. (P) the name of	9.136	3.2.230	3.2.228
48. (P) why	9.147	3.2.118	3.2.121
49. (H) (P) *Nay* then	9.153	3.2.124	3.2.127

[If the word "Nay" is an unauthorized addition—and there is no good evidence to support emending it—the error could be compositorial rather than theatrical, because "nay then" occurs in the previous line.]

50. (H) (P) begin	9.162	3.2.246	3.2.243
51. (P) Alas	9.194	3.2.344	3.2.342

[In Guildenstern's following reply to Hamlet, the later texts have the superfluous phrase "Believe me" (3.2.346), not present in Q1. If "Alas" could be interpolated, then so could "Believe me."]

52. (H) (P) you shall	9.219	4.2.19	3.5.22
*53. (H) O	16.148	5.1.248	5.1.256
54. Sir	17.59	5.2.221	5.2.191

[This monosyllable occurs after a caesura in a verse line divided between two speakers. See no. 37 above.]

55. O	17.98	5.2.311	5.2.281

[Metrical in Q1.]

56. of our chiefest	17.128	5.2.379	5.2.350

[The verse context in Q1 is different than the later texts.]

Altogether, Irace identifies 103 words as "possible" additions by actors. Even if all these examples were convincing, they would represent a mere 0.6 percent of the text : one word out of every 155. This is a minuscule data-sample on which to base so drastic a hypothesis. And the data-sample is anything but random. Irace with Q1 (like Jenkins with the Folio) has carefully searched the text for words and phrases that would support the theory of interference by actors.

But even the 103 words that Irace found do not stand up to detailed investigation. One alleged example is not even an addition in Q1 (no. 26). Of the 55 remaining variants, 17 are prose, making it impossible to differentiate between Q1 and the other texts on formal grounds. Even the examples that occur in verse are ambiguous. In six cases, Q1's "addition" actually produces *more* metrical regularity than the later texts (2, 12, 13, 29, 27, 32). In five cases, the Q1 "addition" is irregular only if it is inserted into the Q2/F context; the line in Q1 itself is metrical (18, 21, 27, 39, 55). In eight cases, *all three texts* are metrically irregular, but irregular in different ways (4, 11, 17, 19, 28, 30, 31, 45). In four cases the "addition" does produce metrical irregularity, but could easily result from a common compositorial error, and thus tells us nothing about the memories of actors (16, 24, 30, 49). Thus, of the 38 alleged examples in verse, 16 are useless as evidence, and another six actually contradict the theory. That leaves us with a mere 16 "additions" that produce more metrical irregularity in Q1 than in Q2 or F. But all those irregularities can be paralleled elsewhere in Shakespeare, and indeed elsewhere in *Hamlet*, in lines that editors do not stigmatize as corrupt: an extra unstressed syllable at the end of a line (14), an extra stressed syllable at the beginning of the line (1, 6, 7, 10, 11, 17, 18, 20, 22, 33, 53), a hexameter (2, 23, 25), an extra syllable at the caesura (8, 32, 54).

So, of Irace's 56 examples of actors' additions, what's left?

Nothing.

Actually, less than nothing. *Six of her examples contradict her theory.* The theory is even more profoundly damaged by the ease with which proponents of memorial reconstruction can detect alleged interpolations. All three early texts of *Hamlet* (and most other dramatic texts of the period) contain words and phrases that could, by these loose criteria, be stigmatized as actors' additions. We cannot use such data as evidence that the memory of an actor corrupted one text, unless we concede that the memory of an actor corrupted *all the texts*. Moreover, most of Irace's examples are in Hamlet's speeches—like most of the apparent "interpolations" Jenkins found in the Folio, and most of the examples I culled from the 1604 quarto. In all three texts, a disproportionate number of such "additions" occur in the title role. This pattern suggests that these features are in some way relevant to the character of Hamlet (who, if not mad, is at least emotionally volatile) or relevant to the actor for which the role was designed.

This kind of "evidence"—offered by Irace, and cited approvingly by Taylor, Thompson, and other twenty-first-century scholars—allegedly proves that *one* text (Q1) is an actor's memorial reconstruction, but it actually forces us to dismiss *all three* texts as the product of an actor's memory. So this "evidence" is meaningless. But what may seem to be an entirely negative conclusion actually has two positive corollaries.

First, it means that the "bad" 1603 text is, in this respect, as "good" as the other two. Second, it reminds us that Shakespeare was an actor who wrote for actors. As a writer, he was capable of extraordinarily creative metaphors, unique phrases, and perfect iambic pentameters. But he also, as a writer, played continuously with interjections, repetitions, the linguistic small change and rhythmical irregularities of ordinary speech. When describing the texts of a poet who was also a player, an actor's interpolation is indistinguishable from a writer's.

Despite the obvious logical weaknesses of Irace's work on *Hamlet*, it was still being cited, repeatedly and approvingly, by Lene B. Petersen in a dense monograph published by Cambridge University Press in 2010.[49] Petersen makes use of much more sophisticated statistical software than Irace, but her procedures are often unexplained, self-contradictory, inaccurate, or incomprehensible: as Gabriel Egan observes, in a long and detailed review, "Readers who are baffled should not blame themselves."[50] A very different statistical analysis of the variants in *Hamlet* has been provided by Charles Adams Kelly. He looks at the distribution of blocks of texts present *only* in Q2, or *only* in F, that leave "no trace" in Q1. The 15 largest such passages contain 257 lines, representing about 6 percent of the total number of lines in the traditional conflated text.

> It might be thought that memorial reconstruction could miss 6% of the text while recalling over 1500 concordant lines. But, this is like throwing 1500 darts into a dart board and never hitting a 6% area of the target. The probability of this is so infinitesimally small that there are over 40 zero's following the decimal point.....[51]

Kelly is an independent scholar, and his account of the texts of *Hamlet* is full of amateur errors. But Egan nevertheless singles out Kelly's statistical observation as an important and original contribution: "It is statistically unlikely that [the reporter] would consistently fail to remember parts that are Q2-only or F-only. But that is precisely what he does, and the only plausible explanation is that the Q2-only and F-only parts were not present in what he was trying to remember."[52] In itself, Kelly's evidence does not disprove memorial reconstruction; but it does force any theory of piracy to assume that the version being performed and reported lacked *both* the material unique to the second quarto *and* the material unique to the Folio. Although Kelly's assumption that the 1603 version represents an earlier version of Shakespeare's play is not the *only* theory that would account for that pattern, it is certainly the *simplest*.

Others are better equipped than I am to arbitrate between the competing statistical claims of Petersen and Kelly. But anyone with an interest in literature can understand the foundations of Petersen's argument. Her statistics are all based, like Irace's, on an indefensible assumption. Petersen compares Shakespeare's plays to ballads, folk tales, and other genres of oral literature that evolve through repetition into simpler, more economical "goal-forms," and on the basis of this comparison she concludes that the first edition of *Hamlet* is a later version of the play, one honed by performance into a more minimal folk form. But her initial hypothesis ignores the fundamental distinction between a scripted play and an orally transmitted tale. Consider the well-known "telephone game," where you whisper something to the person next to you, who whispers it to the next, and so on, until it reaches the end of the circle, where you discover (unsurprisingly) that the original message has been transformed by its oral transmission. This model applies well enough to songs, because they are often passed orally from one illiterate person to another, and even today most people are musically illiterate, unable to read a musical score but perfectly capable of picking up a tune once they have heard it a few times, or even one time. This mechanism of oral transmission explains why, in all three texts of *Hamlet,* the lyrics of the gravedigger's song differ from the words written by Thomas Lord Vaux and printed in 1557: Shakespeare presumably had *heard* the song, 30 or 40 years after it was written. Now, alter the nature of the telephone game by changing the technology of communication: instead of each person whispering a message to their neighbor, each hands the neighbor a text containing that message: at the end of the circle, the text has not changed. The scripted drama of early modern England was undoubtedly modified, in performance, by moments of improvisation and occasional failures of memory. But when one actor in a long-running play retired or died or moved to another company, the next actor to play that character was handed a manuscript "part," a written text that had been copied from the licensed manuscript playbook. But even that analogy is misleading, because there is no reason to believe much, if any, change of cast occurred between the first performance of the canonical *Hamlet* and the creation of the manuscript printed by Ling in 1603. At most, three years, not three decades, had passed.[53]

Petersen's model also postulates an inevitable evolution toward simplicity, and therefore equates the simplest text, linguistically, with the latest text, chronologically. That may be true of ballads and folk tales, but it is not true of authorial revision in a manuscript or print culture. As everyone knows, when Henry James revised his novels their sentences became, not simpler, but more complex. No one denies that the first edition of *Hamlet* is shorter, and linguistically and formally simpler, than the later editions; we do not need computers and linguists to tell us that. Before Petersen, Leah Marcus had already analyzed the gradual evolution of the printed texts of *Hamlet* from 1603 to 1623 in terms of a movement from orality toward literariness, which in turn explained the preference of literary critics for the least "oral" text.[54] But the brevity and simplicity of the first edition is intrinsically ambiguous. It could be the result of corruption (going in one temporal direction) or of the evolution toward complexity (going in the opposite temporal direction). Petersen's statistics do nothing to resolve that ambiguity. They just mystify it.

I have been a little hard on Kathleen Irace and Lene Petersen. In fact, the errors of logic and evidence that I have tried to point out in their work are endemic to all nineteenth- and twentieth-century theories of memorial reconstruction. I have focused on their work because they are the latest, and most influential, champions of the revived, re-costumed theory. Experience has taught me that any attempt to say something positive about the 1603 quarto will still immediately be dismissed, if it does not first confront the theory of memorial reconstruction. A bad theory has to be dismantled, before a new one can be built.

My negative remarks about Irace and Petersen are actually quite mild, by comparison with what scholars have said about anyone who challenges the theory of memorial reconstruction, particularly in relation to *Hamlet*. Why do scholars—who are supposed to be like Horatio, the man "that is not passion's slave"—become so angry, so contemptuous, when the theory of memorial reconstruction is challenged or ignored? This question is related to another: why have so many intelligent, serious, erudite, and hardworking scholars believed in such a wobbly theory? Exasperated outsiders like Eric Sams have explained this historical fact by attacking the entire profession of Shakespeare editing, and beyond that the entire profession of Shakespeare scholarship, and beyond that the entire academy. But in my own experience, few Shakespeare editors, Shakespeare scholars, or professors of literature are the blinkered idiots that Sams imagines them to be. Most are seeking answers to difficult questions. Most are fascinated by human artistry. They have dedicated their lives to celebrating and preserving the aesthetic achievements of the past. Hampered by the paucity and ambiguity of the available evidence, struggling with jigsaw puzzles that lack many of the most important pieces, they labor for a lifetime, for little material reward, in good faith and with intellectual integrity.

So why, and how, could they get it so wrong, so long, in this particular case? "If a theory is stated often enough, confidently enough and over a long enough period of time," Albert B. Weiner observed, "it somehow loses its theoretical nature and is transformed into an established fact," and "the theory of memorial reconstruction" was, for most of the twentieth century, "so widely accepted, and...stated with such confidence, that a young student can only with the greatest diligence and industry discover that it ever was a theory."[55] Hardin Craig, himself a veteran Shakespeare editor, in dismissing Pollard's theory of pirate-stationers and the "even vaguer and less well-supported theory of memorial reconstruction," pointed out that "the vaguer a false hypothesis is, the more extensive are its possibilities," and that memorial reconstruction "is variously stated according to the fancy of its users and the needs of the argument."[56] The very vagueness, evasiveness, and flexibility of the theory *logically* undermined its validity, but made it *practically* useful to many people. After all, there are many reasons to be fascinated by *Hamlet*, and many Shakespeare problems worth solving; the mantra of "memorial reconstruction" allowed Shakespeare fandom to focus on those other (perfectly legitimate) interests, without having to unravel all the textual tangles. It's easier to juggle two balls, than three, and so it's tempting to throw away one of the three balls. The 1604 and 1623 texts are closer to each other than either is to the 1603 edition, and both of them are stylistically more accomplished. The differences between the two later texts are enough to exercise the time and intelligence of textual critics.

Craig's and Weiner's explanations for the popularity of the theory of memorial reconstruction are general observations about the sociology of knowledge. However, I refuse to assert, here, that *no play* was *ever* memorially reconstructed by an actor or actors. I have not examined every case, and in this book I am focusing on *Hamlet*. Why, despite the demonstrable weakness of the evidence, has this theory been so often invoked in discussions of the first edition of *Hamlet*?

One reason is that the theory focuses on two real, quantifiable, and important facts. The 1603 edition repeatedly sets prose as verse, and also misaligns much of the verse. Such carelessness naturally suggests that the quarto text was produced by someone indifferent to literary and formal distinctions that were important to Shakespeare and remain important to modern critics, actors, and teachers. But such mislineation is not evidence of piracy. It occurs in other early modern printed and manuscript plays that cannot be stigmatized as memorial reconstructions. Thomas Middleton mislined his own verse when making a copy of *A Game at Chess*. Paul Werstine, surveying playhouse manuscripts, points out that copyists often introduce mislineation. More generally, Werstine insists that a "bad" text may just be a "good" text that has been badly copied.[57] But of all the possible agents of transmission, actors were the people least likely to ignore lineation. The formality of verse helps actors memorize their lines; they pay more attention to line endings than almost any other reader. Therefore, although in this respect the first edition is undoubtedly "bad," that very badness points away from actors, and towards more normal forms of manuscript copying.

The second fact that has encouraged theories of memorial reconstruction is that, although some parts of *Hamlet* vary wildly between the first quarto and the two later editions, other parts remain relatively stable in all three texts. The Prologue's single sixteen-word three-line rhymed speech (9.92–4) is identical in all three texts. Lucianus, likewise, speaks only one six-line rhymed speech (9.165–70), but its 40 words are effectively the same in all three versions.[58] So are the 149 words of one of the Danish ambassador's speeches, reporting on his embassy to Norway (7.31–51).[59] The speeches of Marcellus in 1.1, 1.2, 1.4, and 1.5 are much less stable than these—but more stable than those of any other major character.[60] Memorial reconstruction will not explain the *pattern* of these pockets of textual stability in the surrounding swirl of variation, but those pockets do tell us something important about *Hamlet*.

In his own critique of memorial reconstruction, Lukas Erne pointed out that the Marcellus scenes "contain the play's exposition" and are "essential for the audience's understanding of the plot."[61] But Erne's explanation is actually even less satisfactory than Irace's. Horatio and the Ghost, after all, are more important to the play's exposition than Marcellus, but their speeches vary more than his. And Erne does not mention Voltemand, Lucianus, and the Prologue, who are much more stable than Marcellus. One could argue that the play needs Voltemand's speech about his embassy to Norway, which single-handedly keeps the Fortinbras subplot alive in the middle of the play. But Erne argues that Q1 is, primarily, a deliberate abridgement of the enlarged versions of the play, and we know that Fortinbras was eliminated entirely in performances from the Restoration until the early twentieth century. The play-within-the-play is Hamlet's first move against his stepfather, catalyzing everything that happens in the last half of the play; but the highly variant speeches of the Player Duke/King and Player Duchess/Queen are much more important to that agenda than the innocuous Prologue:

> For us and for our tragedy,
> Here stooping to your clemency,
> We beg your hearing patiently.

Likewise, for "the plot" what the murderer Lucianus *says* is less important than what he *does* (pour poison in the sleeper's ear) and how Hamlet describes his action ("He poisons him . . . for his estate"). And if the actor-pirate hypothesis had not limited our attention to the collected speeches of individual characters, we would notice that the invariant patch of text here includes Hamlet's two preceding sentences: "Leave thy damnable faces and begin. Come, the croaking raven doth bellow for revenge."

What unites the invariant, or less variant, patches of text is that, beyond their functionality, they are not very interesting, dramatically or psychologically or poetically. They do the job, but in the context there's not much more they can do. No aspiring actor dreams of some day being good enough, or lucky enough, to play Marcellus, or Voltemand, or Lucianus. No aspiring writer dreams of emulating these sentences. These are not Shakespeare's most memorable lines, and we should reject any theory that makes them the best-remembered lines of the play in performance, the lines that actors most wanted to keep or that spectators most wanted to preserve in their notebooks. The difference between variant and stable areas of the text cannot be plausibly graphed as a function of any conceivable intermediary of textual transmission. Rather, it suggests, to me, the priorities of a writer.[62] For instance, almost all scholars agree that an anonymous play published in 1591, *The Troublesome Reign of John, King of England*, was a major source for Shakespeare's *King John*. But only two verse lines in the play are identical, and they are spoken by different characters who must have been played by different actors: "Poitiers and Anjou, these five provinces" (*King John* 2.1.528, spoken by King John) and "For that my grandsire was an Englishman" (5.4.42, spoken by Melun). Long ago, F. P. Wilson cited these two lines as evidence for the orthodox view that *Troublesome Reign* preceded *King John*. Otherwise, Wilson found it hard to explain why anyone who "remembered so much of the plot and here and there some of the words [of *King John*] did not remember any of the language which we think of as characteristically Shakespearian, only colourless matter-of-fact words."[63] The same reasoning suggests that the 1603 edition of *Hamlet* represents a play written before the canonical version, rather than a memory of that canonical version. *King John* retains so little of *Troublesome Reign* because Shakespeare did not write that earlier play. The later editions of *Hamlet* retain more identical lines from the first edition because Shakespeare himself wrote all three versions of the play. But the kind of line that remains invariant is, in both *King John* and *Hamlet*, something functional and ordinary, rather than something extraordinary or memorable.

Hamlet, his mother, his stepfather, his father, his friend Horatio, his beloved Ophelia, her father, her brother, and Fortinbras—those characters and their interactions obviously fascinated Shakespeare, and it is easy to imagine that fascination continuing, provoking him to play with their speeches and their characters. He was also fascinated by even smaller roles, like the braggart courtier ("Osric") in the final scenes, the Gravedigger clown, the travelling players, the servant of Corambis/Polonius, Hamlet's school friends summoned to court and eventually dispatched to execution. He could even do something more with the sentry who begins the play and then almost immediately leaves it. But the Prologue, Lucianus, and Voltemand were just necessary nonentities, and Marcellus not much more. They were not interesting enough to justify expansion, development, updating, rethinking. Their textual stability simply indicates that they were there from the beginning, and did not change.[64]

Why has this explanation of the invariant material not been obvious to everyone from the outset? An historically specific answer is suggested by the first modern response to the 1603 edition. The copy now in the British Library, when found in Dublin in 1856, had been interleaved by an earlier owner.[65] Onto those inserted pages, facing the original edition, that unknown eighteenth-century reader had pasted cuttings from the 1718 edition of *Hamlet* "As it is now Acted."[66] He or she also transcribed onto those leaves comments on the play from Lewis Theobald's 1733 edition of *The Works of Shakespeare*. In other words, the first known post–Jacobean reader of the 1603 edition immediately and anachronistically compared it to two things: (1) a modern performance-text, based on the theatrical interpretations and interventions of William Davenant, Thomas Betterton, and Robert Wilkes; and (2) a modern scholarly edition. Theobald's edition systematically combined material from the 1604 and 1623 versions, thereby producing the even more "enlarged," conflated megatext that has dominated our thinking about the play from the beginning of the eighteenth century. This first Enlightenment reader, and all subsequent readers, knew the modern *Hamlet* first, and brought that previous experience watching *Hamlet*, reading *Hamlet*, and reading about *Hamlet* to their encounter with the alien 1603 text.

The direction of our reading of *Hamlet* has always privileged the expanded, later text. We go *from* the "expanded" *to* the not-expanded. Since the beginning of the eighteenth century, *no one has encountered the first edition first*. So we do not see the differences between the 1603 edition and the enlarged editions, as we should, in terms of what those later editions left untouched; we see the differences instead in terms of what the 1603 edition preserved, and we seek an explanation for the pattern of *its* changes. Modern editors and scholars routinely describe the text printed in 1603 as "shortened" or "abridged" or "abbreviated." Passages present in the 1604 or 1623 editions are said to have been "omitted" or "cut" or "deleted" from the 1603 edition. Material in a different place in the 1603 text is said to have been "moved" or "transposed" or "misplaced." When the 1603 edition uses a different word than the later ones, we are told that it has "altered" or "substituted"—or "misremembered"—the familiar later word. Such prejudicial language, in what is supposed to be an objectively descriptive textual apparatus, is rightly criticized by Randall McLeod.[67] But the prejudice accurately reflects the vector of our own experience. When we read the 1603 text, our reading is inevitably, inescapably haunted by our memory of the expanded canonical text. With the best will in the world, a modern scholar cannot not-remember the expanded version. So all our readings of the 1603 edition are biased by our previous reading of something else. A judge can order that irrelevant later testimony to be stricken from the record, but cannot erase it from the memories of the jurors.

That anonymous eighteenth-century reader was obviously a well-educated adult. By the early nineteenth century, readers were encountering the canonical *Hamlet* at a much earlier age. In 1807, Charles Lamb adapted the expanded play into one of his *Tales from Shakespear*, specifically intended for children.[68] In 1817, William Hazlitt, 39 years old, wrote of "that Hamlet the Dane, whom we read of in our youth"—and declared "It is *we* who are Hamlet."[69] Decades before the 1603 edition was reintroduced to the world, reading the canonical *Hamlet* had become a foundational experience, affecting not only our view of that play, but our view of ourselves, and our sense of what literature should be. The Lamb who translated Shakespeare's play into a "Tale" also famously argued that Shakespeare's tragedies were "diminished by the makeshifts of staging." Hazlitt, too, declared that "We do not like to see our author's plays acted, and least of all, *Hamlet*."[70] This anti-theatrical prejudice became fully institutionalized in the twentieth century, when scholars interested in performance broke away from English departments to form their own separate programs and schools dedicated to theatre.[71]

What distinguishes memorial reconstruction, as a theory, is that it blames actors, and actors alone, for what are perceived as the deficiencies of a text. Our own anachronistic memories of the canonical *Hamlet* easily convince us that the 1603 version is "deficient." Our culture's prejudices against theatre then easily convince us that actors are responsible for that deficiency.

A full account of these prejudices in action would require a lengthy defense of every verbal difference between the first edition and the later, more familiar texts. But let me give just one example, singled out by a reader of an earlier version of this book as a particularly compelling proof of memorial reconstruction. The textual variant occurs late in the play, in the scene where the King enters alone with Laertes.

> KING: Hamlet from England! Is it possible?
> What chance is this? They are gone, and he comes home.
> LAERTES: O, he is welcome! By my soul he is:
> At it my jocund heart doth leap for joy
> That I shall live to tell him, thus he dies.
> KING: Laertes, content yourself. Be ruled by me
> And you shall have no let for your revenge.
> LAERTES: My will, not all the world.
> KING: Nay, but Laertes, mark the plot I have laid.
>
> (15.1–9)

The King presumably enters holding a piece of paper, which contains the news that astonishes him; such entrances are common in Shakespeare's plays, and the original stage directions sometimes specify the letter, and sometimes do not.[72] Alternatively, we may imagine that he has just received the news offstage. In either case, the scene immediately establishes a clear contrast between the two characters. The younger man needs no urging to murder Hamlet. While the older, more experienced King is still asking questions and trying to absorb the news, Laertes is already anticipating, imaginatively, the moment when he thrusts his sword into Hamlet's body. The King responds by trying to calm him down and manage him, but at the same time promises that there will be no "let" (obstacle) to his intended "revenge." Laertes interrupts to declare that his own "will" (desire, determination) is the only possible obstacle; "all the world" will not stop him, otherwise. The King's "your revenge" is immediately transformed into, and redefined as, "my will"; the King's "no let" is echoed by, and redefined as, "not all the world." This chiasmic structure (ABBA) is common in Shakespeare, and particularly in the first quarto of *Hamlet*.[73] "My will, not all the world" ends with a full stop in the first edition, as do most speeches, but that might be interpreted, by actors or modern editors, as an exclamation mark (as in the 2006 Arden edition) or as a dash, if we imagine the King intervening to stop Laertes in mid-sentence. At some level, "Nay but" is certainly an interruption. The idiom occurs elsewhere more than 40 times in Shakespeare's plays, and on five of those occasions it is followed, as here, by a vocative: "Nay, but Beatrice" (*Much Ado* 4.1.312); "Nay, but Ophelia" (Q2 4.5.34); "Nay, but my lord" (*Troilus* 3.1.80); "Nay, but fellow" (*Coriolanus* 5.2.59); and "Nay, but hark you, Francis" (*1 Henry IV* 2.5.57).

Do you find this passage "perfectly unintelligible"? It's elliptical, but idiomatic, as good dramatic writing often is; sometimes hard to parse, grammatically, but easy enough to grasp. It isn't great poetry, but in my experience actors and audiences have no difficulty understanding it.[74] Indeed, for 100 years after the first quarto was rediscovered, no reader seems to have felt that it required explication or comment. But in 1924 a German scholar, Bastiaan Adriaan Pieter van Dam, described this exchange as "a perfectly unintelligible dialogue." Van Dam pointed out that the canonical text gives Laertes the phrase "My will, not all the world" (F 4.5.135) or "My will, not all the world's" (Q2 4.5.136) in an earlier scene.[75] Assuming the priority of the canonical version, Van Dam describes the presence of this phrase in a different context in Q1 as a "transposition" and "corruption," caused by "an actor's slip." He goes on to describe the memorial mechanism of the alleged error.

> The player who acts the part of Laertes hears the last words of [15.7], "no let for your revenge," which remind him of the last half of [Q2 4.5.135]: "*King*. Who shall stay you [from revenge]?," upon which he, by reflex action so to speak, answers with [15.8, "My will, not all the world"], that is to say the second half of [Q2 4.5.136]. The actor personating the King of course notices the mistake, and by means of the words, which really do not belong to his part, "Nay, but Leartes, mark," very cleverly sets the dialogue right again.[76]

Van Dam attributes his own accurate memory of the phrase to the inaccurate memory of an actor. When, in the course of reading Q1, Van Dam encountered "My will, not all the world," he remembered it from an earlier scene in the more familiar canonical text. But in order to explain this change of position as one actor's error, he first had to transpose, himself, the cue-word "revenge," which he places in square brackets, because it is *not actually present* in the question-cue from 4.5. Like most advocates of memorial reconstruction, he either ignores, or is sloppy about, the importance of cues. Furthermore, Van Dam also has to assume, and assert, that the first edition also contains changes to the text made by a *second* actor playing the King, who "very cleverly" adjusts his own line by interpolating a phrase that "sets the dialogue right." So the "perfectly unintelligible" text becomes "very cleverly...right." No one has ever identified the actor playing Laertes, or the actor playing the

King, as the pirate-actor responsible for the 1603 edition. Van Dam's conjecture thus fails to fit the actor-centered pattern of textual variation that is, allegedly, the signature of memorially reconstructed texts. Van Dam's imagined scenario also requires us to assume that *someone* revised the text, but insists that the someone cannot have been Shakespeare.

Van Dam does not quote either passage, in either quarto, in its entirety, and a reader of his conjecture may not appreciate how radically different the two contexts are. The transposition of "My will, not all the world" is not an isolated textual variant. In the canonical version, the beginning of the earlier scene is much longer, in a way that emphasizes the role of Laertes and the political threat of rebellion. After Ophelia's first exit, the King has a long, reflective speech (not present in Q1), followed by the entrance of a messenger (not present in Q1), warning of the approach of Laertes and his "rabble," followed by their entrance (not present in Q1) and Laertes's dialogue with them and their exit (not present in Q1). Only then does the canonical text reach the beginning of the dialogue between Laertes and the King, with the line (identical in all three texts) "O thou vile King! Give me my father" (Q1 13.49; Q2 4.5.115–16; F 4.5.114–15). Here, once again, we encounter a textually stable moment: like the others I've already discussed, it is not verbally striking, and could easily have been written at the beginning of Shakespeare's career. It is not spoken by, or in the presence of, anyone ever considered to be the pirate actor. But it serves a necessary structural function efficiently, and it might have been kept by a revising author. Then, after Ophelia's second exit in that scene, the familiar version again contains a much longer, and very different, dialogue between the King and Laertes, emphasizing the political context: provisions (not present in Q1) for a council or jury, chosen by Laertes, which will judge whether the King was responsible for the death of Polonius, and, if the King is found guilty, give Laertes the "kingdom" (4.5.195–201). The canonical text follows this with a short scene between Horatio and a sailor with a letter, which describes Hamlet's capture by offstage pirates. Then comes another political conversation between Laertes and the King, the entrance of a messenger, and the reading aloud of Hamlet's letter to the King (4.7.1–51); none of all this is present in Q1. In other words, by the time we reach the moment when Laertes responds to the news of Hamlet's return, the character and situation of the bereaved Laertes have already, in the canonical version, been fully established, and so has his relationship with the King. In that context, their exchange (4.7.57–9) makes sense: the King asks "Will you be ruled by me?" and Laertes responds, respectfully, "Ay, my lord, / So you will not o'errule me to a peace" (with "rule" answered by "oe'rrule");

the King's rejoinder, "To your own peace," changes the general "a" to the specific "your," and thereby transforms "peace" from the absence of violence to the presence of personal emotional satisfaction. All this additional and variant material in the canonical version is written in Shakespeare's mature, inimitable seventeenth-century style.

In the first edition, the relationship between Laertes and the King develops very differently. The political threat to the King is much less important, and is dropped the moment that Ophelia reenters. After her second exit, the King reveals to Laertes that he already has plans in motion to dispose of Hamlet: "Think already the revenge is done" (13.122), he says, promising Laertes that he will receive confirmation within a few days. This confidence is immediately contradicted by the scene, present only in the first edition, in which Horatio informs the Queen that Hamlet is "safe arrived in Denmark" (14.1), and the two make plans together to assist the Prince. Consequently, when the King and Laertes reenter, together, Laertes at once discovers that the King's earlier promise of revenge on Hamlet has been broken, and the audience knows that a counterconspiracy is already afoot. So in Q1 it makes sense that Laertes reacts to the news by setting his "will" against "all the world" (including the King to whom he is speaking, and the counterconspiracy that the audience knows about).

Van Dam dismissed the idea of Shakespeare's deliberate "rewriting," because he paid no attention to this larger dramatic context. Instead, he isolated a single phrase, which he remembered from his own reading of the canonical text; he then conjecturally attributed the position of that phrase in the first edition to transposition by a single actor's (miscued) memory, supplemented and "very cleverly" complemented by another actor's revision of the text to make sense of the first actor's error. But it would be simpler and more economical to assume that the same mechanism explains both the transposition of one phrase and all the other structural and verbal changes to this sequence of scenes. The actor who remembered "My will, not all the world," and transposed it to a different scene, could have been Will Shakespeare. He had, after all, a special fondness for the noun "will" (as demonstrated, most conspicuously, by the Sonnets). The phrase memorably and efficiently sums up the psychology of Laertes in the second half of the play, and Shakespeare never tired of alliterative binary oppositions. The phrase no longer fit its original context, dramatically, but it could be inserted into the expanded, rewritten return of Laertes in 4.5. Most spectators would not notice—indeed, most readers still do not notice—that the phrase actually does not fit the revised context as well as it fit the original context.

In Q1, the impersonal noun "will" responds directly to the impersonal noun "let." But that impersonal noun "will" does not so obviously or directly respond to the personal pronoun in the King's question: "*Who* shall stay you?" We would expect the pronoun "who" to be answered by the pronoun "I." Moreover, in the canonical version, Laertes speaks the phrase in a context where a significant fraction of "the world" seems to be on his side: we have just seen him enter "with his followers," who are compared to "the ocean" overrunning lowlands (Q2 4.5.99–100) and are now apparently standing just offstage. In Q1, by contrast, Laertes is all alone when he speaks those words, his never-seen followers have long disappeared, and the world does indeed seem to be against him.

Van Dam casually invokes "an actor's slip" and an actor's memory, but his conjecture actually depends on his own reading and his own memory, not on any practical understanding of actors, their memories, their relationship to their written parts, or the relationship of Shakespeare the actor to Shakespeare the playwright. This unsubstantiated denigration of actors is all too typical of twentieth-century theories of piracy. So it should not surprise us that some of the latest damning criticisms of memorial reconstruction have not come from a bibliographer, or an editor, or a literary critic. They have come instead from a theatre historian who specializes in archival work on early modern performance practices. In 2013, Tiffany Stern observed that "the actor-pirate theory" behind all claims about memorial reconstruction "does not take acting into account." "For an actor-pirate," she observed, "trained to remember a text by sound and rhythm, a synonym is less obvious than the correct word;" "it would be surprising if an actor-pirate, shrewd enough about sense to recall synonyms, is also ignorant enough about sense to recall entirely wrong words that sound similar." Discussing Hamlet's speech about "this player" whose "visage waned, Tears in his eyes, distraction in his aspect, A broken voice" (lines not present in Q1), Stern notes that these "lines in particular, might be expected to stick in the mind of an actor, for they are about the trade of playing." Discussing Q1's "frequent mislineation," Stern notes that an actor "is likely to have been conscious of line endings—he needed to observe, particularly, when they were enjambed—which would have been an aid to memorization."[77]

Unfortunately, while hammering these additional nails into the coffin of the pirate-actor theory, Stern simultaneously attempts to resurrect the spectre of the pirate-spectator.

CHAPTER 3

Piratical Reporters?

"My tables: meet it is I set it down"

The first edition of *Hamlet* was not pirated by its publishers and was not pirated by actors. But the determined search for pirates continues. Although theories of memorial reconstruction dominated the twentieth century, the earliest attempt to discredit the first quarto, and the most recent, both offer an alternative theory of piracy. Only months after the 1825 facsimile again made the text publicly available, *The European Magazine* published "A Running Commentary on the Hamlet of 1603." It claimed that the earliest edition of *Hamlet* was "the production of a careless reporter," its text "having been surreptitiously taken down piecemeal in the theatre by a blundering scribe."[1] That 1825 article was quoted, and endorsed, in the first paragraph of an enthusiastically applauded paper, published in November 2013 by Cambridge University Press as the lead article in *Shakespeare Survey*, and written by the most influential theatre historian of her (and my) generation, Tiffany Stern, professor of early modern drama at the University of Oxford.[2]

The 1825 article was written by Ambrose Gunthio. His position was actually more complicated than Stern suggests, and significantly differed from her own. For one thing, Gunthio quoted several "new lines worth preserving" in the first edition, which he regarded as "improvements" on the traditional text.[3] He applauded a ten-line exchange between the King and Laertes (13.119–29), unique to the first quarto: "questionless 'tis Shakespeare's." He singled out, in that passage, the line "To bury grief within a tomb of wrath," which he considered "very fine." His other favorites included "Both of them are keys / To unlock chastity unto desire" (3.67–8) and the King's response (13.43–6) to Ophelia's madness:

> A pretty wretch! This is a change indeed.
> O Time, how swiftly runs our joys away!
> Content on earth was never certain bred.
> Today we laugh and live, tomorrow dead.

These passages might not be much to postmodernist taste; they reflect, and appeal to, an earlier aesthetic, which valued pithy generalizations and pathos. But Gunthio recognizes those qualities as Shakespearian; critics still often celebrate the way that Shakespeare personalizes and particularizes abstract nouns. Notably, Gunthio's favorites are all perfectly regular, end-stopped iambic pentameter, much more characteristic of Shakespeare's earliest work than of his verse at the beginning of the seventeenth century.

Ignoring Gunthio's praise of material unique to the first quarto, Stern focuses on his "careless reporter" theory, which was less original. Gunthio specifically cited, as a precedent, Samuel Johnson's view of the early printed texts of *The First Part of the Contention* (*2 Henry VI*) and *Richard Duke of York* (*3 Henry VI*): Johnson was "inclined to believe them copies taken by some auditor who wrote down, during the representation, what the time would permit him, then perhaps filled up some of his omissions at a second or third hearing, and when he had by this method formed something like a play, sent it to the printer."[4] Gunthio's only originality was to apply to the newly discovered 1603 edition of *Hamlet* Johnson's speculation about those two other plays. But Gunthio recognized that Johnson's theory could not, by itself, satisfactorily explain the phenomena. The accuracy of "Voltimand's narrative of the embassy to Norway" forced him to conjecture that the reporter "procured a faithful transcript of the speech in question" from the actor who played that small role, who "was of course one of the inferior performers." Acknowledging that Q1's "Corambis" could not possibly be an error, he concluded that it was "therefore doubtless the name originally given to the character" (345). The name "Polonius" must therefore represent a later revision. Likewise, one of the Queen's speeches "appears evidently to be Shakespeare's first rough draft." He also recognized that the 1603 text represents Gertrude in a substantially different way.[5] Gunthio hypothesized three agents at work on the manuscript behind the 1603 edition: a reporter taking notes on performances, an accurate transcript of one minor actor's part, and Shakespeare (producing a first draft that he would later revise). Stern retains only the note-taker.

Stern believes that "Gunthio" was a pseudonym for John Payne Collier. That identification is based on circumstantial evidence, and may not be correct.[6] However, Gunthio's "careless reporter" did anticipate one key element of Collier's later views about *Hamlet*.[7] In 1843, Collier asserted that the 1603 edition was *not* the play "as originally written by Shakespeare" (as the 1825 reprint had assumed). Instead, Collier claimed, it was a derivative and corrupt text. He attributed the edition to "some inferior and nameless printer, who was not so scrupulous" and who "surreptitiously secured a manuscript of the play" (191). As I have already shown in chapter 1, there is no reason to believe Collier's libel on the printer Valentine Simmes or the publisher Nicholas Ling. The fact that "only a single copy" of the 1603 edition has survived, Collier took as evidence that "but a few were sold" because "its worthlessness was soon discovered" (191). But at least two English book collectors, who together acquired and preserved 122 playbooks, owned a copy of "Hamlet prince of Denmark 1603," so "its worthlessness" must not have been apparent—even in 1647, when six more recent editions contained allegedly better, and certainly longer, texts of *Hamlet*.[8] In any case, Collier's theory was soon undermined by the discovery of a second copy of *Hamlet* (and by the single copy of the undoubtedly authoritative first edition of *Titus Andronicus*). Collier's bibliographical "evidence" for dismissing the 1603 edition does not stand up to serious scrutiny, and suggests that his entire account of the play is driven by what psychologists call "confirmation bias": he was determined to find evidence for an hypothesis to which he was already committed.[9] Collier was so convinced of his own views that he felt justified in inventing evidence to prove them: this may explain why Collier became the most notorious forger in the history of Shakespeare scholarship. After the bogus bibliographical claims of his preface, Collier then proceeded to speculate about the imaginary manuscript that had been "surreptitiously" acquired. Unlike Gunthio, Collier specified, for the first time, what he called "shorthand" as the method used by the reporter. The word is anachronistic; it is first recorded in 1636. But the thing Collier described—"a method of speedy writing by means of the substitution of contractions or arbitrary signs or symbols for letters, words"—did exist in Shakespeare's lifetime, under the name of "brachygraphy" or "stenography." Collier's story is worth quoting in full, because of the long shadow it casts from 1843 to 2013:

> It will be unnecessary to go in detail into proofs to establish, as we could do without much difficulty, the following points: 1. That a great part

of the play, as it stands, was taken down in short-hand. 2. That where mechanical skill failed the shorthand writer, he either filled up the blanks from memory, or employed an inferior writer to assist him. 3. That although some of the scenes were carelessly transposed, and others entirely omitted in the edition of 1603, the drama, as it was acted while the shorthand writer was employed in taking it down, was, in all its main features, the same as the more perfect copy of the tragedy printed with the date of 1604. It is true that in the edition of 1603, Polonius is called Corambis, and his servant Montano, and we may not be able to determine why these changes were made in the immediately subsequent impression; but we may perhaps conjecture that they were names in the older play on the same story, or names which Shakespeare at first introduced, and subsequently thought fit to reject. We know that Ben Jonson changed the whole *dramatis personae* of his "Every Man in his Humour." (191)

Collier tells a story, but provides no proof: he treats his conclusions as self-evidently true. The unsubstantiated tale he tells is also remarkably complicated. Even Collier is forced to break it down into a succession of separate claims: (1) shorthand, combined with (2) memory *or* (3) a second writer, combined with (4) names imported from a lost play by someone else, *or* (5) authorial revision of the names, on the model of Jonson's thorough rewriting of *Every Man in his Humour*.[10] Amazingly, this last conjecture invokes the very spectre of authorial revision that the whole theory is designed to disprove. If we can imagine that Shakespeare changed the names of Corambis and Montano, why can we not imagine that Shakespeare transposed scenes, or rewrote passages? More generally, by invoking so many different agencies and circumstances Collier gives the impression that he is producing a sophisticated scholarly theory. In fact, there is nothing intellectually sophisticated about this procedure. He is simply multiplying fictional entities to explain away inconvenient textual facts. He also gives himself plenty of options (memory *or* a second author, names from a lost play *or* from Shakespeare's revision). Rhetorically, this makes the overall theory seem more plausible. If someone objects to the first option, proponents can switch to the second; if someone objects to the second, they can switch back to the first. Two options may seem twice as probable as one; four options may seem four times as probable. But the probability of each option needs to be considered separately; they do not add up; by increasing the number of required conditions, you actually reduce the probability of any hypothesis.[11] The proliferation of options makes Collier's speculation harder to falsify, but a good empirical theory should be falsifiable. Collier is here using what debaters call "shotgun tactics": he just launches lots of poorly substantiated claims, leaving any opponent the huge task of spending time refuting each one of them.

Paul Werstine has criticized older theories about memorial reconstruction because they always require additional, subsidiary speculations.[12] Likewise, Collier's improbable, multiplying complication has persisted in all subsequent theories that begin with a member of the audience writing down notes on *Hamlet* as it was performed. Stern, in the latest incarnation of this story, recognizes that none of the shorthand systems publicly available at the beginning of the seventeenth century can, in itself, explain the 1603 text of *Hamlet* (or any other printed text of a Shakespeare play). Her innovation is to combine shorthand with other forms of "swift writing." But this variation on the old hypothesis piles up a rickety superstructure even more complicated than Collier's, or anyone else's. She presupposes (1) not just one person but "groups of people" taking notes (2) in order to express their own frustrated, pathetic "'authorial' leanings" and "to reach print" by combining their words with Shakespeare's, *or* simply (3) "for the money" they could earn by selling their notes to (4) an unscrupulous stationer who consciously published a bad text "*in order* to force the 'real' version from the author." These imaginary note-takers used (5) "alphabetic shorthand," combined with (6) "any form of handwriting they liked," attending the play (7) not once but on "any number of occasions," supplementing their notes on *Hamlet* with (8) notes taken at productions of "other plays," assisted by (9) "memory," including possibly (10) "a memorizer," like the supermnemonic spectators later documented in Spain but not England, and (11) "an amender" or "inferior poet," responsible for (12) the "creation" of newly "invented" material, combined with (13) "specific performance variants" reflecting in some cases (14) a different "localized version" *or* (15) "what Shakespeare once intended" but later changed.[13] Unlike Collier, Stern scatters these various subsidiary hypotheses over 23 pages, rather than compressing them into a single paragraph where their complexity would be more apparent. Nevertheless, Stern again demonstrates how many speculative epicycles must be invented in order to sustain the initial assumption of note-taking.

As with Gunthio and Collier, Stern's final supposition eats its own tail, raising the ghost of revision that the theory claims to exorcise. This fact, in itself, tells us something positive and important about *Hamlet*. Every theory of a spectator-pirate, like every theory of an actor-pirate, is forced to presume, at some point, that *Hamlet* was revised by Shakespeare, and/or by Shakespeare's own acting company (where he was a major shareholder, part-owner of their theatre, an actor, and without doubt their most important source of profitable play-scripts). But if all theories about the text of *Hamlet* require such revision, why do we need all these other speculations? Our initial hypothesis should be that the one agent *must* be present in any theory, and that historically *could* have been present, is the cause of *all* the major variations between the 1603 edition and the later "enlarged" versions. That initial hypothesis may be wrong, but it must first be proven wrong before we resort to conjectures about other agents. Stern does not attempt to disprove it; like Collier, she assumes, from the beginning, that the 1603 quarto is "bad," and then speculates about how it got so bad.

Unlike Collier, Stern is not a forger. Unlike Collier, Stern supports her conjectures with a full scholarly apparatus of footnotes and cross-references. But Stern's conjectures begin by assuming, as did Collier, that the 1603 text originated in notes taken in the theatre during performance. But what evidence supports that assumption? Collier in 1843 did not provide any of his alleged "proofs," though he claimed he could do so "without much difficulty." However, he did unveil the first pebble in the foundation of that theory in 1856 in a letter to *The Athenaeum*, cited and endorsed by Stern.[14] To establish his own credentials as an expert witness, Collier (who was born in 1779) testified, "I have written shorthand all my life," using "the shorthand I was taught in my boyhood." His claims about Q1 *Hamlet* are immediately followed by announcement of another alleged discovery: "It is capable of most distinct and undeniable proof," Collier declares, "that Heminge and Condell printed [*The Taming of the Shrew* in the 1623 Shakespeare Folio] from a previous edition in quarto." No one believes Collier's "proof." Here, as with every claim that Collier made from the 1820s to the 1870s, we cannot simply assume he was telling the truth.

But the weakness here goes beyond the personal veracity of Collier to a more general problem in all claims about note-taking reporters as an explanation for the 1603 edition of *Hamlet*. Collier was homeschooled and demonstrably did use shorthand for many years, earning a living as a newspaper reporter. But the profession to which Collier and his father belonged did not exist in 1603. There were no journalists then, and no Parliamentary reporters. As the historian Michael Mendle observes, "Amongst the most fascinating but least studied developments of the 1640s was the emergence of what today would be called the reporter—the agent of a publisher or interested party who attended a trial or an execution or other event to capture as much of it as possible and report it, as the basis for a free-standing tract."[15] Like "Gunthio" and Collier, Stern speculates that the manuscript behind the 1603 quarto of *Hamlet* was produced by an "agent of a publisher," paid for taking notes at a live event and then writing them up for print publication. But that speculation presupposes the existence of an occupation that first emerged, for very specific historical reasons, four decades later, *in the early 1640s*.

The larger issue, in other words, is anachronism. Collier read the text of the 1603 edition from the perspective of his own experience in the early nineteenth century, and he projected that experience back onto the early seventeenth century. Stern does the same. She compares the 1603 edition of *Hamlet* to "pirated products today," when "rogue audiences film blockbusters and put the results on the internet."[16] She thereby compares a 1603 text printed on a muscle-powered handpress to digital images captured on miniaturized iPhone cameras and downloaded onto a global network with file-sharing software. But what is possible now was not possible then. Stern, like Collier, projects her own professional experience backward in time. In the twenty-first century, every scholar (including me) uses digital databases, and Stern is rightly famous for her pioneering and creative data-mining. Finding and downloading excerpts from many different texts, Stern rearranges and compiles her notes into PowerPoint presentations for academic audiences.[17] Her PowerPoint rhetoric (briefly flashing a string of photoquotations from primary sources) creates an enviably impressive spectacle of abundant evidence culled from a wide range of texts, and Stern's unscripted command of that displayed material is hypnotically authoritative. I have never seen anyone do this so well. She often gives these presentations on several occasions in different academic venues, and the fact that her verbal commentary on the notes is unscripted allows her to modify it to suit the specific location. Finally, using word processing software that enables easy transposition and editing, Stern turns her PowerPoint files into a sequential prose narrative, supplying discursive links to connect the collected notes. Before her hypothesis about the 1603 edition of *Hamlet* was written down or published, it was performed for an audience of fellow academics, taking notes on her notes about note-takers, and afterward giving her additional notes of their own, which were all then consolidated and "sent to the printer." This process is almost exactly what Stern imagines, and asks other academics to imagine, happening in 1603. Collier's audience immediately understood his invocation of reporters using shorthand, and Stern's audience immediately understands her invocation of collective note-taking. We have all experienced it. But there were no digital databases in 1603, no photoquotations, no PowerPoint, no word processing software, no personal printers at home, no cheap paper, no academic conferences, no iPads or laptops for note-taking in lecture halls, no emails to facilitate the sharing of notes, and—equally important—none of the social behaviors or institutions associated with those technologies.

Although Stern does what she does exceptionally well, I do not mean, here, to focus on a single personality. I am trying to call attention to a methodology, one which seems natural to my generation, and even more natural to my students. But that methodology is inextricably linked to particular text technologies and institutions, which were developed only recently. The research techniques employed by Stern—and by many of the rest of us—were not available to Collier, or E. K. Chambers, or W. W. Greg, or the editors of the 1986 Oxford Shakespeare. They were certainly not available in 1603. Projecting our own experience and assumptions onto the blank screen of the past is a mistake that is extraordinarily easy for *any* of us to make. It takes constant effort to remind ourselves that "the past is a foreign country," where they did things differently than we do. The problem for a modern scholar, here, is not entirely dissimilar to the problem for a modern actor: trying to imagine an existence different from your own, trying to "live" in a different skin, often a skin hundreds or thousands of years (or miles) away.

Stern's important work as a theatre historian has, from the beginning, depended on her use of late seventeenth- and eighteenth-century evidence to flesh out our understanding of rehearsal and performance in Shakespeare's lifetime.[18] That intellectual method may be legitimately and usefully applied to habits and material practices, like the use of actor's parts or sides, which demonstrably did not change for centuries. But anachronism becomes much more problematic when applied to emergent practices and technologies that were rapidly changing in the seventeenth century.

For instance, Stern's speculation about *Hamlet* rests, literally, on an assumption about the physical materials that enabled early modern note-taking. In order to avoid "the pens, ink, sand, knives, paper and blotting-paper that permanent text required," Stern observes, note-takers used "tablebooks," that is, "small notebooks that could be written on with graphite pencils or soft-metal pens."

> Tablebooks had several advantages: they encouraged continuous writing, as they were not reliant on dipping a pen in ink; they were portable—surviving examples are 16mos in 8s; and they were economical, as they could be wiped clean with damp bread or a wet sponge once their notes had been transcribed onto a permanent medium.[19]

Her summary here, and her adjacent quotations of primary materials, are sourced from two important articles on early modern tablebooks, published independently in 2004.[20] But Stern significantly misrepresents their findings. First, she here includes "graphite pencils" among writing implements that might have been used to take notes during performances of *Hamlet* between 1600 and 1603. But Stallybrass, Chartier, Mowery, and Wolfe specifically deny that pencils would have been used with tablebooks in Shakespeare's lifetime. For one thing, graphite pencils were a relatively new technology, first recorded in Germany in 1565, and until the late seventeenth century used primarily by artists and draftsmen; C. Ainsworth Mitchell, surveying books in the Bodleian Library and the British Museum, found no examples of graphite before 1630.[21] The *Oxford English Dictionary*'s earliest record of the word *pencil* in its modern sense, in 1573, comes from *The Art of Limning*, a drawing manual: it recommends beginning "with a pencil of black lead, or with a coal made sharp at the point" to "trace all thy letters."[22] In context, this is clearly not normal or extensive writing, but letter-tracing subordinated to a larger visual context, with the pencil treated as the equivalent of a sharpened lump of coal. The next recorded example, from 1583, occurs in a manuscript account book, and specifically describes a subscription on a ticket. The next example, in 1612, refers to students making notes in their books, recommending that textbooks be marked up in ink: "But for all other books...note them with a pencil of black lead," so "that you may rub out again when you will." A marginal note explains what "pencil" means: "black lead thrust into a quill."[23] Here at last (nine years after the first edition of *Hamlet*) we have "noting" with a pencil, but the noting here consists of occasional notes made in printed books; it does not imagine an attempt to transcribe a whole speech or sermon or play with pencils. By the mid-1640s, clerks of Parliament found pencils extremely useful, but the earliest Parliamentary diary written with graphite was Sir Nathaniel Rich's in 1614.[24] But one knight in Parliament, more than a decade later, does not provide a precedent for multiple pirate-spectators at the Globe.

Stern's invocation of pencils may seem superfluous, because tablebooks were undoubtedly used (and often sold with) a soft-metal stylus. But "graphite pencils" contributes to the rhetorical multiplication of concrete possibilities that characterizes all her speculation: with so many plausible alternatives, she implies, how can anyone doubt that the 1603 text could derive from notes taken during performances? But the historical improbability of "pencils" is important, because modern readers will anachronistically associate that word with a modern, cheap, convenient little object (which in fact took centuries to develop and mass-produce). And pencils, then as now, could be used with tablets of ordinary writing paper. The stylus, by contrast, worked only on tablebooks with specially treated multilayer paper, resembling pasteboard, and that special paper in turn required special bindings. "The treated paper and the binding," not surprisingly, "added significantly to their cost."[25] Although their reusability in one sense made tablebooks "economical," early modern writers and modern scholars all recognize that they did wear out with repeated use.

How many repeated uses of a tablebook would be required to produce the 15,893 words in the text of *Hamlet* printed in 1603? The answer depends, obviously, on the size and number of specially treated sheets in each book. Far and away the most common format was just a pair of two blank leaves, fastened together, and that format seems implied by most of the contemporary references to tables, tablets, and tablebooks. Some of Stern's readers may not realize that the technical bibliographical description "16mos in 8s" describes a book the size of a modern Palm Pilot (or Iphone). That explains why Hamlet, like other characters in early modern plays, can be carrying his "tables" onstage, initially in his pocket, subsequently in his hand. Stern cites a stage direction from *Love's Labour's Lost*, which calls for Nathaniel to "*draw out his Tablebook*." But Nathaniel takes it out in order to write down one word, "peregrinate," which he applauds as "A singular and most choice epithet" (5.1.15). The earliest citation of the word "tablebook" recorded by the *Oxford English Dictionary* occurs in 1596, when the specified material object is used "to gather phrases."[26] Stern's scholarly sources give many examples of such minimalist note-taking, which connect the "diminutive size" of tablebooks to the humanist emphasis on gathering quotable sentences and "epitomizing." Stern's own first example, placed between the two descriptions of "tablebooks" I quote above, refers to a man who "in the midst of the sermon pulls out his tables in haste, as if he feared to lose that note"—which tells us that he was not attempting to write down a whole sermon, but instead quickly taking out "his tables" to make a note about a particular point the preacher had just made.[27]

Stern later cites Thomas Dekker's 1603 description of the accession of King James ("it were able to fill a hundred pair of writing-tables with notes, but to see the parts played ... on the stage of this new-found world") as evidence of a playwright writing about "plays that were comprehensively gathered" by note-taking spectators.[28] Of course, Dekker was not describing a scripted commercial play performed in a purpose-built theatre, which spectators could not enter without paying to see the enclosed spectacle; he is instead describing a free outdoor event, while invoking the ancient, commonplace idea of the world itself as a theatre. And Dekker's "hundred pair of writing-tables" actually undermines Stern's argument. Even at the low end of the market, such tables could cost sixpence a pair, which for a hundred pair adds up to two and a half pounds. Since a publisher would not normally pay more than two pounds for the manuscript of a play, Stern's evidence would put the cost of taking notes significantly higher than the price that could be earned for them—even before we take account of the cost of ink and paper, once the perishable notes were collected and transferred into a more "permanent medium." The notes were erasable, and the tablets could be reused, but reuse would require repeated costly visits to the playhouse, not to mention deterioration of the writing surface.

Finally, where would these tablets be placed, during a performance? Stern herself cites an example of note-takers in a church, in 1641, "turning the communion tables into a surface on which to write," and in the 1620s note-taking Members of Parliament "probably balanced their notebooks and materials on their knees—something that would account for the appalling script—but others may have availed themselves of writing boxes," which provided "a portable writing surface."[29] Hamlet while standing can write a few words in his tables, but standing hardly seems practicable when writing so many notes on so many thick pasteboard pages for two hours, surrounded by other spectators. Placing tablets "on their knees" would require the note-takers to pay extra, to sit in the galleries. And while acting companies were accustomed to spectators who took out their tablets to write down a few jokes, or quotable phrases, or new words, would their suspicions not have been aroused by a spectator, or spectators, who sat taking notes throughout the entire performance? In 1631, Richard Brathwaite described a "corranto-coiner," that is, someone in the business of gathering small articles of news for the earliest printed newspapers, the *corantos* of the 1620s and early 1630s: "He carries his tablebook still about with him, but dares not pull it out publicly."[30] Here we see the embryo of the 1640s "reporter" described by Michael Mendle. But even in 1631 the reporter must keep his tables concealed.

The corranto-coiner in 1631 had a new, well-organized, profitable, guaranteed commercial market for his notes, and he also had access to highly developed systems of abbreviated writing, including shorthand. We are dealing, then, not only with the evolution of material objects, but with the evolution of specific technical practices that facilitated rapid transcription. This problem was addressed in the first half of the twentieth century, when claims about the use of shorthand to create reported texts of Shakespeare's plays, made by Collier and other nineteenth-century scholars, were for the first time systematically examined from a specifically historicist perspective—and rejected as anachronistic.[31] Stern acknowledges the force of the evidence that the 1603 *Hamlet* could not have been reported by one member of the audience using the shorthand systems known to have been available at that time. However, she sidesteps those arguments by claiming, first, that unbeknownst to us, many more shorthand systems might have existed in 1603, and second, that shorthand could have been combined with "speedy" longhand note-taking. This is another example of Stern's multiplication of imagined agents: from one reporter to many, from one tablebook to a hundred, from one system for note-taking to many.

Stern justifies this multiplication (her key innovation) by claiming that "note-takers filled Parliament." Her evidence for this claim comes from an important recent book by the historian Chris R. Kyle. However, unlike Stern, Kyle repeatedly emphasizes the chronological evolution of such practices, which "grew exponentially in the 1620s" in conjunction with the larger "news revolution of the 1620s." In the increasingly contested political atmosphere of that decade Parliamentary diaries "proliferated and became records of speeches made on the floor of the chambers, rather than legislative business and procedural minutiae"; "the sheer volume of material in the 1620s dramatically increased"; "1621 marked a watershed"; "the contrast between the extant parliamentary diaries of the 1620s and previous parliaments is stark." Instead, Stern selectively cites Kyle's few earlier examples of such practices, treating them as typical rather than innovative. Even so, her first sighting of a Parliamentary note-taker does not occur until 1607, four years after the 1603 edition of *Hamlet*. As late as 1614 "only one of the diaries can be said to be a substantial account of the parliamentary proceedings." Performed plays consist almost entirely of live speech, mostly in the form of dialogue, but "in the Elizabethan period, very little debate is captured" in any Parliamentary records, and only in the 1620s do we see "a shift...towards debate and attempts at verbatim speech recording."[32] Kyle's record of all Parliamentary committee lists identifies only a single slim example from 1606, and another like it from 1610; the remaining 31, all more substantial, come from 1620–28.[33] Parliament does not provide a pre-1603 precedent for lots of spectators taking notes in the theatre.

Stern evades the insuperable obstacles faced by theories of a single pirate-actor, or a single pirate-reporter, by claiming that *groups* of note-takers worked together to pirate a playtext. She writes, casually, of "the audience" or the "congregation" as the collective source of a reported text, as though every single person attending a sermon or a play pooled their notes and memories afterward. To support this conjecture, she quotes Kyle's example of "many writing and noting" during a speech by King James. But she does not record the date of that speech (1610)—seven years after the 1603 *Hamlet*. Nor does she acknowledge how atypical that situation was, even in 1610. Kyle explains that "in the Elizabethan and early Jacobean periods, the most common form of parliamentary writing was the oft-copied opening and closing speeches made by the monarch or Lord Keeper."[34] Why? Because those speeches were the most important in the entire Parliament. They were much shorter (and more important) than a play.

Stern also refers to collective note-taking in churches. But her examples come from 1619, 1641, 1644, 1651, 1656, and the 1690s (in Germany).[35] Closer in time to *Hamlet*, she cites the preface to a sermon printed in 1605, seeking additional texts taken down by others.[36] But this clearly differs from *Hamlet*. The original preacher was dead (as Shakespeare was not), so notes by others provided the only potential avenue for improving the text; the printing press itself was being used, explicitly, to advertise for other sources. Obviously, there had been no prepublication conspiracy, and in fact we do not know whether any other note-takers responded, or existed. In only one case does a coalition of note-takers predate the 1603 *Hamlet*. In 1596, a preacher prefaced the printed edition of one of his sermons by naming *and thanking* six of his "loving parishioners" for "conferring together" and "penning" the text, "to make [his] simple skill liked."[37] Again, this cannot be compared to the alleged "piracy" of 1603 *Hamlet*: the preacher himself clearly coconspired with his parishioners to reconstruct his own spoken text.

This example points to a fundamental problem in comparing the note-takers in houses of worship or houses of Parliament to the alleged note-takers in Elizabethan playhouses. Preachers and Parliamentarians were not usually reading prepared texts, and so their spoken words could only be captured, remembered, or circulated at all by note-takers. In these circumstances, a reported text might be welcomed by the author, the publisher, and the reading public. In the 1620s, members of Parliament kept notes on the substance of speeches and debates, as Kyle shows, in order to inform their constituencies, and to enhance their own political effectiveness. They "saw themselves as important actors playing a role in an increasingly vital political forum"; they were men "of considerable standing in their regions and in some cases on a national scale."[38] Those Parliamentarians resembled Hamlet himself, an important political figure who, in the fifth scene of the play, has a conversation with a king, who brings him news with shattering political implications. When the royal Ghost leaves, Hamlet bursts into a passionate speech about memory, his father, and the "damned, pernicious villain" who murdered him. Then he says, "My tables, meet it is I set it down." At that point, we would expect him to take out his "tables." But although Hamlet considers it "meet" (appropriate) to "set...down" what he has learned, he does not attempt to record every word or sentence that the Ghost has spoken. Instead, he summarizes the gist of the business: "That one may smile, and smile, and be a villain"—to which he adds the careful condition: "At least, I am sure it may be so in Denmark" (5.78–82). Hamlet is not planning to sell his notes to a printer; he is writing for himself. Parliamentarians made such notes, and so apparently did spectators in the early modern theatre: not attempting to record a whole play, or even a whole scene, but preserving an incandescent fragment that they might be able to recycle in their own lives.[39]

Sermons were much more amenable to note-taking than dramatic dialogue or Parliamentary debates. In transcribing sermons the note-taker "could easily become familiar with a preacher's idiosyncrasies of style and manner, he might easily practice his craft upon such material," and "there was a tradition of such reporting."[40] Sermons, which were "delivered in a quiet place in measured tones by a single speaker, on familiar themes clearly structured and repeated, and in customary religious and biblical language, could have been taken down in longhand by an auditor as well as students now take lecture notes." Consequently, sermons in the period openly advertise that they were taken "by ear," using some form of shorthand. Reporters proudly identify themselves, expecting their public service to be recognized and appreciated. Richard Knowles describes a characteristic Elizabethan note-taker (who in 1605 had the sermons of Edward Philips published at his own expense) as "an enthusiastic young student...earnestly recording for private study (quite possibly writing his notes in longhand or private notation) the congenial preaching of a divine he admired. Many years later he prepared his notes on those (possibly formative) sermons and readied them for publication in order to do posthumous honor to their author and to edify the world." Neither the initial note-taking, nor the eventual preparation for publication, was driven by the profit motive.[41]

The situation that Stern imagines, behind the curtain of the 1603 edition of *Hamlet,* could hardly be more different. God and government were, and are, to almost everyone, much more important than new commercial plays. Audiences in the playhouses were hearing actors speak words that had been prewritten by a playwright, pre-authorized by a censor, and pre-copied by a theatrical scribe at least once (for preparing individual actors' "parts") and perhaps twice (for the licensed playbook, or a patron). An authoritative text always existed, so the cobbling together of notes could never be anything other than inadequate and underhanded. No *play* ever advertised itself as having been "taken" by shorthand, or "by ear." The alleged reporters of the alleged bad quartos never identified themselves, were never thanked by authors, and were never solicited to bring their notes forward in order to correct an existing text. Early modern consumers recognized that note-takers might produce the best possible text of a sermon, but evidently no one believed that such a text could adequately represent a full-length play.

This basic contrast between plays and sermons makes it impossible to accept Stern's speculation that note-takers in the theatre published their text of *Hamlet* as "a proud display" of the play's "performance heritage." This might be true of a modern academic, or of an eighteenth-century tourist describing in detail David Garrick's performance of Hamlet, but "heritage" is the wrong word to describe a performance of what was at the time a new play in repertory in a culturally suspect commercial theatre. Anyone interested in the play in performance could just go see it in the theatre, being performed by the same company that the noter had witnessed. Middleton's uniquely popular theatrical and political sensation *A Game at Chess*, which was shut down by the government and banned, and therefore could not be seen by anyone who had missed the nine successive packed-out performances in August 1624, was the subject of more contemporary comment than any other play of the period; it would have provided a perfect stimulus for collections of note-takers to cobble together a reported text, to satisfy the curiosity of those who had heard about the play but not seen it; but even in that ideal case (two decades after the first edition of *Hamlet,* when shorthand and collective note-taking were becoming more common), neither of the two printed editions has ever been considered a "reported" text or a "bad" quarto.[42] Stern's conjecture that such a text was "a printed puff for the noter" is equally absurd, because the alleged "noter" of *Hamlet* (or any other play) was never publicly identified. The same objection applies to her conjecture that print "enabled the noter to see his words published," and "to mingle their words with their hero's."[43] We may now link "Shakespeare and the Bible" as equivalently canonical, but no one made that equation in Shakespeare's lifetime.

This leaves only one possible motive for publishing a play-text based on notes taken during performance: the production of "a saleable article" (Gunthio, 340) "for the money" (Stern, 20). But Gunthio's unsubstantiated economic assumption makes more sense than Stern's, because at least he presupposes only a single reporter. Stern imagines a team. The more reporters are required, the smaller the share of each collaborator in the profit from sale of the pirated manuscript; the more often the play was seen, the greater the cost of attending the theatre; the more notes taken and then later written out in longhand, the greater the investment in materials and time. Moreover, the reporters' investment would have been speculative. Collier, as a professional reporter, knew that he would be paid for the notes he had been commissioned to take. Stern's imaginary note-takers could have had no such assurance. Neither Ling nor Trundle would have paid them in advance to acquire such a manuscript, because neither had an established interest in publishing commercial plays, or in preserving their "performance heritage."

Stern moves from speculations about the motives of note-takers to speculations about the motives of stationers, and of Nicholas Ling in particular. But she is not a bibliographer or a book historian, and her conjecture depends upon an entirely anachronistic assessment of the relative value of sermons and plays in the early modern book market.[44] She observes, correctly, that the same stationer sometimes published the first edition of a sermon and then a second, "corrected" edition, too—but she then leaps to the conclusion that the publisher deliberately published "bad" texts in order to "flush out good ones." This conjecture makes two assumptions. First, it presumes that texts of sermons taken down by note-takers were, from the perspective of early consumers, intrinsically "bad." This assumption is, as I have already shown, and as other scholars have demonstrated, anachronistic. Reported texts of plays could never satisfy playgoers or readers of literature, but reported texts could be the best available accounts of the substance of what a preacher said about sin and salvation. Second, what Stern calls "blackmail"—publishing "a text in noted form *in order* to force the 'real' version from the author"—might make economic sense with successful preachers like Henry Smith, Thomas Playfere, and William Perkins, but it does not make sense for *Hamlet*.

Stern compares Ling's publication of *Hamlet* to his publication of Henry Smith's sermon *The Affinity of the Faithful*. Mark Bland has calculated that Smith's sermons generated 125 editions between December 1588 and 1614.[45] All were of single authorship, and all were clearly attributed to Smith. During the same period, only 40 comparable Shakespeare editions (of single authorship, and clearly attributed to him) were printed, and almost half of those (19) were poems, not plays.[46] In Shakespeare's lifetime, in the book trade as a whole, Shakespeare's plays (21 editions) were much less predictably profitable than Smith's sermons (six times as many editions). Ling's personal experience tells the same story. He began publishing Smith in 1591, and by 1602 had produced at least six editions of his sermons; in those years he published nothing by Shakespeare. Moreover, reprints and larger books produced more profit for the publisher than risky first editions and small books (with correspondingly small profit margins). Only two of Ling's editions of Smith were first editions; the rest were reprints. Ling's larger collection of three reprinted Smith sermons was itself reprinted three times within eight years. Smith was undoubtedly a valuable intellectual property, for which Ling might theoretically have taken the financial risk of publishing an edition he knew to be inadequate. Moreover, Smith's sermons were repeatedly published in editions taken "by ear," which were repeatedly replaced with editions "corrected" by the author. Smith must not have written down full texts of his own sermons; he spoke from notes, and notes of one kind or another were the only texts available. Consequently, publishing a reported text was not, as Stern claims, "blackmail." There was no alternative method for preserving Smith's sermons, and Smith was demonstrably willing to collaborate with stationers by correcting such texts.

By contrast, the history of Shakespeare's plays in print up to 1603 would not have encouraged the risk of blackmail. Although allegedly "bad quartos" of *The First Part of the Contention*, *Richard Duke of York*, *Richard III*, *Romeo and Juliet*, *Henry V*, and *The Merry Wives of Windsor* had all been published by 1602, only one of the six had been replaced by a "good quarto."[47] *Romeo and Juliet* was "Printed by John Danter" in 1597; a second edition, described on the title page as *"Newly corrected, augmented, and amended,"* was published by Cuthbert Burby two years later. Neither edition attributed it to Shakespeare. As far as Ling and the book trade was concerned, there was *no precedent* for Shakespeare replacing a "bad" text with a good one. Even if Ling had known who wrote *Romeo and Juliet*, this precedent would not have encouraged him to blackmail Shakespeare or his acting company. After all, a different publisher brought out the "corrected" second quarto of *Romeo*. But even that edition was not a good omen, from the perspective of Ling in 1603: the corrected *Romeo* had not yet been reprinted, and therefore cannot have sold particularly quickly. Ling's *Hamlet* is, in fact, the *only* example of an allegedly "bad quarto" (attributed to Shakespeare on the title page) replaced by an allegedly "good quarto" (attributed to Shakespeare on the title page).

Finally, Ling's "bad" and "good" editions of *The Affinity of the Faithful* bear no resemblance to his two editions of *Hamlet*. As with other corrected sermons, the differences between the two editions are minor.[48] In the other examples Stern describes, "the first 'bad' text is from notes; the second is authorial." She implies that the same is true of *The Affinity of the Faithful*, which she cites as an example of Ling's alleged ability "to acquire 'good' sermons and plays through printing 'bad' ones." But in fact Ling's first two editions of Smith's sermon do not say that it was printed by "charactery" (shorthand). Instead, it is the third edition that declares itself to be "Nowe the second time Imprinted, corrected, and augmented, according to the Coppie by Characterie, as he preached it."[49] It is the "corrected" edition (not the first or second) which advertises that it was printed from a manuscript ("the Coppie") that had been taken down using shorthand ("by Characterie"). Noticeably, Ling does not attribute the corrections and augmentations to the author. Did Ling mean to suggest that the improved edition had been reported using the more reliable, new techniques of shorthand, rather than the older tradition of note-taking, responsible for the first edition? Whatever he meant, this is not a convincing parallel for *Hamlet*. Ling's "good" edition of this sermon, like the 1599 "good" edition of *Romeo and Juliet*, explicitly advertized that it was "corrected." Ling's second edition of *Hamlet* did not. Nor did Ling resemble the stationer, cited by Stern, who offered any customer who had "cast away his money upon the former edition" that he would replace it, "for nothing," with the newly imprinted "true copie." However we look at them, Ling's two editions of *Hamlet* do not resemble any of Stern's examples of alleged "blackmail."

What's left of Stern's hypothesis, if we strip away these anachronistic and inapplicable examples of Parliamentary diaries, collective note-taking at sermons, and extortionate stationers? Nothing but the discredited parallel between "bad quartos" of Shakespeare's plays and shorthand texts of Elizabethan sermons. That parallel has already been considered, and rejected, by Shakespeare scholars and historians of shorthand. Stern's tweaking of the old theory does nothing to answer the old rebuttals. Like all proponents of memorial reconstruction and shorthand, she simply assumes that variations between Ling's two quartos are "errors" in the first, that material added in 1604 was "omitted" from 1603, that material missing in 1604 was "added" to 1603, that material transposed in 1604 was "misplaced" in 1603. She cites examples of allegedly "aural errors," ignoring the often-observed fact that "confusions of similar-sounding words or phrases are easily explained by the common experience of a scribe's or compositor's (or anyone's) inexactly reproducing words temporarily held in his mind as he worked." In other places Stern diagnoses "memorial corruption," but *Hamlet* "is no different from any other Shakespearean play in offering examples of simple typesetting errors, especially of a compositor's substitution of a homophone for a word held in his memory while setting." She attributes to shorthand the slight variations in some names (Cornelia/Cornelius, Voltemar/ Voltemand, Rosencraft/Rosencrantz, Guilderstone/Guildenstern), though other scholars have warned that we should "discount variants so graphically similar that they are often or usually explained by editors as understandable misreadings of manuscript forms." Proper names are especially easy for copyists to get wrong, and so are foreign words; consequently, foreign proper names are more likely to be misread than any other words. We don't need shorthand, or a reporter, to account for the first edition's error "Plato" for "Plautus" (7.298); a very similar error ("Pluto" for "Plutus") occurs in two texts of *A Game at Chess* (5.3.116), and examples are also found in errata lists for other books printed by Simmes.[50] To all these speculations, the answer is the same: "Where ordinary explanations of Q1's features exist, there is no compulsion to accept a less likely explanation such as swift and secret stenographic copying."[51] As an historian of shorthand objected, 80 years before Stern's essay was published, "always there is a far simpler explanation."[52]

Like other discredited advocates of the shorthand hypothesis, Stern foregrounds "synonyms." She begins her tabulation of evidence for note-taking by asserting that the 1603 edition "is known for its synonyms," but she does not quantify such variants, and she prejudicially defines "synonym" to mean that the reading of the 1604 text has been "needlessly replaced" in the 1603 text by a word with similar meaning. But almost a century ago Hereward T. Price's examination of Spenser's *Faerie Queene* demonstrated that "synonyms have been substituted for the poet's original words even in rime, and where shorthand" [or any form of reporting] "is out of the question."[53] In the print shop, compositors could and did sometimes substitute a synonym for the word in the text they were setting. This is not only generally true; it is specifically true of the print shop of Valentine Simmes. The 1603 edition was apparently set into type by a single workman, the so-called Compositor A, whose work has also been identified in other plays printed by Simmes, including reprints of plays.[54] We can, in such cases, compare what Compositor A *should* have set with what he *did* set, and the error he most frequently committed was, not surprisingly, substitution. He replaced the correct word with another word with a similar meaning.[55] But he was also occasionally responsible for transposed words, interpolated words, and omitted words—and even an omitted line. When Q1 *Hamlet* has Horatio enter, saying "Here my lord" (9.42), even though

Hamlet has not called for him, Stern agrees with Irace that this is "a clear indication that Q1 *Hamlet* was derived from a longer version."[56] Something is certainly missing in the 1603 edition. But the "longer version" may simply have consisted of a short manuscript line, Hamlet's "Horatio!" or "What ho, Horatio!" (3.2.49), accidentally skipped by Compositor A.[57] We know that he had skipped a longer line ("My staffe, I yeeld as willing to be thine") when setting the second edition of *The First Part of the Contention*, three years earlier.

Compositor A cannot account for all the small verbal variants that distinguish Ling's two editions of *Hamlet*. Others undoubtedly originated as mistakes made in the printing shop of James Roberts, who set the type for the 1604 edition.[58] But compositors introduce fewer synonyms than authors. For the last two scenes of *A Game at Chess*, we possess two different manuscripts in Middleton's own handwriting, and they are full of synonymous words and phrases.[59] Moreover, we need not assume that the manuscript printed by Simmes in 1603 and the manuscript printed by Roberts in 1604 were both in Shakespeare's own handwriting. Recent scholarship has identified scribal transcripts behind the first editions of *Richard II* (1597), *Richard III* (1597), and *1 Henry IV* (1598), and behind most of the plays in the 1623 Folio (including *Hamlet*).[60] So it's entirely possible that we must take into account the errors introduced by at least one unidentified copyist in the manuscript behind at least one of the two Ling quartos. I could fill a long book debating which of these agents (compositors, scribes, author) is most likely to be responsible for every difference between Ling's two editions of *Hamlet*. The 1603 edition undoubtedly contains errors, introduced by the printer or by the scribe(s) who prepared the manuscript. But we don't have to agree about the relative probabilities in every case. What matters is that known and necessary agents of normal textual transmission will account for all the differences, thus sparing us from having to invent imaginary piratical note-takers.

Stern might reasonably object, at this point, that I have been ignoring the most important evidence of all: three seventeenth-century documents, which she interprets as proof that plays were reported by groups of note-taking spectators.[61] In 1608, Thomas Heywood prefaced *The Rape of Lucrece* with an epistle "To the Reader":

> Though some have used a double sale of their labors (first to the stage, and after to the press), for my own part I here proclaim myself ever faithful in the first, and never guilty of the last. Yet since some of my plays have

(unknown to me, and without any of my direction) accidentally come into the printers' hands—and therefore so corrupt and mangled (copied only by the ear) that I have been as unable to know them, as ashamed to challenge them—this therefore I was the willinger to furnish out in his native habit: first being by consent, next because the rest have been so wronged in being published in such savage and ragged ornaments.[62]

Heywood's testimony here undeniably establishes that two or more of his plays *had* been printed, without his permission, in execrable texts. In 1615, Sir George Buc declared that those who know "brachygraphy" (one specific system of shorthand, or perhaps any system of shorthand) "can readily take a sermon, oration, play, or any long speech, as they are spoken, dictated, acted, and uttered in the instant."[63] Buc undeniably claimed, here, that shorthand *could* be used to transcribe a play. In 1639, the eighth edition of Heywood's *If You Know Not Me, You Know Nobody* added a new Prologue by Heywood; this prologue had already been published two years earlier in a miscellaneous collection of Heywood's poetry and prose.[64] Heywood claimed that his play had been

> well received, and well performed at first:
> Graced, and frequented; and the cradle age
> Did throng the seats, the boxes, and the stage
> So much, that some by stenography drew
> The plot: put it in print, scarce one word true:
> And in that lameness it hath limped so long.
> The author, now to vindicate that wrong,
> Hath took the pains, upright upon its feet
> To teach it walk: so please you sit and see't.

Heywood explicitly claimed here that shorthand was used to generate a manuscript of his play, which was then sold to a printer. *If You Know Not Me* had been published by Nathaniel Butter in 1605, so Heywood was making this claim 30 years after the event, when shorthand was much better developed and more widely used, and when the rise of printed news had created regular employment for reporters. Not everyone has been persuaded by Heywood's retrospective diagnosis.[65] But William Proctor Williams, editing the play for the forthcoming Oxford edition of Heywood's works, believes Heywood.[66] No one can deny that Heywood was accusing someone of stealing his play and circulating it in a defective version; he felt strongly enough about it to publish that accusation twice, in separate books. Heywood does not use the word "piracy," but he does specify unauthorized mechanical reproduction.

This example from 1637, reprised in 1639, satisfies the foundational principle enunciated by Adrian Johns ("some person, thing, or act has to have been characterized as piratical by contemporaries themselves in order for it to count").[67]

Actually, Heywood published the accusation three times, because his 1608 preface is most easily explained as a reference to the same piracy. *If you know not me, You know nobody: Or, The troubles of Queen Elizabeth* had been entered in the Stationers' Register by Nathaniel Butter on 5 July 1605; it was published by Butter, with a title page woodcut of Queen Elizabeth, in 1605, 1606, and 1608. On 14 September 1605, Butter entered his rights to Heywood's sequel, *The Second Part*, which took the Queen's story up to the defeat of the Spanish Armada in 1588; Butter published that sequel in 1606 and again in 1608. Heywood, by 1608, had endured five "corrupt and mangled" printings of his two plays on Elizabeth. By contrast to his specificity in the 1630s, his vagueness in 1608 ("some of my plays") would be understandable, because *The Rape of Lucrece* was also published by Butter, who would not want to damage sales of his two 1608 reprints. Sir George Buc's claim, in 1615, might also allude to the same incident: Buc had been the government licenser of all printed plays since 1606, and therefore could have read Heywood's preface. In 1610, Buc became Master of the Revels, the official censor to whom all new playbooks were submitted before their performance, and he would also have known Heywood in that capacity. All three smoking guns may therefore be aiming at the same target.

Heywood undoubtedly believed in 1608 that the execrable quality of the printed texts of *If You Know Not Me* was due to bootleg transmission "only by the ear," and he later supplemented that hypothesis by specifying that "the ear" had been assisted by some sort of shorthand. But the sincerity of Heywood's (or anyone else's) accusation does not prove its accuracy. Heywood may well be our only witness, and any competent defense attorney could dismantle his credibility. The vagueness of Heywood's testimony suggests that he did not know who, exactly, pirated the text, and if he could not confidently identify the culprit he could not confidently identify the method. Heywood might, in other words, have leaped to the same conclusion that Stern does: sermons were taken down "only by the ear," so perhaps the same thing could be done with a play. Heywood was an outraged playwright, not a forensic scientist, bibliographer, or textual critic.

But let's give Heywood the benefit of the doubt. Let's suppose that *If You Know Not Me* was indeed transcribed by note-takers in the audience, and then sold to a stationer, purely for financial gain. If that is true, does the first quarto of *If You Know Not Me* explain the first quarto of *Hamlet*? No. Heywood specifies, in the 1639 reprint, that the pirates "first drew the plot." This may mean simply that they wrote down an outline of the play's story, but the noun "plot" also had a technical meaning in the early modern theatre: the plot was the breakdown of a play into a sequence of scenes containing specified characters and props.[68] Playwrights themselves "first drew the plot" (and pitched it to a company of actors) before writing the actual dialogue, and Heywood makes the same distinction: the pirates successfully "drew the plot" (a relatively short and simple outline) but could not successfully capture the dialogue ("scarce one word true"). The first quarto of *Hamlet*, by contrast, does not get the plot right: notoriously, it does not even identify the characters correctly, it invents a new scene, it transposes the order of crucial events. But many of the words are "true," including sentences and speeches reproduced verbatim. The pattern of alleged "corruption" in the 1603 *Hamlet* thus inverts Heywood's description of the results of "stenography" in the 1605 *If You Know Not Me*. The 1603 title page names the playwright and provides uniquely expansive evidence about previous performances; the 1605 quarto does not identify the author, or suggest any access to insider information. The 1603 quarto was never in the seventeenth or eighteenth century accused, by anyone, of being illicit or corrupt; the 1605 quarto was indicted by the author.

Heywood's publisher, Nathaniel Butter, differed as much from Nicholas Ling as the two quartos did. He was born in London in 1583, the son of a London stationer; unlike Ling, he grew up in a metropolis with a thriving commercial theatre industry. Butter ended his apprenticeship on 20 February 1604, and entered his first text in the Stationers' Register on 4 December of that year. That is, Butter started his career after Ling published the 1603 *Hamlet*, and he probably published his first title at about the same time that Ling published the 1604 *Hamlet*. He belongs to a different generation, and a different breed of stationers. By the end of 1605, Butter had published four plays. Throughout his career Butter specialized in cheap, ephemeral texts, like news books and plays; he was cofounder of the news syndicate that, in the 1620s, revolutionized the relationship between print technology and the mass-marketing of current events. That focus brought Butter into repeated conflict with the regulations of the Stationers' Company and the government. *If you know not me* was "news," a brand-new, spectacular commercial success in the theatre (as Heywood tells us, in detail). Distressing as it may be for us to acknowledge, *If You Know Not Me*, with nine quarto editions before 1642, was more popular than *Hamlet*, which managed only five. *If You Know Not Me* was also "news" because it put Queen Elizabeth herself directly on stage, something only possible after her death. *Hamlet* was not news: by 1603 it was, according to traditional scholarship, three or more years old, and it was in any case an adaptation of a medieval story that had already been dramatized at least 14 years earlier. *If You Know Not Me* did something that no one could have done before; *Hamlet* was just a remake.

From Ling's perspective, *Hamlet* was worth the risk of publishing because it was literature; from Butter's perspective, *If You Know Not Me* was worth the risk of publishing because it was breaking London news. If anyone was going to inaugurate a new relationship between print and performance, it was the aggressive young Butter, not the cautious old Ling. If anyone was going to transfer techniques from sermon reporting and news reporting to play-reporting, it was the innovator Butter, not the conservative Ling. If anyone was destined to be the target of the first accusation of dramatic piracy, it was the controversial Butter, not the invisible Ling. *If You Know Not Me* may be the inaugural example of note-taking spectators pirating a play, or just the inaugural target of a misplaced accusation of such piracy, but in either case it marks a watershed. And that breakthrough moment in the history of piracy postdated the first edition of *Hamlet*.

* * *

In addition to recycling the claims made by previous advocates of shorthand or memorial reconstruction, Stern adds something new of her own. She recognizes that parts of the 1603 edition resemble the later texts more closely than other parts (although she prejudicially describes this fluctuation in terms of "relatively accurate" or "relatively inaccurate"). This pattern is, as I showed in chapter 2, an important feature of the data, and any valid theory must provide a convincing cause for these shifts. A revising author is the simplest solution. But Stern proposes a new alternative. "Firstly," she observes, reasonably enough, that "the clarity of the performer affected the quality of the notes," and that the peculiarities of "a speaker impacted the accuracy of the notes." She then observes that "Some players will, in their natures, and some by choice, have spoken more slowly and distinctly than others." She then conjectures that "some speeches, and some characters... are more clearly captured than others" because "the speakers themselves were louder or clearer."

In other words: the actors in the Chamberlain's Men who best communicated with an audience were the ones who played the Prologue,

Lucianus, and Voltemand. The actor impersonating Marcellus was not nearly so clear, but even he was much, much more intelligible than the veteran shareholders entrusted with Hamlet and the play's other famous characters. Burbage did not speak as "distinctly" or "clearly" as the unknown theatrical genius who spoke the deathless poetry of Voltemand. Even more remarkably, these lesser actors were "louder" than the leading members of the company. The ability to project the voice is the most basic of all technical skills required of an actor; it would have been absolutely fundamental to the success of a company working in large amphitheatres, or playing in inn-yards and other outdoor spaces while touring (which the Chamberlain's Men did every year until the second decade of the seventeenth century). In a world without microphones or close-ups, a professional actor could not have made a living without having mastered projection and articulation. The actors most likely to be allowed to slow down (and therefore take up a disproportionate amount of stage time) would be those who were most important to the company or the play. Hired men who slowed down a performance for their relatively unimportant speeches would not be hired again. Stern's theory forces her to presuppose an inverse pyramid of competence in the acting company. Her explanation of the radical fluctuations in the stability of *Hamlet*'s text is, if anything, even more implausible than memorial reconstruction.

Stern's argument for note-taking also forces her to contradict, or forget, her own work as a theatre historian. She contends that, in the text of the first edition, Ophelia's part is "virtually unplayable," because it contains five repeated cues ("a nunnery go").[69] Since the actor only had his own part, with almost no time for group rehearsal, such repetitions would allegedly create chaos in performance. Stern is here quoting Paul Menzer, but his own analysis of cues also acknowledges that there are repeated cues in both the second quarto and the Folio. As with the arguments for memorial reconstruction, Stern's attempt to prove piracy in the first edition leads, logically, to the conclusion that all three versions have been corrupted by the same mechanism. Menzer, recognizing the problem, offers a variety of explanations: "perhaps cue repetition did not disturb actors; perhaps learning by parts did not depend on cue memorization as much as we may think... or, perhaps, Shakespeare is wittingly creating an effect."[70] Stern does not cite Menzer's qualifications here. More remarkably, she does not cite her own earlier work on Renaissance rehearsals. Her book with Simon Palfrey, on actors' parts, contained a whole chapter on repeated cues, especially in Shakespeare's early work.[71] The nunnery scene, in which the repeated cues appear, is a dialogue between Hamlet (played by Burbage) and Ophelia (played by an unknown boy actor). "Boy actors in adult companies were apprenticed to a sharer rather than the company itself," Stern wrote in 2000, "and part of the job of that sharer was to teach" the boy how to act. Whereas experienced actors memorized and prepared their parts alone, boy actors often "studied" a part with an older actor. Stern cited references to this practice in Middleton's *Your Five Gallants*, where the Boy studies with Fitzgrave, and in Richard Brome's *The English Moor*, where Arnold teaches Buzzard how to play an idiot boy. She also gave an example from *The Return from Parnassus*, where Burbage himself was portrayed instructing an apprentice; on another occasion, John Heminges instructed "his boy." In other cases, boy actors were rehearsed under the direction of a playwright (Ben Jonson, George Peele, Anthony Munday).[72] Therefore, the boy who played Ophelia in the first performances of *Hamlet* could have been instructed by Burbage (whose own part contained the parts of the dialogue that Ophelia's part did not) or by the author Shakespeare (who had written the repeated cues, and had access to the whole script of the scene, in his head or on paper). In either case, the boy actor would have been prepared, in advance of group rehearsal, for the repeated cues, and would have been no more confused by them than any modern actor.

Why did someone so intelligent as Stern propose so implausible a theory, and one which required her to forget her own work? We may begin to see an answer to that question by looking at another twenty-first-century discussion of the texts of *Hamlet*. Lukas Erne's *Shakespeare as Literary Dramatist*, published by Cambridge University Press in 2003 and in a revised edition in 2013, has been more talked about among academic Shakespearians than the 2006 Arden *Hamlet,* in part because its influence extends far beyond one play. Erne's title announced a foundational challenge to performance-oriented approaches to Shakespeare, and his analysis of the texts of *Hamlet* needs to be understood within that larger intellectual agenda.

The link between Stern and Erne can be seen clearly enough in their separate rejections of the groundbreaking article published in 2008 by Zachary Lesser and Peter Stallybrass, which I discussed in chapter 1. Lesser and Stallybrass called the 1603 edition "The First Literary *Hamlet*," because it used quotation marks to signal especially quotable passages. In 2013, Erne objected to that conclusion, because it

> does not distinguish between Q1 *Hamlet* as a book and as a text. While their article persuades me that the book of Q1 *Hamlet* has considerable

"literary value," the text of Q1 does not but is important for something else, namely its theatrical proximity... Its textual theatricality contrasts with the textual literariness of Q2...[73]

How does Erne *know* that the quotation marks belong to the printed "book," but not the underlying manuscript "text"? He simply asserts the distinction, because it is vital to his own (conservative) interpretation of the play.

Stern also recognizes and rejects the challenge posed by Lesser and Stallybrass, but she attempts to provide evidence for an alternative explanation. She points out that, "throughout the late seventeenth and eighteenth centuries," quotation marks like those in the 1603 edition were used in printed playbooks to "signal cuts."[74] Here, again, we encounter the problem of anachronism. More seriously, Stern's claim that the marked passages in Q1 *Hamlet* were omitted from performance self-evidently contradicts her claim that Q1 *Hamlet* represents what spectators saw and heard in performance. To cover up that contradiction, she resorts to the further conjecture that someone, "revisiting the theatre, observed [that a passage] had been cut." She is therefore forced to speculate (1) that passages present in all three early versions of *Hamlet* were actually omitted from the play in very early London performances, and (2) that they were cut in some performances but not others, and (3) that one of the conspiracy of note-takers noticed the cut—while failing to notice most of the performance, and (4) that the note-taker *thought the cut was worth signaling to readers*, even though (5) at the time, such signals always had a different meaning. This is desperate, though no more desperately complicated than the rest of the note-taking hypothesis. But Stern, to her credit, at least recognizes and accepts that a scholar who dismisses Q1 must attempt to provide some historical, material mechanism by which it came into being. Erne simply evades that responsibility.

Erne discusses the 1603 edition of *Hamlet* in two chapters of *Shakespeare as Literary Dramatist*. The first, on "bad" quartos and their origins, surveys a century of scholarship on the theory of memorial reconstruction generally, and specifically in relation to the "bad" first editions of *Romeo and Juliet*, *Henry V*, and *Hamlet*. Erne is skeptical about whether those texts were produced by a process involving memorial reconstruction by a single actor. He distances himself from the "twentieth-century absorption with arresting a particular actor and charging him with producing a 'bad' quarto."[75] He dedicates a paragraph to Maguire's 1996 book, and he endorses Paul Werstine's 1999 conclusion that "twentieth-century Shakespeare textual criticism has not been able to maintain the memorial-reconstruction hypothesis on the basis of qualitative evidence."[76] He also attacks, at length, and persuasively, an element of most theories of memorial reconstruction (including Irace's): the claim that bad quartos represent the plays as they were performed by an acting company on tour in the provinces.[77] In all these respects Erne echoes the revisionist ferment of the late twentieth century, and in all these respects I agree with him.

Nevertheless, Erne asserts that the first quarto of *Hamlet* "*is* a bad text" (his italics). How then did it get so bad? His answer is contained in the next, climactic chapter of his book, which contrasts "theatricality" and "literariness." The "short, theatrical texts...record...the plays as they were orally delivered on stage," whereas the "long, literary texts...correspond to what an emergent dramatic author wrote for readers in an attempt to raise the literary respectability of playtexts." The exact mechanism by which such textual reflections were created does not matter much. Erne does not absolutely reject, or absolutely endorse, the theory of memorial reconstruction, but sets it alongside theories of dictation, shorthand, and other mechanisms by which actors might have written down what they performed. Like Stern, he provides a buffet of "possible" mechanisms, and lets his readers choose whichever they find most convenient or persuasive. The particular mechanism matters less to Erne than what he calls "the most important implication of Greg's 'memorial reconstruction' theory." For Greg, what was "most important" was the identification of an historical mechanism to explain textual facts; for Erne, what is "most important" is what satisfies a critical desire "that the text so diagnosed is recognized as derivative rather than original, a *re*-construction rather than an early draft" (his italics). In support of that argument, he cites scholars whose work had already been refuted by Maguire and Werstine: not only Irace, but earlier work by Burkhart (1971), Hart (1942), and Thomas (1992). Erne thus endorses the key assumption of theories of memorial reconstruction, that the first edition does not represent a first version of the play, but instead represents a debased and later *re*-construction of it. But in Erne that debasement is not accidental or occasional, not the result of provincial tours or of an individual dishonest actor playing a small part. For Erne, the debasement is systemic. *It shows us what happened to all Shakespeare's plays when they left his desk and entered the theatre.* Erne is committed to "demonstrating that the first quartos of *Romeo and Juliet, Henry V*, and *Hamlet* are related to what Shakespeare and his fellows performed in London." He argues that "'Bad' quarto language that does not match its counterpart in the 'good' text may thus often reflect a version of what the players spoke on stage."[78] Notice that the singular actor-reporter of earlier theories has here become a plural "fellows" and "players." Like Stern, Erne moves from a single imaginary bad apple to an equally imaginary band of botchers.

Erne repeatedly describes the process which produced Q1 *Hamlet* as "revised," "reworked," "reworking," "restructuring," and "rearrangement." He thus reiterates the anachronistic vector that has governed all readings of the 1603 text since it was rediscovered in 1823: backward from the enlarged text that we know to the shorter, unfamiliar first text. Erne's assumption allows him to provide a critical "reading" of the differences between the 1603 text and the later versions. That reading resembles the differential interpretations of *King Lear*, *Hamlet*, *Othello*, *Henry V*, and *Romeo and Juliet* that had been so prominent and influential an element of the revisionist wave of the 1980s and 1990s—except that the method has, in Erne's hands, been turned on its head. The revision does not produce a better text, or even a text equally valuable but simply different. Instead, the "revised" text is now "less multi-layered and complex" than the original; it eliminates the original "strong sense of interiority and psychological complexity"; it "disambiguates" the major characters.[79] Everything that we value about Shakespeare, about *Hamlet*, disappeared when the play was transferred from reading to staging.

This claim may seem plausible in the twentieth-first century. Regular theatregoers, and especially those who take a special interest in revivals of Shakespeare, will have seen productions that massacre the text, radically abridging it, changing its staging, messing with its language. But those parallels are, of course, anachronistic. They presume theatrical and cultural conditions that did not exist in Shakespeare's lifetime. Erne does not identify a specific material, historical mechanism by which the manuscript behind the 1603 edition of *Hamlet* was produced. He is simply sure that some such mechanism *must* have existed.

Erne relies, in part, on a single remark by Peter W. M. Blayney. In 1647, Humphrey Moseley published a collection of the plays of Francis Beaumont and John Fletcher, and in his preface to "the readers" he explained why his expensive edition was better than the manuscripts of the same plays then in circulation: "When these *Comedies* and *Tragedies* were presented on the Stage, the *Actours* omitted some *Scenes* and Passages (with the *Authour's* consent) . . . and when private friends desir'd a copy" of a particular play, the actors "then (and justly too) transcribed what they *Acted*." According to Blayney, "What Moseley has been trying to tell us since 1647 is . . . the commonplace and innocent origin of the kind of text that Pollard called a Bad Quarto."[80] Blayney is one of the most outstanding early modern bibliographers of his generation, but he is a specialist in printed books and their makers, not theatrical manuscripts. The first comprehensive reexamination of all surviving playhouse manuscripts was published by Paul Werstine in 2013. "Erne is surely right," Werstine says, "to characterize Shakespeare as a literary dramatist who wrote for the page as well as the stage." But Werstine rejects Blayney's interpretation of Moseley and, even more emphatically, the construction put on Moseley's and Blayney's words by Erne. There is, Werstine says, "no comparison" between variant texts in the Fletcher canon and Shakespeare texts like Q1 *Hamlet*. Erne had claimed that "the gap left between the long and short, the literary and the theatrical texts of *Romeo and Juliet*...and *Hamlet*" was the result of playhouse abridgement, but Werstine's careful survey of theatrical manuscripts demonstrates that "such a gap yawns so wide as to render incredible any claim that 'bad quartos' of *Hamlet* and *Romeo and Juliet* could represent performances guided by playhouse [manuscripts] containing the texts found in the Second Quartos of the same plays."[81]

Werstine is equally damning about another theory appropriated by Erne. In 1999, Andrew Gurr suggested that "good quartos" and "bad quartos" should be redefined as "Maximal and Minimal Texts." Gurr speculated that the maximal versions had been written by Shakespeare and licensed for performance by the Master of the Revels, and that "Shakespeare and his fellows were in the habit of trimming and redrafting his scripts for use on the stage quite drastically."[82] Gurr's theory was based on the assumption, also endorsed by Erne, that performances could last no longer than two hours. Michael J. Hirrel has since marshaled contemporary evidence that the time devoted to the performance of plays "varied substantially, perhaps from as little as an hour and a half to as much as three hours and a quarter." Thus, the 1623 edition of *Hamlet*, and even the longer 1604 edition, "could have been performed with time to spare.'[83] Gurr's theory is unnecessary. But that theory also, Werstine shows, "runs afoul of empirical evidence in several ways." Passages were occasionally cut, or added, in theatrical manuscripts (although on nothing like the scale imagined by Gurr and Erne). But "what generally separates actual theatrical texts from" the so-called bad quartos, including Q1 *Hamlet*, "is a marked reluctance to rewrite in the former. There is good reason not to regard such Quartos as paradigmatic of playhouse manuscripts."[84]

Werstine demonstrates that the foundations of Erne's theory are as rickety as the foundations of Stern's. Neither Erne nor Stern offers a plausible explanation of how the 1603 edition of *Hamlet* came into existence. But both are nevertheless convinced that it *must* somehow represent the play in performance, and *must* somehow have come into being after the later, expanded versions. Despite differences of detail, Erne and Stern agree on one thing: we *must*, at whatever cost, by whatever means necessary, save Shakespeare from any association with the 1603 text.

The theories of Blayney, Gurr, Erne, and Stern are all attempts to recover from the intellectual collapse of memorial reconstruction, while at the same time avoiding the conclusion that Ling's 1603 edition of *Hamlet* represents Shakespeare's own first version of the play. But their alternatives are no more plausible, probable, or sustainable than memorial reconstruction. They don't work. Indeed, they cannot be right. If the 1603 edition represents a later, explicitly theatrical version of the long play that Shakespeare wrote at the turn of the century, then why is that first edition closer than the later versions to Shakespeare's source?

When scholars dispute the relationship of the three early texts of *Hamlet*, they are trying to establish what is called a "stemma" of transmission, like a family tree; the most reliable text would be the one "closest" to Shakespeare's own manuscript, which would be the "source" of textual authority. But once we recognize that every writer begins as a reader—as I urged in my prologue—then we also recognize that behind the textual, writerly source of Shakespeare's *Hamlet* (an authorial manuscript) lies a readerly source: the book that Shakespeare was reading before he started writing. At the top of the stemma of transmission of *Hamlet*, at the top of the family tree, is the reading that preceded the writing.

Everyone agrees that the story of "Amleth" in Volume V of François de Belleforest's *Les Histoires Tragiques* inspired Shakespeare's play, directly or indirectly, and Margrethe Jolly has recently examined the French text against Ling's two editions of *Hamlet*. The 1603 edition, she concludes, "has more borrowings [from Belleforest], despite being the shorter play." Even more striking than the raw totals is their density: because Q1 is only 55 percent of Q2's length, "proportionally, the borrowings occur at almost twice the density in Q1 than in Q2." Shakespeare must have read Belleforest at least once, probably twice. He is much more likely than a pirate actor, or a collective of pirate note-takers, to be responsible for Q1's stronger connection to the play's French source. Therefore, "the simplest explanation for the findings" is that Q2 contains Shakespeare's "revision" of his earliest version of the play, represented in Q1.[85] In other words: of all the surviving printed texts of *Hamlet*, the one at the top of the stemma, the one closest to Shakespeare's *original* intentions, is the first edition.

This overview also illuminates particular variants. For instance, Stern observes that one of the lines unique to the 1603 edition occurs near the beginning of Hamlet's climactic encounter with his mother: "but first we'll make all safe" (11.7), he says, in order to insure the privacy and security of their conversation. Stern claims that Q1's line preserved "the experience of watching *Hamlet*," and therefore constitutes proof that the text of Q1 was compiled by a "noter" in the auditorium, rather than by Shakespeare.[86] Once again, Stern's theory is complicated, because the alleged note-taker, viewing the behavior of an actor, did not, as we would expect, record that experience by jotting down a stage direction, but instead invented six words that should have been, but were allegedly not, *heard*, rather than *seen*. As always with Stern and these theories of piracy, there is a simpler explanation. Shakespeare used the relatively rare phrase "all safe" twice elsewhere, at the beginning and end of his career.[87] In Belleforest, Hamlet had been warned, in an earlier episode, that he was entering a trap.

> So he enters his mother's "chambre" with his "glaive" ("sword") in his hand, full of suspicion and expectation that here is another trap. Belleforest as a novelist underlines this by placing Amleth in the chamber, and in the very next clause indicating Amleth's suspicions: "[il] se douta de quelque trahison" ("he suspected some treachery"). Then, before he even speaks to his mother, Amleth feigns his "folles et niaises" ("mad and naïve/simple") mannerisms as usual... In Q1, Hamlet shows that he too is suspicious when in the fourth line after his entrance he declares "but first we'll make all safe."

Q1's unique half-line, Jolly concludes, "makes complete sense when the French source is known," and "suggests that the playwright was in places reading Belleforest quite closely."[88] Ling's first edition does preserve "the experience of" something: not the experience of a spectator watching a performance and then inventing words that were never spoken, but the experience of a playwright, transforming a French narrative into an English play. That experience, that reading, and that invention were all Shakespeare's—as the title page of Ling's first edition declared.

CHAPTER 4

How Old Is Young?

"Young Hamlet"

There are no pirates in the first edition of *Hamlet*. That text cannot be convincingly attributed to a piratical publisher, a piratical actor, or a piratical spectator. There are errors in the printed text, of course, as there are errors in all early printed texts of Shakespeare's plays—and, indeed, in all books produced by Gutenberg's complicated hand-press printing machine. But since the rediscovery of the 1603 edition, almost two centuries ago, no one has ever provided convincing evidence that the first quarto of *Hamlet* is a radically illegitimate text, produced by some fundamentally unauthorized person or mechanism of transmission. No early witness ever impugned Nicholas Ling's authority to publish it or the quality of its text. The manuscript from which it was printed may not have been in Shakespeare's own handwriting; it was probably a copy, perhaps even a copy of a copy, and it undoubtedly contained the kinds of mistakes introduced when people copied manuscripts. But the errors of copyists and the errors of printers can be found in the 1623 collection of Shakespeare's *Comedies, Histories, and Tragedies*, and in all the "good quartos" printed in Shakespeare's lifetime. Editors vary in their willingness to emend, but no serious scholar doubts Shakespeare's authorship of other printed texts just because they are imperfect. In the three preceding chapters, I have tried to show that there is no good reason, and no good evidence, for claims that the first edition of *Hamlet* fundamentally differs from any of those other texts, which form the basis for all modern editions of Shakespeare's works. The first quarto is innocent until proven guilty.

Anyone persuaded by the three preceding chapters must accept the authority of the title-page of Ling's first edition. Ling was the first person to claim, in print, that *Hamlet* was written by William Shakespeare, and the first person to claim, in print, that *Hamlet* was performed by the acting company to which Shakespeare belonged. Everyone accepts the accuracy of those claims. Ling was also the first person to publish hundreds of lines and phrases reproduced in subsequent editions of *Hamlet*, and everyone accepts Shakespeare's authorship of that material. Once we have eliminated the various unsubstantiated accusations of piracy, then we must also accept that Shakespeare wrote the rest of the text of the first edition (not counting normal errors). In place of the implausible, improbable, anachronistic conjectures of modern criticism, we must trust the text published by Nicholas Ling and legitimated by the London book trade in Shakespeare's lifetime.

But no one believes that the material unique to the first edition could have been written by Shakespeare in the early seventeenth century. Stylistically, even the most cursory comparison of that text with *Twelfth Night*, *Troilus and Cressida*, *Othello*, *King Lear*, or "The Phoenix and the Turtle," suggests that the text *printed* in 1603 must have been *written* long before 1603. As it happens, the first reference to an English play about Hamlet was published long before 1603. That first document, in 1589, does not name an author, but it does say that the play was full of "tragical speeches," and Shakespeare's *Hamlet* contains more famous tragical speeches than any other play in English. In this chapter, and the two to follow, I will assume that the first quarto is a legitimate text of a play written by Shakespeare, and I will consider how best to reconcile the reliable, empirical, material historical evidence of that printed text with our conjectural understanding of Shakespeare's evolving style and his changing relationship to the early modern theatre.

This approach may require some adjustment to our prevailing theories about Shakespeare's early career. It forces us to imagine a Shakespeare who, as Leah Marcus puts it, "was not yet sounding like 'Shakespeare.'"[1] Consider, for instance, Sonnet 145. You will not find it in many anthologies of English poetry. Most scholars, including such mainstream Shakespearians as Stanley Wells and Peter Holland, believe that it is Shakespeare's earliest surviving writing:

> Those lips that love's own hand did make
> Breathed forth the sound that said "I hate"
> To me that languished for her sake;
> But when she saw my woeful state,
> Straight in her heart did mercy come,
> Chiding that tongue that ever sweet

> Was used in giving gentle doom,
> And taught it thus anew to greet:
> "I hate" she altered with an end
> That followed it as gentle day
> Doth follow night who, like a fiend,
> From heaven to hell is flown away.
>   "I hate" from hate away she threw,
>   And saved my life, saying "not you."

The penultimate line apparently puns on "Hathaway," the surname of the woman who in 1582 became Mrs. "Anne Shakespeare." This simple poem might therefore have been written in the early 1580s. It differs, formally, from all the other poems published in the 1609 edition of *Shakespeare's Sonnets*. Contemplate, for instance, the difference between the "Hathaway" sonnet (above) and Sonnet 107 (below), which most scholars believe was written in 1603, soon after the death of Queen Elizabeth and the peaceful accession of King James:

> Not mine own fears, nor the prophetic soul
> Of the wide world, dreaming on things to come,
> Can yet the lease of my true love control,
> Supposed as forfeit to a confined doom.
> The mortal moon hath her eclipse endured,
> And the sad augurs mock their own presage.
> Incertainties now crown themselves assured,
> And peace proclaims olives of endless age.
> Now with the drops of this most balmy time
> My love looks fresh, and death to me subscribes,
> Since, spite of him, I'll live in this poor rhyme,
> While he insults o'er dull and speechless tribes.
>   And thou in this shalt find thy monument,
>   When tyrants' crests and tombs of brass are spent.

The question we must ask about the first edition of *Hamlet* is: could that text also have been written in the 1580s? Are the stylistic and intellectual differences between it and the more familiar, seventeenth-century version of *Hamlet* greater than the differences between Sonnets 145 and 107?

My approach thus differs from previous attempts to establish the legitimacy of the first quarto. Critics like Paul Edmondson, Philip McGuire, Kirk Melnikoff, and Steven Urkowitz have defended the integrity of Q1 by showing that it portrays particular episodes of the play, and particular characters (Horatio, Fortinbras, Polonius, the King, and Laertes), differently than the enlarged canonical versions.[2] As an actor, I find those arguments plausible, but I won't repeat them here, because they do nothing to establish when, or why, those differences originated. Moreover, such arguments have been easily appropriated by defenders of the various theories of piracy: proof that Q1 is an actable script does not convince people who already believe that Q1 was written down by actors or spectators. I will instead focus on evidence that distinguishes (1) the date when one version of *Hamlet* (printed in 1603) was written by an actor-playwright for a particular company of actors, from (2) the date when another version of *Hamlet* (printed in 1604) was written by the same actor-playwright for a particular company of actors—but not necessarily the same company.

* * *

A manuscript elegy of 1619 remembers various roles played by the recently deceased leading actor of Shakespeare's company, Richard Burbage. One of those roles was "young Hamlet," and the anonymous elegist remembers, "Oft have I seen him [Burbage] leap into the grave."[3] This independent eyewitness account seems to confirm a stage direction in the scene of Ophelia's burial, a direction that occurs in both the early 1603 quarto and the 1623 Folio: after Laertes leaps into his sister's grave, "Hamlet leaps in after Leartes" (16.145–6; 5.1.247.1).

Burbage apparently was an actor for "35 years," beginning in about 1584.[4] Modern scholarship dates Shakespeare's original manuscript of *Hamlet* to some period between late 1599 and early 1601.[5] Most scholars also assume that Q1 derives, in some way or another, from performances that took place between late 1599 and 1603. If those theories are correct, then Burbage played the role for the first time no later than 1599, and perhaps as late as 1601. At that time, Burbage would have been between 32 and 34 years old. The actor who succeeded Burbage in the role, Joseph Taylor, was 33 years old when Burbage died. Thus, according to the theory that has dominated Shakespearian criticism for a century, both Burbage and Taylor first played Shakespeare's Hamlet when they were over 30. This assumption neatly fits the text of the play printed in 1604. That "enlarged" edition goes out of its way to specify, very precisely, that Hamlet was born "on that very day" that "our last King Hamlet overcame Fortinbras," which was also "that day" when the Clown began digging graves, "thirty years" ago (5.1.135–53).[6] This "thirty years" echoes the repeated insistence, in the 1604 text, on the "thirty" years of marriage of the "Queen" and her husband the "King" (who is poisoned while sleeping in his garden) in the inset "Mousetrap" play (3.2.148, 150, 151).[7] These characters in the play-within-the-play are clearly meant to suggest the old King Hamlet and his Queen Gertrude; their 30 years of marriage, before his death, would place the birth of their only son, 30 years ago, in the first year of their marriage.

Building upon much earlier scholarship, Bart van Es has argued convincingly that Shakespeare wrote all his protagonists from 1599 to 1607, and especially Hamlet, specifically for Burbage, and that the great tragedies of that period result from the playwright's close artistic collaboration with his leading actor (who was also, starting in 1599, a leading investor).[8] But van Es does not mention that Shakespeare seems to have written the role of Hamlet with his leading actor's *age* in mind. Nowadays, rock stars in their sixties and seventies continue to reprise hit songs written when they were in their teens, and in earlier centuries star actors continued to play for years characters that they had created earlier in their career; fans grow accustomed to those performances, and look forward to their repetition. However, new roles written specifically for a particular actor are not likely to ignore completely his aging body—which will continue to age if, as writer and actor hope, the play is a success and remains in the repertoire. During the period van Es surveys, Shakespeare was certainly conscious of the fact that Burbage was no longer in his twenties: Henry V (1599), in the first scenes of his play, is specifically dissociated from the former "courses of his youth" and "wilder days," and *Twelfth Night*'s Orsino is by his own account "too old" for Viola (1601), and *Measure for Measure*'s Vincentio is "the old fantastical Duke" (1603), and Othello "declined into the vail of years" (1604), and Lear an "old man"(1605), and autumnal Macbeth "fall'n into the sear, the yellow leaf" (1606), and the "old" lion Antony an "old ruffian" (1607). Shakespeare even, apparently, wrote the role of Hamlet with his leading actor's girth in mind: by the seventeenth century, to judge by the sole surviving portrait, Burbage was a little "fat and scant of breath," as Hamlet is said to be in the 1604 edition and all its successors (5.2.269).[9] The enlarged *Hamlet* first printed in 1604 was specifically, explicitly written for a leading actor in his thirties. But "with Hamlet as a man of 30," A. A. Jack objected,

> the whole story Shakespeare was handling goes to pieces. Had Hamlet been 30 he would himself on his father's sudden death have ascended the throne amid general acclamation.... A man of 30 would not have been at "School" at Wittenberg, nor packable off, like a schoolboy, by

his uncle, to visit an obliging English King. . . . A boy might be expected to forget his feigned idiocy when offered the affections of a young girl, or to betray himself confidentially to his mother when in her chamber with her alone, but these are tests specially appropriate for adolescence, not maturity.[10]

The awkwardness here suggests that Shakespeare had inherited a story with a younger protagonist, but was forced to adapt it to suit an older actor. Scholars have assumed that the story Shakespeare inherited was the lost "Hamlet" of 1589. But we do not need to invoke a lost play. We possess a printed *Hamlet* with the adolescent protagonist that the story requires.

The text printed in 1603 does not contain the lines that specify Hamlet's age, or his winded plumpness, does not identify the couple in the "Mousetrap" as King and Queen, does not date their marriage "thirty" years ago.[11] Moreover, that text gives a different date for Yorick's death: not "twenty three" or "three and twenty years" ago, as in the second quarto and the Folio (5.1.163–4), but a mere "dozen year[s]" previously (16.86). That 23 years of the later editions fits well enough with their "thirty" for Hamlet. But in the 1603 quarto Hamlet could remember Yorick as a boy, could have been carried on his back 20 times, could have kissed him a 100 times (16.109–11), without being more than 16 or 17 years old.[12] All of the indications of a later age for Hamlet, present in the later texts, are absent from the first edition. Indeed, the 1603 text, read by itself without any assumptions about its relationship to the later printed texts, does nothing to suggest that Hamlet has passed the threshold into his twenties.

All three texts of the play refer to "young Hamlet." But the pattern of those references in the first edition differs substantially from the later ones. The play (unlike its source) contains two men named "Hamlet" and two men named "Fortinbras." Critics have often celebrated Shakespeare's complex mirroring of father and son, in the two parallel royal families of Denmark and Norway, but to avoid confusion in the theatre the father must always be clearly distinguished from the son of the same name. So, in the first scene "Fortinbras of Norway" (1.70; 1.1.85) is introduced, and killed off, before we hear of "young Fortinbras" (1.79; 1.1.98). In the next scene, the living Fortinbras is again contrasted with his uncle, "old Norway," who is "bedrid" (2.2–3; 1.2.20, 35). Likewise, we see the ghost of the dead King of Denmark, and hear his name—"valiant Hamlet (For so this side of our known world esteemed him)" (1.72–3; 1.1.87–8)—before his son is introduced: at the end of that scene, Horatio suggests "Let us impart what we have seen tonight / Unto young Hamlet" (1.125–6; 1.1.174–5). Indeed, the lines I have quoted in this paragraph are identical in all three texts. They are spoken by Horatio and Claudius, and the actors who played those roles have never been suspected of pirating or reporting the text. From the perspective of any theory of piracy (by publisher, actor, or spectator) we would not predict that these lines or phrases would be perfectedly transmitted. But the textual stability here makes sense in terms of authorial revision. It reflects a necessary initial clarity in any exposition of the plot, especially for an audience (which has to catch these relationships on the fly, aurally). In all three versions, the play's protagonist is not mentioned until the end of the first scene, and we do not see him until after we have already seen the "grizzled," salt-and-pepper, "sable silver" beard of the ghost of his father.[13] And in all three texts, Hamlet belongs to the play's youngerage-cohort: younger certainly than his dead father, his stepfather, and his mother, and younger than Ophelia's father, too. All these older characters lived many years intimately in the company of the dead king, and they naturally refer to the Prince of the same name as "young." In the generational divide that structures *Hamlet*, a 30-year-old can easily be the leader of the "young" faction.

But the first edition emphasizes Hamlet's youth in more specific ways, not present in the other texts. It is not just that Q1 calls him "young" four times where Q2 and F do not (6.38, 7.59, 7.224, 11.1).[14] More conspicuously, Hamlet is twice addressed with the vocative "boy." In the scene where he meets privately with his mother, in the later texts Polonius says "He will come straight" and the Queen replies "I hear him coming." When he enters and begins berating the Queen, she retorts, "Why, how now, Hamlet!" (3.4.1, 6, 12). But in Q1, that scene begins with Corambis saying "I hear young Hamlet coming," and after Hamlet enters, the Queen's retort to him is "How now, boy!" (11.1, 10). In the much earlier scene, when Marcellus and the others enter searching and calling for "Lord Hamlet," the line "Illo, lo, so, ho, come, boy, come" is spoken in Q1 by Marcellus (5.87), not Hamlet, as in Q2 and F(1.5.118). So the referent for "boy" in Q1 is Hamlet, whereas in the later editions the referent is Marcellus. Ambrose Gunthio, otherwise so skeptical of the 1603 text, actually praised this variant: "In the first quarto the words are doubtlessly appropriated to the true speaker" because this phrase "was the falconer's call to lure back a *stray bird*, and therefore proceeds with peculiar impropriety from the object sought for."[15] They seek Hamlet; he is not seeking them. "Boy" is much more obviously appropriate to a teenager than to a 30-year-old man. Indeed, in 249 cases in surviving legal records in London and Norwich from 1556 to 1685 "boy" was never used for anyone beyond their teens.[16]

Another variant also relates to the issue of Hamlet's age. In the later editions of the play that we all know, the King rejects Hamlet's "intent / In *going back* to school in Wittenberg" (1.2.112–13. my italics). But in the first edition that rejection comes much earlier in the scene and the play, in the first speech addressed to the protagonist, where the King instead rejects Hamlet's "intent, *going* to Wittenberg" (2. 28, my italics). The later editions begin with Hamlet's desire to return, after an indeterminate period, to the famous university in Wittenberg. The first edition instead introduces him to the audience as someone who, apparently, aspires to go to Wittenberg for the first time, which would be appropriate for a teenager but not a 30-year-old.[17] In early modern England, most students started university at the age of 14.

All these textual variants indicating a difference in the imagined age of the protagonist come in scattered speeches by Marcellus, the Queen, the King, Corambis, Ophelia, the husband and wife of the Mousetrap, and the Gravedigger. They cannot be explained by any pattern of memorial reconstruction or note-taking. Thus, piracy will not account for the pattern of textual stability or the pattern of textual variation in the early texts. These variants also relate to the larger differences in the relationship between the printed texts and the play's source, which I noted at the end of chapter 3. Margrethe Jolly demonstrates that "Belleforest's characterization of Amleth as youthful is pervasive; it is also consistent." In Q1, "again the references are pervasive...and consistent." In Belleforest, Amleth is not simply described as "jeune" (young), but also as "Adolescent" and "enfant." Specifically, he has not yet reached the age of majority ("à perfection d'age").[18] In Elizabethan England, a reader would have understood this last phrase to mean that Hamlet was not yet "of age," which in normal circumstances would mean that he had not yet turned 21.[19] However, a different definition of adulthood applied to princes and heirs to the throne. In France, the royal age of majority was 14, and in 1559 Francois II had ascended the throne at the age of 15; his brother Charles IX was declared of age in 1563, when he was just 13. So Belleforest probably imagined Amleth in his very early teens. But a reader in Elizabethan England would probably have been more influenced by sixteenth-century English royal precedents. Henry VIII had succeeded to the throne when he was just shy of his eighteenth birthday. His son, Edward VI, was only nine years old when he was crowned; a regency council was created to govern the realm until he turned 18, at which point (if he had lived) he would have acquired full monarchical powers. It's not clear how much Shakespeare knew about Denmark, beyond what he read in Belleforest, before 1603; but in April 1588 the successful warrior king Frederick II of Denmark and Norway died; his son and heir became Christian IV at the age of 12, but did not begin to govern the country until 1596, when he was 18. Shakespeare, reading Belleforest, would probably have understood that Prince Amleth was not yet 18. As a playwright, he would not have wanted a protagonist in his early teens, because such roles would normally be played by a boy actor, and in all three texts Hamlet is beyond the range of such a performer. But a 17-year-old prince could certainly have been played convincingly by a young adult professional actor. (Burbage in 1589 would have been only 21 or 22 years old.)

Jolly shows that the agreement of Belleforest with Q1 over the issue of Hamlet's age is part of a larger pattern in the English treatment of the French source. But she actually misses the most compelling consequence of her evidence. The 1603 text does *not* specify that Hamlet is 30 years old, does *not* describe him as "fat and scant of breath," does *not* have him remember fondly a man who died 22 years ago. Instead, the first edition systematically creates the impression of an adolescent Hamlet, a man who, at the beginning of the play, has not crossed, or only just crossed, the threshold of adulthood—or who crosses it during the course of the play. How are we to explain these differences between the 1603 and 1604 editions? If the first edition represents the play as performed in the early seventeenth century, how can any witness of performance—whether an actor or a note-taking spectator—have failed to notice that Hamlet/Burbage was 30-something? Any theory that the first edition represents a reconstruction (memorial or otherwise) of performances of the enlarged 1604 text must assume that (1) Shakespeare at the turn of the century wrote a play with the age, physique, talents, and limitations of his leading actor in mind, and that (2) the acting company then *altered* Shakespeare's script, in order to make it *less* appropriate for their leading actor, while at the same time (3) bringing various details of the *later* text closer to the author's *earlier* reading. The second element of this hypothesis is as wildly implausible as the third. Theatrical adaptation adjusts a text to the requirements of a theatrical venue, a special occasion, an acting company, or a leading actor; the theory of actor-piracy or spectator-piracy here presumes instead that theatrical adaptation not only ignored that logic but also reversed it, turning a text designed for the leading actor into something *less* suitable for him. Likewise, an author's reading of a printed source affects the first version of a text more closely and directly than a later revision; but here, the theory of actor-piracy or spectator-piracy presumes that the later revision is closer to the initial reading. Any theory that the first edition of *Hamlet* represents a performed version of the play, chronologically later than the enlarged version, cannot be correct. It violates the simplest practical principles of theatrical logic and, at the same time, the simplest practical principles of the chronological relationship between reading, writing, and revision.

In Erne's particular version of this theory, Shakespeare and all the actors of the company, including Burbage himself, collaborated in rewriting, reworking, and restructuring the script for London performances, in a way that made it harder for Burbage to perform convincingly. Erne does not see the absurdity of this hypothesis because he is, like everyone else, reading the chronology of the texts in reverse, moving from the familiar enlarged text backward toward the first edition. He is also reading a text that he considers to be the work of a "literary dramatist." He is not thinking like an actor.

Shakespeare was an actor. Although we cannot be sure exactly when he began acting, or stopped acting, he was certainly an actor when the enlarged, canonical text of *Hamlet* was written.[20] And from the perspective of an actor, there is a much simpler explanation for these differences between the 1603 edition and the later printed texts. The first edition of *Hamlet* is closer to the play's source because it represents the earliest version of the play, one written by a young man, in which the protagonist was also a young man, played by a young actor. The later editions are not as close to the French source because they represent a later version of the script, which has been revised for many reasons—one of them being the fact that the actor who will play the title role has, in the interim, grown capable of much more complex and impressive feats of personation, but also gotten older, a little plumper, perhaps less inclined to overstrain himself physically. Since the actor in question is also the leader of the company, artistically and financially, the new version will have to accommodate him, even if that creates some awkwardness in the story.

* * *

In the later editions of *Hamlet*, the protagonist can still be vaguely "young," but not specifically underage. In all three versions of the play, Ophelia compares Hamlet to a flower, but Q1's "only flower of Denmark" becomes, in the later editions, the "rose of the fair state" and "blown youth, / Blasted with ecstacy" (3.1.151, 158–9): better poetry, but also describing Hamlet as "blown" and "blasted," fully blossomed, overripe, a little past his first flowering.²¹ The original Hamlet compared himself to Nero (9.234), who became emperor when he was only 17 years old, and murdered his mother when he was 22. But the older actor, playing an older character, can still fear that he might turn into Nero (3.2.384), because matricide is taboo at any age. The only difference between the two classical allusions is that the younger Hamlet prays, "let ne'er the heart of Nero enter this *soft* bosom," and the older one prays "let not ever / The soul of Nero enter this *firm* bosom" (my italics). Changing one word turns the original soft boy—what Shakespeare elsewhere calls a "tender juvenile"—into a firm man.

Hamlet's age has implications beyond a single adjective. How could it not? The age of a prince, and heir apparent, is a fact of extraordinary political and social importance. To begin with, a change in Hamlet's age affects his relationship to some other characters. But not all of them. For instance, Hamlet's age makes no difference whatsoever to Lucianus, the Prologue, or Voltemand, the roles that are textually the most stable in all three versions of the play. It makes a little difference to Marcellus—as noted already, he calls Hamlet "boy" in the first edition—but not much: Marcellus is an uneducated soldier and Hamlet is a prince, in all three texts, and the relative age of that prince does not matter much to their onstage social interaction.

Only one major role seems completely unaffected by the change in Hamlet's age: the king's counselor. In all three texts, Corambis/Polonius is the play's oldest onstage character. After his death, Ophelia in her mourning remembers (13.36–7; 4.5.187–8) that "his beard" was "white as snow," and that his "pole" (= head) was "flaxen" (= white). By contrast, the dead King's beard is only "grizzled," meaning that it contained a mixture of black and white hair; there is no evidence of him being white-haired, and the exclusive focus on the beard implies that only it is "grizzled." Physiologically, the hairs of the male human beard are the first to begin turning white, so the description of Hamlet's father could put him anywhere between his thirties and his sixties. In any case, Hamlet's father is younger than the white-bearded, white-haired counselor. And whatever changes occur in the other characters, their relationship to Corambis/Polonius does not change: eavesdropper, busybody, university-educated know-it-all, older than anyone, father to Ophelia and Laertes, court counselor, coconspirator with the King, spy on Hamlet, obstacle to young love, victim of Hamlet's wit and then of Hamlet's sword. This fact explains why the speeches of Corambis change when he becomes Polonius, but his *cues* remain exceptionally stable.[22] Unlike Voltemand, Lucianus, the Prologue, and much more than Marcellus, the old counselor is an interesting character, an old buffoon (like the conventional "senex") combined with a cunning, experienced, dangerous political operative. A revising playwright might well remain interested in that interesting character, and so might continue to tinker with him, expanding and rewriting his speeches. But in contrast to speeches, cues are generated by, and express, one role's *relationships* to the play's other roles, and the counselor's relationships do not change. Authorial revision provides a simple explanation for the transformation of the speeches, but the relative stability of the cues, of Corambis/Polonius.

By contrast, Hamlet's age does make a difference to the portrayal of the play's other important courtier, the one who first appears in the final scene, bringing Hamlet a message from the king. In the first edition this character is an unnamed "Braggart Gentleman" (17.4). But in the later versions he is given a name and an age: "young Osric" (5.2.176, 236; also 5.2.80.1 in the Folio). All this happens soon *after* the later texts have insisted upon Hamlet's 30 years, and the effect is surely to contrast Hamlet's maturity with the mocked immaturity of Osric. Just before Hamlet's death, "Young Osric" reenters to announce, "Young Fortinbras with conquest comes from Poland" (5.2.334). Again, this suggests, in the later versions, a contrast between the tragic prince and the "young" who will survive him.

Given the structural pairing of Hamlet with Fortinbras and with Laertes, if Hamlet in the first edition is younger then so, presumably, are they. In all three texts, Laertes appeals to the king for permission to leave the court, so it is not clear whether he has reached the age of majority: he might, or might not, be over 21. But only in the first edition is Laertes a student, returning to his studies: Corambis, sending his servant Montano to Paris with money for his son, says "bid him ply his *learning*" (6.3, my italics).[23] In the later versions, Laertes is simply an aristocratic young man in search of cosmopolitan experiences, away from his father's constricting oversight. He might well be in his twenties. In all three versions, Laertes is considered the better fencer, and Hamlet is therefore given favorable odds.[24] In the later texts, "fat and scant of breath" suggests a reason for the oddsmaker's handicapping: that Hamlet is less athletic, and perhaps less young, than Laertes.[25] No explanation is given in the first edition, leaving open the possibility that its Hamlet might be less accomplished simply because he is actually younger, and therefore less experienced, than its Leartes.

The age of Laertes in turn affects Ophelia, his sister. None of the texts specifically say that she is the younger sibling, but in my experience of watching, directing, and acting in the play, he always comes across as older than her, whichever text is being performed. More objectively, the much shorter text of Q1 contains four additional references to Ophelia's youth, not found in the later editions:

> But this mischance of old Corambis' death
> Hath piercéd so the young Ofelia's heart... (13.6–7)
> O see where the young Ofelia is! (13.14)
> O my Lord, the young Ofelia... (15.40)
> Bore the young lady up, and there she sat... (15.45)

In all three versions, Ophelia is younger than the play's parental generation. But as with Hamlet, the question is: how young? In her mid-twenties? or in her teens? A young woman in her twenties would be more appropriate for a 30-year-old Hamlet, and in the twenty-first century such a couple would be perfectly acceptable in a film or play. But the older romantic pairing inevitably raises questions. Is Hamlet a 30-year-old virgin? A young prince, who is also the sole living child and presumed heir of a king, usually has his pick of women. Moreover, in medieval and early modern Europe an heir to the throne would have been married off, for dynastic reasons, long before his thirties. Prince Arthur, the eldest son and heir of Henry VII, was betrothed when he was ten, and married by proxy when he was 12; he married in person and shared a bed with his bride when he was 15. Arthur's younger brother, the future Henry VIII, was betrothed when he was 12, and married that woman just before his eighteenth birthday.[26]

If we switch our focus from political to theatrical history, we are faced by the same problem. The relationship between Hamlet and Ophelia reads like first love, the usual subject of Elizabethan romantic plots. Unless an Elizabethan audience was told otherwise, it would assume that convention. In Shakespeare's plays, Kate is definitely older than her sister Bianca, and Petruccio is almost always portrayed as older than the would-be student Lucentio. But in *The Taming of the Shrew* Kate's age demonstrates that no one wants to marry her. By contrast, no one considers Ophelia an unmarriageable shrew. Likewise, Benedick and Beatrice do not seem as young as Claudio and Hero, but *Much Ado About Nothing* explains their maturity in terms of a mutual resistance to marriage, with clear suggestions of a long-standing emotional tussle between them. By contrast, in all three versions Hamlet and Ophelia are, instead, set in relief against an *older* couple, the Queen and King. The "enlarged" text of *Hamlet* provides no explanation for the chronological maturity of its romantic male lead.

In his most famous love story, Shakespeare tells us twice that Juliet is 13 years old (1.2.9, 1.3.13), and he also tells us that "Younger than she are happy mothers made" (1.2.12), that "Younger than [she], / Here in Verona, ladies of esteem, / Are made already mothers" (1.3.71–3), and that Lady Capulet gave birth to Juliet when she was about 13 herself (1.3.74–5). Historically, Margaret Beaufort was 13 years old when she gave birth to Henry Tudor (Queen Elizabeth's grandfather). Aristocratic women like Ophelia, in particular, "ladies of esteem," were often married young. Ophelia in the 1603 edition could easily be, like Juliet, just 13 years old. A modern audience would find this objectionable, but Elizabethan spectators obviously would have accepted it as a social reality.

In all three versions, Ophelia is consistently identified as a virgin ("maid," "maiden") who must protect her "honor" (virginity). In all three versions, both her brother and her father, in lecturing Ophelia about Hamlet, treat her as though she needs to be instructed in the most basic facts. In the enlarged texts of the play, her brother immediately stresses the political issues raised by the relationship.

> His greatness weighed, his will is not his own.
> He may not, as unvalued persons do,
> Carve for himself, for on his choice depends
> The safety and health of this whole state,
> And therefore must his choice be circumscribed
> Unto the voice and yielding of that body
> Whereof he is the head. Then if he says he loves you
> It fits your wisdom so far to believe it
> As he in his particular act and place
> May give his saying deed, which is no further
> Than the main voice of Denmark goes withal.
>
> (1.3.17–27)

Polonius, too, stresses the social gap between her and "the Lord Hamlet," who sends her a "command" to meet with him; "with a larger tether may he walk / Than may be given you" (1.3.122–5). An Elizabethan audience, or a Jacobean reader, might well assume that even an Ophelia in her twenties knows relatively little about politics; it was not a topic most women were expected, or encouraged, to investigate for themselves. We might also recognize that her male relatives at least do her the courtesy of explaining politics to her. But none of this is present in the first edition, where Laertes and Corambis instead stress only the general unreliability of men's promises, the general volatility of male passion: "do not trust his vows," Laertes warns her; "Perhaps he loves you now... But yet take heed, my sister" (3.4–6). Corambis is equally caustic and abstract: "What, do not I know when the blood doth burn / How prodigal the tongue lends the heart vows?" and "lover's lines are snares to entrap the heart" (3.60–61, 66). These warnings are retained in the later texts, but in Q1 they monopolize the conversation. In the first edition, our first impression of Ophelia stresses only her emotional naivete, her complete ignorance of the rituals of male courtship.[27]

The younger Ophelia is, the more understandable the behavior of her male relatives becomes. If she is in her early or mid-teens, it's not surprising that she accepts her father's command that she end the relationship with Hamlet; her acquiescence in her father's plot to "entrap" and eavesdrop on Hamlet is equally understandable, and more likely to be forgiven by an audience (even if Hamlet does not forgive it). But a younger Ophelia will also have less emotional resilience when subjected to Hamlet's brutal treatment of her in the nunnery scene and the play scene. That innocence and vulnerability in those middle scenes will, in turn, render her collapse into madness more believable, but also more pathetic.

* * *

I have until now limited my analysis of the age of *Hamlet*'s characters to direct textual and historical evidence. But at this point it may be useful to pay some attention to stage history. The discovery and republication of the 1603 edition in 1825 almost immediately began to affect texts of *Hamlet*, incorporating isolated words, phrases, or stage directions into the texture of the conflated, enlarged canonical text.[28] Performances of Q1 itself have become increasingly common, since William Poel's inaugural, under-rehearsed, amateur production in 1881.[29] Irace's introduction to her 1998 edition includes a stage history of Q1, as does Thompson and Taylor's more extensive and sophisticated 2006 introduction.[30] I am not interested, here, in an historically or textually comprehensive survey of performances of Q1 (in whole or part). Instead, I will focus only on what recorded modern performances may tell us about the implications of the early textual variants affecting age. I will also focus on productions not already described by the Cambridge or Arden editions.

The difference age makes can be demonstrated by Trevor Nunn's 2004 modern-dress production at the Old Vic, "with a bunch of students playing *Hamlet*."[31] Nunn had first directed the play when he was 18. In 2004 as in 1958, his script was a conflated text of the canonical version, but he recognized that "the story did not make proper sense if the actors are as mature as they generally are when they get to play it."[32] His unauthorized and erratic combination of material from different versions created inconsistencies, and it obviously cannot help us solve the historical problem of the relationship between the three early texts of the play.[33] But Nunn's use of younger actors, playing younger characters, was revealing. His Ophelia, Samantha Whittaker, was at the time only 19 years old, and her "infinitely touching Ophelia [was] first discovered bopping along to The Strokes in her school uniform."[34] Whittaker played her "childish, gym-slipped" Ophelia as a "teenage girl who has a crush upon Hamlet."[35]

My own 2011 production of the play did not have the financial or human resources of the Old Vic, and did not receive the same quantity or quality of reviews. I would never dare to compare myself to Trevor Nunn; however, unlike Nunn's production, the one I directed did use the text of the first edition throughout.[36] It was advertised as "Young Hamlet," and tickets were much cheaper than those in London; the sold-out production so appealed to an overwhelmingly young audience that we added an extra performance.[37] My Ofelia was played by Maria Souza, who had trained in theatre at Purdue University and at the New Jersey Shakespeare Festival. She looked younger than her 24 years, and I told her to play Ofelia as though she were a student in a Catholic high school, a beautiful, well-dressed but prim "good girl" who carried a rosary. She was very much Daddy's little princess, hugging her father and turning to him for advice or reassurance. Lacking a mother, she also tried repeatedly to connect with the Queen, a neediness conveyed by blocking, touch, and eye contact. In the nunnery scene, Hamlet became violent, threatening her with a knife and almost raping her onstage before abandoning her to the indifference of her father and the king. Clearly, neither the performer nor the character had ever experienced anything so traumatic, but we got feedback from many young women about how powerfully this scene spoke to their own shock and bewilderment, completely unprepared when confronted for the first time with a physically abusive boyfriend. Souza's Ophelia was notably gun-shy in her next meeting with Hamlet, in the Mousetrap scene: emotionally jerked around by Hamlet's inexplicable, and unpredictable, lurching changes of tone, and deeply embarrassed by Hamlet' s smutty jokes (and gestures). She looked to her father and the Queen for explanation or support, but both were preoccupied with other issues. After two scenes of traumatic abuse, the transition to madness was immediately intelligible to the actor and the audience.

One of the many reasons I cast Souza is that she could sing, a cappella, convincingly. The early texts differ in the order of Ophelia's mad songs. In the enlarged version, she begins with the sexual songs, and then, in the presence of Laertes, sings the dirge for her father. That arrangement makes sense, and it stresses the shared grief of the siblings for their dead parent. But the 1603 edition instead begins with the mourning song. This had the advantage, for Souza, of immediately giving Ophelia an onstage emotional reaction to the news of her father's death. When she returns, the sexual songs were particularly shocking because she had been, until then, so prim, but also because her sexuality was acted out in front of her brother. She was dressed in a slip, and wound up on her back, on the floor, with her feet toward Laertes, legs slightly apart, knees raised, unmistakably mimicking intercourse. Laertes and the King both turned away, while the Queen moved to help her up and offstage. The city's leading theatre critic described Souza's Ophelia as the "most moving and consistent" performance in the play.[38] This entire interpretation depended on Ophelia beginning the play as a naive adolescent, not a woman in her twenties.

The age of Ophelia cannot be separated, on stage or in the early texts, from the age of the Queen.[39] In the enlarged versions of 1604 and 1623, the Queen has a 30-year-old son, which means that she can hardly be younger than 43 (and might easily be 50 or older). In the 1603 edition, her son is almost certainly younger than 18, which means that she could, by early modern standards, be no more than 30. That difference will obviously affect the actor's, and the audience's, attitude toward her sexuality, her remarriage, her relationship to her son, her second husband, and Ophelia. Imogen Stubbs (figure 4.1), who played the role in Nunn's production, made "something fascinating out of Gertrude: a besotted wife, a fitness-freak and an adoring mother who ruffles her son's hair and realizes too late he is telling the truth."[40] She was "outstanding as a glamorous, sex-obsessed Gertrude who cracks up completely in the confrontation with Hamlet in her bedroom and ends up on the bottle"; "very seductive," she was "constantly canoodling" with her new husband Claudius.[41] In her later essay on that performance, Stubbs precisely articulated the problem with traditional interpretations of the Queen as "a dignified empress," asking "Why is this forty-year-old so obsessed with his sixty-year-old mother getting remarried?"[42]

Without having seen or read about her Gertrude, I had reached many of the same conclusions as Stubbs.[43] My Gertrude entered the

Figure 4.1 A 30-something Gertrude (Imogen Stubbs) tries to pacify a sulky, adolescent Hamlet (Ben Whishaw) in the second scene of *Hamlet*, dir. Trevor Nunn (Old Vic, 2004). Photo by Alastair Muir.

play dancing happily with her new husband, played by Kevin Johnson, a handsome black actor who is also an accomplished dancer; we both have a background in American musical theatre, and we used that experience to craft the physical relationship between the royal couple. But unlike Stubbs, I was performing the 1603 text of the play. That version creates a very different, more intimate relationship between the 30-something Queen and the teenage Ophelia. This is particularly apparent in the scenes of Ophelia's madness. The canonical version of those episodes conspicuously distances the Queen from Ophelia. In both enlarged texts, the Queen at first refuses even to see her, and is told about her madness by someone else, a man who has until that moment had no discernible relationship to the vulnerable younger woman (4.5.1–13). In the 1623 text, that someone is Horatio, who has to persuade the Queen to grant Ophelia entrance. In the 1604 text, that someone is an anonymous Gentleman, who persuades Horatio, who himself orders the

Gentleman to admit Ophelia, overriding the Queen's resistance. When she does enter, the Queen does not respond, and Ophelia speaks of her in the third person, very formally ("Where is the beauteous majesty of Denmark?"). No one, reading this passage, would be likely to conclude that the Queen and Ophelia were close. By contrast, in the 1603 edition it is the Queen herself who first describes Ophelia's offstage madness:

> But this mischance of old Corambis' death
> Hath pierce'd so the young Ophelia's heart
> That she, poor maid, is quite bereft her wits.
>
> (13.6–8)

The King responds to this by changing the subject, focusing instead on Laertes and the political problem. But the Queen then insists again on talking about the orphaned daughter, and is the first to respond to her appearance: "O, see where the young Ophelia is!" (13.14). Both these speeches by the Queen emphasize Ophelia's youth. And when Ophelia exits, from the scene and the play, in the first edition the Queen apparently accompanies her (13.115).[44] In my production, she fell against the Queen, who then protectively helped her offstage, and this image of the two women clinging to each other was the last time that the audience saw Ophelia alive.

This exit in turn related to the Queen's later description of Ophelia's death. The familiar canonical version is justly celebrated for its poetic landscape-painting, which has inspired more artists than anything else that the Queen or Ophelia say. It makes death beautiful.

> There is a willow grows askant the brook
> That shows his hoary leaves in the glassy stream.
> Therewith fantastic garlands did she make
> Of crowflowers, nettles, daisies and long purples,
> That liberal shepherds give a grosser name
> But our cold maids do dead men's fingers call them.
> There on the pendent boughs her crownet weeds
> Clambering to hang, an envious sliver broke,
> When down her weedy trophies and herself
> Fell in the weeping brook. Her clothes spread wide
> And mermaid-like awhile they bore her up,
> Which time she chanted snatches of old lauds
> As one incapable of her own distress,
> Or like a creature native and endued
> Unto that element. But long it could not be

> Till that her garments, heavy with their drink,
> Pulled the poor wretch from her melodious lay
> To muddy death.
>
> (4.7.164–181)

I must admit that, having taught the canonical Queen before, I was a bit dismayed to lose this gorgeous, show-stopping, literally purple passage when I came to play the 1603 text of the Queen. But I soon realized that the unfamiliar version has much more immediacy, and creates a far more personal sense of grief. To begin with, when the Queen enters, the King immediately reads the emotion on her face and in her body before she speaks a word: "How now, Gertrude? Why look you heavily?" (15.39). And the Queen's first utterance here is an inarticulate moan, "O," like the "O" of her response to Ophelia's first mad entrance—an exclamation that she never uses in the canonical version. And that groan or sigh is immediately followed by the name, and another reminder of youth: "O, my lord, the young Ophelia." In the later texts, the Queen never once speaks Ophelia's name in this scene, or refers to her age. Instead, that later, older Queen first enters with a philosophical reflection, followed by a statement of fact: "One woe doth tread upon another's heel, / So fast they follow. Your sister's drowned, Laertes" (4.7.161–2). That Queen emphasizes Ophelia's relationship to her brother, not her own relationship to Ophelia. But in the first version of this moment, the Queen has no time or energy for reflection or landscape. She is obviously in the first shock of bereavement.

> O my lord, the young Ophelia
> Having made a garland of sundry sorts of flowers,
> Sitting upon a willow by a brook,
> The envious sprig broke, into the brook she fell
> And for a while her clothes spread wide abroad,
> Bore the young lady up: and there she sat
> Smiling, even mermaid-like, 'twixt heaven and earth,
> Chanting old sundry tunes uncapable
> As it were of her distress, but long it could not be
> Till that her clothes, being heavy with their drink,
> Dragged the sweet wretch to death.
>
> (15.40–50)

I have repeated, here, the original punctuation, which does not contain a single full stop until it finishes. It is rushed, barely grammatical, not leisurely or measured. For an actor, this is a remarkably different moment. It isn't so pretty, so obsessed with inanimate, inhuman, enameled detail. The Queen doesn't get to the unbearable word "death" until the very end. Audiences of the first version would not have known that Ophelia dies, and the Queen does not tell them, or Laertes, until she can no longer avoid it: she is reliving the sequence of events as they happened. By contrast, many spectators of the revised version would already have known Ophelia's fate, and the canonical version ensures that the foreknowledge is shared by everyone, including the listeners onstage. The focus then shifts from the news itself, to the cold way that news is delivered.

In the first edition of the Queen's speech, Ophelia starts as "young" and ends as "sweet" (words that don't appear in the later, canonical texts). Three times in the earlier version of these two Ophelia scenes, the Queen insists on Ophelia's youth. She is focused, not on herself, but on the tragedy of a young girl, who could easily be her own adolescent daughter, the daughter she never had. These details of the early version suggested, to me, a much closer relationship between the two women. The Queen is the older, stronger, mother-figure while Ophelia is alive, but when Ophelia dies she reacts the way any mother would react to the death of her young daughter. But unlike Stubbs, I did not aspire to create "a pathetic Gertrude" (as one reviewer described her 2004 performance), or "a woman who seems powerless to comprehend her situation."[45] And unlike Stubbs and Nunn, I do not believe that "the domestic" world and "the family" dominate or exclude political issues.[46] Michael Billington, recognizing that *Hamlet* is "a deeply political play," complained that "Nunn gives us little sense that Elsinore is a deeply corrupt tyranny poisoned by usurpation."

Billington focused on the politics of the play as a whole. He did not recognize, and Nunn's production did not encourage audiences to recognize, the gendered specificity of the play's political issues. In all three early versions of the text, Hamlet's mother is a Queen, not just a rich, upper-class, spoiled mother. Indeed, she was a Queen before she was Hamlet's mother, and a Queen before she remarried. For a late Elizabethan audience, in 1600 or after, the age of a Queen was of obvious and pressing political importance. By the time any English play about Hamlet was written, Elizabeth I's biological clock had run out of time: everyone knew that she had passed the point at which she might ever give birth to an heir. It wouldn't matter, politically, whether Hamlet's mother was 43, or 50, or 60, because at any of those ages she was, in the early modern world, too old for a viable pregnancy. Therefore, in the canonical enlarged versions of *Hamlet*, Gertrude's sexuality has no political consequences. Knowing that the Queen cannot bear him a son, Claudius can publicly declare to his nephew and stepson, "Let the world take note, You are the most immediate to our throne " (1.2.108–9).

But no such declaration is present in the 1603 edition. A 30-year-old Queen could obviously conceive, and give birth, again. Indeed, in at least one recent production, she was visibly pregnant throughout the play.[47] If she has another child, by the new king, then the new king will have an heir of his own, who could displace Hamlet. Therefore, the King does not publicly announce that Hamlet is "the most immediate" to his throne. And therefore, when Hamlet tells his mother, "If ever you did my dear father love, / Forbear the adulterous bed tonight... In time it may be you will loath him quite" (11.91–4), he is not simply obsessed with his mother's sexuality: he is also pleading with her not to produce a rival heir. An alternative Prince of Denmark would not only oust "young Hamlet" from the succession but also oust the old King Hamlet from his place in the future royal line, turning his branch of the family tree into a dynastic dead end.

The dynastic uncertainty created by a young Queen explains why the Ghost reappears in this scene. More particularly, the Queen's youth and fertility explains why, in Q1 alone, the Ghost enters here "in his nightgown" (11.57.1). Modern readers and spectators probably associate an old man in a nightgown with Scrooge in *A Christmas Carol*, or the equally asexual narrator of the nineteenth-century poem *'Twas the Night Before Christmas*. But in early modern plays a male nightgown could be as sexualized as female nightgowns are now.[48] Moreover, the father of a 17-year-old Hamlet could be in his thirties, too, like Gertrude, and only a little older than his younger brother. In the context of Q1's age-map, the nightgowned Ghost may intend to remind his widow, and certainly reminds Hamlet and the audience, of the sexual basis behind Hamlet's claim to legitimacy, and of the sexual threat posed by the Queen's remarriage. In the later versions of the text, that threat has disappeared, and the nightgown disappears too.[49]

The earliest extended critical response to the 1603 edition, Ambrose Gunthio's in 1825, recognized that the Queen in that edition differs significantly from the Queen of the canonical enlarged text. Earlier interpreters had already worried over "the question whether Shakspeare intended that the Queen should be supposed privy to the murder of her husband." But the long-lost first edition gives her two lines, in this scene, not present in the 1604 or 1623 texts, which resolve any ambiguity: "as I have a soul, I swear by heaven / I never knew of this most horrid murder" (11. 85–6). Gunthio recognized the importance of these lines, and went on to connect them to major variants in later scenes: "This declaration she sequently seems to make good, by displaying a natural indignation on discovering the plot against Hamlet, and even abetting him in his design upon the King." Gunthio acknowledges that this must have been Shakespeare's "original intention." But then he confuses the issue by seemingly reversing the direction of the change: "Her character, in short, is *raised* from that of an insignificant personage, whose innocence at best is problematical, to that of a prominent agent in the drama, with no particular fault but her objectionable marriage."[50] Preferring the 1603 edition's portrayal of the Queen, Gunthio slips into reading backward from the familiar enlarged text to the unfamiliar earlier one, as though Shakespeare had revised the play to disambiguate the Queen. Unlike Gunthio, and the entire Enlightenment/Romantic critical tradition that he represents, we now actually celebrate Shakespeare's portrayals of complex ambivalences, and we should have no difficulty imagining that, in revising *Hamlet*, Shakespeare deliberately rendered the Queen *more* ambiguous.

But Gunthio was right to see that the Queen is a more "prominent agent" in the first edition. Her agency is political, and it springs from her womb. In Q1, she was not a coconspirator in the murder of her first husband. But in Q1, once old Hamlet was dead, she became simultaneously pivotal and vulnerable: what G. B. Shand calls a "captive queen."[51] Like Isabella in Marlowe's *Edward II*, or Margaret in Shakespeare's *Richard Duke of York / 3 Henry VI*, she was the mother of a prince who (in Q1) was not yet old enough to rule on his own. For a month she was the Queen Mother, like Isabella after the murder of Edward II, or like Catherine de Medici in France, who from 1559 to 1588 was arguably the most powerful woman in Europe, powerful because of her fertility (unlike Elizabeth I, whose power depended on her virginity). But as a widow, young Hamlet's young mother would, in Q1, also have been in immediate danger of losing the regal status she had enjoyed for many years, either to her own son (if he became king quickly), or to her powerful and ambitious brother-in-law (if he usurped the throne). The man who murdered his brother was, as all versions of the play demonstrate, also perfectly willing to murder his brother's son. By rapidly marrying the dead king's brother, Q1's young Queen Mother had not only protected her young son but also preserved her own power.

All of this disappears in the enlarged, familiar, canonical version of the play, with its 30-year-old Hamlet. But with a teenage Hamlet, Elizabethan audiences would immediately have recognized the Queen's pivotal political position, and would have seen her, from the outset, as a political agent. When she first appears, the canonical text gives Claudius an opening speech 39 lines long, and 54 lines before she opens her mouth. But in the 1603 edition, the King's opening speech is only ten lines long; he mentions her at line 30 ("your mother"); he speaks only 30 lines before she intervenes, decisively:

> Let not thy mother lose her prayers, Hamlet.
> Stay here with us. Go not to Wittenberg. (2.48–9)

Three short sentences, all with imperative verbs: the turning point in the scene. In the canonical text, she is pleading ("*I pray thee*, stay with us"); but there is no begging in the first edition, and no preceding speeches where she pleads with Hamlet, then he sarcastically answers her, then the King takes over the conversation. Like any "good" wife in sixteenth-century Europe, the Queen in the first edition publicly decorously subordinates herself to her husband; she is a consistently pious woman with none of the vices usually associated with widows who remarry.[52] But she is also a confident woman with power who cannot be ignored or disobeyed.

Consequently, in the first edition, Hamlet's private conversation with her, after the "Mousetrap," is not just an emotional turning point, but a political one. Hamlet has to determine whether the Queen/Mother conspired in his father's murder—because, if she did, then she is an obstacle to his revenge, or even a necessary target of that revenge. But if she did not conspire against his father, she may become Hamlet's most important ally. By the end of the scene, she has, in Q1 only, become her son's coconspirator. When he asks her, "Mother, but assist me in revenge," she kneels and replies

> Hamlet, I vow by that [high] Majesty
> That knows our thoughts and looks into our hearts,
> I will conceal, consent and do my best—
> What stratagem soe'er thou shalt devise. (11.95–100)[53]

Hamlet has not failed here. "It is enough," he says, and he is right. He has eliminated the King's right-hand man, Corambis, and persuaded the Queen/Mother to ally herself with the rightful heir against the usurper (figure 4.2). In our production, this was the moment when mother and son were most intensely emotionally connected.

Three scenes later, in Q1 only, the Queen meets Horatio, to conspire with him and Hamlet against the "subtle treason" of "the King" (14.4). I directed that scene in an experimental performance paper at the Blackfriars Conference in 2005, employing the same actors then playing Gertrude (Tracy Hostmyer) and Horatio (Eric Schoen) in a production of the canonical *Hamlet* in repertoire at the same time. In place

Figure 4.2 The Queen (Terri Bourus) kneels and swears to conspire with her son Hamlet, still dressed in the threateningly offensive teenage combination of Marine Corps jacket and swastika armband (Thomas Cardwell) in *Young Hamlet*, dir. Terri Bourus (Hoosier Bard, 2011). Photo by John Gentry.

of the somewhat insipid, domesticated Gertrude of the familiar text, the Q1 scene in performance revealed a Queen more like Queen Margaret, or Queen Isabel—or Elizabeth I.[54]

> I grieve and dare not show my discontent,
> I love and yet am forced to seem to hate,
> I do, yet dare not say I ever meant,
> I seem stark mute but inwardly do prate.
> I am and not, I freeze and yet am burned,
> Since from myself another self I turned.

This, the opening of Elizabeth I's most famous poem, articulates a gendered understanding of political role-playing. Like Elizabeth, the Queen of the first edition of *Hamlet*, dependent on the approval and tolerance of powerful men, must play a role, and act out her stately performance, while simultaneously working behind the scenes to manipulate and control the state. Only in the first edition, only in that scene, do we see the Queen acting politically, independently of either the King or his counselor. She concludes the scene "With thousand mother's blessings to my son" (14.33), leaving no doubt about her alliance with the Prince against the King. In the final scene, she dies warning the Prince against "The drink, the drink, Hamlet, the drink" (17.86). At that point, Hamlet has already been fatally poisoned by Laertes's foil, but the Queen's last words unveil the king's whole conspiracy, and allow Hamlet to kill his father's murderer before his own death. Without the Queen/Mother's help, Hamlet would never have succeeded in his revenge.

The age of the Queen/Mother thus intertwines, dramatically and politically, with the age of the Prince of Denmark. Hamlet's age, with which I began, affects the play more profoundly than the age of any other character. In Nunn's 2004 production, Hamlet was played by Ben Whishaw, then only 23 years old, nominated for a best actor award a mere year after he had graduated from the Royal Academy of Dramatic Art (figure 4.3). "No Hamlet," wrote Nicholas de Jongh in the *Financial*

Figure 4.3 An out-of-control teenage Hamlet (Ben Whishaw) in the "Mousetrap" scene in *Hamlet*, dir. Trevor Nunn (Old Vic, 2004). Photo by Alastair Muir.

Times, "has made a more powerful or emotional impact. With his light, tremulous voice, painfully thin body," and "all the gangliness of adolescence," Whishaw was "the most raw and vulnerable Hamlet" veteran reviewer Charles Spencer had ever seen: "No wonder that this inadequate prince finds it so hard to revenge. Whishaw brilliantly captures an adolescent deep in the depths of clinical depression... Yet he is also the most lovable of Hamlets."

Whishaw established that an adolescent Hamlet could work, theatrically and psychologically. Another South Bank *Hamlet*, the summer 2011 production directed by Dominic Dromgoole, also featured a very young protagonist, Joshua McGuire (figure 4.4). Charles Spencer, who had raved about Whishaw, described McGuire as "a young, touchingly vulnerable Hamlet," who "delivers the soliloquies with freshness and spontaneity."[55] For Paul Taylor, he was a "pint-sized," "toff undergraduate" with "an excruciated smile under a mild shock of curls," an "intensely touching" Hamlet who was "young, unjaded and open-hearted."[56] For Lyn

Figure 4.4 A teenage Hamlet (Joshua McGuire) comforted by Ophelia (Jade Anouka) in a touring production of *Hamlet*, dir. Dominic Dromgoole (Shakespeare's Globe, 2011). Photo by Fiona Moorhead.

Gardner, McGuire suggested "something of the sullen prep-schoolboy, but also a self-dramatising teenager fatally damaged, emotionally, by his father's death and mother's hasty remarriage"; she praised his "teenage impetuosity" and the "charming gawkiness" of Jade Anouka's Ophelia.[57] Another reviewer singled out Anouka's "sweetly innocent" Ophelia for her "childlike madness."[58]

Beyond their two adolescent leads, these two productions had little in common. Audiences and reviewers saw Whishaw's awkward teenage Hamlet in a Victorian, proscenium-arch theatre, as part of an upholstered production that used the enlarged canonical text (which, even with some cuts, lasted three hours and 40 minutes). By contrast, Spencer saw McGuire play Hamlet in a sleeveless tee shirt at Shakespeare's Globe, the reconstructed outdoor Elizabethan amphitheatre of which Dromgoole is artistic director. Dromgoole's "stripped down *Hamlet*" was a touring production, which had trimmed the play to the length of the 1603 quarto. "With a running time well shy of three hours," Spencer described it as "fast, fresh, and lucid," and "one of the shortest Hamlets you are likely to see." He "particularly admired the production's clarity." Dromgoole recognized that Elizabethan theatre companies "toured all the time," and that this affected the way they performed plays in their metropolitan home base, too.[59] His production used a hybrid script, but instead of conflating the different early versions to produce a megatext, he put the language of the Folio version onto the skeletal structure of the first quarto. He turned to the first quarto because he wanted to avoid the "big, hefty, heavy, serious *Hamlet* with all of the extraordinarily odd cultural baggage that accretes to it," wanted to "get away from all of this sort of angst and neuroses and fake pain which has sort of occluded" the play "in the twentieth century with lots of very tortured post-Freudian interpretations." The 1603 structure gave him "a way of freeing the play up and of finding a very fresh approach to it," in part because "it tells a driving story, and occasionally it flips over to something cruder and bolder." He also, occasionally, incorporated some of the language unique to the 1603 edition, because it "is so choice and so beautiful and also so distinctly Shakespearean, such as the stuff about catchphrases at the end of the advice to the players, where it is very hard to see any other voice but Shakespeare's there." For instance, the first Quarto's "No King on earth is safe if God's his foe" (10.33) has "a sort of brutality" that may be "really clunky, but it is quite gorgeously clunky," and a "great closer" to the scene.[60] Dromgoole's production thus restored the 1603 edition's young Hamlet and young Ophelia to the structure of the 1603 edition and some of its language, while at the same time restoring many Elizabethan performance conditions and practices. But he did not restore the original Queen, or the play's original political situation. Like Nunn's production, this one was primarily a "domestic tragedy" about "the agonies of teenage angst and the fragile dynamic of family."[61]

My own production was based entirely on the 1603 edition, with a running time of only two hours and ten minutes.[62] The difference here was not simply textual: like Dromgoole's production, mine used early modern performance practices, so we had none of the Old Vic's massive set or elaborate props, no scene or lighting changes, no proscenium-arch separation of actors from audience. Philip Fisher had praised Whishaw for "slowing every soliloquy," so "that the meaning could be savoured." By contrast, in Dromgoole's production all the actors did indeed speak their lines "trippingly on the tongue," and McGuire's young Hamlet, in particular, spoke "at a hectic lick, while always observing the distinction between mere speed and dramatic momentum."[63] My own Hamlet, Thomas Cardwell, was also a 23-year-old British Equity actor, who looked even younger on stage, especially in contrast to a grandfatherly Corambis (figure 4.5). Like McGuire, he disappointed some reviewers who wanted the mature canonical Hamlet, paralyzed by Romantic

Figure 4.5 A teenage Hamlet (Thomas Cardwell) berates a grandfatherly Corambis (Stephen Scull) in *Young Hamlet*, dir. Terri Bourus (Hoosier Bard, 2011). Photo by John Gentry.

introspection. But Cardwell, acting the unadulterated 1603 part, was praised for very different reasons: as an "impulsive, punkish," "edgy," and "less philosophical hero," one "less apt to weigh all sides of a question," whose "To be or not to be?" was handled "with more dispatch than the version everyone knows."[64]

Cardwell's Hamlet was not just an adolescent, but the particular adolescent portrayed in the 1603 edition. His immaturity—and playfulness—was signaled by the Mickey Mouse tee shirt he wore in the "Mousetrap" scene (figure 4.6). His "dispatch," his "less philosophical" character, reflect features of the first quarto that have been noticed in many performances. All the productions of Q1 that Ann Thompson and Neil Taylor had "read about or seen from 1881 to 2003" evoked perceptions of "its speed and narrative drive" and "its lack of introspection and 'literary' elaboration." Gunnar Sjögren described a 1968 Swedish production as a "swift and thrilling version." Nicholas Shrimpton praised a 1985 production at London's Orange Tree theatre for its "clarity, energy

Figure 4.6 Hamlet (Thomas Cardwell) in the "Mousetrap" scene in *Young Hamlet*, dir. Terri Bourus (Hoosier Bard, 2011). Photo by John Gentry.

and tension," singling out Peter Guinness's performance of Hamlet as "the most entirely satisfactory piece of tragic acting of the year." Guinness himself called it *"Hamlet* with the brakes off," and its speed pleased both audiences and performers. Peter Holland was impressed by the "merciless pace" of a 1992 touring production, which "reconnected the audience to the pleasures of narrative rather than the different virtues of introspection." The 1999–2000 Red Shift production "was designed to appeal to young audiences and it clearly succeeded, delighting and surprising those whose study of the play had not led them to expect anything so energetic and exciting."[65] These are also qualities praised in "Dromgoole's wonderfully engrossing touring production for Shakespeare's Globe," based on the structure and brevity of the 1603 quarto: "you only have to see the rapt faces of the audience to realise that this production makes an emotional impact that often eludes snazzier versions of the play."[66]

To these well-documented examples, I can add some others. Nicholas Pullin played the title role in 1992 in the first professional American production of that earliest text, directed by Michael Muller in Fort Worth, Texas. Pullin, remembering that open-air Shakespeare in the Park production, says that "the play itself played like gangbusters— and enabled a number of rethinkings of roles to fit very naturally to the play," including "a comparatively young Ghost" and "a very active Hamlet."[67] In April 1999, Pullin again performed scenes from Q1, this time playing the King in an experimental production at Loyola University, Chicago.[68] Three scenes from the 1603 edition were performed alongside corresponding scenes from the Folio; these were followed by the one scene unique to Q1 (Sc. 14, the conspiratorial meeting of the Queen and Horatio).[69] Afterward, Pullin said that "Q1 works better." For him, it "explains things about the characters that one can never understand in the Folio version, in spite of the fact that the two versions are obviously connected." Tim Decker, who played Hamlet at Loyola, felt that performing the Q1 version of "To be or not to be?" was "more fun, and far more logical and interesting" in terms of character development; "I mean, . . . I feel as if this is the way Hamlet *should* express himself. That is how I would feel in this situation." All of the performers enjoyed acting the 1603 edition, and everyone, including the director (Steve Scott), agreed that it was different from, and better in performance than, the other so-called bad quartos.[70]

By now, it should be clear to everyone that the 1603 edition works in performance. I want, instead, to emphasize a rather different point, which does not simply reiterate the old contrast between literature and performance. The *way* that the 1603 edition works directly relates to the *age* of its protagonist. Which is to say, the nature of the action reflects the nature of the character, whether we are reading the play or watching it performed. In all three versions, Hamlet learns of his father's murder in the fifth scene; when the Ghost exits, Hamlet is alone, and accepts the obligation of revenge. And in all three, he achieves that revenge when he kills the usurper in the play's final scene. In the traditional conflated text of *Hamlet*, there are 3,077 lines between the exit of the Ghost and the murder of the king—a stretch of text longer than most entire Elizabethan plays.[71] In the version printed in 1603, there are only 1,588 lines between the Ghost's exit and the King's death. These numbers tell us two things. First, they help explain why the first part of the play, up to the end of the fifth scene, is relatively stable in all three versions of the text: this is not an effect of memorial reconstruction, or note-taking, but of an authorial revision that concentrated on what happens between the Ghost's exit from the play and the King's death. Second, these numbers tell us that, in the later, canonical text of the play, it takes Hamlet almost twice as long to kill the King.

The length of this interlude between stimulus and response can also be calculated in another way. In all versions of the play, after the First Player's speech about Hecuba, Hamlet rebukes himself, in a famous soliloquy, for not having yet revenged his father's death: "O what a rogue and peasant slave am I...Am I a coward?" (Q2 2.2.485–521). He then, echoing Seneca, makes a decision to act—"About, my brain!" (Q1 7.426; Q2 2.2.522; F 2.2.582)—and hammers out a plan to test the Ghost's testimony: "The play's the thing / Wherein I'll catch the conscience of the king" (Q1 7.134–5; Q2 2.2.539–40; F 2.2.599–60). Once Hamlet rebukes himself, the audience becomes sensitive to the passing of time, and the related issue of Hamlet's determination and ability. In the canonical texts of the play, this self-rebuke is Hamlet's first soliloquy after the fifth scene. But in the first edition, the order of the soliloquies is reversed. Hamlet's first soliloquy after the fifth scene is "To be or not to be?" (7.115–36); the self-rebuking "Why, sure I am a coward" speech comes much later (7.404–35). During the twentieth century, some critics, directors, and filmmakers preferred the order of these soliloquies in the first edition, because the sequence of action is much clearer, and because it makes psychological sense for Hamlet to go from suicidal despair ("To be or not to be") to active self-rebuke, followed by a specific plan to test his opponent.[72] But we can also, again, quantify the issue. The canonical conflated text contains 2,364 lines between Hamlet's self-rebuke, which raises the issue of delay, and the completion of his revenge—a stretch of text longer than *The Comedy of Errors* or *The Tempest*. By contrast, in the first edition that gap contains only 1,063 lines. The canonical text more than doubles our sense of delay. It also lengthens and strengthens Hamlet's self-criticism in that soliloquy. Phrases present in the canonical text of that speech, but not the first edition, give him "the motive and the cue for passion," and he is "Prompted to [his] revenge by heaven and hell"—and both "cue" and "prompt" require an immediate response. He also, in the canonical text, calls himself "dull and muddy-mettled" (suggesting some constitutional deficit, rather than a difficult environmental problem he has not yet overcome) and "unpregnant of my cause" (as though he has not yet even conceived, and therefore is at least nine months away from completion of his task).

Because the canonical Hamlet takes twice as long to do his duty, criticism has, naturally enough, focused on Hamlet's "delayed" revenge. Coleridge's famous description of Hamlet—as a man "living in meditation, called upon to act by every motive, human and divine, but the great purpose of life defeated by continually resolving to do, yet doing nothing but resolve"—was written more than a decade before the rediscovery of the 1603 version.[73] Hazlitt claimed that Hamlet's "ruling passion is to think, not to act" eight years before he could have read the 1603 text of the play.[74] Both these English Romantics were anticipated by a German Romantic, A. W. Schlegel, who in 1808 described *Hamlet* as "a tragedy of thought inspired by continual and never satisfied meditation," which is "calculated to call forth the very same meditation in the minds of the spectators." Schlegel berated Hamlet's "far-fetched scruples" as "often mere pretexts to cover his want of determination," citing "the resolutions which he so often embraces and always leaves unexecuted" as evidence for "the weakness of his volition." The whole play, Schlegel argued, "is intended to show that a consideration which would exhaust all the relations and possible consequences of a deed to the very limits of human foresight, cripples the power of acting."[75] As proofs of this interpretation, Schlegel quoted Hamlet's own lines:

> And thus the native hue of resolution
> Is sicklied o'er with the pale cast of thought,
> And enterprises of great pitch and moment
> With this regard their currents turn awry
> And lose the name of action.

(3.1.83–7)

>   some craven scruple
> Of thinking too precisely on th'event
> (A thought which quartered hath but one part wisdom
> And ever three parts coward)
>
> (4.4.39–42)

This Romantic interpretation has cast a long shadow: "This is the tragedy of a man who could not make up his mind" provided the opening epitaph of Olivier's Oscar-winning 1948 film *Hamlet*, and was quoted most recently in Jude Morgan's historical novel *The Secret Life of William Shakespeare*.[76] But none of the lines above, quoted by Schlegel and his successors, appears in the 1603 edition. In that earliest text, Hamlet does not dawdle. As Peter Guinness remarked, after performing Hamlet in the first quarto version, "the speed of the narrative opened up the politics of the play."[77] In the original story—told in Latin by Saxo Grammaticus in the twelfth century, translated into French by Belleforest in the 1570s, translated into English and dramatized by the first quarto in 1603, and filmed in 1993 by the Oscar-winning Danish director Gabriel Axel as *The Prince of Jutland*, with a teenage Christian Bale as Amleth and an alluring Helen Mirren as his mother Geruth—the revenger is not even an adult, legally.[78] He's just a teenager. His opponent has all the power of a crowned king, cunning and ruthless, perhaps twice his age, more experienced, legitimated by his fraternal relationship to the dead king and by his fresh marriage to the Queen Mother. Michael Billington objected that Ben Whishaw's Hamlet failed to create "any sense that he poses a real physical danger to Claudius; you can see why he would get on the king's nerves, but the idea that this skinny student would actually avenge his father's murder is preposterous." For the teenage Hamlet of the original story, and of the first edition of the play, the obstacles to his revenge do seem insuperable, not only to the protagonist but also to his readers or his audience. That is what made it such a compelling myth. It depends upon the classic narrative tension created by "irresistible force meets immovable object." And the young, "less philosophical" hero does in fact overcome the obstacles—"with more dispatch than the version everyone knows." In the first edition (which Taffety Punk Theatre Company, in their 2012 production, called "the bad-ass quarto"), we are not surprised that it takes Hamlet 1,588 lines to kill the usurper. We are surprised that the boy manages it at all.

In the version everyone knows, Hamlet is older, slower, more poetic, and more philosophical. Not just because Burbage was older and slower.

Shakespeare was older, too, perhaps slower, but certainly more poetic, more sophisticated, and more philosophical. In that enlarged version, Hamlet is more than a decade older, and the death of Yorick happened more than a decade earlier, than in the first version. Might this suggest that more than a decade had passed between the writing of the first version of the play and the writing of the second? If the fuller Shakespearian version of *Hamlet*, the canonical *Hamlet* that has dominated our culture since the Restoration, was written at the beginning of the seventeenth century, was the earlier version of *Hamlet* written more than a decade earlier?

As it happens, the first known reference to an English play about *Hamlet* was published in 1589.

Just a coincidence, no doubt.

But, just to be sure, perhaps we should pay some attention to that play of 1589.

CHAPTER 5

Young Shakespeare?

"The chronicles and brief abstracts of the time"

Before the 1603 edition was rediscovered in 1823, Shakespeare scholarship had already decided that *Hamlet* was written in 1600. The man who decided was the Irish lawyer Edmond Malone, the greatest Shakespeare scholar of the eighteenth century, who for more than 35 years attempted "to ascertain the order in which the plays of Shakespeare were written." From 1778 until his death in 1813 Malone wrote three treatises on the subject, each longer and better documented than its predecessor. His final version, which put *Hamlet* in 1600, was published posthumously in 1821, filling 180 pages of his biography of *The Life of William Shakespeare*.[1] Malone's biography was published separately, but it also filled one of the 21 volumes of Malone's revised edition of Shakespeare's works, completed and seen through the press by James Boswell. The Malone-Boswell "Variorum," with its selective summation of eighteenth-century scholarship, remained the single most influential Shakespeare commentary throughout the nineteenth century, endlessly recycled and repackaged.[2] Malone's *Life*, in particular, was the foundation of biographical and chronological scholarship on Shakespeare for more than a century. When Ling's first edition of *Hamlet* was republished in 1825, it entered a world already convinced that Shakespeare's most famous tragedy was written at the beginning of the seventeenth century. The "new" text had to be situated in relation to an already canonical Shakespeare chronology. But the verse of that rediscovered first edition seems, to me and almost all observers, incompatible with Shakespeare's style in 1600.

Although many scholars debated and tinkered with details of Malone's chronological edifice, no one attempted an equally thorough, equally authoritative reassessment of the entire structure until E. K. Chambers published, in 1930, his two-volume *William Shakespeare*, with its modest subtitle, "A Study of Facts and Problems." By 1930, memorial reconstruction was all the rage, and Chambers embraced it without reservation. All theories of piracy, memorial reconstruction or reporting assume that the manuscript behind the 1603 quarto text is actually later than the manuscript behind the 1604 quarto text, speculating that the first edition postdates performances of the "enlarged" play. As a consequence of that speculation, Chambers simply dismissed the 1603 edition as an irrelevance, and followed Malone in dating Shakespeare's composition of *Hamlet* in 1600.[3] The next attempt to construct a timeline for Shakespeare's plays, based on an up-to-date survey and extension of all relevant scholarship, was Gary Taylor's 1987 "Canon and Chronology." Taylor, too, accepted the theory of memorial reconstruction, and therefore ignored the first edition as an irrelevance, and therefore followed Malone in dating *Hamlet* in 1600.[4] Effectively, all canonical chronologies of Shakespeare's works, from Malone to the present, ignore the 1603 edition of *Hamlet*. As a result, mainstream scholarship on the date of *Hamlet* has occupied itself, almost entirely, with trying to pinpoint exactly when, in the 14 or 15 months between late 1599 and early 1601, the "enlarged" play was written.

Malone had decided that *Hamlet* was written no earlier than 1600 on the basis of two documents. First, he had reexamined a long manuscript note by the Cambridge humanist Gabriel Harvey. Harvey observed that "the younger sort takes much delight in Shakespeare's *Venus and Adonis*: but his *Lucrece*, and his *Tragedy of Hamlet, Prince of Denmark*, have it in them to please the wiser sort."[5] This is the first document that unequivocally identifies Shakespeare as the author of a tragedy about Hamlet. Harvey wrote that note in his copy of the 1598 edition of Chaucer's *Works*, but Malone had "found reason to believe, that the note in question may have been written in the latter end of the year 1600." Harvey "speaks of *translated Tasso* in one passage; and the first edition of [Edward Fairfax's *Godfrey of Bulloigne*, a translation of Torquato Tasso's epic poem *Gerusalemme Liberata*], which is doubtless alluded to, appeared in 1600." Second, Malone noted that "all the theatres except the Fortune and the Globe were inhibited by an Order of council in June, 1600," and he believed that restriction explained the play's reference to "the late innovation" that had caused an "inhibition" of playing (Folio 2.2.330–1).

Both Malone's pieces of evidence are disputable, and have been disputed. First, the phrase "late innovation" occurs only in the 1623 edition of *Hamlet* (alongside a unique reference to the Globe theatre).[6] It does not necessarily tell us anything about the date at which the texts of the play printed in 1603 and 1604 were written. As Malone himself said, on two other occasions, "the allusion in question... probably was an addition; for it is not found in the quarto of 1604... nor did it appear in print till the publication of the folio in 1623."[7] Second, Harvey speaks of the Earl of Essex in the present tense, so his note was almost certainly written before the Earl's execution on 25 February 1601. But that date establishes only that Shakespeare must have written a version of the play while Essex was still alive. He *might* have written it long before the Earl died. Victoria F. Stern, a specialist on Harvey, dates his reference to *Hamlet* to June 1599.[8] The other Shakespeare titles that Harvey mentions, in the same sentence, are *Venus and Adonis* (published in 1593) and *Lucrece* (published in 1594). Whether it was written in 1598 or early 1601, Harvey's note does not say that Shakespeare's *Hamlet* was new, and in fact associates it with work written long before 1600.

Harvey's note establishes that a version of Shakespeare's *Hamlet* must have been written, at the very latest, earlier than February 1601. But Malone does not establish *how much earlier*. We know that an English play about Hamlet had been written by the autumn of 1589, when Thomas Nashe referred to "whole *Hamlets*... of tragical speeches." I'll return to the full context of Nashe's comment later in this chapter, but for the moment it's enough to point out that, obviously, Harvey's note *could* refer to the 1589 tragedy. Harvey might have seen that earlier version performed in Cambridge or London, but by 1593 he seems to have left London for good, and by 1598 had retired to his hometown, the village of Saffron Walden, where he apparently remained until his death in 1631.[9] How, then, could Harvey have seen a performance of *Hamlet* in 1600? If we assume that Harvey's knowledge of the play derived from performance, then his note, *whenever it was written*, almost certainly refers to London performances of a *Tragedy of Hamlet, Prince of Denmark*, written by Shakespeare, no later than 1593.[10] Of course, Harvey might have read the play, as he read *Venus and Adonis* and *Lucrece*—but unlike those poems the play was not in print in 1598 or 1600, so Harvey would have needed to read it in a literary manuscript. But would the Chamberlain's Men have allowed immediate manuscript circulation of a brand new play by their leading dramatist? That seems unlikely. They had no reason to trust, or single out, a disgraced, retired Cambridge scholar as the recipient of such a copy; he was not a possible patron. But the Chamberlain's Men might not have objected to manuscript circulation of an older play, especially one that was at least nine years old by the time that Harvey bought the 1598 edition of Chaucer; indeed, since the Chamberlain's Men did not exist in 1593, they might not have been able to control the circulation of copies of that earlier play. Harvey's note, so often cited as evidence for the date of the canonical *Hamlet*, may actually, more importantly, establish Shakespeare's authorship of the earlier, noncanonical *Hamlet* of 1589.

Malone knew about Nashe's 1589 comment, quoted it—and dismissed its relevance, *before the 1603 edition was rediscovered*. Malone claimed that Nashe was referring to a lost play, written by someone other than Shakespeare. The obvious question is: how could Malone be so certain that Shakespeare did *not* write a play that Malone could *not* read?

* * *

Beginning in 1778, all Malone's Shakespeare chronologies emphatically declared that Shakespeare could not have started writing plays until 1591. Obviously, someone who wrote his first play in 1591 could not have written the Hamlet play that Nashe mentioned in 1589. On the basis of such reasoning, Malone denied Shakespeare's authorship of five plays: the 1589 *Hamlet*, *Titus Andronicus*, and the original versions of the three plays on the reign of Henry VI. No serious scholar nowadays doubts Shakespeare's hand in *Titus* or the *Henry VI* plays, though all four are probably collaborative. Malone's argument about the 1589 *Hamlet* cannot be separated from his discredited argument about four early Shakespeare plays.

But what made Malone so confident that Shakespeare never wrote a play until he was 27 years old? Malone's argument is simple: Shakespeare, "the new prodigy of the dramatic world," would surely have been noticed and celebrated from the first moment that he appeared, and Shakespeare wasn't noticed until 1592. Just as he assumed that Gabriel Harvey would have known all about Shakespeare's *Hamlet* within weeks of its first performances, Malone assumed that Shakespeare's first plays would immediately have attracted the attention of important cultural critics. There is, of course, a certain circularity in Malone's argument: if Nashe was referring to Shakespeare's *Hamlet*, then Shakespeare's playwriting was first noticed in 1589, not 1592. But Nashe does not cite Shakespeare by name, and it is names that concern Malone. His logic is worth quoting at length:

> The reasons that induce me to fix on that period [1591] are these. In [William] Webbe's *Discourse of English Poetry,* published in 1586, we

meet with the names of most of the celebrated poets of that time; particularly those of George Whetstone and Anthony Munday, who were *dramatic* writers.

Three years afterwards [in 1589], [George] Puttenham printed his *Art of English Poesy*; and in that work also we look in vain for the name of Shakespeare. [In a footnote, Malone records that Puttenham does name "for tragedy, the Lord Buckhurst and Master Edward Ferrys...the Earl of Oxford and Master Edwardes of her Majesty's Chapel, for comedy and interlude."]

Sir John Harrington, in his "Apology for Poetrie," prefixed to the Translation of Ariosto (which was entered in the Stationers' [register] Feb[ruary] 26, 1590–1, in which year it was published), takes occasion to speak of the theatre, and mentions some of the celebrated dramas of that time; but says not a word of Shakespeare, or of his plays.

Webbe, Puttenham, and Harrington were all cited in 1778, in Malone's first version of the chronology, and again in 1790.[11] In the 1821 version, Malone added a long, undated quotation from Sir Philip Sidney's criticism of the early English stage; since it is "impossible to believe that our great poet [Shakespeare] could be included in this censure," Malone concluded that Shakespeare cannot have been writing for the stage before Sidney's *Defense of Poesy* was written.[12]

None of Malone's evidence is reliable. To begin with the last claim: Sidney died in October 1586, and modern scholarship dates his work on the treatise to "*c*.1580."[13] Sidney's testimony thus predates Webbe, and comes from a time when Shakespeare was still in his teens. As for Webbe, he does not refer to the plays of either Whetstone or Munday.[14] Malone and other Shakespearians think of Whetstone as a playwright, because his only play was a major source for Shakespeare's Jacobean *Measure for Measure*. But this is an anachronistic misrepresentation of Whetsone's career and reputation. Whetstone's preface to *Promos and Cassandra* announces that it had never been performed, and criticizes the commercial theatre, so Webbe's praise of Whetstone's "Faculty of Poetry" does not endorse, or reflect any interest in, the venues where Shakespeare's plays were performed. Whetstone (born in 1550) began publishing in 1575, in a poem praising George Gascoigne; his name was attached to printed poetry 11 years before Webbe praised him, and 18 years before Shakespeare appeared in print (in *Venus and Adonis* in 1593).[15]

In contrast to Whetstone, Munday was indeed a professional writer of commercial plays. But unlike the country boy Shakespeare, Munday was born in London (in 1560); the son of a stationer, he officially entered the London book business himself in 1576 (as an apprentice to the printer John Allde), and debuted in print in 1577. His only known play before 1586 was *Fedele and Fortunio* (1585), a translation of an Italian drama by Luigi Pasqualigo, which was remarkable chiefly for its continental credentials and its performance at court.[16] Before then, Munday had already published the formally varied verse of his *Mirror of Mutability* (strongly influenced by *The Mirror for Magistrates*), his lengthy romance *Zelauto*, his anti-Catholic memoir *The English Roman Life* (published by Nicholas Ling), and he had begun what became a series of translations of continental romances. Munday earned his living as a busy, productive writer of a wide range of profitable genres. He was conspicuous in print long before Shakespeare.[17]

The four dramatic writers noticed by Puttenham in 1589 were all much older than Shakespeare, all belonged to the aristocracy or upper gentry, and all had courtly rather than commercial credentials. "Lord Buckhurst" is now better known as Thomas Sackville (born *c.*1536), coauthor of the court sensation *Gorboduc* (1561) and contributor to the 1563 edition of *Mirror for Magistrates*. But Sackville's last poem, bidding farewell to poetry and committing himself to a political life, had been written in 1566, when Shakespeare was two years old.[18] That was also the year that another of Puttenham's dramatists, Richard Edwards, died. "Master Edwards" had been born in 1525, and his dramatic career at "her Majesty's chapel" was remarkably brief (1564–6).[19] "Master Edward Ferrys" is Puttenham's mistaken identification of the courtier George Ferrers (1510–79), whose literary career stretched from 1551 to 1575; Puttenham included him among poets of the reign of Edward VI, before Shakespeare was born.[20] The youngest of Puttenham's dramatists was the Earl of Oxford, Edward De Vere (born in 1550). His poetry started appearing in print in 1576 (17 years before Shakespeare), but it also circulated in manuscript; Puttenham must have seen manuscript sources, because his book printed one of Oxford's poems for the first time. None of Oxford's plays is known to survive, but he was patron of a company of actors from 1580 to 1602.[21] That company might have performed some of their patron's work—or Puttenham might have mistakenly assumed that something performed by the Earl's company was the Earl's play.[22] Puttenham belonged to what Steven W. May has called "genteel" but "out of court" society; he was disgraced long before Shakespeare left Stratford-upon-Avon, and he showed no interest in commercial theatrical activity in London.[23] Even if he had been interested, his 1589 book might have overlooked a play first performed in 1589.

"Supposing Shakespeare to have written any piece in the year 1590," Malone insisted, "Sir John Harrington's silence concerning him in the following year appears inexplicable."[24] But Malone again exaggerated the witness's interest in the commercial theatre. Harington named no contemporary playwrights, and recorded the titles of only four Elizabethan plays, one tragedy and three comedies. The first three of the four were Latin academic plays.

> That which was played at Saint John's [college] in Cambridge, of *Richard the third*.... Then for Comedies: how full of harmless mirth is our Cambridge *Pedantius*? and the Oxford *Bellum Grammaticale*? or to speak of a London Comedy, how much good matter, yea and matter of state, is there in that Comedy called the play of the Cards? in which it is showed how four Parasitical knaves rob the four principal vocations of the Realm, *videl*, the vocation of Soldiers, Scholars, Merchants and Husbandmen. Of which Comedy I cannot forget the saying of a notable wise counselor that is now dead [marginal note: *Sir Francis Walsingham*], who when some (to sing *Placebo*) advised that it should be forbidden, because it was somewhat too plain, and indeed as the old saying is, *sooth boord is no boord*, yet he would have it allowed, adding it was fit that *they which do that they should not, should hear that they would not*.[25]

Harington's only "London" play had been performed by the Children of the Chapel before Queen Elizabeth in 1582, nine years before his preface was published.[26] That lost comedy belonged to the old-fashioned genre of the allegorical morality play. Harington cited it, moreover, primarily to cue the comment by Walsingham, Elizabeth's notorious enforcer of political and religious orthodoxy. Given Harington's agenda (defending poetry against ethical and political criticism), and his preference for old-fashioned academic or allegorical drama, the fact that the one commercial play he mentioned was not by Shakespeare is not at all "inexplicable."

I have dedicated so much attention to Malone's flimsy argument because Malone's authority has shaped mainstream assumptions about Shakespeare's career for more than two centuries. Without Malone, without his assumption that Shakespeare would have been *named* in print almost immediately after his work began appearing in the theatre, we have no reason to assume that Shakespeare wrote his first play in 1591. E. K. Chambers, for instance, begins his account of Shakespeare's theatrical career exactly where Malone did, with Robert Greene's 1592 attack on "Shake-scene" and his "tiger's heart wrapped in a player's hide." But only a few pages earlier Chambers, in the preceding chapter on the English theatre before 1592, had concluded, "The fragmentary history of the evidence makes a dramatic history of the period extremely difficult. The work of *even the best-known writers* is uncertain in extent and chronology" (my italics).[27] This should have alerted Chambers to the fact that we cannot take the absence of Shakespeare's *name* from records of the late 1580s as evidence for the absence of Shakespeare.

"Are we to suppose," E. A. J. Honigmann asked, "that a dramatist who wrote with such extraordinary 'easiness,' who appears to have been endowed with an exceptional quickness of wit and invention and to have been in other respects precocious, composed his juvenilia in his late twenties?"[28] Other major twentieth-century scholars, like Peter Alexander and F. P. Wilson, also expressed dissatisfaction with the orthodox assumption that Shakespeare was a "late starter."[29] That assumption is also undermined by two early modern testimonials, both by Ben Jonson. The Induction of *Bartholomew Fair* (written in 1614, while Shakespeare was still alive) described any spectator who "will swear *Jeronimo,* or *Andronicus,* are the best plays yet" as "a man whose judgment...hath stood still these five-and-twenty or thirty years." If we accept—as Malone did not—that Shakespeare wrote most or all of *Titus Andronicus*, then this passage dates at least one of his tragedies no later than 1589. In the prefatory poem "In the memory of my beloved, The Author Mr. William Shakespeare," printed in the 1623 Folio, Jonson celebrated "how far thou [Shakespeare] didst our Lily outshine, / Or sporting Kyd, or Marlowe's mighty line." These three playwrights, whom Jonson described as Shakespeare's "peers" in the immediately preceding line, all wrote influential plays in the 1580s. Jonson himself, born in 1572, seems to have lived in London with little if any interruption until 1591, so he is a credible witness for London theatrical events in the late 1580s. Scholars since Malone have offered alternative interpretations of these Jonson passages, but at face value both seem to assert that Shakespeare was writing plays by the late 1580s.

I do not want to substitute a new categorical claim for an old one; I am not asserting that Shakespeare *must* have started writing plays in the 1580s. Instead, I am simply stating the obvious: he *could* have started in the late 1580s. And if we accept that possibility, then we, unlike Malone, are free to read Nashe's testimony, and Harvey's testimony, with an open mind. We can place Nashe and Harvey in the context of a sequence of documents that trace the theatrical history of Hamlet before 1600.

* * *

The most influential reference to *Hamlet* between 1589 and 1602 comes from Thomas Lodge in 1596. Lodge described a "devil" or "fiend" who "walks for the most part in black under color of gravity, and looks as pale as the Vizard of the ghost which cried so miserally at the Theater like an oyster wife, *Hamlet, revenge.*"[30] Unlike most other nouns in the sentence (color, gravity, ghost, wife), the capitalized noun "Theater" suggests that it is a proper name, referring to the first theatre built in 1576 and owned by the Burbage family. The Theater was the London home of the Chamberlain's Men from sometime in late 1594 or early 1595 until at least mid-1598.[31] We can therefore be reasonably confident that, by 1596, the Chamberlain's Men were performing a revenge play about Hamlet, which featured a ghost.[32] This play must have been based on the revenging Amleth in Belleforest's *Histoires Tragiques.* In the French novella, the ghost is not a major character, and does not speak, but Belleforest twice refers to the "*ombre*" (shade, spirit) of Hamlet's father, which could have inspired the English playwright.[33] Lodge also tells us that, in the play, Hamlet's revenge was commanded by a ghost, who "cried... miserally" (miserably) to him with the imperative verb "revenge." This happens in all three early texts of Shakespeare's play (Q1 5.20; Q2 1.5.25; F 1.5.25). Lodge's ghost "looks... pale," and Shakespeare's ghost is consistently described as "very pale" (Q1 2.146; Q2 1.2.232; F 1.2.230). The pallor of Lodge's ghost is compared to the pallor of a "devil" or "fiend"; in Shakespeare's play, Hamlet suspects that the ghost he has seen may be a "devil" (7.430; 3.1.534; 3.1.594). Finally, Lodge juxtaposes the ghost who commands Hamlet with a male who "walks for the most part in black." In all three versions of Shakespeare's play, Hamlet first walks onstage dressed in black, wearing a "sable suit" (Q1 2.33) or "inky cloak" and "customary suits of solemn black" (Q2 1.2.77–8; F 1.2.75–6). The texts do not call for him to change his costume until later in the play, when he feigns madness. Shakespeare's play thus seems to imagine a Hamlet who "walks... in black" to meet a "pale... ghost" who calls on him to "revenge."

Understandably, when Lodge's allusion to Hamlet was first discovered, in the eighteenth century, scholars assumed that it must refer to Shakespeare's play. In 1778 and 1790 Malone concluded, on the basis of Lodge's testimony, that Shakespeare wrote *Hamlet* in 1596. But Malone changed his mind in the chronology published in 1821, and modern scholars, accepting Malone's later date, object that the words "Hamlet, revenge" are not spoken, in exactly that form, in any early text of Shakespeare's play.[34] On the basis of this discrepancy, they conclude that the phrase "Hamlet, revenge" is evidence for the existence of a lost *Ur-Hamlet*, which was the source for Shakespeare's own later play.

The claim that "Hamlet, revenge" comes from a lost play ignores three facts about Lodge's quotation. First, Lodge's two words are the only "text" of any part of any early play about Hamlet that we *know* represent a memorial reconstruction of something heard by a member of an audience. No play about Hamlet was in print in 1596; Lodge must have seen that play at the Theater, and must have been remembering a performance, a day or a month or a year or years later. *Lodge's quotation is the least reliable testimony to the exact verbal content of the early play that we possess.* Scholars have taken the word of a text that is indisputably a memorial reconstruction (Lodge) over the evidence of a text impossible to attribute to memorial reconstruction (Ling's 1603 edition).

This may seem to be special pleading on my part. But consider the history of famous misquotations from films.[35] In the case of film, we can check a popular quotation against the original performance. So we know, for instance, that in the celebrated 1942 film *Casablanca* Humphrey Bogart never actually says "Play it again, Sam." Instead, that famous misquotation compresses and rearranges the dramatic context: "You played it for her, you can play it for me. If she can stand it, I can. Play it!" The words are addressed to a character named "Sam," but the vocative does not appear in these lines.[36] Like the two words "Hamlet, revenge," the iconic three words "greed is good" are not contiguous in Michael Douglas's Oscar-winning performance in the film *Wall Street* (1987). My father's swimming coach, the film star Johnny Weismuller, never said "Me Tarzan, you Jane" in *Tarzan, the Ape Man* (1932) or any other film, and Dustin Hoffman did not say "Mrs. Robinson, are you trying to seduce me?" in *The Graduate* (1967), and Clint Eastwood did not say "Do you feel lucky, punk?" in *Dirty Harry* (1971), and Captain Kirk did not say "Beam me up, Scotty!" (*Star Trek: The Voyage Home*, 1987), and Darth Vader did not say "Luke, I am your father" (*The Empire Strikes Back*, 1980). I have taken all these examples from Yahoo's online list of "Ten Famous Movie Misquotes," which is not trying to prove a point about *Hamlet*. Nevertheless, you will notice how many of these examples involve misplaced or interpolated vocatives ("punk"), especially names as vocatives (Sam, Jane, Mrs. Robinson, Scotty, Luke). In these films, the quoted character is speaking to someone particular, and the misremembered vocative contextualizes and helps explain the quotation. The *Hamlet* performed by the Chamberlain's Men at the Theater was not filmed, but human neurons undoubtedly played the same tricks on audiences in the 1590s as they did in the twentieth century. For exactly the same reasons that we misquote movies, Lodge's memory could easily have compressed the onstage three-dimensional action of,

GHOST (*speaking to Hamlet*) Revenge!

into the two-dimensional text,

"Hamlet, revenge!"

William Shatner played Captain Kirk, and James Earl Jones spoke the lines of Darth Vader, and when we misremember quotations from movies we are often remembering the idiosyncratic voice and performance style of a particular actor. But any actor playing the Ghost in Shakespeare's play is likely to emphasize, in one way or another, that imperative verb "revenge": it is the entire purpose of the character and the scene.

Scholars who take Lodge's 1596 quotation as evidence of a lost play also overlook a second important fact about its context. Lodge's own motivation, in this passage, was not to provide an accurate, literal, scholarly text of *Hamlet*, or even a play-text that would satisfy a publisher like Nicholas Ling or his customers. Early modern texts are full of misquotations, accidental or deliberate. Lodge's primary intention here was to vivify his own prose by alluding, intelligibly, to something particular and memorable that was familiar to many of his readers. The allusion thus tells us not only that a play on Hamlet already existed by 1596; it tells us that the play had been successful enough that Lodge could expect readers to recognize his sarcastic reference to it. Indeed, if it had been a failure, Lodge wouldn't have needed to mock it; he mocks it because he resented its success. Lodge's book, *Wit's Misery*, is a satire on contemporary vices, divided into the seven deadly sins, and this passage on *Hamlet* belongs to his discussion of Envy. The traditional, emblematic pallor of Envy's skin is compared to the pale face of the Ghost. But the Ghost's words, "Hamlet, revenge," are immediately followed by "he is full of infamy and slander." The ambiguous "he" leaves open a suggestion that the Ghost's account is slanderous, or that his cry for revenge springs from devilish envy, or that all revenge springs from envy; the black clothing of Hamlet himself, then, would indicate his envy of the happiness of his newly married mother and stepfather. But in the larger context of this chapter Lodge seems to be suggesting a contrast between an emblematically envious writer and "poets," "men of wit," and "scholars." The ambiguous pronoun "he" does not distinguish between "Envy" and the envious writer: "many fools there be that, because he can pen prettily, hold it Gospel whatever he writes or speaks." (Shakespeare, as an actor-playwright-poet, both "writes" and "speaks.")

Why Lodge connected *Hamlet* to envy must remain a matter of interpretation. More important, and less debatable, is the fact that nine prose lines following his sneering allusion to *Hamlet*, Lodge celebrates the "divine wits" of five living English writers: "[John] Lyly, famous for facility in discourse; [Edmund] Spenser, best read in ancient Poetry; [Samuel] Daniel, choice in word, and invention; [Michael] Drayton, diligent and formal; Th[omas] Nashe, true English Aretine." Lyly, Daniel, Drayton, and Nashe all wrote plays (as did Lodge himself). Shakespeare does not make Lodge's list of admirable English writers. By Malone's reasoning we might therefore deduce that Shakespeare had not written any of his plays or poems by 1596! However, Lodge's refusal to name, or praise, Shakespeare is not unusual. The first explicit printed praise of Shakespeare *as a playwright* did not appear until 1598, and even in the early seventeenth century *Hamlet* was parodied more often than praised. The crucial fact here is that Lodge contrasts the unnamed author of *Hamlet* with five named living writers. Given the structure of contrast here, we would expect the unnamed author of *Hamlet* to be a living writer. After all, why satirize a dead man? Lodge thus implicitly eliminates, as possible authors of the early *Hamlet*, not only himself and the praised living playwrights Lyly, Daniel, Drayton, and Nashe, but also the dead playwrights Greene, Watson, Marlowe, and Kyd. That leaves few known playwrights who might have been writing for the commercial theatre in 1589, and were also still alive in 1596: the most conspicuous candidates would be Anthony Munday, George Peele, and Shakespeare. Of those, the one that Lodge had the most obvious reason to satirize was Shakespeare. Lodge's friend and collaborator Robert Greene famously attacked Shakespeare in 1592. Lodge himself might reasonably have resented the runaway success of Shakespeare's *Venus and Adonis*, published in 1593, which appropriated the genre of the mythological Ovidian epyllion; Lodge's *Glaucus and Scilla*, published in 1589, had pioneered that genre, using the same six-line stanza that Shakespeare copied in *Venus and Adonis*—which completely eclipsed Lodge's poem. I cannot prove that Lodge resented or disliked Shakespeare, and I cannot prove that Shakespeare was the target of Lodge's mockery of the early *Hamlet*. But we can say that Shakespeare is one of the few plausible candidates. We can also imagine that Shakespeare, uneducated country shopkeeper's son, might envy (or might be thought to envy) the "university wits" of the 1580s and 1590s, including Lodge himself.

Satirical literary allusion is not bound by editorial principles of maximum accuracy (or fairness), but by the practicalities of intelligibility and the aesthetics of contrast. It seems unlikely that the professional actor playing the ghost *actually* sounded like a fishwife selling fresh oysters in a busy London market, yelling to attract customers. Lodge's clever mockery of the commercial theatre, comparing the tragic actor to a low-class street vendor, will entertain a reader only if its specific target is unmistakably clear. In the phrase "Hamlet, revenge," the vocative "Hamlet" identifies which ghost, which play, and which author Lodge was negatively comparing to the works of Lyly, Spenser, Daniel, Drayton, and Nashe.[37]

The third fact ignored by scholars who construct an imaginary lost play from Lodge's two words "Hamlet, revenge" is that the quotation gets repeated after Shakespeare's play was written, performed, and printed. Samuel Rowlands echoed it in 1620: "I will not call *Hamlet Revenge* my greeves, / But I will call *Hang-man Revenge* on thieves."[38] This is 20 years after the canonical date of Shakespeare's tragedy, and 16 years after publication of the enlarged 1604 edition. Rowlands cannot be quoting any of the three printed texts of *Hamlet* that would have been available to him in 1620, so either he is quoting Lodge (24 years after the only edition of *Wits Misery*) or, like Lodge, he is remembering the play in performance. His readers, in 1620, would be much likelier to understand an allusion to a play still being regularly performed, than to understand an allusion to Lodge's unremarkable pamphlet. Are we to imagine that, after Shakespeare had written his own *Hamlet* in 1600, the Chamberlain's Men continued to perform the lost old "Ur-Hamlet" play, with its line "Hamlet, revenge"? Not likely.[39] Instead, Rowlands, like Lodge before him, seems to be slightly misquoting (and italicizing) an iconic theatrical moment. Also like Lodge, he is contrasting (in this case comically) "Hamlet, revenge" with something else (in this case, "Hang-man, revenge"). Likewise, in Dekker and Webster's play *Westward Ho*, printed in 1607 and apparently performed in 1605, a character says "Let these husbands play mad *Hamlet*; and cry revenge."[40] Here, "Hamlet" and "revenge" are again juxtaposed with the verb "cry," but here it is "mad Hamlet," not the Ghost, who cries for revenge. In Dekker's *Satiromastix*, Captain Tucca says, "My name's Hamlet revenge."[41] This play was printed in 1602, and most scholars believe that it was performed by the Chamberlain's Men after they performed Shakespeare's canonical *Hamlet*. Again, the allusion to Hamlet creates a contrast with the immediately following words, which deride "Horace," a.k.a. Ben Jonson, who in his brief and unsuccessful career as an actor had performed "Suleiman" at the less reputable Swan Theater in "Paris Garden."[42] The contrast works at multiple levels: Suleiman against

Hamlet, Paris Garden against the Theatre or the Globe, and Captain Tucca (based on Captain Jack Hannam) against Horace (based on Ben Jonson). Why does Tucca call himself "Hamlet, revenge"? Perhaps because he is a soldier, like the Ghost.

All four of these allusions (in Lodge, Rowlands, *Westward Ho*, and *Satiromastix*) collocate "Hamlet" and "revenge," and none of them actually name Shakespeare. But Lodge's passage in 1596 is the only one that, according to the traditional theory, need refer to a lost early play. The simplest explanation for all four is that all four refer to the same play, Shakespeare's, by an understandable compression of its most iconic features.

Finally, a fifth early reference ties Lodge's highlighted "Hamlet, revenge" to a text performed by the Chamberlain's Men. As I mentioned in chapter 1, when the printer James Roberts recorded his ownership of the Chamberlain's Men's play in the Stationers' Register in July 1602, he gave its title as "The Revenge of Hamlet." Presumably that was the title on the manuscript that had been read and approved by the censor, Zachariah Pasfield. By the time Shakespeare's play was printed sometime in the second half of 1603, that title had been changed, by someone, to "The Tragical History of Hamlet," a title repeated in the 1604 and 1623 editions. But if an alternate title of the play had been "The Revenge of Hamlet" (as the legal record by Roberts suggests), then that title would have been pasted on printed playbills around London whenever it was performed—and Lodge's allusion would have been clear even to readers who had never seen the play, but had seen the playbills.

Lodge's allusion to *Hamlet* is, thus, perfectly compatible with the hypothesis that he was referring to a performance of the version of the play first printed in 1603. Nevertheless, let's suppose for a moment that Lodge was alluding to an entirely lost play about Hamlet, written by someone other than Shakespeare. Lodge's allusion would still tell us something important: that the Chamberlain's Men were performing another text about Hamlet by 1596, before Shakespeare wrote the familiar version of the play printed in 1604. This fact immediately eliminates a practical objection often raised against the idea that Shakespeare revised his own work.[43] In this case, we are left with only two scenarios: either Shakespeare in the early seventeenth century wrote a major revision of his own earlier *Hamlet* play, or Shakespeare in the early seventeenth century wrote an entirely new play to replace an older *Hamlet* play written by someone else. In either case, the Chamberlain's Men would have had to pay for preparation of a new manuscript playbook, and pay for preparation of new manuscript "parts" for the actors;

they would have had to pay for rehearsals of the new text, and possibly pay for a new license from the Master of the Revels; they would have had to worry about actors accidentally remembering the wrong (old) text instead of the right (new) text. Consequently, in this particular case there can be no economic, or practical, objection to the theory of authorial revision. Either way, the Chamberlain's Men faced the same problem. In fact, in this situation authorial revision would be *more* economical, and *more* practical. A brand new play by a new writer would certainly have had to be submitted to the censor, and therefore would certainly have entailed a fee for licensing; a revision by the same author of an older play might not, or might be charged a lesser fee for relicensing.[44] And if the 1603 edition is printed from a manuscript of Shakespeare's original version of the play, then he seems to have made sure that the "parts" of the Prologue, Lucianus, and Voltemand would not need to be rewritten. The stability of the three printed texts, in those three parts, would then not be the result of an improbable doubling of actors and an improbable memorial reconstruction, but of an actor-playwright deliberately minimizing some of the costs and consequences of a rewrite. In the case of *Hamlet,* revision is the more economical hypothesis, not only intellectually but also financially.

I have devoted so many pages to Lodge's two words "Hamlet, revenge" because they are *the only basis* for claims about a lost early play that differed from the 1603 edition of Shakespeare's *Hamlet.* Malone's misinterpretation of those two words created an entire "ghost" play, which has bedeviled Shakespeare scholarship for two centuries.

* * *

Lodge's 1596 allusion clarifies an ambiguous reference to Hamlet in 1594. The financial notebooks of the theatrical entrepreneur Philip Henslowe are an invaluable source of information about the nuts-and-bolts business operation of the early English theatre. On 3 June 1594, Henslowe started recording receipts of box office takings for performances by the Lord Admiral's Men and the Lord Chamberlain's Men, in the theatre at Newington Butts. Either they were temporarily working together, or (more plausibly) they were alternating performances in the same theatre.[45] This is in fact the first documented reference to performances by the company patronized by the Lord Chamberlain, which would become the most famous and most stable theatre company of the English Renaissance. Among the plays Henslowe listed are "andronicus" (5 June, twelve shillings, and 12 June, seven shillings, presumably *Titus*

Andronicus) and "hamlet" (9 June, eight shillings). Neither play is marked as "ne," though other plays are so marked. Scholars continue to debate the exact meaning of "ne," but most people believe that it means "new" or "newly adapted" or "new to this particular theatre," and certainly the plays so marked have much higher takings.[46] The receipts for "hamlet" are about average for the plays that are not "ne," but they are lower than the takings for the 5 June performance of "andronicus," and unlike that play "hamlet" was not repeated in this period. All this strongly suggests that "hamlet" was not, in June 1594, a new play. It also suggests that it was either older, or less popular, than *Titus Andronicus*.

Because Lodge in 1596 identifies "Hamlet" as a play performed at "the Theater" (occupied by the Chamberlain's Men), and because Henslowe's records of years of performances by the Admiral's Men do not include any Hamlet play, it seems reasonable to assume—as scholars have traditionally done—that the "hamlet" of June 1594 belonged to the Chamberlain's Men, not the Admiral's Men. We can also be reasonably confident that, when the Chamberlain's Men were created in mid-1594, "hamlet" was not a new play, but a part of the theatrical repertoire that they inherited from some other company. Which company?

It may well be impossible to answer that question. Holger Syme and James Marino have reminded us of how little we actually know about the London theatre even from 1594 to the end of the century.[47] The absence of evidence in those later years looks like a feast by comparison with the documentary dearth for the late 1580s and early 1590s. Nevertheless, those very gaps in our knowledge are important when considering a piece of positive evidence that has puzzled scholars. The title page to the 1603 edition declares that Shakespeare's *Hamlet* had been "diverse times acted...in the City of London: as also in the two Universities of Cambridge and Oxford, and elsewhere." All three claims are hard to reconcile with a *Hamlet* first written in 1600. To begin with, "the City of London" was, at the time, a much more specific geographical referent than it may now appear: it indicated a legal and political jurisdiction that did not include the suburban theatre districts to the north and south of the old walled city.[48] The last known performances by the Chamberlain's Men "in the city of London" had taken place in the winter of 1594–5, at the special request of their patron.[49] The obvious explanation for this anomaly would be that the Chamberlain's Men, at the Cross Keys Inn "in the City of London" in the winter of 1594–5, performed the same Hamlet play they had performed in Newington Butts (outside the City) earlier in 1594 and also performed at the Theater (outside the City) in 1595 or 1596: in other words, that the Hamlet play of 1594 is the Hamlet play printed in 1603. But some scholars have argued that performances at the Cross Keys Inn, and elsewhere in the City, continued throughout the 1590s, and as late as 1600.[50] However, these arguments run up against Malone's very evidence for dating *Hamlet* in 1600: the June 1600 order of the Privy Council, restricting performances to two playhouses, both outside the City limits. If the Folio reference to "the late inhibition" refers to that restriction, then it provides evidence that the canonical *Hamlet* was written *after* performances in the City had been prohibited. How, then, can the 1603 title page be referring to performances of the canonical version? It must allude, instead, to performances of the play that the Chamberlain's Men owned in the mid-1590s.

The title page claims about Oxford and Cambridge are equally confusing to anyone who accepts Malone's chronology. Oxford documents record payment "for the king's players" in the fiscal year 1603–4 (which began on 29 September 1603). The King's Men, who were touring that summer, had returned to London by 21 October 1603. We could therefore postulate that the King's Men played *Hamlet* in Oxford in early October 1603, and that Ling learned of this performance when they returned to London, and that he then incorporated a reference to it on the title page, which would in turn have had to be printed late in the year. In the absence of firm evidence for exactly when in "1603" the first quarto was published, that scenario is at least possible.[51] But it has seemed doubtful to many scholars, including the editors of *Records of English Drama* in 2004.[52] In any case, that conjecture would still leave unexplained the references to Cambridge and to the City of London. The last recorded visit of the Chamberlain/King's Men to Cambridge was in the fiscal year 1594–5; again, that would suggest that the play performed in 1594 was the one published in 1603. However, the authoritative account of Cambridge performances in *Records of Early English Drama* doubts that *Hamlet* could have been performed even in 1594–5: "In view of the many prohibitions at Cambridge, including the privy council letter of 29 July 1593 and various payments to companies in lieu of performance, it may be questioned whether the Lord Chamberlain's players would have been permitted to play."[53]

Faced with so many difficulties, some scholars have claimed that the title page of the 1603 edition is deliberately lying.[54] This conjecture simply reiterates the old, unsubstantiated claims that Nicholas Ling was an unscrupulous publisher. As I demonstrated in chapter 1, there is no evidence of anything improper about either of Ling's *Hamlet* editions, and massive evidence that Ling operated by the normal, ethical publishing practices of the time. Here again, Ling is a scapegoat, used by scholars who are not specialists in the book trade to explain away the deficiencies of a reigning theory about Shakespeare. Good scholarship does not throw away documentary evidence, and title pages are crucial evidence for the performance history of most early modern plays. In this case, the independent records of 1594 and 1596 have already established that the Chamberlain's Men were performing a Hamlet play that must have been part of their residual repertoire, inherited from some other, pre-1594 company. The only thing preventing us from making sense of the 1603 title page is Malone's assumption that the earlier *Hamlet* cannot have been Shakespeare's.

The movements of Shakespeare and his plays in the period before June 1594 are difficult, perhaps impossible, to track. Many scholars have conjecturally connected him to the short-lived Pembroke's Men, but that company came into being after 1589 (when *Hamlet* is first mentioned). It therefore seems unlikely that any version of *Hamlet* originated with Pembroke's Men. It has also often been suspected that, before the formation of the Chamberlain's Men, Shakespeare was associated with a company of players under the patronage of Lord Strange.[55] If, as Andrew Gurr conjectures, Shakespeare moved, with Burbage, from Strange's Men to Pembroke's in 1591, that would explain why the modified Strange's Men (led by Alleyn) did not perform *Hamlet* in any of their performances at the Rose in 1592–3. Gurr suggests that Strange's Men became significantly more important after their "acquisition of remnants of Leicester's Men in late 1588," so that "by the end of 1589 they seem to have been competing on fairly equal terms with the Admiral's" Men.[56] If Gurr is right, the *Hamlet* to which Nashe refers would fit tidily into that period between late 1588 and 1589. But this is all highly conjectural. We do not know which company performed the 1589 *Hamlet*, and we do not know what happened to it in the five years before it reappears in the repertoire of the Chamberlain's Men. Whatever company or companies performed the play before 1594, if it were Shakespeare's play then he might have brought it with him, as he seems to have brought with him other plays he had written before 1594.

Whatever company or companies owned *Hamlet* before the creation of the Chamberlain's Men, they might have taken it to one or both of the universities before 1594—and Shakespeare, or some other veteran member of the company, might have provided that information to Ling. Shakespeare, of course, had the strongest incentive to do so; those performances in both Oxford and Cambridge offered him a different kind of academic credential than Greene, and were an implicit reply to the criticisms of Lodge and Nashe. The universities seem to have been more amenable to performances by commercial troupes before the mid-1590s. Frederick S. Boas, who first attempted to trace the history of dramatic performances at Oxford and Cambridge, noted that Lord Strange's Men performed in Oxford in the fiscal year 1592–3. "Why," Boas asked, "should not *Hamlet*, as it appears in the First Quarto, have been written between 1592 and 1594?"[57] This explanation assumed that the First Quarto could not be the play described by Nashe, and it runs up against the objection that Strange's Men may have split into two companies by the beginning of 1592; certainly, Alleyn's Strange's Men never acted *Hamlet* at the Rose in 1592–3. But "my Lord Strange's players" had visited Cambridge in the fiscal year 1591–2, and this might have been before they split into rival companies.[58] Certainly, in November 1589 Strange's Men were performing in the City of London (at Cross Keys Inn).[59] The Strange's Men of 1589–91 could thus account for the advertised performances in Cambridge and in the City.

Of course, other pre-1594 companies visited Oxford and Cambridge, too. The Lord Admiral's Men were in Cambridge in 1588–9, and in Oxford five times between 1586 and 1595.[60] But no one has made a good case for an early association between Shakespeare, or *Hamlet*, and the Lord Admiral's Men. However, Shakespeare has been conjecturally associated, by good recent scholarship, with the Queen's Men, early in his career.[61] The Queen's Men played at various venues in the City of London, and were often at Cambridge and Oxford between 1586 and 1597.[62] They were still active and important in the later 1590s.[63] Assuming that *Hamlet* originated with the Queen's Men would force us also to assume that Shakespeare brought it with him—which, of course, would require us to assume that he wrote it.

Scott McMillin demonstrated that, from 1580 to 1610, only three acting companies regularly performed plays in which the protagonist had to memorize more than 800 lines, and in the 1580s and 1590s those roles were divided between just two leading actors, Edward Alleyn and Richard Burbage.[64] In McMillin's chronological order and with McMillin's line counts, the roles are:

- Hieronimo, 1018 lines in Kyd's *Spanish Tragedy* (1587?), apparently belonging to the Lord Admiral's Men and to Strange's, and therefore Alleyn; but later associated with the Chamberlain's Men and certainly performed, at some time, by Burbage.[65]
- Tamburlaine, 877 lines in Marlowe's *Tamburlaine*, Part Two (1588?), Lord Admiral's, played by Alleyn

- Barabas, 1138 lines in Marlowe's *Jew of Malta* (1589), Strange's in 1591 and later the Admiral's Men, played by Alleyn
- Richard III, 1145 lines in Shakespeare's *Richard III* (1592–3), Strange's? Pembroke's? eventually Chamberlain's Men, played by Burbage

Shakespeare's *Hamlet* is also one of those long roles, played by Burbage, but McMillin counted lines only in the "enlarged" text, for which he repeated the traditional early-seventeenth-century date. The canonical *Hamlet* fits into a pattern of long Burbage roles from 1599 to 1607. However, if McMillin had counted lines in the 1603 version he would have realized that it, too, belongs in this category: the "young Hamlet" of the first edition speaks 823 lines.[66] It would therefore seem to represent a text originally performed by either Alleyn or Burbage. Unfortunately, Burbage's movements are as hard to track, before 1594, as Shakespeare's own. But this evidence does suggest that the 1603 text could represent an early Shakespeare-Burbage collaboration, just as the 1604 text represents a later Shakespeare-Burbage collaboration. Certainly, Q1 *Hamlet* fits what Manley and MacLean describe as the innovative "company style of the Strange's Men," which distinguished them from all earlier companies:

> the use of framed or inset performance... to transform the immediate emotional impact of sensational actions transpiring in the mise-en-scène into critical awareness of performance in the theatrical here-and-now; the use of acting styles that replaced stereotypical markers of status and allegorical personification with the embodiment of situation-specific purposes and passions, and the attempt to render, through the impersonation of passion and madness, the experience of individual consciousness in duress... in the complication or confounding of moral judgment by the excess of Senecan violence and cruelty; in the emphasis on illusion and disillusionment... Realpolitik and political persecution... the conscientious resistance to conformity that emerges from the impersonation of individual passion and consciousness.[67]

One other feature of the first edition of *Hamlet* points to Strange's Men. The leading comedian of the Chamberlain's Men, from 1594 to 1599, was Will Kemp. Kemp was replaced by Robert Armin, and critics have often detected a change in Shakespeare's clown roles that reflects the different comic styles of Kemp and Armin. But although Armin's influence has been convincingly detected in the witty jester Touchstone in *As You Like It* (1599–1600) and the witty fool Feste in *Twelfth Night* (1600–1), it has not been easy to fit the "1600" composition of *Hamlet* into that critical narrative. The character that all three texts of *Hamlet* call "clown" (the Gravedigger) does not seem especially well suited to Armin's style; indeed, it looks like other Kemp clowns, not licensed jesters or court "fools" but lower-class, rustic, uneducated jokers who outwit characters from the city or the court.[68] This anomaly can be explained by the fact that Kemp was in the company when the Chamberlain's Men were playing their 1590s *Hamlet*. Kemp's connection to the play could also have begun earlier than 1594. In 1586, Kemp (along with George Bryan and Thomas Pope) had been among the English performers who accompanied the Danish ambassador, Henrik Ramel, back to the Danish court at Elsinore, where they worked for three months under the patronage of King Frederick II.[69] This trip has been offered as an explanation for the Danish authenticity of the names Rosencrantz and Guildenstern, which do not occur in Belleforest's *Histoires Tragiques*.[70] If so, then the 1603 text of *Hamlet* must have been written after the 1586 visit to Elsinore, and indeed after the return of those English actors to England: Kemp left Denmark for continental travels that apparently included Italy, while Bryan and Pope continued on to Dresden. We don't know exactly when any of the three returned, but Kemp was already famous in London by the autumn of 1589, and probably performing with Strange's Men.[71] So the text of *Hamlet* printed in 1603 cannot have been written any earlier than the period 1587–89. And this Danish information links it, once again, to actors who later joined the Chamberlain's Men.

This potential source for the play's Danish names applies to all three printed versions of *Hamlet*. So does another alleged source from the 1580s, identified by Geoffrey Bullough and reiterated by Lukas Erne. This source (invoking Mary, Queen of Scots) is particularly relevant to the play's political focus and its addition of a dead father's Ghost as a major character, something that had clearly already been done by 1596.

> On 10 February 1567, Henry Stuart, Lord Darnley, Queen Mary's husband, was murdered in a plot which had been laid by James Hepburn, fourth Earl of Bothwell, confidant of Queen Mary. It seems likely that Mary was aware of the plot against her husband's life. On 15 May, little more than three months later, the Queen married Bothwell.... two decades later... in 1587... a Latin poem was written in which the Ghost of Darnley addresses his son [King] James VI [of Scotland]. The Ghost of Darnley, James VI, Mary, and Bothwell closely correspond to the Ghost of Hamlet's father, Hamlet, Gertrude, and Claudius.... Casting James VI in the role of Hamlet seeking revenge for the murder of his parent is less than innocuous shortly after Mary's execution.[72]

This source confirms the Danish evidence that Shakespeare's *Hamlet* cannot have been written before 1587. The 1603 edition contains a unique line, "No king on earth is safe, if God's his foe" (10.33), that would have been particularly resonant, politically, after the execution of Queen Mary in 1586, which sent shock waves through Britain and Europe. The text refers to a "king," not a "queen," but any English audience in the late 1580s would have been able to translate male monarch to female monarch.

Another detail present in all three texts helps to narrow the range of possible dates. In the 1603 edition, Hamlet's conversation with the traveling players is much shorter and less specific than the parallel exchange in the 1604 and 1623 texts. But it does include one brief contrast between those adult performers and the boy actors who were their competitors: "the principal public audience that came to them are turned to private plays, and to the humor of children" (7.272–3). "Private" here refers to the indoor hall theatres, which were smaller and more expensive than the outdoor amphitheatres. The private theatres therefore attracted a more elite audience of "principal" spectators: those "belonging to the first rank; among the most important; prominent, leading."[73] The boy companies were revived in 1599, so this contrast would have made sense at any time from 1599 to the publication of the 1603 and 1604 editions. But throughout the 1590s those boy companies in the indoor theatres at Blackfriars and St. Paul's had been dormant. The boys "appeared at court in the seasons of 1587–8, 1588–9, and 1589–90, after which there was a hiatus until 1599."[74] Therefore, the 1603 text could have been written before 1591, or after 1598, but it is very unlikely to have originated in the years between.

To sum up: the Chamberlain's Men were performing, by June 1594, a play about Hamlet and a ghost, which they seem to have inherited from a pre-1594 company. The title page of the 1603 edition suggests that it probably represents a play performed in the City of London before 1595, and at Cambridge before the 1594 formation of the Chamberlain's Men. Whichever company performed it in that earlier period, features of the 1603 text seem to be linked to actors (Burbage, Kemp, Pope, and Bryan) who were active in the late 1580s, and who later became Chamberlain's Men. Because of its knowledge of Danish names not present in the play's primary source, and its suggestive links to a political Ghost narrative, the 1603 text can have been written no earlier than 1587. If the standard scholarly narratives about the theatre history of the late 1580s and 1590s are true, then the 1603 text does not represent performances of the "enlarged" *Hamlet* printed in 1604, but the text of an earlier, shorter version that could have been written only between 1587 and 1590.

* * *

Into this period, between 1587 and 1590, comes Thomas Nashe's late 1589 allusion to *Hamlet*. If we free ourselves from Malone's chronology, the simplest explanation for Nashe's allusion is that it refers to the same text that can be traced from sometime after 1587 to Ling's edition of 1603. Nashe's remark occurs in his preface to Robert Greene's *Menaphon*, a work which was entered in the Stationers' Register on 23 August 1589, and printed the same year. In a pamphlet published in 1592 (and entered in the Stationers' Register on that 8 August), Nashe referred to a "ne[w]" play first performed with great success only five months earlier, on 3 March of that year.[75] Nashe could therefore easily be referring, here in *Menaphon*, to a Hamlet play that premiered earlier in 1589. Given "the characteristic topicality of Nashe's writing," we would not expect the *Hamlet* play to be earlier than 1588.[76] This date would explain why Francis Meres, in 1598, does not include *Hamlet* in his list of 12 plays by Shakespeare.[77] By then, the original play may have been a decade old, and the "enlarged" version had not yet been written. Meres does not mention *The Taming of the Shrew* or any of the *Henry VI* plays, either; Taylor's Oxford chronology places those four plays before March 1592.[78] If *Hamlet* dated from 1589, then the Meres omissions would all come from the very beginning of Shakespeare's career.

Like Lodge, both Nashe and Greene had university educations, and Nashe's preface is titled and addressed "To the Gentlemen Students of Both Universities."[79] Because it is so important and so disputed, the passage must be quoted at length. (I have modernized the spelling, but not punctuation or the use of italic.)

> I'll turn back to my first text, of studies of delight; and talk a little in friendship with a few of our trivial translators. It is a common practice nowadays amongst a sort of shifting companions, that run through every art and thrive by none, to leave the trade of *Noverint* whereto they were born, and busy themselves with the endeavors of Art, that could scarcely latinize their neck-verse if they should have need; yet English *Seneca* read by candlelight yields many good sentences, as *Blood is a beggar*, and so forth: and if you entreat him fair in a frosty morning he will afford you whole *Hamlets*, I should say handfuls of tragical speeches. But O grief! *tempus edax rerum*, what's that will last always? The sea exhaled by drops

will in continuance be dry, and *Seneca* let blood line by line and page by page, at length must needs die to our stage: which makes his famished followers to imitate the Kid in *Aesop*, who enamored with the Fox's new-fangles, forsook all hopes of life to leap into a new occupation; and these men renouncing all possibilities of credit and estimation, to intermeddle with Italian translations: wherein how poorly they have plodded, (as those that are neither provenzal men, nor are able to distinguish of Articles,) let all indifferent Gentlemen that have travailed in that tongue, discern by their two-penny pamphlets: and no marvel though their home-born mediocrity be such in this matter; for what can be hoped of those, that thrust *Elysium* into hell, and have not learned so long as they have lived in such spheres, the just measure of the Horizon without an hexameter. Sufficeth them to bodge up a blank verse with ifs and ands, and otherwhile for recreation after their candle stuff, having starched their beards most curiously, to make a peripatetical path into the inner parts of the City, and spend two or three hours in turning over French *Doudie*, where they attract more infection in one minute, than they can do eloquence all days of their life, by conversing with any Authors of like argument.[80]

In his treatment of this passage, Malone consistently denied that it could refer to any version of Shakespeare's *Hamlet*. He began, in 1778, by disputing whether *Hamlets* was a proper name, because in the second edition of *Menaphon* (the only one he had seen) the word was not italicized. But by 1790, having seen the first edition, he admitted his mistake, accepting that the "handfuls of tragical speeches" influenced by the Roman dramatist Seneca belonged to a play: "It is manifest from this passage that some play on the story of *Hamlet* had been exhibited before the year 1589."[81] Likewise, in 1778 Malone argued that "it is by no means clear, that Shakespeare was the person whom Nashe had here in contemplation" because the word *Noverint* indicates someone with legal training, and "Shakespeare was not bred to the law." In 1778, Malone regarded this objection as "decisive." But by 1790, having single-handedly edited all Shakespeare's plays and poems, the lawyer Malone had changed his mind: Shakespeare's "knowledge of legal terms is not merely such as might be acquired by the casual observation of even his all-comprehending mind; it has the appearance of *technical* skill; and he is so fond of displaying it on all occasions, that I suspect he was early initiated in at least the forms of law; and was employed, while he yet remained at Stratford, in the office of some country attorney, who was at the same time a petty conveyancer, and perhaps also the Seneschal of some manor-court." Malone's conjecture about Shakespeare's legal training has been endorsed by many subsequent scholars, including most recently Bart van Es, who points out that legal training was often the prelude or companion to a literary career.[82] If the lawyer Malone was impressed with Shakespeare's technical legal knowledge, Shakespeare's contemporaries may also have been impressed, leading Nashe or others to assume (as Malone did) that Shakespeare had been trained as a country lawyer's clerk. But we can reject Malone's 1778 objection even without endorsing Malone's 1790 conjecture about Shakespeare's legal training. Ronald B. McKerrow, the only modern scholar to have edited and annotated all Nashe's work, pointed out that *noverint* need not be literal: "Nashe elsewhere refers to *noverint*-writers as if representative of the lowest class of work connected with the pen."[83]

Although two of Malone's original objections had, by his own admission, collapsed, he still remained "inclined to think that" the *Hamlet* mocked by Nashe "was not Shakespeare's drama." His resistance is not surprising: he was deeply invested in the belief that no play of 1589 could have been written by Shakespeare. But only one specific objection remained constant from 1778 to 1821: "Our author, however freely he may have borrowed from Plutarch and Holinshed, does not appear to be at all indebted to Seneca." The phrasing of Malone's objection here is misleading. Plutarch and Holinshed provided narrative sources for the characters and plots of whole plays, and Seneca is not the narrative source for any Shakespeare play; but any play on *Hamlet*, whoever wrote it, must have adapted the narrative of Belleforest (or Saxo Grammaticus), not Seneca. What is at issue, for Nashe and for any comparison with Shakespeare, is Senecan phrasing or fragments or conventions, not whole Senecan plots. Malone's grand assertion that Shakespeare was "not ... at all indebted to Seneca" may have appealed to the eighteenth- and nineteenth-century emphasis on Shakespeare as an "original genius," but it cannot possibly be sustained. Shakespeare was specifically compared to Seneca in 1598.[84] As Madeleine Doran recognized, "*Hamlet* without Seneca is inconceivable."[85] Geoffrey Bullough, best known for his study of Shakespeare's sources, did not discuss the 1589 *Hamlet,* but he had "no doubt" of Seneca's influence on Shakespeare, especially "young Shakespeare," at the start of his playwriting career.[86]

Robert S. Miola, with no ax to grind about the 1589 *Hamlet*, has written an admirable book about Seneca's influence on Shakespeare's tragedies, arguing that "Senecan tragedy is as important to *Hamlet* as to *Titus Andronicus*." Miola foregrounds Seneca as an exemplar of "majesty of style" generally, and more particularly of revenge tragedy, ghosts, tyranny, madness, soliloquies, self-dramatizing protagonists, narrative speeches describing offstage events (like the duel between old

Fortinbras and Hamlet's father, or the death of Ophelia, or "the rugged Pyrrhus"), and the "domina-nutrix convention, that dialogue between passionate protagonist and restraining confidant" (in this case, Hamlet and Horatio).[87] Miola ignores the 1603 edition, but all three texts of Shakespeare's *Hamlet* foreground a structurally indispensable ghost, come from the underworld, clamoring for revenge—an unmistakably Senecan plot-device, not present in Belleforest or any earlier known version of the Amleth/Hamlet story. Likewise, all three texts dramatize a corrupt court and a corrupt dynastic house, characterized by fratricide, incest, adultery, usurpation, madness, poison, multiple murders, suicide, and the threat of matricide; in all three texts, the murderous, lecherous, ambitious uncle recalls the Aegisthus of Seneca's *Agamemnon*. All three texts explicitly name "Seneca" (and the Emperor "Nero," Seneca's student), along with "imperious Caesar," the Roman actor "Rossius," Julius Caesar, Brutus, Hercules, Pyrrhus, Priam, Hecuba, Aeneas, Dido, Hecate, Mars, Vulcan, Pelion, Olympus, and Alexander. In all three, Hamlet himself is compared to "a chorus" (7.143), like those in Seneca's tragedies; in all three, a villain with the Roman name Lucianus gives a typically Senecan speech associating "midnight" with "Thoughts black," "drugs," and murder (9.165–70). Miola demonstrates that Hamlet's two most famous soliloquies (the meditative "To be or not to be" and the self-rebuking "What is Hecuba to him?") have sources in Seneca, as does the soliloquy when he decides not to kill the praying king but instead wait until his victim is engaged in "some act / That hath no relish of salvation in't, / Then trip him that his heels may kick at heaven"; so do the famous Pyrrhus speech, the conjunction of Pelion and Olympus in the speech just before Hamlet leaps into the grave, and Hamlet's comparisons to Hercules in his first two scenes.[88] These are all "tragical speeches" in the 1603 edition that Nashe could have correctly recognized as Senecan. Nashe might also have realized, as Miola does, that the climactic encounter between Hamlet and his mother, and the portrayal of Ofelia/Ophelia, both seem specifically indebted to "English Seneca," in the form of John Studley's translation of *Agamemnon*.[89] More generally, all three texts are filled with quotable "sentences," maxims of the kind that made Seneca so amenable to the humanist cultural agenda and the English grammar school curriculum—and of the kind specifically highlighted in Ling's 1603 and 1604 editions of *Hamlet*. Seneca's work is deeply engaged with the problem of tyranny, and only the 1603 edition of *Hamlet* refers to "a tyrant's reign" (7.127). It is easy to see why Nashe might associate the *Hamlet* printed in 1603 with Seneca, and particularly with the translation of Seneca into English.

Modern scholarship has demolished Malone's case against Shakespeare's authorship of the 1589 *Hamlet*. But Malone distracted attention from the weakness of that evidence with a conjecture that started a wild goose chase for an alternative author. "Perhaps the original *Hamlet* was written by Thomas Kyd," he suggested. He gave four pieces of evidence for this conjecture. The passage contains a possible pun on his name ("the Kid in Aesop"); Kyd imitated Seneca; Kyd translated a French Senecan tragedy by Robert Garnier; and "in Kyd's *Spanish Tragedy*, as in Shakespeare's *Hamlet,* there is, if I may say so, a play represented *within* a play."

Malone's arguments in favor of Kyd are all weak. Shakespeare's canon contains more examples of a play-within-a-play than Kyd's: *The Taming of the Shrew, Love's Labor's Lost, A Midsummer Night's Dream, The Tempest,* and *The Two Noble Kinsmen*, not to mention *Hamlet.* Every tragic author of the period imitated Seneca.[90] Malone does not acknowledge that Nashe's jibe at an author reliant on "English Seneca" suggests that he is referring to someone with no apparent knowledge of Seneca in the original Latin. Kyd's only influential play was *The Spanish Tragedy*, which quotes Seneca's *Octavia, Agamemnon, Troades,* and *Oedipus*, in Latin, in a single speech by Hieronimo.[91] No one could plausibly have claimed that Kyd knew only the English translations of Seneca's tragedies. But the Senecanism of the 1603 edition of *Hamlet* could easily have been attributed to the English translations of the Roman playwright. As for Kyd's translation of Garnier, it was not published until 1594, and seems to have been written in 1593; it cannot possibly explain Nashe's 1589 reference to men who "spend two or three hours in turning over French *Doudie*" in the "inner parts of the City." David Riggs more accurately paraphrases Nashe's sentence as ridicule of "popular playwrights" who "spend their idle hours leafing through French crap at the bookstalls in the churchyard of St Paul's Cathedral."[92] This suggests someone who cannot afford to buy or study books, but instead simply browses through them in bookshops. It could hardly apply to Kyd's translation of Garnier, which demonstrably required sustained writing with the French text at hand. By contrast, the author of the 1603 *Hamlet* could have gotten everything he needed from Belleforest's short tale by reading it in a bookstore—especially if, like actors in the rapidly changing Elizabethan repertory system, he had a quick memory. And which is Nashe more likely to have disdained as "French crap": Garnier's neoclassical tragedy about the Roman matron *Cornelia*, or Belleforest's anthology, and in particular his translated medieval romance of Amleth?

Of Malone's evidence, only the possible pun on Kyd's name remains. McKerrow's rejection of that argument, more than a century ago, seems often to have been forgotten, but it has never been answered, so it is worth reciting in full.

> We must remember that this is not the only fable to which Nashe refers in this Preface. Two pages earlier... he speaks of "the Glow-worm mentioned in *Aesop's* Fables." There happens to have been no writer of the name of "Glow-worm."... and therefore no attempt has been made to give a personal application to the passage. Here, *in a precisely similar way*, he speaks of "the Kid in Aesop"; is the fact that there happens to have been a person of the name of "Kyd" any justification whatever for seeing in this case a personal allusion, when it is acknowledged that there is none in the other?... Nashe wishes to illustrate the way in which the Senecan writers had, in their search for something new, turned, to their own undoing, to translation from Italian; he happened to know one fable (and can anyone suggest a better one, or even simply another?) which was suitable, and he used it. What more natural? The interpretation put upon the passage may well remind one of Nashe's own complaint... "In one place of my book, *Pierce Penniless* saith but to the Knight of the Post, *I pray you how might I call you*, and they say I meant one *Howe*, a Knave of that trade, that I never heard of before.[93]

Unlike Malone or the other Shakespeare scholars who have cited the 1589 paragraph about *Hamlet*, McKerrow was an expert on Nashe, interpreting the passage by reference to the full range of Nashe's other work. "It is certainly *possible*," McKerrow acknowledges, "that Kyd was one of the 'sort' of dramatists who are attacked," but he could not see how Kyd's authorship of the 1589 *Hamlet* could "be deduced from Nashe's words." This is cautious and sane, and it convinced W. W. Greg, who "could feel no certainty either that Nashe had Kyd in mind or even if he had that it proves him to have written *Hamlet*."[94] Kyd is a possible candidate, but only one possibility among others.

Nevertheless, scholars seriously invested in Kyd have sought to maximize his importance by identifying him as the certain author of the 1589 *Hamlet*.[95] The most recent champion of Kyd's entire canon, Lukas Erne, makes the best possible case. Briefly acknowledging but not quoting McKerrow's full rebuttal, Erne focuses instead on another part of Nashe's paragraph. Combining the phrases "intermeddle with Italian translations" and "two-penny pamphlets" (which in Nashe are separated by 32 intervening words), Erne contends that only Kyd satisfies both criteria. Admittedly, few extant translations from Italian were printed in 1586 to 1589, and one of them was by Kyd: *The Householder's Philosophy*, a 1588 translation of Tasso's *Il Padre di Famiglia*. But that translation was not, as Erne implies, a two-penny pamphlet: it contains eight and a half sheets of paper, and would have cost four pence, at least (even without addition, in the second issue, of three sheets of "a dairy book for all good housewives").⁹⁶ Erne's own argument here rules out Kyd, since none of his extant works was a two-penny pamphlet. Besides, at least one play from the 1580s was translated from Italian (Munday's 1585 *Fedele and Fortunio*), and there may well have been more: only a tiny fraction of plays performed in the 1580s made it into print.⁹⁷

More generally, the argument by Malone, Boas, Freeman, and Erne depends on the assumption that Nashe was targeting, in this long passage, only a single author. But Nashe introduces the topic with the promise of plurality: his initial "a few of our trivial translators" is followed by "companions...themselves...their...they...followers...these men...they ...men...their...their...those...they...them...their...their...they ...they...their...Authors." McKerrow, who was not editing Shakespeare or Kyd, concluded that Nashe was "speaking not of one writer, but of a group—probably, but not certainly, of dramatists. He did know of a Hamlet play, but the passage throws no light upon its authorship."⁹⁸ E. K. Chambers, who dismissed Q1 *Hamlet* as a memorial reconstruction, concluded that "Nashe's reference is quite inconclusive."⁹⁹ George Ian Duthie, who also considered Q1 *Hamlet* a "bad quarto," nevertheless objected that "not one of the phrases" in Nashe's passage "points directly at Thomas Kyd." Duthie admitted that "one or two of them might possibly serve as corroboration of an attack on Kyd *inter alios*" [among others], but the argument for Kyd's authorship of any *Hamlet* requires the entire passage to refer to him alone.¹⁰⁰ Honigmann, another consistent advocate of memorial reconstruction, nevertheless dismissed the case for Kyd: "From Nashe's Epistle no valid clue for the authorship of the old *Hamlet* can be inferred," and it might even have been written by Shakespeare.¹⁰¹

I stress these scholarly rejections of Malone's conjecture about Kyd because I want to emphasize that my rejection of Malone here is not controversial, and not invented to justify my interpretation of the 1603 edition of *Hamlet*. You do not have to abandon your belief in all bad quartos or all memorial reconstructions, in order to abandon a belief in an allegedly lost *Hamlet* allegedly written by Kyd. You do not have to accept the eccentric claims, by Eric Sams, that Shakespeare never collaborated, and wrote the whole of *Fair Em*, *Locrine*, *The Troublesome Reign*, and *Edmund Ironside*.¹⁰² Rather, simply, Nashe's passage does not prove, or disprove, that either Kyd or Shakespeare wrote a *Hamlet* tragedy in the late 1580s.

What Nashe does tell us about that early *Hamlet* is that it was written by a single author. Although the beginning and end of Nashe's diatribe are dominated by plurals, the middle sentence about *Hamlet*, and that sentence alone, is governed by singular pronouns ("if you entreat *him* fair in a frosty morning, *he* will afford you whole *Hamlets*, I should say handfuls of tragical speeches"). Maybe this sentence was a late addition to the paragraph; maybe the *Hamlet* play premiered just before Nashe's epistle went to press. But certainly this single *Hamlet* author belongs, for Nashe, to a category of "trivial translators," "shifting companions" who have abandoned their natural sphere of employment and gate-crashed the precincts of Art. These uneducated pretenders differ from Nashe, Greene, and the "Gentlemen Students of both Universities" that the preface addresses. They were not gentlemen, and they were not credentialed by a university. Nashe's criteria would apply to at least three Elizabethan playwrights: Anthony Munday, Kyd, and Shakespeare. None of those three men attended university; all three wrote texts translated from French and Italian sources.[103] If we combine Nashe's allusion to *Hamlet* with Lodge's, then Peele is eliminated (because he is explicitly praised by Nashe) and so is Kyd (because he was dead by the time Lodge wrote). That leaves Munday and Shakespeare as the two most likely candidates, on the basis of the external evidence from 1589 to 1596. Munday wrote most of his plays in collaboration, and he was never praised as a tragic playwright, in his own time or since. Shakespeare wrote most of his plays alone, and he has been repeatedly specifically praised for his tragedies, from the 1590s to the present. Although Shakespeare wrote a number of collaborative plays early in his career, it would not be odd even for an apprentice playwright to write one or more plays entirely on his own.[104] Shakespeare therefore seems the most probable of the two candidates—even without the testimony of Harvey, whose note is more likely to refer to the earlier play than to one written in 1600..

To summarize: Malone's insistence that the 1589 *Hamlet* cannot have been written by Shakespeare is unwarranted. On the basis of the external evidence, Shakespeare remains the most plausible candidate—and the only one whose name is ever elsewhere associated with a play about Hamlet. That open possibility allows us to ask a question Malone could not: might the 1603 edition of *Hamlet* (which Malone never saw) have been written by Shakespeare in 1589?

* * *

Two details of *Hamlet*, stable in all versions of the text, connect to Shakespeare's early life in Warwickshire. First, the protagonist's name had, by 1589, been changed from "Amlethus" or "Amleth" to "Hamlet."

Second, the play departs from Belleforest by creating the character of a young woman, connected to Hamlet, who is drowned in suspicious circumstances, then buried in a way that suggests she committed suicide, provoking a discussion of sixteenth-century English legal precedents. There is a small village less than two kilometers from Stratford-upon-Avon called Tiddington. There, in December 1579, a young woman, "the remarkably named Katherine Hamlett," drowned in the Avon River.[105] An inquest was held on 11 February 1580 to address the questions raised by the church and court regarding the manner of her death.

> The jurors, consisting of three gentlemen or freeholders of Alveston, and ten humbler neighbors, gave it as their opinion that the deceased "going with a milk pail to draw water at the River Avon, standing on the bank of the same, suddenly and by accident slipped and fell into the river and was drowned."[106]

The records of the inquest state that Hamlett's drowning was judged to have been a "misadventure," an accidental death, "per infortunium . . . et non aliter nec alio modo ad mortem suam devenit" (i.e., "she came to her death by a mishap, and in no other way"). In spite of the verdict, however, there was at least a strong suspicion that Katherine Hamlett had in fact committed suicide, since she was buried on 18 December 1579, "with 'maimed rites' or none, to be taken up at the inquest later."[107] The means of her burial, along with the inquest, indicate a possible suicide, an issue that would later be addressed by Shakespeare in *Hamlet*, when Ofelia is buried without traditional rites, very like Katherine Hamlett.[108]

> Leartes   What ceremony else? Say, what ceremony else?
> Priest   My Lord, we have done all that lies in us,
>   And more than well the church can tolerate:
>   She hath had a dirge sung for her maiden soul,
>   And but for favor of the king and you,
>   She had been buried in the open fields,
>   Where now she is allowèd Christian burial.
>   (16.130–36)

Even Harold Jenkins concedes that the connection between Katherine Hamlett and the story of Ofelia may "admittedly, be more than a coincidence."[109]

In 1585, Shakespeare became the father of fraternal twins, a daughter christened Judith, and a son, who would be his only male descendant.

That son's name is spelled "Hamnet" in the parish register and in modern biographies (beginning with Malone). But without any standardized spelling, the same name could easily have been pronounced, and spelled on other occasions, "Hamlet."[110] The child had most likely been named after Shakespeare's friend, Hamlet Sadler, connecting Shakespeare even more profoundly to the name found in the English tragedy from 1589 on.[111] The two spellings were demonstrably interchangeable.

Shakespeare, in other words, had a particular, personal, local, early interest in the name "Hamlet," and a particular, local, early reason for connecting that name to a drowned young woman, suspected of suicide. These circumstances originated in the period 1579–1585, and they would explain Shakespeare's interest in a 1575 French story about an "enfant" or "Adolescent" named Amleth. Young Shakespeare might have encountered that French story through his friendship with the stationer Richard Field, who in 1593 and 1594 would print *Venus and Adonis* and *Lucrece*, the first works publicly attributed to Shakespeare, the only works printed in his lifetime for which he provided signed dedications. In 1579, Field had left Stratford to begin an apprenticeship with the London printer Thomas Vautrollier, who died in 1587. In 1588, Field began collaborating with Vautrollier's widow Jacqueline, whom he then married in 1589. When Shakespeare left Stratford-upon-Avon for London, sometime in the second half of the 1580s, Field may well have been the only Londoner that he knew well. Shakespeare could have found, in the shop where Field worked, many of the English books that would be important sources for his plays. Moreover, Thomas Vautrollier and his wife Jacqueline were both French, exiled Huguenots, and those French booksellers are more likely than most London stationers to have taken an interest in imported French books, such as Belleforest's *Histoires Tragiques*.

All these connections are circumstantial. They do not prove that Shakespeare wrote *Hamlet* in 1589, or that the *Hamlet* of 1589 was the one printed in 1603. But no other playwright has so many personal links to the Hamlet story in the 1580s. All these links were emotionally charged: the birth of his first and only son, named for a close friend, the nearby and disputed and possibly suicidal drowning of a young woman about his age, his arrival as a provincial stranger in London, browsing books in the shop of a childhood friend who was also his only London contact with his hometown. These events would have been much more vividly present to Shakespeare in the late 1580s than in 1600. It seems unlikely that Munday or Kyd or any other English playwright had so many reasons to write a *Hamlet* play in the late 1580s. These personal connections to the Hamlet play first printed in 1603 would have been vivid to Shakespeare at the same time as the Danish sources for names in the 1603 edition, and the 1587 poem about the Ghost of a murdered royal father. Everything here points to the late 1580s.

So, perhaps, does the name "Corambis." It has been argued that the name is a Latin pun, based on *cor* meaning "heart" and *ambo* and/or *bis* meaning "both, double" (as in "two-faced" or "ambiguous"). This meaning would obviously be appropriate for the character in the play, but it would also pun on the motto of William Cecil, Lord Burghley, *cor unum* ("one heart"). Where Burghley asserted his constancy, the name *Corambis* instead insists on duplicity. This point has been pressed by anti-Stratfordians, which goes some way to explaining why sane scholars have ignored it.[112] But Burghley's motto had been public knowledge since 1578, when it appeared in print, so the pun does not presuppose insider knowledge beyond the reach of a common player.[113] And the parallels between Elizabeth's most powerful minister and the Danish court counselor have been recognized by scholars—E. K. Chambers, John Dover Wilson, A. L. Rowse, among others—with no conspiratorial ax to grind.[114] But Burghley died on 4 August 1598. Why would Shakespeare satirize Burghley after his death? For anti-Stratfordians like J. Thomas Looney, the link between Burghley and *Hamlet* is one among many proofs that Shakespeare did not write *Hamlet* (or anything else).[115] But if we abandon the chimera of Malone's chronology, and entertain the possibility that Shakespeare wrote the first version of *Hamlet* in 1588–89, an allusion to Burghley makes sense. Corambis's servant Montano, sent to France with the mandate "by indirections find directions out" (an episode for which there is no equivalent in any of the known sources) might then suggest Sir Francis Walsingham, creator of the Elizabethan espionage network, who had also served as ambassador to France, and who died in 1590. Two playwrights from the 1580s, Marlowe and his roommate and friend Thomas Watson, apparently worked for Walsingham, so the London theatrical world was not too distant from the kind of spying rampant in the court of *Hamlet*.[116] Shakespeare's neighbors and relatives in Warwickshire had been directly affected by the success of the Burghley/Walsingham network in exposing and executing the Catholic conspirators in the Somerville and Throckmorton plots in 1583–4. Whether or not Shakespeare was ever a Catholic, he would have been aware of the role of the Elizabethan intelligence network in defending a monarch that Catholics considered a usurper, who inherited the crown after the death of her sibling. We do not need to commit ourselves to a particular interpretation of Shakespeare's sectarian views in order to recognize that the portrayal of

Corambis and Montano in the first edition of *Hamlet* would have been particularly resonant, for a Warwickshire playwright with Catholic friends and neighbors, and for London audiences, in the late 1580s.

Traditional modern scholarship nevertheless rejects Shakespeare's responsibility for the 1589 play and/or for the 1603 text of *Hamlet*, because that first edition is a so-called bad quarto. It "is indeed bad," Leah Marcus acknowledges, "and will continue to be as long as we rank the early texts of the plays on the basis of their adherence to culturally predetermined standards of literary excellence."[117] If we judge the 1603 edition against the standard set by the poetic power, psychological complexity, and philosophical depth of the enlarged 1604 version, or the even larger conflated text of modern editions, we will be disappointed. But, as we have seen, none of the claims about bad quartos, piracy, memorial reconstruction, shorthand, or note-taking plausibly explain the 1603 text. "I am not saying," David Kastan has written, "that Q1 *Hamlet* is as good a play as the *Hamlet* we usually read (though I would say that it is a better play than has generally been allowed, and certainly not '*Hamlet* by Dogberry' as Brian Vickers has termed it)."[118]

Modern performances have repeatedly demonstrated that the 1603 text "does very well for an unsophisticated audience."[119] By the beginning of the seventeenth century, London audiences had seen Dekker's *Shoemaker's Holiday*, Jonson's *Every Man in his Humor*, Marston's *Antonio's Revenge*, and more than half Shakespeare's plays, including such complex masterpieces as *Richard III*, *Richard II*, *Romeo and Juliet*, *A Midsummer Night's Dream*, *Much Ado About Nothing*, *Henry IV*, *Henry V*, and *Julius Caesar*. There is no reason to believe that such audiences would be satisfied (as Lucas Erne supposes) by performances accurately reflected in the 1603 text. Erne presumes that all early modern audiences were less sophisticated than we are. It would be more reasonable to distinguish between seventeenth-century audiences and those way back in 1588, or early 1589, when the purpose-built London amphitheatres were only 12 or 13 years old, when Munday, Greene, Peele, Lodge, and Robert Wilson were still popular, when the most successful, groundbreaking recent plays had been *Tamburlaine*, *The Spanish Tragedy*, and *Mucedorus*. The issue here is not a difference between the merely "theatrical" 1603 edition and the sublimely "literary" 1604 edition. In 1589, neither Sidney's *Arcadia*, nor his *Astrophil and Stella*, nor his *Defence of Poesy*, nor Spenser's *Faerie Queene*, had yet been printed. None of Drayton's, Donne's, Marston's, or Jonson's poems had been written. Nicholas Ling regarded the 1603 *Hamlet* as a marketable literary text, in part because Ling's own literary taste reflected the "unsophisticated" fashions of the 1580s and very early 1590s.

Stylistically, the 1603 edition is demonstrably much more old-fashioned than the 1604 and 1623 versions. It uses *hath* 40 times, but does not contain a single example of *has*; by contrast, the 1604 edition has nine, and the 1623 edition 16. The doth/does ratio in Q1 is 20/3; in Q2, it's 27/25; in F1, 27/22. The same preference for obsolescent language can be seen in the first edition's use of individual words like "whilom" (9.102) and "whenas" (11.107), which editors identify as "archaic."[120] The disyllabic "whenas" has clearly been chosen, over modern "when," to pad out the verse line: "Whenas he came, I first bespake him fair" (11.107) contains two such archaic metrical fillers, "whenas" and "bespake." This padding is also evident in other archaic forms present in the first edition: "when that" (15.35, meaning "when"), "for to" (15.3, meaning "for"), and "like to" (3.15, 3.18, meaning "like"). All these linguistic preferences and metrical fillers are much more common in Shakespeare's early verse, as are tautologies like "An eye at which his foes did tremble at" (11.27) and "flaming fire" (5.4).[121]

In 1987, Gary Taylor identified and tabulated four obsolescent forms that are useful for indicating chronology, because they occur more frequently in Shakespeare's early work; Taylor did not bother to count them in the first edition of *Hamlet*, but they are proportionally more common there than in the enlarged canonical text.[122] The old-fashioned "-eth" ending of verbs occurs 12 times: singeth (1.116), waxeth (4.58, also at *Venus* 440), posteth (5.52), closeth (6.13, 16, 17), possesseth (7.93, 11.91), useth (9.29), catcheth (9.38), cometh (9.82.3, stage direction), and toucheth (9.140). Of these, only "singeth" is repeated in the later editions, probably because "sings" would disrupt the meter ("The bird of dawning singeth all night long"). But none of the others can be explained as a metrical choice, either because the modern form is metrically equivalent (waxeth, possesseth), or because the word occurs in prose (closeth, useth, catcheth, toucheth) or in a stage direction (cometh). The first edition simply prefers the old-fashioned form. It also makes more use, in verse, of obsolescent, sounded, syllabic vowel terminations (which some modern editions indicate with an accent).[123]

> With martial stalk he passèd through our watch (1.55)
> Of music which whilom pleasèd mine ear (9.102)
> And so I am revengèd. No, not so, (10.16)
> His shipping is already furnishèd (11.119)
> Hath piercèd so the young Ofelia's heart (13.6)
> Which once unhearsèd, then the world shall hear (13.126)

> And lifted up his head to motïon (2.133)
> And not the smallest alteratïon (9.61)
> Would wash the crime clear from my conscïence (10.2)
> For murderous minds are always jealïous (14.13)

These old-fashioned metrical fillers may be related to Nashe's complaint (in the paragraph where he mentions *Hamlet*) about authors who "bodge up a blank verse with ifs and ands." The verb "bodge up" meant "patch up" or "put together clumsily," and both of those meanings might be applied to these outdated expedients for creating extra syllables. Nashe's "ifs and ands" is a proverbial expression, but its relevance to metrical padding would be use of the old tautology "and if," which editors sometimes modernize to "an if," meaning simply "if." Whether or not Nashe had this pleonasm in mind, it occurs five times, uniquely, in the first edition of *Hamlet*, from the very beginning of the play:

> An if you meet Marcellus and Horatio (1.3)
> An if this be not true, take this from this (7.94)
> An if it prove any otherwise than love (7.108)
> What would he do an if he had my loss (7.408)
> O fie, Horatio! An if thou shouldst die (17.106)

All of these features of the language of the first edition justify the scholarly conclusion that, stylistically, it does not belong to the same period of Shakespeare's career as *Julius Caesar* or *Twelfth Night*. They also contribute to anachronistic speculation that a memorial reconstruction, or a text transcribed by spectators in the theatre, was "botched up" by a "hack poet." But such language, and such verse, is typical of the best poets and playwrights of the late 1580s.

Those who consider the first edition a "bad quarto" often quote the beginning of Shakespeare's most famous soliloquy.

> To be, or not to be—ay, there's the point.
> To die, to sleep—is that all? Ay, all.
> No, to sleep, to dream—ay, marry, there it goes,
> For in that dream of death, when we're awaked...
>
> (7.115–18)

Contrast this with the first four lines of the canonical version from the later editions:

> To be, or not to be—that is the question;
> Whether 'tis nobler in the mind to suffer

> The slings and arrows of outrageous fortune
> Or to take arms against a sea of troubles...
>
> (3.1.55–8)

The later version is, undeniably, much better poetry. But Shakespeare *must* have become a better poet after another 11 or 13 years of writing verse. We should also notice that the 1603 edition begins with four end-stopped lines, with a stressed syllable at the end of each line. By contrast, the first four lines of the 1604 version all end with an extra unstressed syllable, what is sometimes called a "feminine" ending. The end-stopped stress-stopped lines of Q1 are entirely characteristic of Marlowe's mighty line, and of the verse style of the 1580s generally.[124] But as every metrical analyst agrees, Shakespeare over the course of his career made more and more frequent use of that extra unstressed final syllable. He also made more use of strong enjambment, as in the second line of the canonical text: the line ends with the transitive verb *suffer*, but the sentence and the sense carry over to the direct object in the following line ("the slings and arrows"). In both respects, the contrast between the two texts of this passage is typical of the larger contrast between the first version and the later, longer texts. Stylistically, the language and verse style of the first edition makes sense as a play written in the late 1580s, transcribed and printed in the early seventeenth century.

The passages in the 1603 edition identified by scholars as theatrical allusions are also compatible with performance in the late 1580s. Told of the arrival of a troupe of traveling actors, Hamlet responds by cataloguing a list of roles: "He that plays the King shall have tribute of me, the venturous Knight shall use his foil and target, the Lover shall sigh gratis, the Clown shall make them laugh that are tickled in the lungs... and the Lady shall have leave to speak her mind freely" (7.277–83). Thompson and Taylor identify these as "stereotypes of the stage in the 1580s and early 1590s" (1603, 101). The 1604 and 1623 versions of the text add, to this list, "the Humourous Man shall end his part in peace" (Q2 2.2.288–9; F1 2.2.321–2). We might take "Humorous" to mean "comic," but the 1623 text contains both "the Clown" and "the Humourous Man," which seems redundant. However, "humorous" can also mean "showing a particular humour, or psychological type," as in Chapman's *An Humourous Days Mirth* (1597), or Jonson's *Every Man in his Humour* (1598) and *Every Man Out of his Humour* (1599).[125] The later printed texts seem to refer to a theatrical vogue that began in the late 1590s; the first edition does not.

Later, in a passage stable in all three texts, Hamlet's "The croaking raven doth bellow for revenge" (9.164) mockingly misquotes two lines from an anonymous play performed by the Queen's Men, *The True Tragedy of Richard the Third*: "The screeking Raven sits croking for revenge. / Whole he[r]ds of beasts comes bellowing for revenge."[126] That play was first printed in 1594, and Thompson and Taylor follow earlier scholars in dating its original composition and performance as "*c.*1591."[127] Here, an innocent reader might think, is evidence that the 1603 edition cannot represent a text performed by 1589. In fact, the "*c.* 1591" date is just a way of indicating that the anonymous play must be earlier than Shakespeare's *Richard III*, often dated 1592. McMillin and MacLean, who revolutionized our understanding of the Queen's Men, observed that "we know nothing about its authorship and must settle for saying that it was written before it was published." More generally with the Queen's Men, "a chronology based on dates of composition is bound to be virtually useless."[128] "The absence of a clown figure prominent enough to be recorded in the play," David Walsh has suggested, "might indicate that it was first put on by the Queen's Men after Richard Tarlton's death in 1588, although this is not certain."[129] If we accept this suggestion, *The True Tragedy of Richard the Third* cannot be earlier than late 1588, which means that Hamlet's quotation from the play could hardly have been written before the beginning of 1589. It would also have been especially topical in 1589.

Hamlet uses a quotation from a play by the Queen's Men to cue a rhymed iambic-pentameter speech by Lucianus (9.165–70), played by one of the traveling troupe of actors. That quotation-cue thus associates the traveling players in *Hamlet* with "the most active touring troupe on record," the Queen's Men. In 1587, Marlowe's prologue to *Tamburlaine* had famously dissociated his revolutionary play from "jigging veins of rhyming mother wits / And such conceits as clownage keeps in pay." As McMillin and MacLean recognized, the specific target of Marlowe's aesthetic manifesto was the Queen's Men, whose stock-in-trade was "rhyme and clownage."[130] In *Hamlet*, "The Murder of Gonzago" begins with a Prologue of three rhyming tetrameter lines, which provokes another mocking comment from Hamlet: "Is't a prologue or a posy for a ring?" (9.92–6). Hamlet, and *Hamlet*, mock not only the rhyme of the touring troupe, but also their "short" verse lines. The rhymes throughout the inset play, the initial dumb show (9.82.105), the "damnable faces" of the actor before he speaks (9.162–3), would, in 1589, not have been innocent formal devices for differentiating the *Hamlet* play from the "Mousetrap" play-within-the-play; more specifically, the contrast between Hamlet and the touring actors embodied a topical aesthetic contrast between two rival companies. That same contest is evident in the lines, unique to the 1603 edition, on clownage.

> And then you have some again that keep one suit of jests—as a man is known by one suit of apparel—and gentlemen quotes his jests down in their tables before they come to the play, as thus: "Cannot you stay till I eat my porridge?" and "You owe me a quarter's wages!" and "My coat wants a cullison!" and "Your beer is sour!" and, blabbering with his lips and thus keeping in his cinquepace of jests when, God knows, the warm Clown cannot make a jest unless by chance—as the blind man catcheth a hare—masters, tell him of it. (9.29–38)

This passage alludes, unmistakably, to Richard Tarlton, the great Elizabethan clown, "your only jig-maker" (9.147). Tarlton, one of the leaders of the Queen's Men, died in September 1588.[131] In late 1588 or early 1589, it would have been hard for spectators *not* to think of the recently deceased Tarlton when they watched a scene in a graveyard that featured the skull of a "mad rogue," "a fellow of infinite mirth" and physical comedy, famous for his "jests" and "flashes of merriment" (16.104–13).[132] In 1588–9, *Hamlet*—and specifically, the text printed in 1603—would have been as unmistakably metatheatrically topical as *Tamburlaine*.

But unlike *Tamburlaine*, the 1588/1603 *Hamlet* did not pronounce its manifesto in a prologue; instead, it integrated its aesthetic defiance into the play itself. Although Shakespeare liked the device of a play-within-a-play, they are usually amateur (*A Midsummer Night's Dream*, *Love's Labour's Lost*) or supernatural (*The Tempest*). In *The Taming of the Shrew*, they are travelling professionals, but their brief appearance does not allude to London theatrical rivalries or to debates about acting styles. By contrast, *Hamlet*'s traveling players, not present in any of the prose sources for the story, allow Shakespeare to use Hamlet as a spokesman for the playwright or the acting company.

> Pronounce me this speech trippingly o' the tongue as I taught thee. Marry, an you mouth it, as a-many of your players do, I'd rather hear a town-bull bellow than such a fellow speak my lines. Nor do not saw the air thus with your hands but give everything his action with temperance. O, it offends me to the soul to hear a robustious periwig fellow to tear a passion in tatters, into very rags, to split the ears of the ignorant—who for the most part are capable of nothing but dumb-shows and noises—I would have such a fellow whipped for o'erdoing Termagant: it out-Herods Herod! (9.1–11)

The references here to Herod, and probably Termagant too, refer to biblical plays that Shakespeare could have seen as a boy in Warwickshire.[133] The players who "mouth it" are *your* players," which might be the impersonal indefinite use of the possessive pronoun (as in modern "one's"), but in 1589 it might more pointedly have suggested a distinction between "our" acting company and "your" acting company.[134] This passage also occurs in the 1604 and 1623 texts, but it has been altered there in tiny ways: the old-fashioned ethical dative here ("Pronounce me") was removed in the later editions, the old-fashioned "an" and "a-many" were updated to modern "if" and "many." The "town-bull" here (which suggests a small market town like Stratford-upon-Avon, rather than London) was changed to "town crier." The generic "split the ears of the *ignorant*" here was changed there to "split the ears of the *groundlings*," apparently a new word, first appearing in the 1604 quarto. The word "groundlings" presupposes the architecture of the London amphitheatres; the first edition's "ignorant" would be just as relevant to performances at the Cross Keys Inn, or by a touring company in all sorts of venues. In each of these small variations, the first edition's comments on acting better fit the language and the circumstances of the 1580s.

Two other explicitly theatrical allusions in the 1603 text would have been topically relevant in 1589. Hamlet's reference to the great Roman actor Roscius (7.310–11) might allude to Edward Alleyn, the first celebrity actor in the early modern theatre: Alleyn was often compared to Roscius.[135] The same actor may also be implied by Hamlet's complaint that "There be fellows that I have seen play (and heard others commend them—and that highly, too) that, having neither the gait of Christian, pagan nor Turk, have so strutted and bellowed that you would ha' thought some of Nature's journeymen had made men (and not made them well), they imitated humanity so abhominable" (7.15–20). Alleyn's most famous role was *Tamburlaine*, which was certainly being performed by 1587. One of the remarkable features of Alleyn's embodiment of that role seems to have been his "gait." Dekker, in 1603, referred to "stalking Tamburlaine," and Middleton, in 1604, used the same verb: "The spindle-shank spiders, which show like great lechers with little legs, went stalking over his head as if they had been conning of *Tamburlaine*."[136] Alleyn was thus, in early 1589, a highly commended actor, famous for his singular "gait" in a recent successful play that featured Christians, pagans, and Turks.

Thus, explicit theatrical allusions in the first edition of *Hamlet* distance it both from the Queen's Men and Alleyn. That play text also distinguishes itself from Marlowe's "mighty line," and from the aesthetic unity created by two thousand lines of virtually uninterrupted blank verse. Like the early Shakespeare, but unlike Marlowe, the first edition of *Hamlet* is willing to use rhyme in serious passages outside the play-within-the-play.

> And think already the revenge is done
> On him that makes you such a hapless son.
> LEARTES You have prevailed, my lord. Awhile I'll strive
> To bury grief within a tomb of wrath,
> Which once unhearsèd, then the world shall hear
> Leartes had a father he held dear!
> KING No more of that. Ere many days be done
> You shall hear that you do not dream upon.
> (13.118–29)

The later editions get rid of this passage, and of five other couplets unique to Q1 (3.69–70, 8.39–40, 11.165–6, 15.53–4, 17.124–5). By 1600, those couplets would have seemed impossibly old-fashioned. But the plays of the Queen's Men, the most powerful and influential company in the 1580s, were always a conspicuous "medley" of forms, styles, and emotions. So are Shakespeare's. Rather than shying away from the mixture of kings and clowns, tragedy and comedy, denigrated by Sidney and other purists, all editions of *Hamlet* literally bring both together. The first edition's singular "Clown" is a "peasant" (16.74), who converses with the Prince of Denmark about "our last King Hamlet" (87), "Denmark" and "England" (93, 95).[137] Although he does not speak in the second half of the scene, he may be present, silently, when the King, Queen and courtiers enter. But Shakespeare turns the Queen's Men's medley of princes and peasants, prose and song, blank verse and rhyme, tragedy and clowning, into "some necessary point in the play" (9.27). The clown here is confined to a single scene (16.1–107), invented by the playwright, which dramatizes and combines two pivotal events in the plot: the burial of Ophelia and Hamlet's return from England. Shakespeare turns the comedian into a character: a working peasant who contrasts with, but recognizes, the dead court jester Yorick. "Hath this fellow any feeling of himself that is thus merry in making of a grave?" Hamlet asks, and Horatio answers, "custom hath made it in him seem nothing" (16.36–40). The incongruousness of merriment and grave-digging is first a psychological peculiarity, or puzzle, which is then explained as a natural social consequence of the repetitions of manual labor.

Hamlet is responding to the Clown's singing. The play contains six songs; five are sung by a madwoman, their incongruousness a sign of her madness. Unlike the art song in the 1580s plays of Lyly, *Hamlet* recycled familiar old songs sung to old tunes. Here an adult Clown sings, a cappella, a verbally inaccurate version of a popular ballad, originally written by Lord Vaux in the reign of Queen Mary and published in Richard Tottel's best-selling miscellany of *Songs and Sonnets* in 1557, often reprinted.[138] Again, *Hamlet*, in all its versions, draws on material that Shakespeare could have encountered in his youth.

Just as the quotation from the Queen's Men's *Richard the Third* calls attention to *Hamlet*'s aesthetic differences from their repertory, so a quotation from *The Spanish Tragedy* differentiates Shakespeare's play from Kyd's influential revenge tragedy (and Alleyn and the Admiral's Men). Hamlet's "An if the king like not the tragedy" (9.183) quotes Kyd's "An if the world like not this tragedy."[139] This quotation comes less than 20 lines after Hamlet quotes the Queen's Men play, and here again the echo is explicitly parodic: Hamlet follows the line with the flippant "Why then—belike he likes it not, perdie," the added rhyme producing a ridiculous jingle. In the later editions of 1604 and 1623, the quotation from Kyd is modified, changing "tragedy" to "comedy." Editors have justified that change, but it is another example of the 1603 edition being closer to the play's sources, and closer to the 1580s.

Scholars have found several other alleged parallels to *The Spanish Tragedy* unique to the first edition, and taken these as evidence of memorial reconstruction. None of the echoes is certain, and they could be just as easily attributed to Shakespeare's familiarity, in the late 1580s, with Kyd's sensationally successful tragedy, and his conscious or unconscious echoing of a play that *Hamlet* both appropriates and resists. *Hamlet* rejects Kyd's long set speeches, his many Latin quotations, his rigidly formal verse, but all scholars agree that *Hamlet* was deeply influenced by Kyd's play. If Nashe's reference to "the Kid in Aesop" is indeed a pun on Thomas Kyd's name, that fact would not establish Kyd's authorship of the 1589 play, because what Nashe actually claimed is that Seneca's "famished followers... *imitate* the Kid". Seneca's famished followers are imitators of Kyd, not Kyd himself. The 1603 quarto text of Shakespeare's tragedy does indeed imitate Kyd, as Nashe claimed. In *The Spanish Tragedy*, a father mourns and revenges the death of a son; in *Hamlet*, a son mourns and revenges the death of a father; in both cases, mourning leads to madness. Fundamentally, Shakespeare substitutes a young, unmarried revenger for Kyd's old, married one. In the context of the late 1580s, Hamlet's youth is part of the play's metatheatrical contest with Shakespeare's theatrical rivals, the aging star actors of the Queen's Men and the old revenger Hieronimo. Burbage, in 1589, would have been only about 21 or 22. In November 1590, the first explicit reference to Richard Burbage in a London theatre describes him actively participating in a brawl, beating a supporter of a rival faction about the legs with a broomstick.[140] This is an aggressive young man who could certainly have leaped into Ophelia's grave, and thrown and tossed about his mother onstage.

Even when *Hamlet* praises a play from the 1580s, Shakespeare rewrites and repositions it in a way its authors may have found presumptuous. When Hamlet remembers "a speech" about "Aeneas' tale to Dido," it is hard not to think of Marlowe and Nashe's *Tragedy of Dido, Queen of Carthage*, which seems to be from the 1580s. Nashe, in 1589, might well have been irritated by Hamlet's claim that the speech comes from a play that "was never acted—or, if it were, never above twice. For, as I remember, it pleased not the vulgar. It was caviare to the million" (7.328–31). *Hamlet*'s immediate theatrical success would have created a particularly galling contrast. What right had the uneducated Shakespeare, or his character, to sit in judgment on the plays of two graduates of the University of Cambridge? Shakespeare's rendition of the speech about "The rugged Pyrrhus" (340–375) appropriates their classical credentials, but frames them with the surrounding, interrupting naturalistic prose of Hamlet and Corambis. In doing so, Shakespeare, even while praising the neoclassical play, insists on its artificiality, contrasting it with his own creation of a new kind of prose and a new kind of characterization. As in the humanist grammar school, Shakespeare is here competing with rival translators.

At the beginning of the seventeenth century, having been on top of the theatrical world for at least six years, Shakespeare did not need to differentiate himself from the long-dead Kyd and Marlowe, the long-faded Queen's Men, or the disgraced and impoverished Nashe. But in the late 1580s, as a provincial "upstart crow" with no university education, he had the strongest possible motive for distinguishing himself, aesthetically, from those real rivals. And they had every reason to resent his success.

CHAPTER 6

Revising *Hamlet*?

"My father's death"

The first edition of *Hamlet* cannot be explained as a pirated text. But it could derive from the *Hamlet* performed late in 1589, written by Shakespeare, inherited and performed by the Chamberlain's Men in 1594, and still being performed at their playhouse, The Theater, until at least 1595. It may well have been Shakespeare's first play, or the first play that he wrote without a collaborator; it would seem to have been the earliest surviving play entirely by Shakespeare that reached print. It was not published in the 1590s, or the late 1580s, for the same reason(s) that other early Shakespeare plays were not published until long after they were written. In all these ways, it belongs to the normal activities of theatre companies and stationers in the late sixteenth and early seventeenth centuries.

These conclusions have implications far beyond our reading or performance of the 1603 edition. They transform our understanding of the enlarged, canonical text of Shakespeare's tragedy, helping to answer (or at least rephrase) many of the questions that have puzzled and frustrated critics for centuries. They challenge our assumptions about the date and sources of the enlarged version. They newly illuminate the play's relationship to its historical, theatrical, and biographical context. They turn the play's influential articulation of a dramatic aesthetic from a point into a line, from something static and seemingly eternal into something that evolves, responding to changes in its environment. They transform our understanding of the relationship between the 1604 quarto and the 1623 Folio versions, which in turn transforms assumptions about how Shakespeare's most canonical play should be edited. They significantly revise our understanding of the dramatic intersections between literary and theatrical ambition. They position *Hamlet* in a larger critical debate about what happens when great artists, in their maturity, revise work they originally wrote years before.

Let's begin with the most immediate, practical issue: the date. We can now return to, and close, the analysis of the long shadow cast by Edmond Malone's unfortunate chronology. Malone, who died before the rediscovery of the 1603 edition of *Hamlet*, was simply ignorant of the most important fact about the history of the canonical play that he was trying to date, and he therefore misinterpreted the evidence at his disposal.

From Malone to the present, Harvey's note has been crucial to the dating of Shakespeare's most famous work, but in fact it tells us nothing about the canonical *Hamlet*. As Gary Taylor recognized in 1987, all the evidence for dating the familiar, expanded *Hamlet* earlier than July 1602 "depends upon the assumption that Shakespeare himself did not write the [1589] *Hamlet*" and "upon the validity of the hypothesis of memorial reconstruction." In 1987, Taylor accepted both those assumptions, but even he has now abandoned them.[1] Both assumptions have become increasingly implausible, and without them the familiar play is not unquestionably identified, in any surviving document, until Nicholas Ling's publication of an "enlarged" *Hamlet* in late 1604.

It is unlikely that the Chamberlain's Men performed Shakespeare's expanded *Hamlet* before the autumn of 1598. A wide variety of stylistic evidence uniformly suggests that it postdates Shakespeare's other plays from the late 1590s (*Much Ado about Nothing*, *Henry V*, *Julius Caesar*, and *As You Like It*). Together, this evidence tends to confirm that what Hazlitt called "the Hamlet that we read of in our youth" represents an early-seventeenth-century revision of the play.[2] Historical considerations support the same conclusion. It's easy to understand why Francis Meres, in his 1598 list of 12 Shakespeare plays, might have omitted one that had been first performed almost a decade before, that in 1594 had worse box office takings than *Titus Andronicus* (which Meres did mention), and that Lodge mocked in 1596. For commercial reasons, the company may have stopped reviving it entirely, after 1596, and Shakespeare may have found it painful to perform, after the death of his son Hamnet [Hamlet], who was buried on 11 August 1596. But the silence of Meres would be much harder to explain if the company had been performing, in 1598, Shakespeare's new and improved version. Moreover, the 1604 edition adds an extended passage about supernatural omens—"In the most high and palmy state of Rome, / A little ere the mightiest Julius fell" (Q2 1.1.112–19)—clearly based on Plutarch's *Lives of the Noble Grecians and Romans.* Theoretically, Shakespeare might have written that passage at any time after the publication of Thomas North's translation in 1579. But *Julius Caesar* is his first demonstrable use of Plutarch, and scholars generally agree that *Caesar* was written in mid-1599.[3] Likewise, the 1623 edition adds a passage that, in the context of discussing the competition between adult acting companies performing on "common stages," refers to one of those stages as "Hercules and his load," apparently a reference to the Globe Theatre, erected in 1599 (F 2.2.359–60). Consequently, whether we regard the 1604 and 1623 editions as separate versions of the play, or as complementary but partial representations of a single version, neither seems likely to have been written until late 1599 at the very earliest. Finally, this conclusion is supported by the many excellent critics who have seen the traditional *Hamlet*, based upon a combination of the 1604 and 1623 editions, as a play written in the last years of Elizabeth I's reign.[4]

But in which of Elizabeth's last years? Again, the documentary evidence first cited by Malone and echoed by all subsequent scholars is unreliable. When James Roberts entered "The Revenge of Hamlet" in the Stationers' Register on 26 July 1602, he could have been referring to the earlier version of the play, printed the following year; the enlarged version, printed more than two years later, may or may not have existed yet. This means that our earliest certain documentary evidence for the existence of Shakespeare's revised version is Ling's 1604 quarto. All the material in the 1604 and 1623 editions might derive from a single Shakespearean manuscript, as champions of the conflated megatext have long assumed; but we must now say that Shakespeare could have written that omnibus manuscript version at any time between late 1599 and late 1604.[5] Alternatively, the 1604 and 1623 editions might represent two different acts of composition by Shakespeare, in which case the Folio version might, theoretically, have been written as late as mid-1608.[6] But it's equally possible, if we restrict ourselves to the documentary evidence, to imagine that the version first printed in 1623 was composed before the version first printed in 1604.

The preceding evidence puts the initial enlargement of *Hamlet* between late 1599 and the second half of 1604, a much wider range than traditional chronologies allow. In fact, stylistic evidence places the canonical *Hamlet* later than most scholars assume. Eliot Slater's rare vocabulary tests link it most strongly to the tragedies *Troilus and Cressida* (1602), *Othello* (1603–4), and *Lear* (1605) and to the comedy *Measure for Measure* (1603–4); Ants Oras's midline pause tests place it after *Troilus* and *Othello* (1603–4); its proportion of prose puts it most plausibly between *Troilus* and *Othello*; Taylor's colloquialism-in-verse test puts it later than *Troilus* and *Measure*; Barron Brainerd's sophisticated statistical data situated the revised version at about the time of the publication of Ling's "enlarged" quarto (1604–5).[7] Some of these tests may be more reliable than others; I don't claim to be an expert in statistical stylistics, but all these scholars were looking at the whole canon; none of them was pushing a particular theory about *Hamlet*. Their evidence is remarkably consistent in suggesting that the conventional date, "between late 1599 and early 1601," is too early.

Both later versions contain a passage not present in the first edition, which scholars since Malone have suspected may be relevant to the play's date: asked why "the tragedians of the city" are traveling, rather than performing in the metropolis, Rosencrantz replies, "I think their inhibition comes by the means of the late innovation" (Q2 2.2.295–6; F 2.2.330–1). The phrase "the late" does suggest a recent and particular event, and Malone thought that this passage referred to an order by the Privy Council on 22 June 1600: that order banned all but two outdoor London playhouses, and therefore required any other company of adult actors to make a living by traveling.[8] However, as other scholars have argued, in Shakespeare's work the word *innovation* always carried the obsolete, strong sense of "political change, revolution," in which case it might refer to the Essex rebellion of February 1601—or even the death of Queen Elizabeth in March 1603.[9] All these dates assume that "the late innovation" must refer to something in the real, historical, public world of Elizabethan England, and that assumption is by no means certain. The phrase "late innovation" is spoken not long after the unexpected death of King Hamlet, followed by his widow's unexpected marriage "within a month" (Q2 1.2.145) to her brother-in-law, whose ascension to the throne "popped in between th'election and [the] hopes" of the dead King's only son and heir apparent (Q2 5.2.64). That regime-change could certainly have been described and understood, in early modern England, as a "late innovation." The passage, like so many in Shakespeare, does not *have* to be interpreted as an allusion to the real world of the original London audience. But it certainly *could* have been intended and interpreted that way, especially because it occurs in an explicitly metatheatrical context, where the whole discussion of "the tragedians of the city" invites spectators to think about themselves in a theatre in present-tense London, rather than an imaginary medieval Denmark. Perhaps for that reason, Ann Thompson and Neil Taylor single out "the late innovation" as "the best internal evidence" for the date of the enlarged play.[10] Once we recognize that Harvey's note could refer to the earlier *Hamlet*, nothing prevents us from endorsing the view of the many critics who have seen in the revised, canonical *Hamlet* a series of reflections on the fall of the Earl of Essex. Shakespeare had apparently complimented Essex as "the general of our gracious Empress" in *Henry V*, and Essex's inner circle of supporters included the Earl of Southampton, to whom Shakespeare had dedicated *Venus and Adonis* and *Lucrece*.[11] This interpretation would push the date of a revised *Hamlet* to the spring of 1601 at the very earliest.

* * *

"The late innovation" occurs in all versions of the enlarged *Hamlet*. But do the 1604 and 1623 editions represent one revision (and one date), or two? If we look at passages unique to one of those two versions, the text first printed in 1623 actually looks earlier than the text first printed in 1604. The 1623 Folio is the only version of the play to contain a passage claiming that "Denmark's a prison," and that, among the world's "many confines, wards and dungeons, Denmark" is "one o'th' worst" (F 2.2.242–5). Queen Anne, the wife of King James I, was born and raised in Denmark, and after his accession to the English throne in March 1603 this passage would have been gratuitously insulting to the new Queen, and therefore politically dangerous. Would Shakespeare—usually so careful to avoid offending the reigning monarch—have written this passage after May 1603, when he officially became one of the liveried servants of the new King? That seems very unlikely. Combining "the late innovation" with "Denmark's a prison," we might reasonably conjecture that Shakespeare wrote the expanded Folio version of the play between March 1601 and March 1603.

Later in the same scene, the 1623 edition contains another long, unique passage, this one describing "an eyrie of children" who are "most tyrannically clapped for" (F 2.2.336–60). This must allude to the Children of the Chapel at the Blackfriars, who began performing no earlier than the end of September 1600. James P. Bednarz has pointed out that on 4 February 1604, the Children of the Chapel at Blackfriars became the Children of the Queen's Chapel; insulting them might be interpreted as an affront to their patron, Queen Anne.[12] Thus, both of these passages might be unique to the 1623 version because they were retrospectively censored, or self-censored, in the edition of *Hamlet* printed late in 1604.

Before I turn to the third passage unique to the Folio, I'd like to analyze the second one a little more closely. Gary Taylor, summarizing in 1987 a scholarly consensus that has never been challenged, observed that "in every significant structural respect Q1 is closer to F than to Q2; even at the level of verbal detail, the occasional agreements of Q1 with Q2 against F are all attributable to" normal errors and sophistications in transmission. For believers in memorial reconstruction, that meant that the 1603 and 1623 editions both reflected the play in performance. But Taylor acknowledged that, if we consider the 1623 Folio text without reference to assumptions about memorial reconstruction, then it shows no evidence of theatrical origins, and looks instead like "a late and apparently literary scribal transcript."[13] But what was it a transcript of? It must have derived from a manuscript closer to the 1603 edition than to the 1604 edition. Once we abandon theories of piracy, that textual proximity means that the 1623 text derives, at one or more removes, from a manuscript *closer to the original version of the play*. I will not repeat all the evidence here, but the passage about the "eyrie of children" is itself a typical example. The first edition contains the following exchange about "the tragedians of the city":

> HAMLET: How comes it that they travel? Do they grow resty?
> GILDERSTONE: No, my lord, their reputation holds as it was wont.
> HAMLET: How, then?
> GILDERSTONE: I'faith, my lord, novelty carries it away. For the principal public audience that came to them are turned to private plays, and to the humour of children.
> HAMLET: I do not greatly wonder at it, for those that would make mops and mows at my uncle when my father lived now give a hundred—two hundred—pounds for his picture.
> (Q1 7. 266–77)

I've discussed this passage in chapter 5, relating the 1603 text to the children's companies of the 1580s. Here, as in all versions of the scene, the fortunes of an older troupe of actors have been undermined, first and foremost, by theatrical "novelty," which prompts Hamlet to connect the volatility of theatrical fashion to the fickleness of political popularity. The 1623 edition builds on this logical framework, but enlarges it. (I italicize language that appears in the corresponding passage of the first edition.)

> HAMLET: *How* chances *it they travel?* Their residence, both in reputation and profit, was better both ways.
> ROSINCRANTZ: I think their inhibition comes by the means of the late innovation.

HAMLET: Do they hold the same estimation they did when I was in the city? Are they so followed?
ROSINCRANTZ: *No*, indeed, they are not.
HAMLET: *How comes it? Do they grow* rusty?
ROSINCRANTZ: Nay, *their* endeavour keeps in the *wont*ed pace. But there is, sir, an eyrie *of children*... [22 additional lines]...
ROSINCRANTZ: Ay, that they do, *my lord*—Hercules and his load too.
HAMLET: It is not strange, *for* mine *uncle* is King of Denmark, and *those that would make mows at* him when *my father lived* now *give* twenty, forty, an *hundred* ducats apiece *for his picture* in little.
(F 2.2.327–37, 359–64)

Reading the two texts in this order, one sees that the reference to "the late innovation" is superfluous, which (to my mind) increases the probability that it was added for its topical allusion to the Essex rebellion. In order to interpolate this new idea, the first version's "how comes it that" is initially varied to "how chances it" and then (after the additional material about "the late innovation") repeated as "how comes it?" followed by the original question "Do they grow resty/rusty?" (The variant in the final word might be intentional, or might be an easy misreading of one letter in one text or the other.) By contrast, the 1604 edition dispenses with these remnants of the 1603 text. Instead, it almost exactly reproduces the first four speeches of the Folio's expanded version, then skips to its conclusion. I italicize, here, the second quarto's differences from the 1623 text.

HAMLET: How chances it they travel? Their residence, both in reputation and profit, was better both ways.
ROSINCRANTZ: I think their inhibition comes by the means of the late innovation.
HAMLET: Do they hold the same estimation they did when I was in the city? Are they so followed?
ROSINCRANTZ: No, indeed, *are they* not. [26 Folio lines omitted]
HAMLET: It is not *very* strange, for *my* uncle is King of Denmark, and those that would make *mouths* at him while my father lived now give twenty, forty, *fifty, an* hundred ducats apiece for his picture in little.
(Q2 2.2.293–303)

The 1604 quarto is almost identical to the 1623 Folio, except that it lacks 26 lines (eight speeches) about the "eyrie of children"—which (as I've explained above) might have been removed out of deference to their patron, Queen Anne. All of the minor variants in wording between the two later versions might be authorial, but they need not be; they could easily be the result of simple mistakes by a scribe or a printing-house compositor in one text or the other. So, the text underlying the 1604 quarto looks to be later than the text underlying the Folio not only because of the possibility of retrospective censorship in the second quarto, but also because the second quarto here (and elsewhere) seems further from the original version.

There is only one other long passage unique to the 1623 edition, and that variant cannot be explained as a consequence of censorship. In the first edition, the last scene begins with six lines by Hamlet (17.1–6).

> Believe me, it grieves me much, Horatio,
> That to Leartes I forgot myself
> For by myself methinks I feel his grief
> Though there's a difference in each other's wrong.
> *Enter a braggart gentleman*
> Horatio, but mark yon water-fly:
> The court knows him but he knows not the court. (17.1–6)

In both the later versions, the scene begins with a long, added conversation between Hamlet and Horatio, first about Hamlet's aborted trip to England, and then about the wicked king who sent him there to be executed. In both versions, Hamlet then asks "Is't not perfect conscience?" (Q2 5.2.66; F 5.2.67). In the 1623 Folio text, he then continues,

> To quit him with this arm? And is't not to be damned
> To let this canker of our nature come
> In further evil?
> HORATIO It must be shortly known to him from England
> What is the issue of the business there.
> HAMLET It will be short. The interim's mine,
> And a man's life no more than to say one.
> But I am very sorry, good *Horatio*,
> *That to Laertes I forgot myself,*
> For by the image of my cause I see
> The portraiture of his. I'll count his favours;
> But sure the bravery of his grief did put me
> Into a towering passion.
> *Enter young Osricke.*
> HORATIO Peace, who comes here?

The first seven lines of this Folio-only material simply continue the larger addition at the beginning of the scene. The eighth line signals a change of subject with the added word "But" (necessary to create a transition from the added material to the material inherited from the original version). The Folio then rephrases the original first line of the scene ("it grieves me much" becoming "I am very sorry"). Then follow seven words exactly repeated from the first edition (indicated above by italics), and then another line and a half completely rewritten, but conveying the same kind of sympathy for Laertes expressed in the first edition. The Folio then adds two lines with a new idea ("I'll...passion"). After that, we return to the structure already present in the original: the braggart enters, and is commented upon before he speaks. In both texts, the first word after his entrance is "Horatio" (though in the 1603 edition that name is spoken, and in the 1623 edition it is an abbreviated speech prefix).[14]

By contrast, none of the material I have quoted above, in the 1603 and/or 1623 editions, is present at all in the 1604 edition—except for the word "Enter." Hamlet says "Is't not perfect conscience?" and is immediately interrupted by the entrance of a courtier, who immediately speaks. Jenkins, the most accomplished advocate of the old conflation hypothesis, admits that "The absence of these lines from Q2 is difficult to explain except as an accidental omission." But it is difficult to explain only because Jenkins assumes the memorial reconstruction hypothesis. If we don't make that assumption, there is a clear and intelligible development from the 1603 edition to the 1623 edition, and then a smart cut in the 1604 edition. The dramatic intelligibility of the result makes it unlikely to be an accident. Both Gary Taylor and Paul Werstine—who in other respects had and have completely different attitudes toward the text(s) of *Hamlet*—independently connected this unique cut in the 1604 edition to a unique addition in the same scene of that same edition. After the exit of the Braggart/Gentleman/Courtier with the news about the duel and wager, all three texts have a conversation between Hamlet and Horatio, which continues until the arrival of the court for the duel. In the 1603 and 1623 editions, that conversation is uninterrupted (Q1 17. 41–6; F 5.2.146–71). But after Hamlet says "the bubbles are out" (Q2 5.2.174; F 5.2.156), the 1604 edition alone adds a dozen lines (5.2.174.1–186):

> *Enter a Lord*
> LORD: My lord, his majesty commended him to you by young Osric, who brings back to him that you attend him in the hall. He sends to know if your pleasure hold to play with Laertes, or that you will take longer time.
> HAMLET: I am constant to my purposes. They follow the King's pleasure. If his fitness speaks, mine is ready. Now or whensoever, provided I be so able as now.

LORD: The King and Queen and all are coming down.
HAMLET: In happy time.
LORD: The Queen desires you to use some gentle entertainment to Laertes before you fall to play.
HAMLET: She well instructs me.

All editors since Lewis Theobald in 1733 have added "Exit Lord" after Hamlet's last speech here; certainly, the Lord does not speak again, and Hamlet and Horatio continue their confidential conversation, as before. In the 1623 text, Horatio's next line is "You will lose this wager, my lord" (F 5.2.157). In the 1604 text, he says only "You will lose, my lord" (Q2 5.2.187). After the Lord's interruption, the subject has already returned from mockery of Osric to the imminent duel itself, so it's no longer necessary to say "this wager."

Both Taylor and Werstine note that, in this material unique to the 1604 edition, Hamlet's courtesy toward Laertes after the entrance of the court is prompted by his mother's request, whereas in the passage unique to the 1623 edition that courtesy is prompted by his own chagrin ("That to Laertes I forgot myself"). The two versions of the expanded text thus give us two entirely different motivations for the crucial change in Hamlet's behavior to Laertes. For Werstine, this was just one of the rhetorical "narratives" that editors tell themselves, and all such narratives are fictions.[15] But Werstine's argument is as rhetorical as Taylor's, or mine; all language is rhetorical. And I see no way to avoid narratives. Time is part of the deep structure of our universe, and the copying of texts happens in time, and usually in sequence, and Shakespeare throughout his career was interested in providing his characters with motives for changes in their onstage behavior. For Taylor, this scene offered proof that "a coherent literary strategy unites some of the Folio's cuts to some of the Folio's additions."[16] But Taylor (like Philip Edwards and G. R. Hibbard) simply assumed that the absence of the Lord represents a Folio cut, rather than an addition in the 1604 text. Intrinsically, if we look solely at the 1604 and 1623 editions, there is no way to tell which is the cut and which the addition. But if we relate these variants to the first edition, then the vector of change should be apparent. In both cases, the 1623 text is demonstrably closer to the first edition. Since Pollard in 1909, mainstream textual criticism has assumed that the first edition is a "bad quarto," which postdates performances of the canonical play. But that assumption is no longer tenable. If, instead, the first edition represents Shakespeare's first version of the play, then the Folio is closer to that first version, and the second quarto is farther away.

Moreover, in two respects the material unique to the 1604 edition, here, fits into a larger pattern in the evolution of the play from the first version ("1589") to the canonical text. First, the 1603 and 1623 editions both give agency to Hamlet, but the text printed in 1604 shifts agency from Hamlet to his mother. Shakespeare's dramatization of the relationship between mother and son radically changes between the 1580s version and the seventeenth-century versions. In the original, Hamlet's interest in his mother's sexuality made sense, because she was a woman young enough to bear his uncle's child, and thereby permanently disinherit him. By contrast, in the expanded versions, the mother of a 30-year-old Hamlet is beyond childbearing age, and Claudius in the first scene announces that Hamlet is "most immediate to our throne" (Q2 1.2.109, F 1.2.107), and the Danish monarchy is elective (Q2 5.2.64, F 5.2.65). Hamlet's interest in his mother's sexuality thus, in the expanded version, seems obsessive, unbalanced, psychological rather than political, not a crucial strategic alliance but a distraction from his mission. The Lord unique to the 1604 edition takes that psychological emphasis even further, and therefore takes the play even further from its first version and its French source.

Secondly, the passage unique to the 1604 quarto, and the complementary passage unique to the Folio, are about more than the motivation for Hamlet's subsequent behavior toward Laertes. In fact, only 20 words in Q2 are dedicated to that topic (less than 20% of the unique material here). The immediate issue raised by the Lord's entrance and his first speech is, in fact, whether Hamlet will continue to delay: "He sends to know if... you will take longer time" (5.2.177–8). Hamlet's only long speech in this passage directly addresses that issue: "I am constant to my purposes... ready... now... now" (5.2.179–81). In the original version, Hamlet's youth is entirely sufficient to explain the brief time that elapses between learning of his father's murder and revenging it. But in the revised versions, a 30-year-old Hamlet cannot plead immaturity or insufficiency, and the gap between stimulus and response is greatly expanded, so that Hamlet's "delay" becomes a puzzle, a problem, an interesting psychological and ethical issue. The new material goes further than the Folio in addressing this change to the play and the character, by explicitly bringing it to closure: the Lord asks, are you going to delay any longer, and Hamlet finally answers, no.

Thus, the material unique to the second edition here in 5.2 can be directly related to other material unique to that edition, involving Hamlet's relationship to his mother and his delay. In the closet scene,

Hamlet berates his mother's inappropriately habitual sexuality in four extra passages:

> Sense, sure, you have—
> Else could you not have motion. But sure, that sense
> Is apoplexed, for madness would not err
> Nor sense to ecstasy was ne'er so thralled
> But it reserved some quantity of choice
> To serve in such a difference.
>
> (3.4.69–74)
>
> Eyes without feeling, feeling without sight,
> Ears without hands or eyes, smelling sans all,
> Or but a sickly part of one true sense
> Could not so mope.
>
> (3.4.76–9)
>
> That monster custom, who all sense doth eat
> Of habits devil, is angel yet in this,
> That to the use of actions fair and good
> He likewise gives a frock or livery
> That aptly is put on.
>
> (3.4.159–63)
>
> the next more easy,
> For use almost can change the stamp of nature
> And either shame the devil or throw him out
> With wondrous potency.
>
> (3.4.165–8)

In all four cases, the material occurs in the middle of speeches already expanded in both later editions; between the first and second passage above occurs a line and a half ("What devil was't / That thus hath cozened you at hoodman-blind?" (Q2 3.4.74–5; F 3.4.70–71) that differs only slightly from the first edition's "What devil thus hath cozened you at hobman-blind?" (Q1 11.39). The new material occurs in the middle of speeches, and it has sometimes been argued that this is evidence of theatrical cutting, because these lines could be omitted without changing anyone's cue (at the end of a speech).[17] But one could just as easily argue that Shakespeare knew that he could *add* material in the middle of speeches, without affecting anyone's cue. Besides, there is no consistent pattern in the second quarto or the Folio. The unique material between the entrance and exit of the Lord in 5.2 does affect a cue, and so do two other related passages of material unique to the second quarto: the end of Hamlet's long speech just before he sees the Ghost for the first time (Q2 1.4.17–38) and Hamlet's conversation with Fortinbras's Captain, followed by his final soliloquy, "How all occasions do inform against me?" (Q2 4.4.8–65). In the first example, the lines just before and after the additional passage are identical in the 1603 and 1623 editions; in the second, the original short scene of only five lines (spoken by Fortinbras) has been reworded and expanded in both the later editions, giving a short speech to the Captain (4.4.1–8), but only the second quarto gives the Captain more to say. In each case, the material unique to the 1604 text has been fundamental to Romantic and modern interpretations of Hamlet's delay: the first, for its long discussion of "the stamp of one defect" in "particular men" that "in the general censure take corruption / From that particular fault," the second for its acknowledgment that "I do not know / Why yet I live to say 'This thing's to do,'" and its diagnosis of possible explanations (including "some craven scruple / Of thinking too precisely on th'event").

My point here is simple, and I don't want to complicate it here by debating every possible explanation for every variant between the 1604 and 1623 editions. Throughout, the 1623 text is closer, structurally and verbally, to the 1603 text, which (I have argued) represents the original 1589 version of the play. The Folio contains only three extensive passages that are unique to it: two may be unique because they were retrospectively censored in 1603–4, and the third also may be a deliberate cut made in the manuscript behind the second quarto, because it seems to have been replaced by another passage in the same section of the same scene that is unique to that second quarto—and that second passage is related to other material unique to that quarto, which also takes that text further from the original version, in ways already apparent in passages shared by both later editions. The second quarto, in all these instances, seems to belong to the same vector of revision that transformed the 1589 play into the seventeenth-century play, but the second quarto seems further along that vector than the Folio.

Although the 1604 text contains many more unique passages of more than three lines, it is difficult to attribute any of that unique material to retrospective censorship of the 1623 text. The one speech occasionally cited as a possible example of political interference in the Folio is Hamlet's

> This heavy-headed revel east and west
> Makes us traduced and taxed of other nations.
> They clepe us drunkards, and with swinish phrase
> Soil our addition
>
> (Q2 1.4.17–20)

But unlike "Denmark's a prison...Denmark...one o'th' worst," these lines do not name Denmark, even once; nor do the preceding lines. Moreover, since the English were also stereotypically accused of drunkenness, without the word "Denmark" or "Dane" the lines were just as likely to be seen as a comment on England. There is nothing here as explicit or concise as "Denmark's a prison." And the allegedly offending lines constitute only a small part of the unique material here. So this unique 1604 passage is much less likely to be due to censorship, or self-censorship, than the two unique 1623 passages.

For most of the twentieth century, the 1604 edition of *Hamlet* was hailed as the quintessential example of a "good quarto" based on Shakespeare's own "foul papers." To anyone familiar with, or invested in, that claim, it will seem paradoxical or iconoclastic to conclude that the second quarto represents not the first step in the play's evolution, but the last. Nevertheless, the category "good quarto" (celebrating Ling's 1604 edition) always depended on its opposite, "bad quarto" (denigrating Ling's 1603 edition). The collapse of theories of piracy must, therefore, entail an unbiased reconsideration of the 1604 edition. Werstine has already, through his systematic examination of extant theatrical manuscripts, challenged the category "foul papers." Although both the 1603 and 1623 editions have been labeled "theatrical" in origin, in fact neither contains any of the features most confidently associated with playhouse texts. But, as Werstine notes, the 1604 edition does. In the duel between Hamlet and Laertes, when Hamlet scores "A hit, a very palpable hit," the second quarto alone has two marginal stage directions: "*Drum, trumpets and shot*" and "*Florish, a peece goes off*" (Q2 5.2.262; sig. N4v). These are different ways of saying the same thing. "Such duplications of sound and music calls are well recognized as features unique to theatrical [manuscripts]," Werstine observes; "This one indicates that Q2 *Hamlet* has picked up a [theatre] bookkeeper's annotation and has therefore...been printed from a playhouse [manuscript]."[18]

My only quarrel with Werstine's logic is his assumption that the 1604 edition must have been printed *directly* from a playhouse manuscript. It seems to me very unlikely that the King's Men would have entrusted their valuable, unique, licensed manuscript of a relatively recent and popular play to any printing house. What Werstine's evidence demonstrates, more precisely, is that the 1604 quarto *derives from* a playhouse manuscript. The duplication he correctly diagnoses might easily have been reproduced in a manuscript copy of the playbook, just as it was reproduced by a compositor in the printing shop of James Roberts. Anyone who examines Gary Taylor's monumental collation and analysis of the eight different texts of Middleton's *A Game at Chess* will see that even a professional playwright, copying his own work, can carelessly reproduce other people's mistakes, while at the same time casually introducing new verbal revisions of his own; in Middleton's case such carelessness is particularly evident as he got closer to the end of his own play.[19] It therefore seems to me far more likely that the 1604 quarto was printed, not from the playbook itself, but from a copy of that playbook.

And if the manuscript behind the 1604 edition was a copy of the playbook, then—unlike the playbook itself—it represented a text of the play *intended for readers*. It belongs to the history of Shakespeare's transformation into what Lukas Erne would call a "literary dramatist." It also represents, from my perspective, a perfect example of "dramatic intersections." The most theatrical of all texts, a licensed playbook owned by an acting company, was copied to produce a reading manuscript, which was then printed, circulated, and repeatedly reprinted for readers outside the playhouse—and eventually, decades later, became the basis for the so-called players' quartos of *Hamlet*, reflecting performances in the Restoration theatre.

If this analysis is correct, then the manuscript in the printing house of James Roberts in late 1604 represented a version of the text later than the Queen's patronage of the Children of the Chapel, beginning on 4 February 1604, and more generally probably later than the winter season of December 1603 to February 1604, when the King's Men first performed plays in their existing repertoire for the new royal couple. That is, the manuscript postdates the printing of Ling's 1603 edition. It could reflect changes made to the original playbook for the first Jacobean court season in winter 1603–4. But it could also reflect changes made by Shakespeare himself, if he personally prepared that copy of the playbook. In either case, this means that the enlarged *Hamlet* straddles the transition from Elizabeth I to James I. Unlike any other Shakespeare play, the canonical *Hamlet* is both Elizabethan and Jacobean.

We have no way of knowing whether the material unique to the 1604 edition was ever performed by the King's Men, or was instead added by Shakespeare specifically for publication. We have no way of *knowing* whether Shakespeare personally delivered the manuscript to Ling, or whether the King's Men endorsed the second edition. But notably and unusually, the acting company is not credited on the title page of the 1604 edition, which makes no claims about performance anywhere. Perhaps here, perhaps for the first time, Shakespeare followed Ben Jonson's lead, sending to the press a text that included more material than had ever been played.

We can approach this question from another angle. Why would Ling agree to publish the enlarged version? The first explanation must be that the first edition had already sold out, within a year or less. That meant his monopoly ownership of the right to publish *Hamlet* had proven itself to be a valuable intellectual property. Ling therefore had an obvious incentive to publish a reprint. But why an enlarged reprint? Any reprint would have lower overheads than the first edition, because Ling did not have to pay again for licensing. But if he paid, again, full price for a new manuscript of the play, he would be increasing his overheads, and thereby diminishing his profit margin. We might therefore speculate that Ling paid less for the enlarged manuscript than he paid for the original that he had published in 1603. After all, because Ling owned the copyright, that enlarged manuscript could not easily or legally be sold to any other stationer. Ling was the only legal market for that manuscript, and he could therefore afford to drive a hard bargain. And who would be willing to hand over such a manuscript for less, or nothing? Only someone with an exceptionally strong desire to see the enlarged version in print—who also had easy access to the playbook, and could copy it. The King's Men are not mentioned on the 1604 title page, and it is not self-evident that they would have wanted the enlarged version in print, or wanted it so much that they would cut Ling a discount. The person most likely to have satisfied those conditions, of access and motive, was Shakespeare himself. And if Ling was not willing to pay much, or anything, for the new manuscript, then Shakespeare may not have wanted to pay for a professional scribe to copy it. The cheapest way to get a new manuscript to Ling would have been for Shakespeare himself to copy the playbook.

We can say, with considerable confidence, that the 1604 edition represents the terminus of an evolution that began late in 1588, or early in 1589. But my story about how Ling acquired the manuscript is, necessarily, speculative. It assumes, for starters, that the enlarged version of *Hamlet* was unusually important to Shakespeare, personally. Why might that be?

* * *

Shakespeare's final changes to *Hamlet* may date from as late as autumn 1604. But can we establish an earlier date, a date when the enlarged version was first performed, in something resembling the text printed in 1623? What prompted Shakespeare, and the Chamberlain's Men, to revise a play from the distant 1580s?

To answer that question, we can first return to the passage on the "eyrie of children." Most scholars agree that this passage belongs to a period of explicit rivalry between acting companies and their playwrights that has been called "the War of the Theatres," "Poetomachia," or "the Poets' War." Jenkins observed that the phrase "the common stages (as they call them)" quotes Ben Jonson's *Cynthia's Revels* (performed at the Blackfriars in the winter of 1600–1), and James P. Bednarz plausibly argues that the whole passage was written after Ben Jonson's *Poetaster* (also performed at the Blackfriars).[20] The most recent scholarship on the date of *Poetaster* places its first performances in the autumn or winter of 1601.[21] Dekker's quick response to Jonson's second satire, the "Horace" scenes in *Satiromastix*, was performed both by Paul's Boys and the Chamberlain's Men; it was entered in the Stationers' Register on 11 November 1601, but the entry was conditional on approval by the censor.[22] It is therefore possible that Dekker was required to alter the text before it was published (in a quarto dated "1602"), and that the printed text therefore contains more, or different, material mocking *Poetaster* than did the original performances. But from our perspective the most important point is that the latest scholarship on Jonson suggests that this passage in the 1623 text of *Hamlet* cannot have been written earlier than the autumn of 1601. Most editors, including Jenkins, have accepted this evidence, but have assumed that the passage was a later, theatrical addition to the play. But that assumption depends on the usual fantasies about textual piracy. If the 1623 edition derives, instead, from Shakespeare's first expansion of *Hamlet,* then that expansion could not have begun before late 1601.

However, there is another way to look at this evidence linking *Hamlet* to the "throwing about of brains" in the poetomachia of 1600 and 1601, and in relation to the rebellion and execution of Essex in early 1601. Both these events have also been used to date *Troilus and Cressida*. David Bevington, an accomplished, cautious, veteran scholar-editor well known for his mainstream views, in the 2001 Arden edition synthesizes and refines the evidence of many earlier scholars to conclude that the Essex rebellion and the poetomachia are two central elements of the "immediate historical environment" of *Troilus*. Like others, he links the play's experimental satirical mode to the plays of Jonson, Marston, Chapman, and Dekker in 1599–1601; he connects its portrayal of Achilles to contemporary comparisons of Essex to Achilles; he relates Thersites to Marston; he argues that the play responds to Jonson's *Cynthia's Revels*, and that the Prologue (probably written after the rest of the play was completed) responds to Jonson's *Poetaster*. Shakespeare's portrayal of Ajax, in particular, is the "purge" that, according to *The Return from Parnassus, Part Two* in the Christmas season of 1601–2, Shakespeare gave to Ben Jonson ("Our fellow Shakespeare puts them all down, ay, and Jonson... Our fellow Shakespeare hath given him a purge that made him beray his credit"). Bevington concludes that Shakespeare may have begun *Troilus* as early as mid-1601, and probably completed it by late 1601.[23]

It's unlikely that Shakespeare finished both *Troilus* and the enlarged *Hamlet* simultaneously. So which is likely to be earlier? Undoubtedly, the Essex rebellion and the theatrical rivalries of 1600–1 are much more important to the entire structure and tone of *Troilus* than of *Hamlet*, and the "armed Prologue" calls attention to those connections before the play even begins. By contrast, the brief allusion to the "eyrie of children" in the middle of Folio *Hamlet* is, demonstrably, dispensable, and it repeatedly uses the past tense: "there *has been* much to do on both sides... There was *for a while... went* to cuffs... there *has been* much throwing about of brains" (F 2.2.350–57). The tone here, and the acknowledgment of action from both sides, resembles in some respects Jonson's retrospective "Apologetical Dialogue" (appended to the 1602 edition of *Poetaster*). Moreover, the stylistic evidence, as I have already noted, strongly suggests that the canonical *Hamlet* is later than *Troilus*—even though the enlarged *Hamlet* is based on a much earlier play, and retains a significant fraction of that older language. In the absence of any other evidence, we would have to assume that *Troilus* is the earlier play. So if *Troilus* was written in the second half of 1601, then the revision and expansion of *Hamlet* cannot have happened until early in 1602.

The significant historical events that seem to have stimulated *Troilus* began in late 1599 with Jonson's *Every Man Out of his Humour*, continuing through 1600 and the first months of 1601. The event that seems to have most profoundly affected Shakespeare's imagination, in revising *Hamlet*, happened later in 1601. His father was buried in Holy Trinity Church in Stratford-upon-Avon on 8 September. If Shakespeare had written *Hamlet* in 1600, this would simply be an ironic coincidence. But since we now have reason to believe that he revised and expanded the play no earlier than late 1601, it is difficult not to connect one event with the other. It might seem that any version of the story of Amleth or Hamlet would necessarily be preoccupied with the death of fathers. But the phrase "father's death" occurs only once in the first edition: the King, talking about the threat posed by Leartes, refers to "his father's death" (Sc. 13.12). By contrast, the phrase appears eight times in the revised *Hamlet*, far more than in any other work by Shakespeare, and from the first scene to the last. *Hamlet* alone contains 44 percent of the examples in the whole canon. No other Shakespeare play or poem uses the phrase more than once of the death of an adult's father; all eight examples in the canonical *Hamlet* involve the grief of an adult child, and seven the grief of an adult son—more than in all the rest of his work combined.[24] Both Claudius and Gertrude attribute "Hamlet's transformation," his madness, and his melancholy, to "his father's death" (2.2.8, 57); Hamlet himself speaks of "my father's death" (3.2.73); the madness of Ophelia "springs All from her father's death" (4.5.75–6); the rebellion of Laertes is attributed to "his father's death" (4.5.91); Claudius manipulates Laertes by referring repeatedly to "your father's death" (F 4.5.139) and "your dear father's death" (4.5.148); Laertes just before his own death forgives Hamlet for "my father's death" (5.2.314). Each example can be justified in context, but comparison with the first edition makes it clear that the repetition of the phrase is not necessary to the play, narratively or theatrically, and comparison with the rest of the Shakespeare canon demonstrates that the number of occurrences here is wildly anomalous. The death of John Shakespeare is the only obvious explanation for the sharp spike in Shakespeare's uses of this phrase.

But although the one phrase is striking, many other additions and changes to the "enlarged" play reflect a similar emphasis. In 4.7, the word "father" occurs seven times: "your noble father" (4.7.4) "so have I a noble father lost" (26), "I loved your father" (35), "was your father dear to you?" (105), "not that I think you did not love your father" (108), "To show yourself your father's son in deed More than in words?" (123–4), "requite him for your father" (137). In the equivalent episode in the 1603 edition (Sc. 15), the word does not appear at all. Before we see Ophelia mad, we hear that "she speaks much of her father" (4.5.4), and after he sees her Claudio attributes her madness to "conceit upon her father" (4.5.45). Both these speeches are unique to the expanded version.

The revised play's expanded emphasis on dead fathers begins in the very first scene. Speaking of Fortinbras, Horatio refers to "those foresaid lands, So by his father lost" (1.1.102–3), a theme echoed by Claudius in his first speech: "those lands Lost by his father" (1.2.23–4). Shakespeare's own father in the later 1570s lost much of the wealth and status that he had enjoyed when Shakespeare was a boy; in particular, John Shakespeare made his last property purchase in 1575, but in 1579 he was forced to raise money by mortgaging a house and 56 acres, which he then lost when he could not repay the mortgage—and never recovered, despite years of futile and expensive lawsuits.[25]

Gertrude's first speech to her son tells him, "Do not for ever with thy vailed lids / Seek for thy noble father in the dust" (1.2.70–71). That speech does not appear at all in the original version of the play, and it precedes two radically changed and expanded speeches by her son and her new husband. In the 1603 edition, Hamlet creates a dramatic sense of inward "sorrow" based on a simple contrast with "outward semblance," but does so in conventional terms.

> My lord, 'tis not the sable suit I wear,
> No, nor the tears that still stand in my eyes,
> Nor the distracted haviour in the visage,
> Nor all together mixed with outward semblance,
> Is equal to the sorrow of my heart.
> Him I have lost I must of force forgo,
> These but the ornaments and suits of woe. (2.33–9)

In the later texts, this speech is not just longer, better poetry. It is also more complex: not only explicitly metatheatrical from start to finish, but angry, in the way grief often is, and addressed to his mother, not his uncle. I've italicized, below, the few words retained from the first version.

> "Seems," madam? Nay, it is, I know not "seems."
> *'Tis not* alone my inky cloak, cold mother,
> Nor customary suits of solemn black,
> Nor windy suspiration of forced breath,
> No, *nor the* fruitful river *in* the eye,
> *Nor the* dejected *haviour* of *the visage*,
> *Together with* all forms, moods, shapes of grief,
> That can denote me truly. These indeed "seem,"
> For they are actions that a man might play,
> But I have that within which passes show,
> *These but the* trappings *and* the *suits of woe*. (1.2.76–86)

Theories of memorial reconstruction, or note-taking, must assume that an actor backstage, or a spectator in the audience, remembered "suits of woe" but, otherwise, only 15 ordinary words from this famous, remarkable speech. It's much easier to understand the differences, here, as the result of the maturing of Shakespeare's poetic and dramatic art, over more than a decade. And Shakespeare himself would have been expected, after his father's death, to wear mourning for up to a year.[26] Beginning in September 1601, he would have personally inhabited the "inky cloak" of an adult son grieving for his father. But that grieving son was also a professional player, an actor who may well have worn such "suits of woe" on stage, from time to time, performing "shapes of grief" that were merely played. More than most grieving sons, more than most actors, Shakespeare in the months after September 1601 would have *lived* what these lines describe.

In all versions of the play, Hamlet's speech is answered by one from the king. In the first version, the response is the same length as the stimulus, rhetorically and dramatically just as effective, and also equally conventional and generalized.

> This shows a loving care in you, son Hamlet,
> But you must think your father lost a father,
> That father dead lost his, and so shall be
> Until the general ending. Therefore cease laments,
> It is a fault 'gainst heaven, fault 'gainst the dead,
> A fault 'gainst nature, and in reason's common course most certain
> None lives on earth but he is born to die. (1.40–47)

In the later texts, the reply is not only much longer, and much more attentive to the particularity of grief; it keeps the original triple repetition of "father," then doubles it, developing a uniquely dense and complicated echoing and exploration of real and surrogate fatherhood and of the limits of "filial obligation." Again, I've italicized words retained from the 1603 edition.

> 'Tis sweet and commendable in your nature, *Hamlet*,
> To give these mourning duties to your father.
> *But you must* know *your father lost a father*,
> *That father* lost *lost his*, and the survivor bound
> In filial obligation for some term
> To do obsequious sorrow, but to persever
> In obstinate condolement is a course
> Of impious stubbornness, 'tis unmanly grief,
> It shows a will most incorrect to heaven,
> An understanding simple and unschooled,
> For what we know must be, and is as common
> As any the most vulgar thing to sense—
> Why should we in our peevish opposition
> Take it to heart? Fie, 'tis *a fault* to *heaven*,
> A *fault against the dead*, *a fault* to *nature*,
> To *reason* most absurd, whose common theme

Is death of fathers, and who still hath cried
From the first corpse till he that died today
"This must be so." We pray you throw to earth
This unprevailing woe, and think of us
As of a father, for let the world take note
You are the most immediate to our throne,
And with no less nobility of love
Than that which dearest father bears his son
Do I impart toward you.
                                                        (1.2.87–112)

The original "think" becomes "know": Shakespeare by the end of 1601 knew something about grief that he could only have read about and imagined in 1589. He knew that a person cannot be talked out of grief, and that a father cannot be replaced by a surrogate. Moreover, Shakespeare was 35 years old when his father died. The Hamlet of the revised play is not a boy but a man, and his grief can be condemned as "unmanly." This opens up an issue about the protagonist that has echoed down the critical and theatrical history of the canonical version; Sarah Siddons, Sarah Bernhardt, Asta Nielsen, Frances de la Tour, and other actresses have convincingly played the role, precisely because the irresolution of a 30-year-old son in an important way effeminizes him.

This passage makes it clear that the expanded play's intensified focus on the death of fathers coincides with a new understanding of the position of "the survivor." Margreta de Grazia has argued that we should abandon the Romantic and modernist focus on the psychology of the protagonist, and realize that the canonical *Hamlet* is a play about the transfer of property, and particularly of land, between men.[27] When John Shakespeare died, his son William did not inherit "those lands lost by his father," and he may have been particularly reminded of his father's losses in the autumn of 1601, when he had to pay attention to the particulars of the estate. But as the eldest son, William did inherit two houses in Stratford-upon-Avon; within the month, he acquired a parcel of land across from his gardens on the far side of Chapel Lane; on 1 May 1602, he bought 107 acres in "Old Stratford."[28] As a new historicist, de Grazia situates *Hamlet* within broad cultural patterns of patrilineal inheritance and the relationship of persons to land; she is not interested in biographical trivialities. But from September 1601 to May 1602 a biological person named William Shakespeare was more concerned with the inheritance and purchase of landed property than at any other time in his life. He bought nothing between 1596 and late 1601. For anyone interested in determining when Shakespeare the playwright was writing a play centrally concerned with losses and transfers of landed property, the activities of Shakespeare the landowner seem significant.

At the moment when he inherited those two houses in Stratford-upon-Avon, he also acquired a new, and perhaps newly uncomfortable, relationship to his mother. With his father's death William became the family patriarch, the oldest surviving male on either his father's or his mother's side of the family.[29] His mother, a new widow, was now legally dependent upon him. What, in 1589, may have been only an inherited story about an adolescent boy's relationship to his bereaved mother became, in September 1601, the lived relationship of a 30-something son and heir with his bereaved mother. Mary Arden Shakespeare was, by that point, in her mid-sixties: not the young widow required by Saxo Grammaticus, Belleforest, or the 1589 version of *Hamlet*, but something like the "dignified Empress" usually found in performances of Shakespeare's canonical seventeenth-century play.

Finally, the burial of Shakespeare's father must have unavoidably revived memories of the burial of his 11-year-old son Hamnet/Hamlet, in the same place, at the end of another summer, five years before. Malone originally conjectured that Shakespeare's *Hamlet* was written in 1596, the same year as the death of his son. We now know that's impossible; neither the original, nor the revision, can have been written in or shortly after that year (though Shakespeare might have written, at about that time, the additions to *The Spanish Tragedy*, about the grief of a father for his dead son). But Shakespeare in autumn 1601 would again have put on "the trappings and the suits of woe" for the death of the male relative closest to him in the patrilineal system: having lost his only male descendant in 1596, he lost his only male ancestor in 1601. This personal echoing of deaths, of fathers and sons, might well have prompted Shakespeare to think again about his old *Hamlet* play, which he could now approach from the personal experience of the grieving son *and* the grieving father.

In this context, it may be more than a coincidence that the Ghost in *Hamlet* is the only role in his own plays that we have any evidence that Shakespeare performed. That claim was reported by Nicholas Rowe in the first biography of Shakespeare, published in 1709; it probably came to him from Thomas Betterton, who played Hamlet for 50 years, and had allegedly been coached in the early 1660s by William Davenant, Shakespeare's godson, who had seen Joseph Taylor perform the title role; Taylor was a significant professional actor by 1610, a year in which he also had dealings with John Heminges, one of the leaders of the King's Men, and coauthor of the preface and dedication to the 1623 collection. Because the evidence for this bit of casting was published more than a century after the canonical *Hamlet* was written, it may not be reliable, but I am inclined to trust the chain of theatrical gossip from Taylor, Heminges, and Davenant to Betterton and Rowe.[30] But we can also now add two addenda to Rowe's claim. First, it seems unlikely that a 25-year-old Shakespeare would have played the Ghost in 1589. There must have been older and more experienced actors, better suited to the original role. But the canonical text, although it changes the age of Hamlet, his mother, and Ophelia, does not change the description of the Ghost as a warrior, still in armor, with a middle-aged "sable silvered" beard. By late 1601 or early 1602, the actor who had first cried "Hamlet, revenge!" at the Theatre may have died, or retired from acting, and Shakespeare would himself have been old enough, experienced enough, and important enough to the company, to play that role.

Second, Stephen Greenblatt has set the canonical play's invocations of purgatory within the larger context of the Reformation's radical change to religious practices concerning the dead, and to shifting generational attitudes toward that Catholic inheritance. Greenblatt accepts the evidence that John Shakespeare remained Catholic throughout his life, and imagines that, in writing *Hamlet*, "the Protestant playwright was haunted by the spirit of his Catholic father pleading for suffrages to relieve his soul from the pains of Purgatory."[31] I am persuaded by the considerable historical evidence for lingering Catholicism in Warwickshire (especially within the generation that preceded Shakespeare), for the Catholicism of Shakespeare's parents and teachers, and for a recurrent sympathy for some Catholic positions in Shakespeare's plays.[32] I share Greenblatt's conviction that *Hamlet* was "shaped by [Shakespeare's] experience of the world and of his own inner life: his skepticism, his pain, his sense of broken rituals, his refusal of easy consolations."[33] But Greenblatt's biographical argument only makes sense if the canonical *Hamlet* postdates the death of John Shakespeare. Moreover, the strongest evidence for his interpretation of the Ghost/father is the lament that he died "Unhouseled, disappointed, unaneled" (1.5.77), an explicit reference to the Catholic sacrament of extreme unction—which does not appear in the first version of the play. At the other end of the play, Greenblatt's reading of the son's death depends on Horatio's "flights of angels sing thee to thy rest" (5.2.344), which seems to invoke common depictions of angels ferrying souls to purgatory—and which also does not appear in the original version of the play.[34] That is, the canonical play seems to imagine both the dead father and the dead son Hamlet in purgatory. By late 1601, Shakespeare would have had strong personal reasons to add these lines to the original play.

Many scholars are perfectly comfortable with seeking, or acknowledging, dramatic intersections between Shakespeare's plays and the political, social, or intellectual history of his times, but uncomfortable with seeing such intersections between his work and his own life. I would say that the death of his father, of his only surviving male ancestor, was an event in the world outside the theatre that impacted Shakespeare much more directly than the fall of Essex or the formation of the East India corporation.[35] His father's death may, indeed, be the most important "source" for the canonical version of Shakespeare's *Hamlet*, because it was an event that could understandably have prompted him to return to, and revise, the old play.

The personal crisis of his father's death also coincided with an artistic crisis. After the forced retirement of John Lyly from the children's companies in 1590, after the deaths of Robert Greene and Thomas Watson in the autumn of 1592, after the murder of Marlowe in May 1593 and the crippling career-ending interrogation of Thomas Kyd soon after, Shakespeare became more and more prominent among playwrights; as a writer at the intersection of literature and theatre, he had no serious rivals on the London stage from 1594 to 1598. Late in 1598 and then again in 1599, the huge success of Jonson's *Every Man in his Humour* and *Every Man out of His Humour,* performed by Shakespeare's own company, signaled the rise of his first artistically significant rival from a younger generational cohort. Moreover, Jonson was as aggressive as Shakespeare had been, a decade before: *Every Man Out*, published in three editions in 1600 (more than any Shakespeare play had achieved in print), explicitly mocked Shakespeare's newest tragedy, *Julius Caesar*, in much the same way that Nashe and Lodge had mocked Shakespeare's first tragedy, the original *Hamlet*. The polemical "poet's war" of 1600, and the return of the boy companies, further challenged Shakespeare's dominant position. To make matters worse, Shakespeare's response to Jonson, *Troilus and Cressida*, seems to have been his least successful play in more than a decade. The preface in the second issue of the 1609 edition of *Troilus* claims that it was "never clapper-clawed by the palms of the vulgar." E. A. J. Honigmann explains this statement by arguing that the play was never performed, having been refused a license because of censorial sensitivity over its apparent links to the fall of Essex.[36] Other scholars have argued that the play was performed only once, at the Inns of Court. But even editors and critics who postulate that the play was performed at the Globe must concede that there is no evidence of theatrical popularity, then or in the following three centuries. The play has been much admired and performed since the 1960s, but it remains "caviare to the general." Whether politically or theatrically, Shakespeare's experiment in "satyrical comedy" or "satyrical tragedy" seems to have misfired, at the very moment when he was being powerfully challenged by an aggressive, ambitious new generation of playwrights and acting companies.

Shakespeare's first *Hamlet* had been, among other things, an artistic manifesto, written by a new playwright situating himself in a contested field. More than any other play before 1599, it directly dramatizes the new profession of commercial theatre and stages the critical debates about acting styles and dramatic form. It makes sense for him to have returned to it in 1602, as a playwright whose authority was being newly contested by younger writers and new dramatic modes. After the classical *Julius Caesar* and *Troilus and Cressida*, the revived *Tragical History of Hamlet, Prince of Denmark* represented a return to his roots in tragedies (like *Romeo and Juliet*) based upon continental fiction, and in history plays concerned with the politics of succession. No one could compete with him in those genres. But Shakespeare, having in the interim acquired a greater command of Seneca and added Plutarch, also beefed up the Latin credentials of the new version. The original player's speech from "Aeneas tale to Dido" had alluded to Marlowe and Nashe's *Dido, Queen of Carthage*, and more generally to the 1580s vogue for plays based on classical mythology; now, expanded, it could challenge Jonson's self-branding neoclassicism, situating Shakespeare as Vergil to Jonson's Horace. Because the threat of the boy companies had returned, Shakespeare further developed the original brief allusion to them. But he also, more powerfully, expanded and complicated the play's central role, giving the older Burbage a vehicle that demonstrated, irrefutably, that Burbage and Shakespeare together could do what the children and "their writers" could not (and never would). The metatheatrical material that appears for the first time in the enlarged versions includes a specific allusion to Jonson ("The humorous man shall end his part in peace"), but also refines and redefines Shakespeare's earlier self-definition.

> no matter in the phrase that might indict the author of affectation (2.2.380–1)
>
> by very much more handsome than fine (2.2.382–3)
>
> and good discretion (2.2.405)
>
> in the very torrent, tempest and, as I may say, whirlwind of your passion, you must acquire and beget a temperance that may give it smoothness (3.1.5–8)
>
> be not too tame either, but let your own discretion be your tutor. Suit the action to the world, the word to the action, with this special

observance—that you o'erstep not the modesty of nature. For anything so o'erdone is from the purpose of playing whose end, both at the first and now, was and is to hold as 'twere the mirror up to Nature, to show Virtue her feature, Scorn her own image, and the very age and body of the time his form and pressure. Now this overdone, or come tardy off, though it makes the unskilful laugh, cannot but make the judicious grieve, the censure of which one must in your allowance o'erweigh a whole theatre of others. (3.1.16–28)

These passages, and especially the last, are now often cited as universal aesthetic truths. But all this new material discriminates Shakespeare and his veteran fellow actors from the humoral caricatures of Jonson, the affected extremity of Marston, and more generally from the parodic exaggerations and "Scorn" of the boy companies. *Hamlet* was Shakespeare's first aesthetic manifesto, and also his second.

The revised *Hamlet* succeeded, where *Troilus* had not. It initiated the run of unsurpassed masterpieces canonized by A. C. Bradley's *Shakespearean Tragedy*: first *Hamlet* (1602), then *Othello* (1603–4), *Lear* (1605), and *Macbeth* (1606)—to which I would add *Antony and Cleopatra* (1607) and *Coriolanus* (1608). We no longer need to imagine, or explain, a gap of three or four years between *Hamlet* and the run of great Jacobean tragedies. Whether we interpret this artistic explosion in terms of a preoccupation with mortality precipitated by his father's death, or in terms of an aesthetic decision to concentrate on a genre where he and Burbage could crush their theatrical rivals, the revised *Hamlet* represents the beginning of a decisive aesthetic turn in Shakespeare's career. Recognizing that the 1589 *Hamlet* was Shakespeare's, and that its text is preserved in the 1603 first edition, also enables us to recognize the canonical *Hamlet*, the one that transformed literary and theatrical history, as a version that dates from 1602.

That redating of the *Hamlet* we all know also, finally, may explain why James Roberts entered *Hamlet* in the Stationers' Register on 26 July 1602. By then, the Chamberlain's Men probably had an entirely new *Hamlet* in their hands, and perhaps on their boards. They might as well make some money, and get some publicity, by selling the old, old-fashioned, 1589 *Hamlet* to a stationer. James Roberts was the stationer they knew best. He bought the 1589 version, and later sold it to Ling, who published it in 1603. The date that best accounts for the biographical and historical context of the traditional *Hamlet* also best accounts for the bibliographical one.

Epilogue: Conclusions and Rebeginnings

"Tell My Story"

At the beginning of this book I asked four simple questions. It's time now to return to them, and summarize the simple answers that are suggested by all the detailed intervening analysis. But I will reverse the original order of the questions, moving now from the easiest to the most complex.

Why is Hamlet much younger in the first edition than in the other two? Because the first edition was closer to the play's French source, which called for an adolescent prince, which made sense of the play's politics and its revenge narrative. Shakespeare, a young writer, wrote it for a young actor, Richard Burbage, in 1589. The later editions represent a revision of the play, 13 years later, when Burbage and Shakespeare were both older. This change coincided with a major reimagining of the play's political and psychological narrative.

Why was a play called *Hamlet* repeatedly performed in and around London between 11 June 1594, and 24 January 1637, always by the same acting company? Because that company, which was founded in 1594, inherited that play from an earlier company to which one or more of its members had belonged. Burbage was certainly one of those founding members, and Shakespeare probably was, too; they brought with them the 1589 play. Both Burbage and Shakespeare remained with the company until their deaths, and no one else ever had a claim to ownership of any text of *Hamlet*.

Why were the first two versions of *Hamlet* published by one publishing house, and the third by its successor? Because the first edition was not a piracy. For more than two centuries, no one challenged its legitimacy or Nicholas Ling's ownership of the rights to print the play. Ling could therefore publish an expanded edition in 1604, and could pass his intellectual property rights onto John Smethwicke, who as a member of the Folio syndicate in 1623 acquired rights to the third version of the play, apparently supplied at that time by the acting company.

Why were three radically different versions of *Hamlet* published between 1603 and 1623? Because Shakespeare revised the play twice. The first, most radical revision took place in 1602, 13 years after the original version had been staged; it is best represented by the 1623 Folio text. The second revision took place, apparently, in 1604, and unlike the first revision it may have been purely literary; it is best represented by the 1604 quarto text.

And why have these simple answers not been obvious to everyone? Because the first edition was lost during the two centuries when Shakespeare and *Hamlet* were canonized. The first edition simply did not fit those entrenched, inherited ideas about Shakespeare's development, or about the literary and theatrical interpretation of *Hamlet*. Its Shakespeare "was not yet sounding like 'Shakespeare,'" and its Hamlet was not "the Hamlet that we read of in our youth."[1]

The first *Hamlet,* the one mentioned by Thomas Nashe in 1589, is often called the "ur-*Hamlet.*" That Germanic idiom implicitly compares the 1589 play to the "*Urfaust,*" a version of Goethe's masterpiece that he worked on between 1772 and 1775, when he was in his midtwenties. The original manuscript is lost, but a copy was rediscovered in 1886. Goethe continued to work on *Faust* for another 50 years; *Part One* was published in 1808, but he continued to revise it until the edition of 1828–9, and *Part Two* was not published until after his death in 1832. *Faust* is the central masterpiece of the most canonical of German writers, and *Hamlet* is the central masterpiece of the most canonical of English writers, and the first version of both works was lost for more than a century. Like *Faust*—as I hope you are now persuaded—*Hamlet* was repeatedly revised by its author. As *Faust* matured with Goethe, *Hamlet* matured with Shakespeare. It matters so much to us, in part, because it mattered so much to him.

Curiously, Goethe's interest in *Hamlet* lasted almost as long as his interest in *Faust*. His first great success, *The Sorrows of Young Werther* (1774), diagnosed Hamlet as a man "without the strength of nerve that makes a hero," burdened by "his thoughts"; he described the play as a representation of "the effects of a great action laid upon a soul unfit for the performance of it... There is an oak-tree planted in a costly jar, which should have borne only pleasant flowers in its bosom; the roots expand, the jar is shivered." Later in the novel, Goethe concluded that "there are few who at once have Thought and the capacity of Action.

Thought expands, but lames: Action animates, but narrows."[2] This is a classic Romantic view of the canonical version, later more fully articulated by Schiller and Coleridge. More than half a century later, in 1827, Goethe wrote a short essay about the "First Edition of *Hamlet*"—the version of the play that Ling published in 1603, which had been reprinted in Germany in 1825, shortly after Ling's first quarto was rediscovered and reprinted in London.[3]

> In this book Shakespeare's devoted admirers receive a valuable present. The first unbiased reading has given me a wonderful impression. It was the old familiar masterpiece again, its action and movement in no way altered, but the most powerful and effective principal passages left untouched, just as they came from the original hand of the genius. The play was exceedingly easy and delightful to read. One thought one's self in a wholly familiar world, and yet felt something peculiar which could not be expressed...

Like everyone else, Goethe knew and loved the enlarged, revised version of "the old familiar masterpiece" long before he encountered the first edition. Nevertheless, unlike most twentieth-century textual scholars, the great poet was capable of an "unbiased reading." He recognized that the basic structure of the play remained the same ("a wholly familiar world"), and that the most important aspects of its story and the characters persisted from "the original" to all later texts. Goethe also demonstrated that he could imaginatively reverse the vector of his own experience, reading forward from the first edition (which he has just encountered) to the later editions (which he had known for decades).

> Passages, which in the first version are only lightly sketched by the hand of genius, we find more deliberately executed, and in a way that we have to approve and admire as necessary. We come too upon pleasing amplifications, which may not be absolutely necessary, but which are highly welcome. Here and there we find hardly perceptible yet vivid aspersions, connective passages, even important transpositions to make a highly effective speech—everything done with a master-hand with intelligence and feeling, everything thrilling our emotions and clarifying our insight.

By this point in his life, Goethe was one of the most admired European intellectuals of his time. But he did not despise the 1603 edition. He did not dismiss it as "*Hamlet* by Dogberry," or the work of a "hack poet," or a symptom of the debasement suffered by art whenever it enters the theatre. Instead, Goethe read it, and admired it, as a work of literature.

> Everywhere in the first version we admire that sureness of touch which, without lengthy reflection, seems rather as if it had been poured out spontaneously, as a vivifying and illuminating discovery. And whatever excellences the poet may have given to his later work, whatever deviations he employed, at least we find nowhere any important omission or alteration. Only here and there some rather coarse and naïve expressions are expunged.

If you don't trust my literary judgment, trust Goethe's. Entertain his open-mindedness. Read the first edition of *Hamlet*, the one published by Nicholas Ling in 1603, as though it were the first play that young Shakespeare wrote without a collaborator. Imagine that first edition performed in London in 1589 at the Theatre, that first single-purpose English theatrical arena, erected only 13 years before, at the beginning of what would become the greatest artistic wave of commercial popular theatre in English. Better yet, before you read the first version, see it performed. Take your students. Let their young imaginations rejuvenate yours. Introduce them to the first, young Hamlet, before they have read or seen the later, canonical, 30-something remake. They can graduate to the older writer's older protagonist when they are older themselves, and can appreciate its richer, deeper, darker, more complex vintage.

First things first.

Notes

Prologue: Questions

1. Paul Menzer, *The Hamlets: Cues, Qs, and Remembered Texts* (Newark: University of Delaware Press, 2008).
2. Brian Walsh, *Shakespeare, the Queen's Men, and the Elizabethan Performance of History* (Cambridge: Cambridge University Press, 2009).
3. Patrick Cheney, *Shakespeare's Literary Authorship* (Cambridge: Cambridge University Press, 2008).
4. Andrew Murphy, *Shakespeare in Print: A History and Chronology of Shakespeare Publishing* (Cambridge: Cambridge University Press, 2003).
5. See Zachary Lesser, *Renaissance Drama and the Politics of Publication: Readings in the English Book Trade* (Cambridge: Cambridge University Press, 2007), and in particular Zachary Lesser and Peter Stallybrass, "The First Literary *Hamlet* and the Commonplacing of Professional Plays," *Shakespeare Quarterly* 59 (2008): 371–420.
6. Hugh Craig and Arthur Kinney, *Shakespeare, Computers, and the Mystery of Authorship* (Cambridge: Cambridge University Press, 2009).
7. *Hamlet*, ed. Terri Bourus, Sourcebooks Shakespeare (Naperville, IL: Sourcebooks MediaFusion, 2006).
8. *William Shakespeare: The Complete Works*, ed. Stanley Wells and Gary Taylor (Oxford: Clarendon, 1986; rev. 2nd ed., 2005).
9. William Shakespeare, *Hamlet*, ed. Ann Thompson and Neil Taylor (London: Arden Shakespeare, 2006); and William Shakespeare, *Hamlet: 1603 and 1623*, ed. Thompson and Taylor (London: Arden Shakespeare, 2006). Throughout this book, I normally cite the modernized Arden texts of the three versions (as *Hamlet 1603*, *Hamlet 1604*, or *Hamlet 1623*), and their respective line-numbers, unless there is something peculiar to the original printings that is important to the argument.
10. *The RSC Shakespeare: The Complete Works*, ed. Jonathan Bate and Eric Rasmussen (New York: Palgrave Macmillan, 2007).
11. Liam E. Semler, *Teaching Shakespeare and Marlowe: Learning versus the System* (London: Bloomsbury, 2013), 1, 5.
12. My image of the spiral is intended to revise Robert Darnton's model of the "circuit of communication," which has been so influential among

book historians: see "What is the History of Books?" (1982) in *The Kiss of Lamourette: Reflections in Cultural History* (1990), 107–35. Although Darnton's model, based on eighteenth-century French print culture, is complicated by Gary Taylor's model, based on Jacobean London's mix of print, manuscript, and theatre, Taylor retains Darnton's circular logic: see "Preface: Textual Proximities," in *Thomas Middleton and Early Modern Textual Culture: A Companion to the Collected Works*, ed. Gary Taylor and John Lavagnino (Oxford: Clarendon, 2007), 24–8.

13. I have discussed the idea of performance as experiment in two essays: "Poner in Escena: *The History of Cardenio*," in *The Creation and Re-creation of Cardenio: Performing Shakespeare, Transforming Cervantes*, ed. Terri Bourus and Gary Taylor (New York: Palgrave, 2013), 297–318; and Terri Bourus and Gary Taylor, "*Measure for Measure*(s): Performance-testing the Adaptation Hypothesis," *Shakespeare* 10.2 (2014), already available online, forthcoming in paginated print.
14. See Tiffany Stern, "Watching as Reading: The Audience and Written Text in the Early Modern Playhouse," in *How to do Things with Shakespeare*, ed. Laurie E. Maguire (Oxford: Blackwell, 2008), 136–59.
15. Robert Andrews, "Video Nasties Gallery: Fifteen Years of Anti-Piracy Warnings," *The Guardian*, 8 April 2009 (accessed online 22 February 2014).
16. Adrian Johns, *Piracy: The Intellectual Property Wars from Gutenberg to Gates* (Chicago: University of Chicago Press, 2011), 5.
17. Alfred W. Pollard, *Shakespeare's Fight with the Pirates and the Problems of the Transmission of His Text* (London: Moring, 1917), recently reprinted by Cambridge University Press (2010); Johns, *Piracy*, 5 (quoting the variant first line of "To be or not to be"), 13 (piracy "was reputedly rife in the main thoroughfares of Shakespeare's London").

1 Piratical Publishers?

1. Ira Nadel, *Double Act: A Life of Tom Stoppard* (London: Methuen, 2002), 162–94, 390–401.
2. On the history of intellectual property rights, see William St. Clair, *The Reading Nation in the Romantic Period* (Cambridge: Cambridge University Press, 2007).
3. Peter W. M. Blayney, *The Stationers' Company and the Printers of London, 1501–1557*, 2 vols. (Cambridge: Cambridge University Press, 2013), 1:xvii. For misrepresentations of copyright, in particular, see also 2:860–61.
4. Adrian Johns, *The Nature of the Book* (Chicago: University of Chicago Press, 1998), 95.
5. Peter W. M. Blayney, *The Bookshops in St. Paul's Cross Churchyard* (London: Bibliographical Society, 1990).
6. Laurie E. Maguire, "The Craft of Printing (1600)," in *A Companion to Shakespeare*, ed. David Scott Kastan (Oxford: Blackwell, 1999), 438.

7. On the change from Chamberlain's Men to King's Men, see J. Leeds Barroll, *Politics, Plague, and Shakespeare's Theater: The Stuart Years* (Ithaca, NY: Cornell University Press, 1991), 32–3.
8. "Q1" is an abbreviation for "First Quarto," quarto being a bibliographical description of a book printed with sheets of paper folded twice, thereby producing four leaves (i.e., eight pages).
9. William Prynne, *Histrio-Mastix: The Players Scourge, or, Actors Tragedie* (London, 1633), sig. **6v.
10. Lukas Erne, *Shakespeare and the Book Trade* (Cambridge: Cambridge University Press, 2013), 7.
11. I will refer to this edition as "1604" (its actual date of printing and first release) throughout this book. Theoretically, either "1604" or "1605" might be an error in the printing of the title page, but it seems unlikely that a compositor would forget what year it was, and the recurrence of such variants in other books manufactured by different printers (see next note) indicates that it was a routine business practice.
12. For other examples of books published by Ling with two dates on different copies, see STC 11622 ("1594") and 11622.5 ("1595"), 7193 ("1597") and 7193.2 ("1598"), 15685 ("1597"), and 15685.5 ("1598"). "STC" numbers come from *A Short-Title Catalogue of Books Printed in England, Scotland, and Ireland, and of English Printed Books Printed Abroad, 1475–1640*, ed. A. W. Pollard and G. R. Redgrave, rev. ed. 3 vols. (London: Bibliographical Society, 1976–91).
13. On the "clear tendency... for age to depress value," see John Barnard and Maureen Bell, "The Inventory of Henry Bynneman (1583): A Preliminary Survey," *Publishing History* 29 (1991): 5–46, esp. p. 10. Any modern bookseller knows the same thing.
14. Kirk Melnikoff, "Nicholas Ling's Republican *Hamlet* (1603)," in *Shakespeare's Stationers: Studies in Cultural Bibliography*, ed. Marta Straznicky (Philadelphia: University of Pennsylvania Press, 2012), 95–111, esp. 97. The manuscript from which "the 1603 *Hamlet*" was printed might have been Elizabethan, but Melnikoff is specifically referring to the printed book.
15. If Q1 had been printed late in 1603, we might expect some title pages to read "1604." But only two copies of Q1 survive, and only one of those includes the title page. We therefore have no way of knowing whether there were variant title page dates.
16. See William Carroll, ed., *Love's Labour's Lost* (Cambridge: Cambridge University Press, 2009), 181–4, for the lost "1597" first edition; for the 1598 edition as a typical reprint, see Paul Werstine, *Early Modern Playhouse Manuscripts and the Editing of Shakespeare* (Cambridge: Cambridge University Press, 2013), 44–7.
17. The only Jacobean quarto with "Shakespeare" (variously spelled) on the title reprinted before 1642 more often than *Hamlet* was *Pericles*, but that is now recognized as a play coauthored with George Wilkins. I argue that

Q1 *Hamlet* is a different aesthetic object than Q2, and Q2 is certainly not a simple reprint of Q1; consequently, one might argue that these are different books, and should not be lumped together as a single bestseller. But most scholars believe that Q1 and Q2 are different representations of the same play, and I argue that both were written by the same author; in evaluating the success of a book, we normally consider all its versions and revisions (as we do, for instance, in the case of Stoppard's *Rosencrantz and Guildenstern*). If Q1 were a play written by Thomas Kyd, we would need to treat it as a separate book; but I don't know of any scholar who believes that.

18. Zachary Lesser and Peter Stallybrass, "The First Literary *Hamlet* and the Commonplacing of Professional Plays," *Shakespeare Quarterly* 59 (2008): 371–420, esp. 373. The complete lack of documentation for this conjecture is apparent from the absence of footnotes on this page, as opposed to the preceding page (and most others) of this otherwise important article.
19. Peter W. M. Blayney, "The Publication of Playbooks," in *A New History of Early English Drama*, ed. John D. Cox and David Scott Kasten (New York: Columbia University Press, 1997), 383–422.
20. If they wanted copies of the new, "enlarged" edition, they would also presumably want the wholesaler to buy back from them their unsold copies of the first edition—which would, of course, transfer the loss from all those retailers back to the publisher. In either scenario, the publisher would have had a strong disincentive to publish the second edition before the first had sold out.
21. W. Craig Ferguson, *Valentine Simmes* (Charlottesville: Bibliographical Society of the University of Virginia, 1968), 14 (noting that Ling often fails to name a printer).
22. The term "publisher" is anachronistic, but as Blayney notes, "financing and distribution (the basics of what even a modern publisher does) are not the same as retail bookselling, and it is impossible to explain the early trade in printed books without either inventing a word or borrowing an anachronism" (*Stationers' Company*, 1:30–33). I will hereafter use "publisher" for Ling and other stationers performing the same function.
23. R. B. McKerrow, *Printers' and Publishers' Devices in England and Scotland, 1485–1640* (London: Bibliographical Society, 1949), p. 118 (#301). For the near-anagram (Honisucal = Nicholas/Nicholus), see D. Allen Carroll, ed., *Everard Guilpin: Skialetheia or A shadowe of Truth, in Certaine epigrams and Satyres* (Chapel Hill: University of North Carolina Press, 1974), 100.
24. Guildhall Library manuscript 10342 (parish register), fol. 530r.
25. Edward Arber, ed., *A Transcript of the Registers of the Company of Stationers of London: 1544–1640*, 5 vols. (1875–94), 3:365.
26. "'Index 3E:' London Addresses," *Short Title Catalogue*, III: 257 (W9).
27. Gerald D. Johnson, "Nicholas Ling: Publisher, 1580–1607," *Studies in Bibliography* 38 (1985): 203–14, esp. 212–14 ("Ling's shops"). Details of Ling's biography for which I do not cite a source are taken from Johnson's groundbreaking article.

28. "Folio" (often abbreviated to "F1" for the 1623 edition, "F2" for the 1632 edition) is a bibliographical description of a book printed with sheets of paper folded only once, producing two leaves, or four pages, per sheet. Smethwick is named in the colophon as one of four stationers for whom the 1623 edition was printed.
29. Peter W. M. Blayney, *The First Folio of Shakespeare* (Washington, DC: Folger Shakespeare Library, 1991), 17.
30. One of the quarto reprints published by Smethwicke is undated, but R. Carter Hailey has demonstrated that it must have been published in 1625: see "The Dating Game: New Evidence for the Dates of Q4 *Romeo and Juliet* and Q4 *Hamlet*," *Shakespeare Quarterly* 58 (2007): 367–87.
31. Marta Straznicky, "Introduction: What Is a Stationer?" in *Shakespeare's Stationers*, 1–16, esp. 15.
32. For reliable images of all the *Hamlet* quartos from 1603 to 1637, see the British Library webpage "Shakespeare in Quarto."
33. Helgerson, *Forms of Nationhood: The Elizabethan Writing of England* (Chicago: University of Chicago Press, 1992), 1.
34. John F. Pound, ed., *The Norwich Census of the Poor 1570* (Norwich: Norfolk Record Society, 1971), 15, 28, 86 (twice). His elder son Robert also owned one such property (64). See also John Pound, *Tudor and Stuart Norwich* (Chichester: Phillimore, 1988), 131. Unlike Johnson ("Ling," 206), I have used the spelling "Lyng" for the father, John, because that spelling occurs in the Norwich documents, and it is also adopted by David Kathman in his article on "Nicholas Ling" in the *Oxford Dictionary of National Biography* (*ODNB*) (Oxford: Oxford University Press, 2004), accessed online November 2013. All subsequent references to the *ODNB* were accessed online and rechecked that month.
35. *The Register of the Freemen of Norwich, 1548–1713*, ed. Percy Milligan (Norwich: Jarrold, 1934), 108.
36. See Blayney, *Stationers' Company*, 11: a parchment maker "was not a producer of books; his product had other uses, books could be made without using it at all, and as a craftsman he had closer affinities with the Skinners and the Leathersellers than with the Stationers." It is possible that Nicholas Ling's father John was originally a tanner (Milligan, *Freemen*, 42, 120). For "textual culture" as a wider category than the book trade, print, or the Stationers' Company, see Gary Taylor, "Preface: Textual Proximities," in *Thomas Middleton and Early Modern Textual Culture: A Companion to the Collected Works*, ed. Gary Taylor and John Lavagnino (Oxford: Clarendon, 2007), 24–8. Lotte Hellinga notes that vellum "remained in use for manuscript codices as the more durable and more luxurious material," *The Cambridge History of the Book in Britain, Vol. 3: 1400–1557*, ed. Lotte Hellinga and J. B. Trapp (Cambridge: Cambridge University Press, 1999), 93.
37. Pound, *Tudor and Stuart Norwich*, 59; Milligan, *Freemen*, 117–19 (including an Elizabethan and Jacobean John Lynge). For an online list of sixteenth-century Norwich scriveners (and other members of the

book trades), see the *British Book Trade Index*, currently housed by the University of Birmingham, www.bbti.bham.ac.uk.
38. John Barnard and Maureen Bell, "The English Provinces," in *The Cambridge History of the Book in Britain, Vol. IV, 1557–1695*, ed. John Barnard and D. F. McKenzie (Cambridge: Cambridge University Press, 2002), 665–86, esp. 672, 676.
39. David A. Stoker, "Anthony de Solempne: Attributions to His Press," *Library* VI, 3 (1981): 17–32, based on a chapter of Stoker's "A History of the Norwich Book Trades from 1560 to 1760," 2 vols. (London: Library Association Thesis, 1975). On his wine imports, see Pound, *Tudor and Stuart Norwich*, 58; and Norfolk Record Office, Norwich City Records, 16A, Mayor's Court Book, 1569–76, fols. 171, 172.
40. *British Book Trade Index*; Barnard and Bell, "The English Provinces," 673, 676.
41. David Stoker, "'To all Booksellers, Country Chapmen, Hawkers and Others': How the Population of East Anglia Obtained its Printed Materials," in *Fairs, Markets and the Itinerant Book Trade*, ed. Robin Myers, Michael Harris, and Giles Mandelbrote (London: British Library, 2007), 107–36, esp. 114, citing records of a case heard in the Court of Common Pleas (National Archives, CP 40/1297 membrane 1668).
42. H. W. Saunders, *A History of the Norwich Grammar School* (Norwich: Jarrold, 1932); in 1562 Archbishop Parker donated to the school five books, including *Thesaurus Lyngwe Latyne* and *Dictionarium Greco Latino* (262) and in 1560 the future jurist Edward Coke entered the school (263). Early enrollment records are lost, so it is impossible to prove Ling's attendance—but the records for the grammar school at Stratford-upon-Avon are also lost, which does not prevent most scholars from assuming that Shakespeare attended it.
43. Johnson identifies Bynneman as a "printer" ("Ling," 206, 212), but he was also a bookseller, monopolist, and publisher, and those aspects of his business were more relevant to Ling's career.
44. In "Bynneman's Books," *Library*, V, 12 (1957): 81–92, Mark Eccles established that at the time of his death "Bynneman owned 1,082 books at a shop in St. Gregory's by Paul's occupied by Nicholas Ling" (92). For Ling's other connections to Bynneman in 1580–83, see Johnson, "Ling," 207.
45. Stoker, "East Anglia," 120, 110.
46. Pound, *Tudor and Stuart Norwich*, 55–7. The two titles printed in London to be sold in Norwich in 1586, by Nicholas Colman (STC 6564 and 23259), are single-sheet ballads about a damaging storm in East Anglia.
47. Milligan, *Freemen*, 122.
48. For the London and Worcester bookseller Robert Ward, see Alexander Rodger, "Roger Ward's Shrewsbury stock: Inventory of 1585," *Library* V, 13 (1958): 247–68.
49. Johnson assumed that Ling "returned to Norwich" and "remained in Norwich for the next five years" ("Ling," 206). However, he was in

Norwich on 7 August 1585, and then back in London on 6 December. On that day he transferred his apprentice to a younger stationer, John Busby (Arber, *Register*, 2:137). Johnson's essay on "John Busby and the Stationers' Trade, 1590–1640" (in *Library* VI, 7 [1985], 1–15) establishes that Ling and Busby maintained an exceptionally close professional relationship from 1590 to 1594, and suggests that "Ling was the dominant partner all along" (5). Busby had been freed from his own apprenticeship on 8 November 1585, almost six years later than Ling, and less than a month before his first recorded association with Ling. Busby was undercapitalized throughout his career, did not publish anything until 1590, and never owned his own shop. Moreover, his publications in the early 1590s, when they list a place of sale, all use an address that clearly belonged to Ling in 1584 and from 1590 to 1600 ("Busby," 5). Although Johnson does not connect the dots, it seems to me that the obvious explanation for these facts is (1) that Busby worked in, perhaps managed, Ling's shop for a decade after he was freed; and (2) that Ling kept that London shop operational throughout the late 1580s, while also establishing a retail presence in Norwich. This hypothesis would explain why Ling stopped publishing in those years: financing a book is a speculative investment, and while establishing two retail shops Ling could not afford to take other risks. It would also explain the fact that Ling returned to publishing before his father's death, entering a book in the Stationers' Register in London (with Busby) on 6 October, but being "now in" Norwich on 29 November.

50. Burton, *Seven Dialogues* (STC 10457), sig. A2-A4v. In the same year, Ling also published Burton's *Abstract of the Doctrine of the Sabbaoth* (STC 4165a.5). See Burton's *A Sermon Preached in the Cathedral Church of Norwich, 1589* (STC 4178) and C. S. Knighton, "Burton, Thomas (*c.*1545–1616)," *Oxford Dictionary of National Biography*. Among many studies of the city's Elizabethan religious zeal, see Matthew Reynolds, *Godly Reformers and their Opponents in Early Modern England: Religion in Norwich, c. 1560–1643* (Suffolk: Boydell and Brewer, 2005).

51. STC 14923; Arber, *Register*, 3:160 (22 April 1600). Technically, Ling "entered his copy" in the Stationers' Register, which secured a copyright. Here and throughout, I will refer to the action of "entering the copy" as "registering the copyright."

52. Norfolk Record Office, Norwich Consistory Court Wills 608 Flack, registered 29 November 1590; Diocese of Norwich Probate Inventories, DN/INV7/172 (1590–1591). Johnson does not cite the latter, but he does note that Ling was already in possession of one of his father's properties (which I conjecture that he might have been using as a bookshop).

53. Between the end of his apprenticeship in January 1579 and his return to Norwich in mid-1585, Ling published only eight books and a single-sheet Visitation article. By contrast, he published eight books in 1590–91 alone.

54. Zachary Lesser, *Renaissance Drama and the Politics of Publication: Readings in the English Book Trade* (Cambridge: Cambridge University Press, 2007), 18.
55. In an old-fashioned New Historicist move, Melnikoff's "Republican *Hamlet*" stresses Ling's politics, but as evidence of Ling's "republican" investments he cites only three books: *Politeuphuia wits common wealth* (1597), Christopher Middleton's *Legend of Humphrey Duke of Glocester* (1600), and *The Counsellor* (1607). I am not convinced by Melnikoff's interpretation of the passages he quotes, but more important than such subjective judgments is a simple numerical fact: it is surely an exaggeration to claim that these three books establish Ling as "one of the period's leading publishers of political writing" (Straznicky, "Introduction," 12). Even within those three books, only a fraction of the text lends itself to a "republican" reading. One of the three is a narrative poem, another is full of literary quotations, and three political titles are insignificant by comparison with Ling's heavy commitment to vernacular literature. In the 1603 *Hamlet*, the three passages typographically emphasized as sententiae are spoken by Polonius, but none of the three is explicitly political. Melnikoff does not mention Ling's overlap with Coke, or their shared connection to the strong Puritanism of Norwich, which would better support an interpretation of Ling as Parliamentarian, rather than "republican."
56. Jesse M. Lander, *Inventing Polemic: Religion, Print, and Literary Culture in Early Modern England* (Cambridge: Cambridge University Press, 2006), 117. Lander places scare-quotes around "literature" for postmodernist reasons.
57. Raphael Lyne, "Thomas Churchyard," *ODNB*.
58. Nashe, *Strange Newes* (1592), sig. I1; also Thomas Nashe, *The Works of Thomas Nashe*, ed. R. B. McKerrow, 5 vols. (1904–10), rev. F. P. Wilson (Oxford: Blackwell, 1958), I: 309.
59. Johnson does not mention the possible Norwich connection between Ling and Greene, though he does notice that when Ling returned to London he promptly registered an apprentice: "Thomas Bushell, a Norwich native whom Ling may have brought with him from there (Arber ii. 173)" (206).
60. Steve Mentz, *Romance for Sale in Early Modern England: The Rise of Prose Fiction* (Aldershot: Ashgate, 2006), 8. See also Newcomb, *Reading Popular Romance*; and Kirk Melnikoff and Edward Gieskes, eds., *Writing Robert Greene: Essays on England's First Notorious Professional Writer* (Aldershot: Ashgate, 2008).
61. Erne, attempting to demonstrate Shakespeare's primacy in print, shows that Greene's works were not as frequently collected or reprinted as were Shakespeare's (*Book Trade*, 33–35). But his own raw data shows that in 1583–1650 there were 116 editions of Greene, while in 1593–1660 there were only 105 for Shakespeare. My numbers for 1583–1603, focusing on Ling's career, are taken from Erne's tables.

62. Ling may have been introduced to Lodge through Greene; scholars speculate that Greene saw the book through the press while Lodge was at sea: see Alexandra Halasz, "Thomas Lodge," *ODNB*.
63. See Margaret Christian, "*Zepheria* (1594; STC 26124): A Critical Edition," *Studies in Philology* 100 (2003): 177–243. The sequence is most remarkable for its metrical irregularity.
64. Erne, *Book Trade*, 172.
65. On Breton's popularity, see Mark Bland, "The London Book-Trade in 1600," in *Companion,* ed. Kastan, 461.
66. E. A. J. Honigmann, *John Weever: A Biography of a Literary Associate of Shakespeare and Jonson, Together with a Photographic Facsimile of Weever's "Epigrammes"* (Manchester: Manchester University Press, 1987).
67. Lesser and Stallybrass fully describe Ling's relationship to this network in "The First Literary *Hamlet*," where they also relate it specifically to the literary "commonplacing" of passages in both Ling's editions of *Hamlet*. For important earlier scholarship on Ling as editor and anthologist, see William J. Hebel, "Nicholas Ling and *England's Hellicon*," *Library* 4.IV, 5 (1924): 153–60; H. E. Rollins, ed., *England's Helicon: 1600, 1614*, 2 vols. (Oxford: Clarendon, 1935) 2:59–63; James P. Bednarz, "Canonizing Shakespeare: 'The Passionate Pilgrim,' 'England's Helicon' and the Question of Authenticity," *Shakespeare Survey* 60 (2007): 260–1.
68. On Blount, see Gary Taylor's article in *ODNB* and his "Making Meaning Marketing Shakespeare 1623," in *From Performance to Print in Early Modern England*, ed. Peter Holland and Stephen Orgel (New York: Palgrave, 2006), 55–72. He generously allowed me to read his unpublished 2006 McKenzie lectures on Blount, which also influenced Sonia Massai's "Edward Blount, the Herberts, and the First Folio," *Shakespeare's Stationers,* ed. Straznicky, 132–46.
69. Erne, *Book Trade,* 172.
70. Gary W. Jenkins, "Henry Smith," *ODNB*.
71. Compare the Elizabethan bookseller Andrew Wise's commitment to a playwright and a preacher united by "a common aesthetic" and "a vernacular literary style signaled by the epithet mellifluous," described by Adam G. Hooks in "Wise Ventures: Shakespeare and Thomas Playfere at the Sign of the Angel," *Shakespeare's Stationers,* 47–62.
72. Ling published eight editions of Smith, and only two of Shakespeare. Moreover, reprints and big books were more profitable for publishers. Both Ling's Shakespeare editions were small, and only one was a (heavily modified) reprint, which probably did not sell quickly, since it was not replaced until 1611, six years after its publication and four years after Ling's death. By contrast, for a single Smith sermon (STC 22656 in 1591) Ling published the first edition and then two quick reprints (22656.5, 22657), and his larger collection of that sermon and two others, all previously published (22735 in 1599), was itself reprinted three times (22736, 22737, 22738) in eight years. Ling certainly made much more money off Smith than off Shakespeare.

73. Rollins, *England's Helicon*, 27–34.
74. However, the suggestion that Ling owned a copy of the 1609 edition of *Shakespeare's Sonnets* is wishful thinking, since Ling died in April 1607. Erne records this conjecture, without noting its absurdity (*Book Trade*, 215).
75. Edmund Chambers et al., eds., *The Shakespeare Allusion-Book*, 2 vols. (London: Oxford University Press, 1932), 2:478 (63 quotations from the poems, but only 28 from the plays).
76. Erne, *Book Trade*, 172.
77. See Lukas Erne, *Beyond "The Spanish Tragedy": A Study of the Works of Thomas Kyd* (Manchester: Manchester University Press, 2001), 203–16.
78. Lesser and Stallybrass, "First Literary *Hamlet*." In Ling's editions of *Hamlet*, the signposts are quotation marks in the left margin, but Lesser and Stallybrass consider and tabulate all forms of such signposting used in the sixteenth and seventeenth centuries, including the manicule (a hand in the margin with a finger pointing toward a particular spot in main text-block) and italic or some other typeface that distinguishes sententiae from the surrounding text.
79. Werstine, *Playhouse Manuscripts*, 231–3.
80. Carole Rawcliffe, Richard Wilson, and Christine Clark, eds., *Norwich since 1550* (London: Hambledon Continuum, 2005), 36.
81. Paul Slack, *The Impact of Plague in Tudor and Stuart England* (London: Routledge, 1985), 129–30, 151.
82. See Eccles, "Bynneman's Books," and Barnard and Bell, "Inventory".
83. "Ling's shop differs from Bynneman's main shop in larger holdings of books in smaller formats" (Barnard and Bell, "Inventory," 8).
84. H. R. Plomer, "The Eliot's Court printing house, 1584–1674," *Library* II, 2 (1922): 175–84.
85. Presumably Ling could not find, or did not want, a copublisher with these titles because he was the only London stationer with a foothold in Norwich. To these two can be added another title by the former Norwich preacher Burton (STC 4165a.5).
86. Johnson established that this "habit or practice...may be seen in the majority of his work" ("Ling," 203). He entered and published only 16 titles alone (205).
87. Straznicky's useful appendix, in *Shakespeare's Stationers*, contains short biographies of, and recommended scholarly readings about, the other *Hamlet* stationers (Ling, Roberts, Simmes, Smethwick), and the publishers and printers of other Shakespeare plays and poems, but not Trundle; Melnikoff, in the same volume, treats Q1 *Hamlet* as a reflection of Ling's "republican" political sympathies, but says nothing about Trundle's politics.
88. Gerald D. Johnson, "John Trundle and the Book Trade 1603–1626," *Studies in Bibliography* 39 (1986): 177–99. Unless otherwise noted, my statements about Trundle are based on the data assembled in this essay

(although I sometimes interpret that data differently than Johnson, who is committed to the theory that Q1 *Hamlet* was a "bad" quarto).
89. "Thirty-three of [Trundle's] editions give an address of sale in their imprints; of these, twenty-six denote a shop identified with another stationer" (Johnson, "Trundle," 183). Johnson conjectures that the other booksellers had a "more popular location" or more "efficient book-keeping and distribution systems," which may both be true; but every successful small business owner must keep track of what she or he sells. A small shop would be a simpler, or at least supplementary, explanation: enough space to make a living as a retail bookseller of his own and other small, cheap texts, but not enough space for wholesale distribution and storage.
90. Anonymous, *Nobody and Somebody* (1606, Queen Anne's Men); John Day, *The Isle of Gulls* (1606, Children of the Queen's Revels); Thomas Dekker, *If It Be Not Good, the Devil Is in it* (1612, Queen Anne's Men); Joshua Cooke (?), *Greene's Tu Quoque* (1614, Queen Anne's Men); Thomas Middleton and William Rowley, *Fair Quarrel* (Prince Charles's Men, 1617).
91. Farmer and Lesser, "The Popularity of Playbooks Revisited" and "Structures of Popularity in the Early Modern Book Trade," *Shakespeare Quarterly* 56 (2005): 1–32, 206–13; Erne, *Book Trade*, 1–2.
92. *Venus and Adonis, The Rape of Lucrece, The First Part of the Contention, Richard Duke of York, Love's Labour's Lost, Richard II, Richard III, Romeo and Juliet, 1 Henry IV,* and *The Passionate Pilgrim.*
93. Blayney, "Publication," 384–9; and "The Alleged Popularity of Playbooks," *Shakespeare Quarterly* 56 (2005): 33–50.
94. Marlowe's *Jew of Malta* (STC 17412) was entered to Ling and Millington on 17 May 1594; the earliest surviving edition was printed in 1633 for Vavasour. If Ling did publish or copublish a lost early edition of Marlowe's *Jew of Malta*, it must not have been a very successful book, unless we are to assume (implausibly) multiple lost editions. Thus, either Ling had no previous experience publishing commercial plays, or he had a bad experience.
95. Ling was freed on 19 January 1579. Simmes began his eight-year apprenticeship at Christmas 1576, initially and officially to the bookseller Henry Sutton, who did not own a printing press; but at some unknown date before 1583 he became a "servant" to Bynneman. See W. Craig Ferguson, "Valentine Simmes," *Dictionary of Literary Biography*, vol. 170, ed. James K. Bracken and Joel Silver (Detroit: Bruccoli Clark Laymen, 1996), 244. Simmes must have learned the art of printing from Bynneman, and it seems likely that Sutton and Bynneman had a private agreement, outside the official register, by which Sutton put Simmes on the books, thereby allowing Bynneman to acquire an extra apprentice (beyond the number he was allowed by the Company).
96. Ferguson, "Simmes," 246, 248.
97. Alan Craven, "Proofreading in the Shop of Valentine Simmes," *Papers of the Bibliographical Society of America* 68 (1974): 361–72.

98. Compare Drayton's *Matilda* (1594), printed according to one title page by Roberts for Ling and Busby (STC 7205), but according to another title page of the same printing, printed by Simmes for Ling and Busby (STC 7206); this probably indicates shared printing. Likewise, *Greenes never too late* was originally printed in 1590 by Orwin for Ling and Busby (12253), reprinted in 1599 by Simmes for Ling (12253.7), reprinted in 1600 by Roberts for Ling (12254), then reprinted yet again in 1602 by Simmes for Ling (12254.5). Henry Smith's *Three Sermons* (which includes "The Affinity of the Faithful," which I discuss in chapter 3) was originally printed in 1600 by Roberts for Ling (22735), then reprinted for him in 1601 by Simmes (22736)—then in 1604 and 1607 printed for him by yet another printer, Kingston. Thomas Lodge's *Rosalynde* was reprinted in 1596 by Abel Jeffes (another Bynneman apprentice) for Ling and Gubbins (16666), then reprinted in 1598 by Simmes (16667), then in 1604 reprinted by Roberts for Ling alone (16668)—an exact parallel for *Hamlet*, a book printed by Simmes for Ling and another publisher, then reprinted by Roberts in 1604 for Ling alone. Greene's *Ciceronis Amor*, originally published in 1589, was reprinted in 1601 by Simmes for Ling (12226), then in 1605 by Roberts for him (12227).
99. For a full account, see Johnson's interrelated essays on "Ling" and "Trundle" (and "Busby"). Unfortunately, Johnson's groundbreaking emphasis on publishers, rather than printers, was marred by an assumption that some early publishers specialized in "acquiring" copy. There is no evidence for that practice in the late sixteenth or early seventeenth century.
100. Lesser and Stallybrass, "First Literary *Hamlet*," 372.
101. DEEP records "newly imprinted" in 12 printed playbooks from 1560 to 1594, including *Jacob and Esau* (printed by Bynneman in 1568); the online *English Short Title Catalogue*, or *ESTC*, identifies 23 additional nondramatic examples between 1570 (the beginning of Ling's London apprenticeship) and 1604. *ESTC* is not always reliable, but its limitations are likely to underestimate the frequency of these phrases.
102. DEEP records 15 examples of "newly corrected and amended"; *ESTC* identifies 22 additional nondramatic examples from 1570 to 1604 (including Ling's 1604 reprint of his own *Politeuphia, or Wit's Commonwealth*).
103. *Oxford English Dictionary*, "perfect" (*adj.* 5).
104. Between 1570 and 1604, the title page claim "true and perfect" precedes and modifies "doctrine" (1580), "order" (1580, 1589), "news" (1587), "discourse" (1588, 1597, 1602), "friend" (1589), "description of a straunge monstar borne in the city of Rome" (1590), "preparation" (1591), "pronunciation" (1591), "description" (1598), "way of pronouncing" (1573, 1582, 1596, 1602), "declaration" (1600), "gain" (1601), "cure" (1603), and "relation" (1603). Ling sold books as well as publishing them, so he might have stocked any of these titles.
105. The phrase "according to the" is elsewhere followed by references to "Scotish copy" (STC 3967; 10842.3); "written copye" (11050); "coppie

imprinted at Collen" [Cologne] (11693); "Dutch and French copies" (11720); "copy printed in French" (13127); "original printed at Chartres" (13093); "French Coppie" (13098; 11727; 3388); "French copie printed at Verdun" (15213); "copie printed in Collin [Cologne], brought ouer into England by George Bores ordinary poste, the xi. daye of this present moneth of Iune 1590, who did both see and heare the same" (23375); "same copy," that is, the one "Printed at Toures by Iames Mattayer printer to the Kings Maiesty" (6878); "authors third and last edition" *(*4374); "Dutch copie" (18893); "same coppy there imprinted," that is, the one "Printed at Nuremberge by Lucas Mayr ingrauer, dwelling in Kramergesle" (20890); "the Originall" (24651); "copie, printed at Delfe" (12197); and "Spanish and French copies" (19840).

106. "The true copie ... according to the report made to the Kings most excellent Maiestie by the Company of Parish Clearks" (STC 16743 etc.).
107. By Edmund Bollifant for William Aspley (1599, STC 19833.5).
108. See especially Hugh Craig's chapter on the additions in D. H. Craig and Arthur F. Kinney, *Shakespeare, Computers, and the Mystery of Authorship* (Cambridge: Cambridge University Press, 2009), 162–80; Warren Stevenson's *Shakespeare's Additions to Thomas Kyd's* The Spanish Tragedy*: A Fresh Look at the Evidence Regarding the 1602 Additions* (Lewiston: Edwin Mellen Press, 2008); and Brian Vickers's "Identifying Shakespeare's Additions to *The Spanish Tragedy* (1602): A New(er) Approach," *Shakespeare* 8.1 (2012): 13–43. Vickers and Craig disagree with each other's methods, but both reach the same conclusion.
109. See also Ling's uses of a synonym for "enlarged" to describe his own *Politeuphuia*, "Newly corrected and augmented" (1598, STC 15686), and Drayton's *Matilda* and *Gaveston* "newly corrected and augmented" in 1596 (STC 7232).
110. *Batman vppon Bartholomew* (1582), "newly corrected, enlarged and amended"; Luis de Granada, *Memorial of a Christian Life* (1586), "enlarged with new maps and tables"; Holinshed, *Chronicles of Ireland* (1586), "now newlie reuised, inlarged, and *continued to this present yeare*"; Edward Webbe, *The Rare and Most Wonderful Things* (1590), "Newly enlarged and corrected by the Author"; John Partridge, *The Treasury of Commodious Conceits* (1591), "now newly corrected, and inlarged, with diuers necessary phisicke helpes"; Henry Smith, *A preparatiue to mariage* (1591), "The summe whereof was spoken at a contract, and inlarged after. Whereunto is annexed a treatise of the Lords Supper, and another of vsurie"; John Powel, *The assise of bread* (1592), "newly corrected and enlarged"; Anonymous, *Present remedies* (1594), "now newly inlarged by the same Author"; William Warner, *Albions England* (1597), "now reuised, and newly inlarged by the same author"; Du Bartas, *The colonies* (1598), "in diuerse places corrected and enlarged by the translatour"; Richard Percival, *A dictionarie in Spanish and English* (1599), "Now enlarged and amplified with many thousand words"; John Hayward, *The Sanctuarie*

of a troubled soul (1601), "Newly reprinted, enlarged and emended; by the author"; Henoch Clapham, *Three partes of Salomon his Song of Songs* (1603), "The first part printed before: but now re-printed and enlarged. The second and third partes neuer printed before."

111. David McKitterick, *A History of Cambridge University Press*, vol. 1: *Printing and the Book Trade in Cambridge, 1534–1698* (Cambridge: Cambridge University Press, 1992), 285.
112. This calculation ignores the preliminaries, because the title page of Q1 survives in only a single copy, which is missing what was probably the blank cover leaf (A1). I am assuming that both editions included a preliminary half-sheet.
113. For "the customary sixpence for a play of ordinary length," see McKitterick, *Cambridge*, 288, and F. R. Johnson, "Notes on English Retail Book Prices, 1550–1640," *Library* V, 5 (1950): 83–178. Blayney warns against assuming that all quarto playbooks were sold for sixpence.
114. See the website "measuringworth.com" (accessed February 2014). The particular value of this site is that it provides a variety of different ways to calculate the "value" or "equivalency" of historical prices. I have used "economic power" because it seems most relevant to the decisions of a publisher (rather than, say, a retail customer).
115. Alfred W. Pollard, *Shakespeare Folios and Quartos: A Study in the Bibliography of Shakespeare's Plays 1594–1685* (London: Methuen, 1909), 4–10. Pollard expanded this theory in *Shakespeare's Fight with the Pirates* (1917).
116. Arber, *Transcript*, III: 212. This entry (in Register C, f. 84v) is photographically reproduced in S. Schoenbaum, *William Shakespeare: Records and Images* (London: Scolar Press, 1981), 215. Arber adds an editorial "[of]" after "Prince," which is probably a valid correction; but given the other variant in the title it cannot be considered certain.
117. E. K. Chambers, *The Elizabethan Stage*, 4 vols. (Oxford: Clarendon, 1923), 3:186–7; M. A. Shaaber, "The Meaning of the Imprint in Early Printed Books", *Library* IV, 24 (1944): 120–41, esp. 124; F. P. Wilson, "Shakespeare and the New Bibliography," *The Bibliographical Society, 1892–1942: Studies in Retrospect* (London: Bibliographical Society, 1945), 86–7; Leo Kirschbaum, *Shakespeare and the Stationers* (Columbus: Ohio State University Press, 1946), 43–4; Blayney, "Publication of Playbooks."
118. Melnikoff, "Republican," 103–104. Melnikoff cites the Arden *Hamlet*, ed. Harold Jenkins (London: Methuen, 1982), 15. Jenkins himself was channeling Fredson Bowers, who called Q1 "a memorially reconstructed pirate text": see *On Editing Shakespeare and the Elizabethan Dramatists* (Philadelphia: University of Pennsylvania Press, 1955), 55. On memorial reconstruction, see chapter 2. Johnson also presupposes that Trundle supplied a "bad" text ("Ling," 211–12).
119. Ling's shop at the Sign of the Mermaid, from 1582 to 1585, was built against the back of the printing house that Roberts shared with Watkins

from 1580 to 1583: see *A Dictionary of Printers and Booksellers in England, Scotland and Ireland, and of Foreign Printers of English Books 1557–1650* (London: Bibliographical Society, 1968), 229; and Blayney, *Bookshops*, 39–40. Ling and Roberts therefore worked in adjoining premises in 1582-3. Perhaps not coincidentally, during those years Ling first associated with John Charlewood, under whom Roberts had apprenticed. On 21 June 1582, Charlewood and Ling jointly entered in the Stationers' Register Anthony Munday's *The English Romayne Lyfe* (STC 18272), Ling's second book.

120. John Charlewood was assigned the playbill monopoly on 30 October 1587 (Arber II, 477). Roberts acquired the monopoly by marrying his former master's widow, Alice Baylie Charlewood, at Saint Giles Cripplegate on 9 September 1593 (online "Family Search International Geneological Index," accessed 15 March 2001). Roberts was, at the time, himself a widower with seven children (David Kathman, "James Roberts," *ODNB*). The transfer of Charlewood's copyrights, including "The bille for plaies," was subsequently recorded in the registers (Arber II, 651). His printing production tripled after 1593 (*STC*, "Roberts, James," 3:145).

121. STC 16743.2, 16743.3 (1603), 18597 (1606). It is very likely that the two surviving 1603 broadsheets belonged to a series, published weekly; such single-sheet ephemera are the titles most likely to be lost entirely.

122. William Proctor Williams, "'Under the hands of...': Zachariah Pasfield and the Licensing of Playbooks," in *Shakespeare's Stationers*, ed. Marta Straznicky, 63–94, esp. 72.

123. Melnikoff ("Republican," 104) cites David Kastan, *Shakespeare and the Book* (Cambridge: Cambridge University Press, 2001), 27–30 (although Kastan does not use the words "rented" or "promptly"). I independently, simultaneously, proposed the same explanation in "Shakespeare and the London Publishing Environment: The Publisher and Printers of Q1 and Q2 *Hamlet*," *Analytical and Enumerative Bibliography* 12 (2001): 206–28.

124. Erne, *Book Trade*, 159–61. Erne corrects Kastan's claim that "Roberts ... was a printer rather than a publisher" (*Shakespeare and the Book* 29). He also rebuts James Hirrell's conjecture—in "The Roberts Memorandum: A Solution," *Review of English Studies* 71 (2010): 711–728—that Roberts stole plays from the Chamberlain's Men: see *Shakespeare as Literary Dramatist* (Cambridge: Cambridge University Press, 2013), 14–17.

125. Jenkins, ed., *Hamlet*, 16.

126. Tiffany Stern, "'On Each Wall and Corner Poast': Playbills, Title-pages, and Advertising in Early Modern London," *English Literary Renaissance* 36 (2006): 57–89.

127. Including the anonymous Chamberlain's Men's play *Alarum for London*, entered by Roberts on 29 May 1600, but printed in 1602 by Allde for Ferbrand (STC 16754) and Shakespeare's *Troilus and Cressida*, entered by Roberts on 7 February 1603, but reentered on 29 January 1609, by Bonian and Walley, and printed for them that year by Eld (STC 22331-2).

128. Even scholars who accept that Roberts must have sold the copyright to Ling (or Trundle, or both) often assert that the copyright was conditional on Roberts printing the second edition, or that Roberts printed the second edition to make up for Ling having stolen the copyright. But that is all conjecture. As I have demonstrated, Ling often switched between Simmes and Roberts, without there being any question of copyright, or of some pre-existing "rental" agreement.
129. As Barroll notes, the patent of 19 May itself implies that plague had by that date closed the theatres: it authorized the company "to show and exercise publicly... when the infection of plague shall decrease" (*Plague*, 103). This means that their new title would not have been displayed on playbills around the city (where Ling or Trundle might have seen it) until the theatres reopened—which did not happen until spring 1604.
130. Adrian Johns, *Piracy: The Intellectual Property Wars from Gutenberg to Gates* (Chicago: University of Chicago Press, 2011), 17–40.

2 Piratical Actors?

1. For documentary evidence of the "1597" edition, see Arthur Freeman and Paul Grinke, "Four New Shakespeare Quartos?" *TLS* (5 April 2002): 17–18.
2. T. W. Baldwin, *Shakspere's "Love's Labours Won": New Evidence from the Account Books of an Elizabethan Bookseller* (Carbondale: Southern Illinois University Press, 1957). For subsequent scholarship see entry in the Lost Plays Database.
3. Lukas Erne, in *Shakespeare and the Book Trade* (Cambridge: Cambridge University Press, 2013),discusses a few early collectors of playbooks (194–223), but such fans were demonstrably exceptional, accounting for only a small fraction of the initial print-runs of plays. Moreover, none systematically collected multiple editions of a single Shakespeare play, as editors like Theobald began doing in the eighteenth century.
4. Q1 2, Q2 7, Q3 19, Q4 20, Q5 31. For the latest evidence of surviving copies, see Table 6 in Erne, *Book Trade,*, 188–91. More generally, first editions survive in smaller numbers than reprints. Of the 12 first editions of Shakespeare plays printed before Q1 *Hamlet*, for which we can compare reprints in his lifetime, there are 39 copies total, a rate of 3.25 per edition. For reprints (180 copies, 21 editions), the rate is 8.57 per edition.
5. W. W. Greg describes both extant copies of Q1 as "in good condition, though in the Huntington copy a few headlines are shaved and those on the verso pages are obscured by the mounting paper, the leaves being inlaid; both have been to some extent defaced with annotations in pen and ink, more extensive in the [British] museum copy but more serious in the Huntington, where at a number of points, the reading has been deliberately altered": see W. W. Greg, ed., *"Hamlet": First Quarto, 1603* (Oxford: Clarendon, 1965), i.

6. *The Correspondence of Sir Thomas Hanmer, Bart, Speaker of the House of Commons, with A Memoir of his Life*, ed. Sir Henry Bunbury, Bart. (London: Edward Moxon, 1838), 80 (footnote by Bunbury).
7. *First Edition* (1825), unpaginated, unsigned, untitled preface (only recto page between title page of the book and the print-facsimile of the title page of Q1).
8. Tycho Mommsen, "*Hamlet*, 1603; and *Romeo and Juliet*, 1597," *Athenaeum* (7 February 1857), 182.
9. *Oxford English Dictionary*, "hack," $n.^3$ 4.a (accessed 20 January 2014). Mommsen did not identify the source of his quotation.
10. E. H. Mikhail, ed., *Goldsmith: Interviews and Recollections* (New York: St. Martin's, 1993), 29.
11. W. W. Greg, ed., *The Merry Wives of Windsor, 1602* (Oxford: Clarendon, 1910), xxvi–xxvii.
12. For an astute history of "The Rise and Fall of Memorial Reconstruction," see Gabriel Egan, *The Struggle for Shakespeare's Text: Twentieth-Century Editorial Theory and Practice* (Cambridge: Cambridge University Press, 2010), 111–23. He notes Greg's continuing unease about application of the theory to Q1 *Hamlet* (111).
13. Evelyn May Albright, *Dramatic Publication in England, 1580–1640: A Study of Conditions Affecting Content and Form of Drama* (London: Oxford University Press, 1927), esp. 300–310.
14. Laurie E. Maguire, *Shakespearean Suspect Texts: The "Bad" Quartos and Their Contexts* (Cambridge: Cambridge University Press, 1996), 324.
15. Paul Menzer, *The Hamlets: Cues, Qs, and Remembered Texts* (Newark: University of Delaware Press, 2008), 33.
16. Ann Thompson and Neil Taylor, eds., *Hamlet* (London: Arden Shakespeare, 2006), 509
17. Maguire acknowledges but dismisses the "oft-alleged echo" of *Twelfth Night* 2.4.117–19 ("We *men* may say more, swear more, but indeed / Our shows are more than will; for still we *prove* / Much *in* our vows, *but little in* our *love*") at Q1 3.69–70 ("Such *men* often *prove* / Great *in* their words *but little in* their *love*"). Maguire correctly identifies the general idea here as a "conventional saw" (255), but the verbal resemblance in the last phrase is striking. However, the work of MacDonald P. Jackson, John Nance, Gary Taylor, Brian Vickers, and Paul Vincent has demonstrated that such phrasal repetitions are common in Shakespeare; they are, in fact, good evidence of Shakespeare's authorship. Most attribution scholars now accept that Shakespeare wrote parts of *Edward III,* including 2.619 ("Lilies that fester smell far worse than weeds") which is exactly repeated in Sonnet 94.114; but no one believes that either of those texts is a memorial reconstruction.
18. Maguire later acknowledged (personal communication 3 January 2014) that her diagnostic conclusion about Q1 did not correlate with the evidence she offered. She attributed this misfit to her reluctance to disappoint

Harold Jenkins, one of her mentors. (See my discussion, in the Prologue, of the influence of the teacher-student dynamic.)
19. Maguire, *Suspect*, 25, 413.
20. Brian Vickers, "*Hamlet by Dogberry*: A Perverse Reading of the Bad Quarto," *TLS*, 14 December 1993.
21. Gary Taylor and Michael Warren, eds., *The Division of the Kingdoms: Shakespeare's Two Versions of "King Lear"* (Oxford: Clarendon, 1993); George Ian Duthie, *Elizabethan Shorthand and the First Quarto of "King Lear"* (Oxford: Blackwell, 1949) and *Shakespeare's "King Lear": A Critical Edition* (Oxford: Blackwell, 1949).
22. See Taylor's textual introduction to *Hamlet* in Stanley Wells and Gary Taylor, *William Shakespeare: A Textual Companion* (Oxford: Clarendon, 1987), 396–402; and George Ian Duthie, *The "Bad" Quarto of "Hamlet"* (Cambridge: Cambridge University Press, 1941).
23. Taylor, "The Canon and Chronology of Shakespeare's Plays," *Textual Companion*, esp. 80–85.
24. John Jowett, *The Tragedy of King Richard the Third* (Oxford: Oxford UP, 2000).
25. Thompson and Taylor, eds., *Hamlet*, 477. This page does not indicate the dates of Maguire's and Taylor's work, which will be familiar to specialists but, for other readers, could only be determined by checking the bibliography.
26. Kathleen Irace, *Reforming the "Bad" Quartos: Performance and Provenance of Six Shakespearean First Editions* (Newark: University of Delaware Press, 1994), 164.
27. Kathleen Irace, "Origins and Agents of Q1 *Hamlet*," in *The "Hamlet" First Published (Q1, 1603): Origins, Form, Intertextualities*, ed. Thomas Clayton (Newark: University of Delaware Press, 1992), 90–122.
28. The single actor had been identified, independently, by W. H. Widgery and Grant White in 1880–1, and by H. D. Gray in 1910: see Harold Jenkins, ed., *Hamlet* (London: Methuen, 1982), 20–21.
29. *The First Quarto of Hamlet*, ed. Kathleen O. Irace, The New Cambridge Shakespeare: The Early Quartos (Cambridge: Cambridge University Press, 1998), 115–16.
30. James P. Bednarz, *Shakespeare and the Poets' War* (New York: Columbia University Press, 2001), 244.
31. MacDonald P. Jackson, *Studies in Attribution: Middleton and Shakespeare*, Jacobean Drama Studies, vol. 79 (Salzburg: Institut für Anglistik und Amerikanistik, Universität Salzburg, 1979).
32. Thompson and Taylor, eds., *Hamlet*, 561.
33. Ralph Berry, "Hamlet's Doubles," *Shakespeare Quarterly* 77 (1986): 204–12.
34. For "hired man," see among innumerable examples, Jenkins, *Hamlet*, 21; and Gary Taylor's textual introduction to *Hamlet* in *Textual Companion*, 398.

35. This statement is based on the concordances to the roles of individual characters in Marvin Spevack's *A Complete and Systematic Concordance to the Works of Shakespeare*, 9 vols. (Hildesheim: Olms, 1968–80), which is based upon the text of *Hamlet* in the Riverside edition, which combines material from both Q2 and F. I have not checked the figures and proportions in all three versions. However, the memorial reconstruction hypothesis about Q1 is based on the assumption that it derives from something like the Riverside conflation.
36. The memorial reconstruction hypothesis presumes that Shakespeare wrote *Hamlet* just before or just after the turn of the century. Kemp left the Chamberlain's Men in 1599, but as the company's clown he is not likely to have played any of the roles assigned to the alleged reporter, and the "Clown" role of the Gravedigger is not "accurately reported" in Q1.
37. Simon Palfrey and Tiffany Stern, *Shakespeare in Parts* (Oxford: Oxford University Press, 2007).
38. See the positive review by William Proctor Williams in *Notes & Queries* 56 (2009): 452–4. Gabriel Egan's later, more detailed review is damning about the incoherence and inaccuracy of many aspects of Menzer's argument: see "Shakespeare: Editions and Textual Matters," *The Year's Work in English Studies*, vol. 91: *Covering Work Published in 2010* (Oxford: Oxford University Press, 2012), 328–410, esp. 357–67; but Egan does accept Menzer's evidence for greater stability in the Corambis cues, and the "plausibility" of Menzer's argument that the differences between Corambis and Polonius result from "revision" (366).
39. Menzer, *Hamlets*, 60. Menzer also provides, in Appendix 6, a complete transcript of Corambis's part, as represented by Q1, cues and all (223–30).
40. James J. Marino, *Owning William Shakespeare* (Philadelphia: University of Pennsylvania Press, 2011), 87–8.
41. Vadnais, "'According to the scrippe': speeches, speech order, and performance in Shakespeare's early printed play texts," (PhD diss., Ohio State University, 2012), esp. p. 108; accessed online through *OhioLINK Electronic Theses and Dissertations Center*, April 2014. The evidence and arguments marshalled by Vadnais are equally damaging for any theory that the 1603 quarto is the result of note-taking during a performance (discussed in chapter 3).
42. Thompson and Taylor, ed., *Hamlet*, 508.
43. Alan C. Dessen and Leslie Thomson, *A Dictionary of Stage Directions in English Drama 1580–1642* (Cambridge: Cambridge University Press, 1999), 150, 136, 107.
44. Harold Jenkins, "Playhouse Interpolations in the Folio Text of *Hamlet*," *Studies in Bibliography* 13 (1960): 31–47.
45. 1.2.67, 1.5.22, 2.1.49, 2.1.98, 2.2.211–12, 2.2.300, 302, 303, 308, 360, 459, 477, 3.1.19, 48, 166, 3.2.217, 256, 315, 321, 335, 337, 3.3.17, 3.4.213, 4.2.1, 4.3.34, 4.5.33, 38, 64, 170, 187, 4.6.17, 4.7.8, 5.1.145–6, 5.2.14 (line numbers from *Hamlet* [1604], ed. Thompson and Taylor).

46. For this and other metrical variations, see George T. Wright, *Shakespeare's Metrical Art* (Berkeley: University of California Press, 1988).
47. See the unique *Swounds*, where the other texts have the mild interjections "Sure" and "why" 2.2.511.
48. See the textual notes (including full collation of variants) to *A Game at Chess: A Later Form*, in Gary Taylor and John Lavagnino, eds., *Thomas Middleton and Early Modern Textual Culture*, 5.2.52, 5.2.96, 5.3.53, 5.3.61, 5.3.145.
49. Petersen, *Shakespeare's Errant Texts: Textual Form and Linguistic Style in Shakespearean "Bad" Quartos and Co-authored Plays* (Cambridge: Cambridge University Press, 2012), xvi, 63, 65, 73, 78, 79, 84, 210, 223.
50. Egan, "Editions and Textual Matters," 385. Egan's own command of statistical reasoning, and the clarity of his prose, are exemplary.
51. Charles Adams Kelly, *The Evidence Matrix for the 1st Quarto of Shakespeare's "Hamlet"* (Ann Arbor, MI: Howland Research, 2008), 19. A revised, corrected, and enlarged edition of Kelly's argument was published in 2014.
52. Egan, "Editions and Textual Matters," 357.
53. Petersen's work also involves analysis of later German texts of *Hamlet*, *Romeo and Juliet*, and *Titus Andronicus*. But the relationship of Q1 *Hamlet* to the eighteenth-century text of *Der bestrafte Brudermord* cannot tell us anything about the origins of Q1, because the German text involves translation, transnational touring, changes of company and theatre, and sustained adaptation, based probably on the portable printed texts of Q1 and Q2. See Tiffany Stern's "'If I could see the Puppets Dallying': *Der Bestrafte Brudermord* and Hamlet's Encounters with the Puppets," *Shakespeare Bulletin* 31 (2013): 337–52.
54. Leah S. Marcus, *Un-editing the Renaissance: Shakespeare, Marlowe, Milton* (London: Routledge, 1996), 152–76.
55. Albert Weiner, ed., *Hamlet: The First Quarto, 1603* (Great Neck, NY: Barron's Educational, 1962), 24.
56. Hardin Craig, *A New Look at Shakespeare's Quartos* (Stanford: Stanford University Press, 1961), 9.
57. Paul Werstine, *Early Modern Playhouse Manuscripts and the Editing of Shakespeare* (Cambridge: Cambridge University Press, 2013).
58. Q2 has "Considerat" for "Confederate" (3.2.249) and "inuected" for "infected" (251), but most editors agree that these variants are compositorial errors; in early modern usage, "ban" and "bane" (251) are simply spelling variants; F1's unique "usurp" (3.2.251, for "usurps") is also indifferent, and could easily be attributed to a compositor or scribe.
59. Q2's "threescore" for "three" (2.2.73) is extrametrical, and regarded as an error by most editors. The only other substantive variant is harmlessly different in all three texts: "enterprise" is modified by "that" in Q1 (7.49), "this" in Q2 (2.2.78), and "his" in F (2.2.77).
60. "Q1 *Hamlet* is less than 60 percent as long as F, yet Marcellus's role in Q1 retains 92 percent of its length in F—with more than 90 percent of

these lines closely corresponding in the two versions" (Irace, *Reforming*, 123). This means, from the perspective of memorial reconstruction, that the actor completely forgot eight percent of his own lines, and garbled ten percent of the remainder.

61. Lukas Erne, *Shakespeare as Literary Dramatist*, rev. ed. (Cambridge: Cambridge University Press, 2013), 232. Erne rejected memorial reconstruction in favor of his own hypothesis (that Q1 represents the abridged performance script of the play), which I consider in chapter 3.
62. I have written about one modern playwright revising his script, repeatedly, in "'May I Be Metamorphosed': *Cardenio* by Stages," in *The Quest for Cardenio: Shakespeare, Fletcher, Cervantes and the Lost Play*, ed. David Carnegie and Gary Taylor (Oxford: Oxford University Press, 2012), 387–403; and "Poner in Escena *The History of Cardenio*," in *The Creation and Re-creation of Cardenio: Performing Shakespeare, Transforming Cervantes*, ed. Terri Bourus and Gary Taylor (New York: Palgrave, 2013), 197–218.
63. F. P. Wilson, *Marlowe and the Early Shakespeare* (Oxford: Clarendon Press, 1953), 115. The actor who played King John cannot have also played Melun, since Melun exits at the end of 5.2 and John enters immediately at the beginning of 5.3. Wilson did not make this point.
64. Albright's neglected book makes a related point: "Certain characters might become fixed conceptions in the mind of the author early in his work on a play. . . . in reworking a play, there is always the possibility that the changes in plot will not affect some character enough to necessitate a change in his lines" (*Dramatic Publication*, 308).
65. These interleavings were removed and now have a separate British Library shelfmark. I have examined them personally, but they were called to my attention by the accurate account in Arthur and Janet Ing Freeman, "Did Halliwell Steal and Mutilate the First Quarto of *Hamlet?*" *Library* VII, 2:4 (2001): 349–63, esp. 359–63.
66. *Hamlet, Prince of Denmark: A Tragedy* (London: M. Wellington, 1718). This is one of the so-called Players' Quartos (though in fact it is a duodecimo). See Henry N. Paul, "Mr. Hughs' Edition of *Hamlet*," *Modern Language Notes* 49 (1934): 438–43.
67. Randall McLeod, "*Gon.* No more, the text is foolish," in *The Division of the Kingdoms: Shakespeare's Two Versions of King Lear*, ed. Gary Taylor and Michael Warren (Oxford: Oxford University Press, 1983).
68. Charles [and Mary] Lamb, *Tales from Shakespear* (1807). Charles adapted the tragedies, including *Hamlet*.
69. William Hazlitt, *Characters of Shakespear's Plays* (London: Printed by C. H. Reynell, for R. Hunter, 1817), 103, 104.
70. Lamb, "On the Tragedies of Shakspere," *The Reflector* (1811); Hazlitt, *Characters*, 113. Hazlitt and Lamb were both avid theatregoers, but the Shakespeare productions they witnessed were deformed by anachronistic theatrical practices, which magnified the differences between reading the texts and watching them performed. For a valuable defense of Hazlitt and

Lamb, see Edward Pechter, *Shakespeare Studies Today: Romanticism Lost* (New York: Palgrave, 2011), esp. 151–76. My point here is simply that Q1 *Hamlet* was discovered at a moment intrinsically inhospitable to it.
71. On this shift, see Shannon Jackson, *Professing Performance: Theatre in the Academy from Philology to Performativity* (Cambridge: Cambridge University Press, 2004), esp. 40–78.
72. For entrances where modern editors specify the letter, when early editions do not, see for example *Merry Wives* 4.5.0.1, 4.6.0.1 (in each case, the entrance of two characters), *Richard III* 5.2.0.1, and *1 Henry VI* 5.2.0.1.
73. See William Davis, "Now, Gods, Stand up for Bastards: The 1603 'Good Quarto' of *Hamlet*," *Textual Cultures* 1 (2006): 60–89.
74. In my production of Q1 (described in chapter 4), neither actor in that scene had any difficulty with the exchange, or raised any question about it during any rehearsals. Nor did the scene provoke questions from any spectator in any of the talk-backs that followed each of our seven performances.
75. Here, as often elsewhere, the Folio text is closer to Q1. I discuss this pattern in Chapter 6.
76. B. A. P. Van Dam, *The Text of Shakespeare's Hamlet* (London: John Lane, 1924), 19. Van Dam's argument depends in part on the assumption that "My will, not all the world" is the second half of a single verse line, but the phrase is metrically ambiguous, and could just as easily be interpreted (as it is by Taylor and Thompson) as the first half of the next verse line.
77. Stern, "Sermons, Plays and Note-takers: *Hamlet* Q1 as a 'Noted' Text," *Shakespeare Survey* 66 (2013): 1–23, esp. 3, 12, 13, 14, 15.

3 Piratical Reporters?

1. Ambrose Gunthio, "A Running Commentary on the Hamlet of 1603," *European Magazine*, n.s. 1:4 (December 1825): 339–47, esp. 340.
2. Tiffany Stern, "Sermons, Plays and Note-takers: *Hamlet* Q1 as a 'Noted' Text," *Shakespeare Survey* 66 (2013): 1. Stern's 2013 essay is a revision of a PowerPoint presentation she gave at the International Shakespeare Conference at Stratford-upon-Avon in August 2012, where it was enthusiastically received.
3. Gunthio, "Commentary," 346. I have modernized his quotations.
4. Gunthio, "Commentary," 341; see Samuel Johnson, *Johnson on Shakespeare*, ed. Arthur Sherbo and Bertrand Harris Bronson, 2 vols. (New Haven, CT: Yale University Press, 1968), 612.
5. Gunthio, "Commentary," 341, 345, 344, 346. Stern does not mention these other elements of Gunthio's hypothesis.
6. Stern does not cite evidence or a source for her claim that Gunthio was "probably" Collier, but the most recent case for the identification is Bernice Kliman's "All at Sea about *Hamlet* at Sea," *Shakespeare Quarterly* 62 (2011): 180–204. For a different view by two experts on Collier, see

Arthur Freeman and Janet Ing Freeman, *John Payne Collier: Scholarship and Forgery in the Nineteenth Century* (New Haven: Yale University Press, 2004), 1040 (note 7), and 1397 ("Rejected Attributions"). The attribution to Collier originates in what they call the "irresponsible hit-and-run tactics" of Sydney Race, who in the 1950s "challenged the authenticity of at least fourteen more of Collier's documents, questioning the very existence of ten that certainly now exist, and the authenticity of others that had been in place for a century before" Collier cited them (210–11).

7. J. Payne Collier, "Introduction" to *Hamlet* in *The Works of William Shakespeare: The Text Formed from an Entirely New Collation of the Old Editions*, ed. Collier, 8 vols. (London: Whittaker), VII (1843), 189–93. Of course, Collier may simply have read the 1825 article, rather than writing it.

8. W. W. Greg, *A Bibliography of the English Printed Drama to the Restoration*, 4 vols (London: Bibliographical Society, 1939–59), 3:1315–16. Greg provides evidence that the 1647 cataloguer, Henry Oxinden, must have acquired or inherited many of his playbooks from an earlier collector.

9. For "confirmation bias" and related cognitive errors in Stern's recent work, see Gary Taylor, "Sleight of Mind: Cognitive Illusions and Shakespearian Desire," in *The Creation and Re-creation of Cardenio: Performing Shakespeare, Transforming Cervantes*, ed. Terri Bourus and Gary Taylor (New York: Palgrave, 2013), 125–69. As Taylor notes, anyone can be guilty of confirmation bias (including me).

10. I will return to the "lost play by someone else" in chapter 5.

11. For the "conjunction fallacy" in Stern's other work, see Taylor, "Sleight of Mind," 138–44, which draws upon the work by Daniel Kahneman and Avos Tversky, "Extensional Versus Intuitive Reasoning: The Conjunction Fallacy in Probability Judgment," *Psychological Review* 90 (1985): 293–315; and Daniel Kahneman, *Thinking, Fast and Slow* (New York: Farrar, Straus and Giroux, 2011), 158–65.

12. Paul Werstine, "A Century of 'Bad' Shakespeare Quartos," *Shakespeare Quarterly* 50 (1999): 310–33.

13. Stern, "Note-takers," 18, 20, 22, 13, 4, 11, 16, 18, 19, 13, 15, 22.

14. J. Payne Collier, "The Edition of 'Hamlet' in 1603," *Athenaeum* 1510 (4 October 1856), 1220–21; Stern, "Note-takers," 13. She summarizes his explanation for the "right done"/"writ down" variant, but does not quote him (or give the correct page number for his claim).

15. Michael Mendle, "News and the Pamphlet Culture of Mid-seventeenth-century England," in *The Politics of Information in Early Modern Europe*, ed. Brendan Dooley and Sabrina A. Baron (London: Routledge, 2001), 57–79.

16. Stern, "Note-takers," 23.

17. Stern began her career using transparencies and an overhead projector. The pile of transparencies (which could be reshuffled at will) made the comparison with "notes" even more materially conspicuous.

18. See Tiffany Stern, *Rehearsal from Shakespeare to Sheridan* (Oxford: Clarendon, 2000), her first book, based on her doctoral dissertation. For

important critiques of this work, from specialists in the Restoration and eighteenth-century theatre, see the review by Pauline Kewes, *Review of English Studies* 53 (2002): 127–9, and the discussion of *The Rehearsal* in *Plays, Poems, and Miscellaneous Writings Associated with George Villiers, Second Duke of Buckingham*, ed. Robert D. Hume and Harold Love, 2 vols. (Oxford: Oxford University Press, 2007).

19. Stern, "Note-takers," 5.
20. H. R. Woudhuysen, "Writing-Tables and Table Books," *Electronic British Library Journal* (2004): 1–11; Peter Stallybrass, Roger Chartier, J. Franklin Mowery, Heather Wolfe, "Hamlet's Tables and the Technologies of Writing in Renaissance England," *Shakespeare Quarterly* 55 (2004): 379–419. My subsequent statements about tablebooks come from these articles, unless otherwise noted.
21. Henry Petroski, *The Pencil: A History of Design and Circumstance* (New York: Alfred A. Knopf, 1990), 36–60; Ainsworth C. Mitchell, "Pencil Markings in the Bodleian Library," *Nature* 109 (22 April 1922): 516–17; Stallybrass et al., "Hamlet's Tables," 409.
22. Anonymous, *A very proper treatise, wherein is briefly sett forthe the arte of limming which teacheth the order in drawing [and] tracing of letters, vinets, flowers, armes and imagery... necessary to be knowne to all such gentle-menne, and other persones as doe delite in limming, painting or in tricking of armes in their right colors* (1573; STC 24252), sig. Aii recto. *OED*'s definition for this sense (2.a) is ambiguous and misleading: "A tapered or pointed instrument for writing or drawing, consisting of a slender stick of graphite or a similar substance enclosed in a long thin cylindrical piece of wood, or fixed in a case of some other material (as metal, plastic, etc.)." This definition combines writing and drawing, and it anticipates the use of a cylindrical casing, which is not recorded until 1683 (and there described as an innovation, "of late"). EEBO-TCP turns up many apparent examples of "pencil" used of literary writing, but upon examination these turn out to be examples of the conventional trope *ut pictura poesis*, equating poetry with painting. *OED*'s examples at least have the merit of referring, unambiguously, to material acts in which pencils were used to write down words and letters.
23. John Brinsley, *Ludus literarius: or, the grammar schoole* (1612; STC 829.02), 46–7.
24. Chris R. Kyle, *Theatre of State: Parliament and Political Culture in Early Stuart England* (Stanford: Stanford University Press, 2012), 68–9.
25. Stallybrass et al., "Hamlet's Tables," 401–2; Woudhuysen also notes their use as "smart and lavish gifts" ("Writing-Tables," 11).
26. Nashe, *Have with you to Saffron Walden* (1596), cited by Woudhuysen, "Writing-Tables," 9.
27. Stern, "Note-takers," 5, citing Joseph Hall, *The Works* (1625), 187. I have modernized the spelling. Her two subsequent examples come from 1636 (Heywood) and 1641 (Featley).

28. Dekker, *The Wonderfull Yeare* (1603), sig. C1v; cited by Stern, "Note-takers," 8.
29. Stern, "Note-takers," 4; Kyle, *Theatre of State*, 67.
30. Brathwaite, *Whimzies* (1631), sig. B6v-7r; cited by Woudhuysen, "Writing-Tables", 10.
31. William Matthews, "Shorthand and the Bad Shakespeare Quartos," *Modern Language Review* 27 (1932): 243–62, and "Shakespeare and the Reporters," *Library* IV, 15 (1935): 481–500; George Ian Duthie, *Elizabethan Shorthand and the First Quarto of "King Lear"* (Oxford: Blackwell, 1949).
32. Stern, "Note-takers," 8; Kyle, *Theater of State*, 4, 62, 8, 71, 60, 64, 67, 71, 71, 65, 75.
33. Chris R. Kyle, "'It will be a Scandal to show what we have done with such a number'; House of Commons Committee Attendance Lists, 1606–1628," in *Parliament, Politics and Elections 1604–1628*, ed. Kyle, Camden Fifth Series, vol. 17 (Cambridge University Press, 2001), 179–236.
34. Kyle, *Theatre of State*, 80. Stern also ("Note-takers," 17) cites Kyle (p. 68) for an example of one member of Parliament who "made use of" notes by two other MPs to supplement his own; she did not examine (as I have done) the original document (Harleian MS 354, f. 2–8, dated 28 July 1610).
35. Stern, "Note-takers," 18, 4, 8, 21, 18.
36. Stern, "Note-takers," 18, citing William Crashaw's preface to *Perkins his exhortation to Repentance* (1605), A7v (preface by William Crashaw, who originally took it down "with this hand of mine, from his own mouth").
37. Stern, "Note-takers," 18, citing Symon Presse, *A Sermon Preached at Eggington* (1596), A1v.
38. Kyle, *Theatre of State*, 71–2.
39. For spectators recording memorable fragments of Shakespeare, see Gary Taylor, "Feeling Bodies," in *Shakespeare in the Twentieth Century: Proceedings of the Sixth World Shakespeare Congress*, ed. Jonathan Bate (Newark: University of Delaware Press, 1998), 258–79.
40. Matthews, "Reporters," 498.
41. Richard Knowles, "Shakespeare and Shorthand Once Again," *PBSA* 194 (2010): 141–80, esp. 146, 180.
42. See Taylor's textual introductions to *A Game at Chess*, in *Thomas Middleton and Early Modern Textual Culture,* ed. Gary Taylor and John Lavagnino (Oxford: Oxford University Press, 2007), 712–873. I owe this observation to Taylor, who also pointed out to me the relevance of Middleton's synonyms (discussed below).
43. Stern, "Note-takers," 20–21. Stern's psychological speculations about note-takers resemble her disproven speculations about Theobald and his alleged "forgery" of *Double Falsehood*. Even if she were right about Theobald (and the UCLA conference on *Cardenio/Double Falsehood* in January 2014 further undermined her argument), forgery clearly differs from note-taking, and Theobald very conspicuously advertised his presence in *Double Falsehood*.

44. Stern, "Note-takers," 21–2. Stern does not claim to be a bibliographer. Non-specialists can sometimes notice details or imagine possibilities overlooked by people operating within the bubble of a shared set of assumptions. But Stern's only reference to bibliographical scholarship is Melnikoff's (flawed) essay on Ling (p. 22), discussed in chapter 1. Even that does not support her argument.
45. I am grateful to Bland for giving me access to his forthcoming *Renaissance Quarterly* review of Lukas Erne's *Shakespeare and the Book Trade* (Cambridge: Cambridge University Press, 2013).
46. All were of single authorship and clearly attributed to him. In that same period, Lukas Erne identifies only 65 editions from Shakespeare's much larger canon (*Book Trade*, 1, tabulated on pp. 14–15). But one of those is lost, as is the title page of another; at least 17 of the remainder were published without attribution to Shakespeare, and 15 were collaborative (according to the latest stylometric scholarship, which identifies the work of other authors in *Titus Andronicus, Edward III, Pericles, Passionate Pilgrim,* and all three *Henry VI* plays).
47. It is sometimes asserted that the lost 1597 edition of *Love's Labour's Lost* was a "bad quarto," but since its text does not survive we have no way of knowing how it differed from the extant 1598 edition (which does not attribute the play to Shakespeare, and was not reprinted until 1631).
48. Matthews notes that "the differences between the pirated and authorized versions" of the sermons "are largely to be attributed to the preachers' emendations and additions" ("Reporters," 490). Ling also published in 1591 Smith's *Fruitful Sermon*, explicating Paul's first epistle to the Thessalonians (later called "The True Trial of the Spirit"), which was "*taken by characterie*" according to Ling's title page (STC 22664). But he did not publish the revised edition; moreover, "except for a few added lines and small touches of style, especially some condensation of language near the end, the revised edition in the collected sermons is usually virtually the same as Ling's reported text, and is evidently based upon it" (Knowles, "Shorthand", 178). For a fuller account, see Henrie Smith, *A Fruitfull Sermon*, ed. H. T Price (Halle: Verlag von Max Niemeyer, 1922).
49. STC 22657. I have personally examined and collated the British Library copies of Ling's first version (4474.b.68) and the corrected edition (4474.a.20).
50. Ferguson, *Simmes*, 85–6 (including "Tantens" for "Tauteus").
51. Stern, "Note-takers," 13, 12; Knowles, "Shorthand," 168, 172, 171, 169. Knowles is criticizing Adele Davidson's claims that Q1 *Lear* was based on a shorthand text. But Stern recommends Davidson's book ("Noters," 4), and is deeply indebted to it even when she does not specifically acknowledge it. Knowles's arguments apply equally well to Stern's conjectures about Q1 *Hamlet*.
52. Matthews, "Shorthand," 247.
53. H. T Price, *The Text of "Henry V"* (Newcastle-under-Lyme: Mandley & Unett, 1920); Smith, *Fruitfull Sermon*, ed. Price, xv. Price's "even in

rhyme" is important, because Stern claims that variants in rhymes are further evidence of note-taking.
54. Alan E. Craven, "Simmes's Compositor A and Five Shakespeare Quartos," *Studies in Bibliography* 26 (1971): 37–60.
55. Alan E. Craven, "The Reliability of Simmes's Compositor A," *Studies in Bibliography* 32 (1979): 186–97.
56. Stern, "Note-takers," 16, citing Irace, "Origins and Agents," 91.
57. "Horatio!" is the conjecture of Thompson and Taylor (*Hamlet 1603*, 115); the three-word summons occurs in Q2 and F, and was conjecturally inserted in Q1 by Weiner in his edition.
58. John Russell Brown, "The Compositors of *Hamlet* Q2 and *The Merchant of Venice*," *Studies in Bibliography* 7 (1955): 17–40, confirmed and slightly modified by W. Craig Ferguson, *Pica Roman Type in Elizabethan England* (Aldershot: Scolar, 1989), 15.
59. 5.2.16 reverence and respect/reverend respect, 5.2.20 count it strange/think it most absurd, 5.2.31 cunning judgments/strange cunning, 5.2.35 when/if, 5.2.45 by/aside, 5.2.50 others/men, 5.2.69 strict/hot, 5.2.85 were prepared for't/did prepare yourself, 5.2.87 slid/light, 5.2.92 seen/known, 5.2.106.1 with/and, 5.2.114 monster-impudence/bloody villain, 5.2.155 attempt/offence, 4.3.39 specially/especially, 5.2.62 if I should/were I to, 5.3.118 pass/walk, 5.3.120 locked/shut, 5.3.136 those parts/that place, 5.3.188 sfoot/slid, 5.3.191 if/and, Epi.7 in corners/in private. Apparently authorial variants in the six other texts of these two scenes include: 5.2.17 unchasteness/unchastity, 5.2.33 auditory/audience, 5.2.35 office/business, 5.3.40 plump/fat, 5.3.98 crammed/full, 5.3.116 swear/say, 5.3.121 foul/vild, 5.3.135 smile/laugh, 5.3.168 sweetness/meekness, 5.3.195 scant/little, 5.3.198 bag/pit, 5.3.205 mightiest/greatest, 5.3.218 malice/falsehood.
60. Stanley Wells and Gary Taylor, *William Shakespeare: A Textual Companion*, 329–30 (Oxford: Clarendon, 1987) (*1 Henry IV*); John Jowett, ed., *The Tragedy of King Richard III* (Oxford: Clarendon, 2000); William Lloyd, "Scribal Copy for Q1 *Richard II*," *Notes and Queries* 51:3 (2004): 280–3. For the Folio plays set from manuscript copy, see Gary Taylor, "Post-Script," in Taylor and Jowett, *Shakespeare Reshaped* (Oxford: Clarendon, 1993), 237–43.
61. Stern, "Note-takers," 9–10, cites phrases from Buc (1615), then Heywood (1637, 1608), without reference to Maguire's extended discussion in Laurie E Maguire, *Shakespearean Suspect Texts: The "Bad" Quartos and Their Contexts* (Cambridge: Cambridge UP, 1996), 99–105.
62. Thomas Heywood, *The Rape of Lucrece* (London, 1608), sig. A2r.
63. Buc, *The Third University of England* (1615), 984.
64. Heywood, *If You Know Not Me* (1639), sig. A2r; Heywood, *"A Prologue to the Play of Queene Elizabeth as it was last revived at the* Cock-pit, *in which the Author taxeth the most corrupted copy now imprinted, which was published without his consent,"* in *Pleasant Dialogues and Dramma's* (entered in the Stationers' Register, 29 August 1635, published in 1637), sig. R4^v.

65. See, for instance, G. N. Giordano-Orsini, "Thomas Heywood's Play on The Troubles of Queen Elizabeth," *Library* IV, 14 (1933–4): 313–38. But he accepts that the play had been pirated.
66. Williams graciously gave me access to his two conference papers on the topic, one delivered at the Blackfriars conference in 2010, the other circulated in a seminar at the Shakespeare Association of America conference in 2011.
67. Adrian Johns, *Piracy: The Intellectual Property Wars from Gutenberg to Gates* (Chicago: University of Chicago Press, 2009), 7.
68. See Tiffany Stern's own *Documents of Performance in Early Modern England* (Cambridge: Cambridge University Press, 2009) for a description of the surviving plots/plats and an analysis of their function.
69. Stern, "Note-takers," 16, quoting Paul Menzer, *The Hamlets: Qs, Cues, and Remembered Texts* (Newark: University of Delaware Press, 2008), 65.
70. Menzer, *Hamlets*, 68.
71. Simon Palfrey and Tiffany Stern, *Shakespeare in Parts* (Oxford: Oxford University Press, 2007), 165–77. They speculate about artistic motives for the repetition, but I could equally speculate about its motives in the nunnery scene. What matters, objectively, is that repeated cues do appear in Shakespeare's plays, and more often in the early ones.
72. Stern, *Rehearsal*, 58, 67–8.
73. Erne, *Book Trade*, 9.
74. Stern, "Note-takers," 19. She also cites Robert Sanderson's *Two Sermons* (1622), where the author's preface explains that he has used inverted commas (quotation marks) to signal material left out in his own performance of his own text. Obviously, that example is not only two decades later than Q1 *Hamlet*, and in a different genre, but also can do nothing to support Stern's theory of collective note-taking.
75. Paul Werstine, "Narratives About Printed Shakespeare Texts: 'Foul Papers' and 'Bad' Quartos," *Shakespeare Quarterly* 41 (1990): 80; cited by Erne, *Shakespeare as Literary Dramatist*, rev. ed. (Cambridge: Cambridge University Press, 2013), 229. (I cite page numbers from the 2013 second edition throughout, but this part of his argument remains the same as a decade earlier.)
76. Paul Werstine, "A Century of 'Bad' Shakespeare Quartos," *Shakespeare Quarterly* 50 (1999): 327; cited by Erne, *Literary*, 227.
77. Erne, *Literary*, 229–34.
78. Erne, *Literary*, 218, 244, 224, 226, 241, 237.
79. Erne, *Literary*, 260, 261, 258, 259, 263, 258, 259, 263.
80. Humphrey Moseley, "The Stationer to the Readers," in Beaumont and Fletcher, *Comedies and Tragedies* (1647), sig. A4; Peter W. M. Blayney, "Publication of Playbooks," in *A New History of Early English Drama*, ed. John D. Cox and David Scott Kastan (New York: Columbia University Press, 1997), 394; Erne, *Literary*, 173–4.

81. Paul Werstine, *Early Modern Playhouse Manuscripts and the Editing of Shakespeare* (Cambridge: Cambridge University Press, 2013), 224 (citing Erne, *Literary,* 219, 196).
82. Andrew Gurr, "Maximal and Minimal Texts: Shakespeare v. the Globe," *Shakespeare Survey* 52 (1999): 68–87; Gurr, ed., *The First Quarto of King Henry V,* The New Cambridge Shakespeare: The Early Quartos (Cambridge: Cambridge University Press, 2000), ix. Erne relies on Gurr's hypothesis repeatedly (*Literary Dramatist,* 158, 161, 201, 212, 220, 241, 243, 248, 256).
83. Michael J. Hirrel, "Duration of Performance and Lengths of Plays: How Shall We Beguile the Lazy Time?" *Shakespeare Quarterly* 61 (2010): 159–182.
84. Werstine, *Playhouse Manuscripts,* 222–3.
85. Margrethe Jolly, "*Hamlet* and the French Connection: The Relationship of Q1 and Q2 *Hamlet* and the Evidence of Belleforest's *Histoires Tragiques,*" *Parergon* 29.1 (2012): 83–105, esp. 103.
86. Stern, "Note-takers," 15.
87. *Titus Androncicus* 4.4.38, *Cymbeline* 4.2.132. These and other references to Shakespeare (except *Hamlet*) refer to the text and line-numbering of William Shakespeare, *The Complete Works,* ed. Stanley Wells and Gary Taylor (Oxford: Oxford University Press, 2005).
88. Jolly, "F French Connection," 96.

4   How Old Is Young?

1. Leah S. Marcus, *Unediting the Renaissance: Shakespeare, Marlowe, Milton* (London: Routledge, 1996), 107.
2. Paul M. Edmondson, "'A sad story tolde': Playing Horatio in Q1 *Hamlet,*" *Hamlet Studies* 22 (2000): 26–39; Philip C. McGuire, "Which Fortinbras, Which *Hamlet?*" in *Hamlet First Published,* ed. Thomas Clayton (Newark: University of Delaware Press, 1992), 151–78; Kirk Melnikoff, "Nicholas Ling's Republican *Hamlet* (1603)" in *Shakespeare's Stationers: Studies in Cultural Bibliography,* ed. Marta Straznicky (Philadelphia: University of Pennsylvania Press, 2012); Steven Urkowitz, "'Well-sayd olde Mole': Burying Three *Hamlets* in Modern Editions," in *Shakespeare Study Today,* ed. Georgianna Ziegler (New York: AMS, 1986), 37–70.
3. "A Funeral Elegy on the Death of the famous Actor Richard Burbage" (Huntington Library MS HM 198, 99–101), in *English Professional Theatre, 1530–1660,* ed. Glynne Wickham, Herbert Berry, and William Ingram (Cambridge: Cambridge University Press, 2001), 181–3. See also G. P. Jones, "*A Burbage Ballad* and John Payne Collier," *Review of English Studies* 40 (1989): 393–7, and British Library MS Stowe 962, fols. 62b–63b.
4. Andrew Gurr, *The Shakespeare Company, 1594–1642* (Cambridge: Cambridge University Press, 2004), 222.

5. For details, see my fuller discussion of chronology in chapter 5.
6. Harold Jenkins, in his edition of *Hamlet* (London: Methuen, 1982), recognizes that "no arithmetic is necessary to determine that Hamlet must be thirty," but then dedicates four pages to dismissing the "perplexity" this has caused other critics; in particular, he dismisses the variants in Q1, "now that Q1 is recognized as a reported text," by speculating that "the reporter had a poor memory for numbers" (551–4). He does not consider the other evidence I discuss here.
7. Ann Thompson and Neil Taylor, in their edition of *Hamlet* (London: Arden Shakespeare, 2006), note this "stress on 30 years of marriage" (*1604*, p. 308) but do not mention its relevance to Hamlet's age.
8. Bart Van Es, *Shakespeare in Company* (Oxford: Oxford University Press, 2013), 232–48. There is no contemporary evidence that Burbage played Coriolanus, who seems to be younger; another member of the company was clearly capable of long roles, since there is a second one in both *Othello* (Iago, actually longer than Othello, which Burbage played) and *Volpone* (Mosca).
9. In order to deny this correspondence, Mary Edmond has to deny that the portrait represents Burbage, and to argue that "fat" means "sweaty," a meaning for which neither she nor the *Oxford English Dictionary* can produce parallels ("Burbage, Richard," *Oxford Dictionary of National Biography*).
10. Adolphus Alfred Jack, *Young Hamlet*, edited with an "Introduction" by E. D. Taylor (Aberdeen: University of Aberdeen Press, 1950), 4–5. Jack had been Professor and Chair of English Literature at the University of Aberdeen until he retired in 1938; he had died in 1945. The fact that the book was published posthumously probably contributed to the neglect of Jack's argument by subsequent scholars.
11. Q1 dates the marriage "forty" years before (9.98), and calls the player who speaks the word a "Duke" and the player to whom the word is addressed a "Duchess" in the preceding stage direction, in speech prefixes and dialogue (9.139); in the source for the poisoning story, the victim was the Duke of Urbino (Jenkins, *Hamlet*, 507–8). If the couple in the Mousetrap are ducal, the parallel with the royal couple is less emphatic. Even if the Queen and King had been married 40 years ago, she could have had the child less than 20 years ago: see discussion below about the age of queens at marriage. In Q1, when Hamlet refers to Lucianus as "nephew to the king" (9.142), his change of title aggressively strengthens the parallel between the inset play and the Danish court. The stage direction for the preliminary dumbshow also calls them king and queen (9.83.1), but this inconsistency, which may be authorial, does not immediately impinge on "forty." My point is simple: the canonical text explicitly identifies Hamlet's age as 30, and also identifies a royal couple's wedding as 30 years ago; the two numbers reinforce each other, and neither is present in Q1. The later editions have "king" and "queen" for the play-within-the-play, except for a single inconsistent "duke" (3.2.233), 82 lines after the last reference to "thirty" years of royal marriage.

12. Thompson and Taylor conclude that Hamlet is 18 (*Hamlet 1603*, 48, and 16.85–6, note), but that assumes that he *must* have been seven when Yorick died. Shakespeare implicitly specified that, when he wrote the "enlarged" version, and though it is possible that Q1 makes the same assumption, it is not necessary. Thompson and Taylor are assuming, here, that all three texts are versions of the same narrative.
13. Audiences would see the beard before it is described at the end of the second scene (2.152–3; 1.2.240–42). Again, the three texts are stable on this detail: F has "grizzly" and Q1 has "silver," but these indifferent variants could be scribal or compositorial errors.
14. See "young Prince Hamlet" (6.38, Ophelia), "the young Prince Hamlet" (7.59, Corambis), "when I was young I was very idle and suffered much ecstasy in love, very near this" (7.224–6, Corambis comparing himself to Hamlet), "I heare young Hamlet coming" (11.1).
15. Ambrose Gunthio, "A Running Commentary on the Hamlet of 1603," *European Magazine* 1.4 (December 1825): 344. Jenkins cites Rowley's *Birth of Merlin* 2.1.61–3, which confirms this idiom (*Hamlet*, 223), but claims without evidence that it could be "easily extended to any call or enticement."
16. Paul Griffiths, *Youth and Authority: Formative Experience in England 1560–1640* (Oxford: Clarendon, 1996), 24–5.
17. In both quartos, Hamlet later calls Rosencraft/Rosencraus and Guilderstone/Guildenstern his "schoolfellows" (Q1 7.237; Q2 3.4..200); but in itself the word is ambiguous, as it could refer to grammar school or university. In the later version, where Hamlet wants to go *back* to Wittenberg, we naturally interpret it as a reference to university. In Q1 it is ambiguous.
18. Margrethe Jolly, "*Hamlet* and the French Connection: The Relationship of Q1 and Q2 *Hamlet* and the Evidence of Belleforest's *Histoires Tragiques*." *Parergon* 29.1 (2012): 93–4. She does not make the specific point about 21 years of age. She cites evidence of Hamlet's youth from scenes 1, 6, 7, 11, and 16 of Q1, overlooking the examples I cite from Sc. 2 and 5.
19. Jeffrey L. Forgeng, *Daily Life in Elizabethan England* (Westport, CT: Greenwood, 2009), 63.
20. Samuel Schoenbaum, *William Shakespeare: A Documentary Life* (New York: Oxford University Press, 1975) 136, 172, 150; Gurr, *Shakespeare Company*, 239.
21. Compare Cleopatra's complaint that "Against the blown rose may they stop their nose / That kneeled unto the buds" (*Antony* 3.13. 38–9), comparing her own maturity to the "blown rose" (in contrast, implicitly, with her "salad days," when she was the bud).
22. See Paul Menzer, *The Hamlets: Cues, Qs, and Remembered Texts* (Newark: University of Delaware Press, 2008), which I discuss in chapter 2.
23. Q2 and F change this to "let him ply his music" (2.1.69), which is less directive, and refers to a gentlemanly pastime rather than study at school.

Q1 presumably implies the Catholic University of Paris, the most famous in Europe.
24. All three texts specify that the King, in betting that Hamlet will win, has bet on the "weaker side" (17.49; 5.2.238). But this is emphasized in the later versions, where Horatio tells Hamlet that he "will lose," and Hamlet is more confident, but only that he will win "at the odds," that is, not win absolutely, but win more bouts than expected (5.2.187–9)—in the way that someone can win a bet by predicting that a sports team will *lose by a smaller margin* than predicted. In Q1, the King tells Leartes that he will bet "that in twelve venies / You gain not three of him" (15.18–19); in isolation, this would probably be taken to mean "you win not three of him," meaning that Laertes is expected to win 10 of 12. But Thompson and Taylor interpret it to mean the same thing as in the later versions: "you [Laertes] do not exceed him [Hamlet] by three (of the 12) bouts" (*Arden 1603*, commentary, p. 152). The terms are repeated, for clarity, again, in a later scene in Q1, addressed to Hamlet: "that young Leartes in twelve venies at rapier and dagger do not get three odds of you" (17.279). The exact meaning of the bet in Q2 and F is even less clear; Jenkins describes it as "an insoluble problem" (*Hamlet*, 561–3), and Gary Taylor emends it (5.2.128 in the Oxford Shakespeare). But most commentators agree that it implies only that Laertes will get three hits *more* than Hamlet does (Thompson and Taylor, *Hamlet 1604*, 5.2.146–8, commentary).
25. Q2 alone contains a passage that associates Laertes' skill as a fencer with "youth" (4.7.76–9).
26. Edward VI was betrothed at the age of five, but died when he was just 15, before he could be married.
27. The Folio text specifically names "Ophelia his sister" as one of the characters who enters with the court at the beginning of the second scene, and distinguishes her from the "Attendants" who are also specified; although silent in the scene, she participates in a state occasion. Q1 and Q2 are ambiguous about whether she is included among the "attendants" or "others" in that scene.
28. See Marga Munkelt, "Traditions of Emendation in *Hamlet*: The Handling of the First Quarto," in *Hamlet First Published*, ed. Clayton, 211–40; the first example occurs in Samuel W. Singer's 1826 edition of the *Dramatic Works*, published only a year after Q1 was republished.
29. See Linda F. Lunstrom, *William Poel's Hamlets: The Director as Critic* (1984), 13–42, and Marvin Rosenberg, "The First Modern English Staging of *Hamlet* Q1," in *Hamlet First Published*, 241–8.
30. Kathleen O. Irace, *The First Quarto of Hamlet* (Cambridge: Cambridge University Press, 1998), 20–27; Thompson and Taylor, *Hamlet 1603*, 13–39.
31. Philip Fisher, "Hamlet, Old Vic (2004)," britishtheatreguide.info/reviews/hamletOV-rev (accessed December 2013). The 21 July 2004 performance of this production is preserved on film in the National Video Archive of

Performance, which can be seen at the Victoria and Albert Theatre and Performance Department.
32. Imogen Stubbs, "Gertrude," in *Performing Shakespeare's Tragedies Today: An Actor's Perspective*, ed. Michael Dobson (Cambridge: Cambridge University Press, 2006), 29–40.
33. For instance, in order to play Horatio as an undergraduate, Nunn reassigned to Barnardo Horatio's speech in the first scene on the duel between the old King Hamlet and the old King Fortinbras.
34. Charles Spencer, "An Unforgettable and Most Lovable Hamlet," *Telegraph*, 28 April 2004 (accessed online December 2013).
35. Alan Bird, "Hamlet at the Old Vic," 28 April 2004, LondonTheatre.co.uk (accessed December 2013).
36. The Indianapolis arts weekly, Nuvo, praised my direction as the "highlight" of the production ("Review: 'Young Hamlet' at IndyFringe," 8 February 2011, also available on the Hoosier Bard pages of the New Oxford Shakespeare website at IUPUI). However, I doubt that Joe Williams had seen many of Nunn's productions for the RSC or the National Theatre.
37. *Young Hamlet*, dir. Terri Bourus, Hoosier Bard Productions, Indy Fringe Theatre, Indianapolis, 2–12 February 2011. The script was a conservatively edited modern-spelling text of Q1, emending only what seemed to be compositorial errors.
38. Jay Harvey, "'Young Hamlet' Features a Less Philosophical Hero," *Indianapolis Star*, 13 February 2011 (also available on the New Oxford Shakespeare website at IUPUI).
39. The Queen is called "Gertred" in Q1, "Gertrard" in Q2, "Gertrude" in F and almost all modern editions and performances. But she is the Queen in all three.
40. Michael Billington, "Hamlet, Old Vic," *Guardian*, 28 April 2004 (accessible online).
41. Spencer, "Unforgettable"; Fisher, "Hamlet."
42. Stubbs, "Gertrude," 30.
43. The Nuvo review praised my performance, but I was never happy with it, and have resolved never again to act in a play I am directing.
44. None of the three texts specifies when the Queen exits from this scene. But in Q1 she must exit before the end of the scene, because she appears at the very beginning of scene 14, and the law of reentry requires an interval between exit and entrance; moreover, in Q1 after Ophelia's exit the King explicitly talks about "revenge" being done on Hamlet (something that the Queen clearly does not hear). By contrast, in Q2 and F there is no reason for the Queen to leave the stage before the end of 4.5.
45. Bird, "Hamlet."
46. Stubbs, "Gertrude," 30.
47. I am grateful to Ivan Fuller for letting me read his 2003 SETC symposium paper on his New Jersey production of a five-actor *Hamlet* with a Gertrude eight months pregnant: "Playing 'What If' with *Hamlet*." That

production was, however, based on an abridged version of the canonical text, not on Q1, and did not explore the larger issues of age that I am describing here.
48. Dessen and Thomson, *Dictionary of Stage Directions in English Drama: 1580–1642* (Cambridge: Cambridge University Press, 1999). For sexualized examples, see Heywood's *Woman Killed with Kindness* and *Golden Age*, Marston's *Sophonisba*, and Middleton's *Bloody Banquet*.
49. All three texts contain Hamlet's declaration "My father in the [his] habit as he lived" (11.79; 3.4.133), but this is ambiguous. The frontispiece to Nicholas Rowe's edition (1709), without knowledge of Q1, shows him in armor in this scene. Without the specific Q1 stage direction, the phrase could refer to anything that old Hamlet characteristically wore. Once again, if we read *from* Q1 *toward* the later texts, the absence of this direction from Q2 and F looks like deliberate excision of material no longer appropriate to the revised play.
50. Gunthio, "Commentary," 345–6.
51. G. B. Shand, "Gertred, Captive Queen of the First Quarto," in *Shakespearean Illuminations: Essays in Honor of Marvin Rosenberg*, ed. Jay Halio and Hugh M. Richmond (Newark: University of Delaware Press, 1998), 50–69.
52. Dorothea Kehler, "The First Quarto of *Hamlet*: Reforming Widow Gertred," *Shakespeare Quarterly* 46 (1995): 398–413.
53. I have emended this line, adding "high," because the line in Q1 seems to be metrically defective, missing a syllable at that point, and this passage closely resembles the scene in Belleforest, where the Queen Geruthe speaks a very similar sentence: "te jurant par la haute majesté des Dieux" (Israel Gollancz, *The Sources of Hamlet* [London: Oxford University Press, 1926], 220). The phrase "high majesty" appears three times elsewhere in Shakespeare's plays.
54. Terri Bourus, "'With thouwsand mothers blessings': Gertred's Motivations and the Commonwealth of Denmark," Blackfriars Scholars Conference, Staunton, Virginia, 2005.
55. Charles Spencer, "Hamlet, Shakespeare's Globe, Review," *Daily Telegraph*, 6 May 2011 (accessed online February 2014).
56. Paul Taylor, "Hamlet, Shakespeare's Globe, London," *Independent*, 6 May 2011 (accessed online February 2014).
57. Lyn Gardner, "Hamlet—Review: Shakespeare's Globe," *Guardian*, 5 May 2011 (accessed online February 2014).
58. Griselda Murray Brown, "Hamlet, Shakespeare's Globe, London," *Financial Times*, 5 May 2011 (accessed online February 2014).
59. "Dominic Dromgoole on his touring Hamlet," *theatrevoice.com*, interview with Heather Neill recorded on 11 May 2011, accessed February 2014.
60. Dromgoole, "End of Season Interview" (2011), interviewed by Farah Karim-Cooper, Shakespeare's Globe archives.
61. Gardner, "Hamlet."

62. This figure includes only actual playing time. The venue required a 15-minute intermission (in order to make money at the bar). I would have preferred to play it without interruption.
63. Spencer, "Hamlet" (2011); Taylor, "Hamlet" (2011).
64. Harvey, "Young Hamlet."
65. Thompson and Taylor, *Hamlet [1603]*, 36, 23, 26, 27, 27–8, 30.
66. Taylor, "Hamlet" (2011).
67. Nicolas Pullin, personal correspondence, 7 January 2000.
68. "Acting (un)Shakespeare: *Hamlet*, Bad Quarto, Good Play?" dir. Steve Scott; dramaturg, W. B. Worthen; performers Ian Brennan, Tim Decker, Kate Goehring, Nicholas Sandys Pullin, John Shea. Eighth Annual McElroy Memorial Shakespeare Celebration, Mullady Theater, Loyola University, Chicago, 27 April 1999.
69. The parallel scenes performed were Q1 2.1–75 (against Folio 1.2.1–39), Q1 7.355–87 (against Folio 2.2.543–600), and Q1 7.115–198 (against Folio 3.1.55–89).
70. I quote Pullin, Dekker, Scott, and the cast from the discussion following "Acting (unShakespeare)," where I was present and a (not surreptitious) note-taker.
71. Figures for the canonical version, here and in the following paragraph, are based on the conflated edition (Jenkins, *Arden*).
72. For a survey, see Terri Bourus, "The First Quarto of *Hamlet* in Film: The Revenge Tragedies of Tony Richardson and Franco Zeffirelli," in "Text<->Screen," *EnterText* 1.2 (August 2001, accessible online), based on a paper delivered at the "*Hamlet* on Film" conference at Shakespeare's New Globe Theatre London, April 2001.
73. Samuel Taylor Coleridge, *Coleridge on Shakespeare: The Text of the Lectures of 1811–12*, ed. R. A. Foakes (London: Routledge, 1971), 129.
74. William Hazlitt, *Characters of Shakespear's Plays* (London: Printed by C. H. Reynell, for R. Hunter, 1817), 109.
75. August Wilhelm von Schlegel, *A Course of Lectures on Dramatic Art and Literature* (published in German in 1808), trans. John Black, 2 vols. (London: Baldwin, Cradock, and Joy, 1815), 192–5.
76. Jude Morgan, *The Secret Life of William Shakespeare* (New York: St. Martin's, 2014), 185.
77. Bryan Loughrey, "Q1 in recent performance: An interview," in *Hamlet First Published*, ed. Thomas Clayton (Newark: University of Delaware Press, 1992), 131.
78. *Prinzen af Jylland*, dir. Gabriel Axel (1994), released in English as *The Prince of Jutland* (1994). Bale was 20 when the film was released, but only 19 during filming, and Axel's direction emphasizes his youth. This version of the film must be clearly distinguished from the subsequent Miramax travesty, *Royal Deceit*, designed to make the story more appealing to American audiences; Axel, whom I interviewed in 2002 in Copenhagen, angrily disavowed *Royal Deceit*. I gave a fuller account of

the relationship between Axel's original film and Q1 in "I am Hamlet the Dane: Gabriel Axel's *The Prince of Jutland* and Shakespeare's *Hamlet*," an unpublished paper delivered at the European Society for the Study of English (ESSE) conference, Strasbourg, 3 September 2002.

5 Young Shakespeare?

1. Edmond Malone, *The Life of William Shakspeare*, ed. James Boswell (1821), Section 15, "An Attempt to ascertain the order in which the plays of Shakspeare were written," 288–468: for Malone's summary of the chronology, in which *Hamlet* is dated "1600," see 295–6; for his defense of that date, see 369–73. In the main text I have modernized Malone's spelling (which is immaterial to his argument).
2. Textually, the Malone-Boswell text was superseded by the Cambridge edition of 1863–6 edited by W. G. Clark and W. A. Wright, with its thorough collation of variants, and by their enormously popular, one-volume spin-off "Globe" edition (1864). But neither of those editions provided a commentary.
3. E. K. Chambers, *William Shakespeare* (Oxford: Clarendon Press, 1930), 1: 243–576 (chronology), 1: 408–25 (*Hamlet*). In his "trial-table of primary indications limiting initial and terminal dates " for the plays, Chambers does not even list any of the references to *Hamlet* before 1600 (1:246, 249). For scholarly purposes, Chambers was partially replaced by S. Schoenbaum's *William Shakespeare: A Documentary Life* (Oxford, 1975). Schoenbaum provided a narrative, and photographs of documents, rather than transcripts, but he did not attempt to explain or justify the historical sequence of Shakespeare's works. None of the many subsequent biographies contains a comprehensive study of the chronology.
4. Gary Taylor, "The Canon and Chronology of Shakespeare's Plays," in *William Shakespeare: A Textual Companion*, ed. Stanley Wells et al. (Oxford: Clarendon, 1987), 69–144. (Taylor's essay actually considers the authorship and dating of the poetry as well as the plays.)
5. British Library Additional MS 45218, Folio 394 verso: "The younger sort takes much delight in Shakespeares Venus, & Adonis: but his Lucrece, & his tragedie of Hamlet, prince of Denmarke, have it in them, to please the wiser sort."
6. The Folio's reference to "Hercules and his load" (2.2.359–60) apparently refers to the Globe Theatre, rebuilt and renamed in 1599; Hercules carried the world on his shoulders. See Ann Thompson and Neil Taylor ed., *Hamlet [1604]* (London: Arden Shakespeare, 2006), 52–3.
7. Edmond Malone, "An Attempt to ascertain the Order in which the Plays attributed to Shakspeare were Written" in *The Plays of William Shakespeare*, ed. Samuel Johnson and George Steevens, 10 vols. (1778), 269–346, esp. 293, 274; "An Attempt to ascertain the Order in which The Plays of Shakspeare were written," in *The Plays and Poems of William*

Shakspeare, ed. Edmond Malone, 10 vols. (1790), I:261–386, esp. 269–71, 310.
8. Virginia F. Stern, *Gabriel Harvey: His Life, Marginalia and Library* (Oxford: Clarendon, 1980), 127–8.
9. Jason Scott-Warren, "Harvey, Gabriel," *Oxford Dictionary of National Biography* (*ODNB*).
10. Though Harvey may have been in Cambridge occasionally in the mid-1590s, it seems unlikely that the Chamberlain's Men performed there during that period. (See subsequent discussion.) Therefore he would have needed to see the play in London by 1593; but the playhouses were closed in the last half of 1592 and for most of 1593. Malone was unaware of Harvey's movements, and later scholars seem not to have recognized their relevance to his remarks about *Hamlet*.
11. Malone, "Attempt" (1778), 274–6; Malone, "Attempt" (1790), 269–71.
12. Malone, *Life*, 298–302.
13. Katherine Duncan-Jones and Jan Van Dorsten, eds., *Miscellaneous Prose of Sir Philip Sidney* (Oxford: Clarendon, 1973), 59–63.
14. William Webbe, *A Discourse of English Poetrie*, ed. Edward Arber (London: Arber, 1871), 6, 35. Arber identifies Webbe's single sentence on Munday as a reference to *The Mirrour of Mutabilitie* (1579) and *The Paine of Pleasure* (1580).
15. Emma Smith, "Whetstone, George," *ODNB*.
16. Anthony Munday, *Fedele and Fortunio*, ed. Richard Hosley (New York: Garland, 1981).
17. David Bergeron, "Munday, Anthony," *ODNB*. The two 1577 publications are lost.
18. Rivkah Zim, "Sackville, Thomas," *ODNB*.
19. John R. Elliott, Jr., "Edwards, Richard," *ODNB*.
20. H. R. Woudhuysen, "Ferrers, George," *ODNB*. Puttenham's mistake was echoed in 1598 by Francis Meres.
21. Alan H. Nelson, "De Vere, Edward, seventeenth earl of Oxford," *ODNB*. For a fuller biography see Nelson's *Monstrous Adversary: The Life of Edward de Vere, 17th Earl of Oxford* (Liverpool: Liverpool University Press, 2003).
22. Such a mistake would have been easy to make during that early period, when plays were usually identified by acting company rather than author.
23. Steven W. May, "George Puttenham's Lewd and Illicit Career," *Texas Studies in Literature and Language* 50.2 (2008): 143–176, esp. 170–71.
24. Malone, "Attempt" (1790), 271. This reiteration occurs, after a discussion of Dryden's and Rowe's claim that Shakespeare might be the "Willy" in three stanzas of Spenser's *Tears of the Muses* (printed in 1591).
25. Harington, "An Apologie of Poetrie," *Orlando Furioso in English Heroical Verse* (1591), vi. I have modernized the spelling.
26. On "The Game of the Cards," see Martin Wiggins (in association with Catherine Richardson), *British Drama 1533–1642: A Catalogue*

(Oxford: Oxford University Press), *Volume II: 1567–1589* (2013), 307–8 (#732). Wiggins is unaware of the printed marginal note identifying Walsingham.
27. Chambers, *Shakespeare*, 1: 58–9, 55.
28. E. A. J. Honigmann, *Shakespeare's Impact on his Contemporaries* (London: Macmillan, 1982), 55. Honigmann's own case for an earlier start to Shakespeare's career was, unfortunately, based on the theory that the anonymous *Troublesome Reign of John, King of England* (printed in 1591) was a memorial reconstruction of Shakespeare's *King John*, a claim thoroughly discredited by recent scholarship: see George Peele, *The Troublesome Reign of John, King of England*, ed. Charles R. Forker, Revels Plays (Manchester: Manchester University Press, 2011), among others.
29. Peter Alexander, *Shakespeare's Henry VI and Richard III* (Cambridge: Cambridge University Press, 1929), 200; F. P. Wilson, *Marlowe and the Early Shakespeare* (Oxford: Oxford University Press, 1953), 113 ("The fact is that the chronology of Shakespeare's earliest plays is so uncertain that it has no right to harden into an orthodoxy"). In the nineteenth century, Malone's "late-start" chronology had been challenged by Charles Knight in *Studies of Shakspere* (London: Routledge, 1849) and by Thomas Kenny in *The Life and Genius of Shakespeare* (London: Longman, 1864).
30. Thomas Lodge, *VVits Miserie, and the vvorlds madnesse discouering the deuils incarnat of this age* (London: 1596), 56. I have modernized the original typography (from black letter and roman, to roman and italic): "**he walks for the most part in black vnder colour of grauity, & looks as pale as the Vizard of ye ghost which cried so miserally at ye Theator like an oister wife,** Hamlet, reuenge " (sig. h4v).
31. Gabriel Egan, "The Theatre in Shoreditch 1576–1599," in *The Oxford Handbook of Early Modern Theatre*, ed. Richard Dutton (Oxford: Oxford University Press, 2009), 168–85.
32. I discuss later in the chapter documentary evidence that the Chamberlain's Men owned a "Hamlet" play by 1594, which confirms this (standard) interpretation of Lodge's noun "the Theator." If Lodge had intended the generic noun, he could have written "playhouse."
33. Margrethe Jolly, "*Hamlet* and the French Connection: The Relationship of Q1 and Q2 *Hamlet* and the Evidence of Belleforest's *Histoires Tragiques*," *Parergon* 29.1 (2012): 89–90.
34. See, for instance, Chambers, *Shakespeare*, 1:411 ("The Ghost does not call 'Hamlet, revenge' in the Shakespeare texts"); Thompson and Taylor, *Hamlet [1604]*, 46 ("the two words 'Hamlet' and 'revenge' are not actually contiguous in any of" the printed texts); and James J. Marino, *Owning William Shakespeare: The King's Men and their Intellectual Property* (Philadelphia: University of Pennsylvania Press, 2011), 75 ("Those last two words...cannot be found in any surviving texts of the play"). Even Leah S. Marcus, in her revisionist defense of Q1 in *Unediting the Renaissance: Shakespeare, Marlowe, Milton* (London: Routledge, 1996),

cites the fact that "the two words are not quite juxtaposed" as her "own main difficulty" with accepting that Q1 is the Ur-Hamlet (149).
35. Paul Menzer, discussing "Hamlet, revenge," independently, parenthetically mentioned that "*Casablanca* does not actually include the line, 'Play it again, Sam'" (*The Hamlets: Cues, Qs, and Remembered Texts* [Newark: University of Delaware Press, 2008], 137); but he did not further explore the matter, or its implications for his own assumptions (about Q1's origins, or about the 1589 play).
36. Gabriel Egan has called my attention to the fact that Ilsa also says "Play it once, Sam" and "Play it, Sam". Those lines may also be contributing to the famous misquotation. In any case, "Play it again, Sam" does not occur in the film, just as "Hamlet, revenge" does not occur in the texts of *Hamlet*.
37. If we are going to imagine "actors' interpolations" in *Hamlet*, then it would be much easier to assume (1) that the actor who played the Ghost regularly interpolated the word "Hamlet" before the word "revenge," or at least did so once, at the performance Lodge attended, than to assume (2) that all three early printed versions of the text contain scores of actor's interpolations, and that all three therefore derive from memorial reconstruction or the notes of spectators.
38. S. R., *The Night-Raven* (1620), sig. D2. Chambers and others who quote this allusion omit the second line of the couplet and/or the italics.
39. Even less likely is the suggestion by Martin Wiggins (*British Drama*, #813, II:438) that the "lost" 1589 play contained the phrase "things called whips." That conjecture is based upon a single source, Robert Armin's *A Nest of Ninnies* (1608): "There are, as *Hamlet* says, things called whips" (sig. G3v). As Wiggins notes, Armin must have performed in the "Shakespearean" [meaning "enlarged, canonical"] *Hamlet*, which certainly existed by 1604, and which most scholars date to 1599–1601: why then should Armin quote, instead, a 20-year-old play that was not in print and no longer in anyone's repertoire? And why should we base textual theories on the presumed literal accuracy of a clown? Do we presume that modern stand-up comedians are always literally accurate? The phrase "things called whips" also occurs in *2 Henry VI* and the additions to *The Spanish Tragedy*; the latter was performed by Burbage and (according to recent scholarship) the additions may have been written by Shakespeare. As Wiggins acknowledges, Boas thought Armin misremembered, meaning to say "Heronimo" instead of "Hamlet" (since Burbage played both roles). But the mistake might also have been compositorial, since compositors are particularly likely to misread unusual proper names; "Hamlet" is more familiar, as an English name, than "Hieronimo." The substitution might also have been authorial and deliberate (and comically obvious to Armin's readers).
40. Thomas Dekker and John Webster, *West-ward hoe as it hath beene diuers times acted by the Children of Paules* (London: 1607), sig. H3.
41. Dekker, *Satiro-mastix* (London: 1602), sig. G3v. For commentary on this passage see Cyrus Hoy, *Introductions, Notes, and Commentaries to texts in*

"The Dramatic Works of Thomas Dekker," 4 vols. (Cambridge: Cambridge University Press, 1980), I:262–3 (on this passage) and I:200 (on Captain Tucca).
42. Chambers misinterprets the context to suggest that *Hamlet* had been performed at Paris Garden (*Shakespeare*, 1:411).
43. See Roslyn L. Knutson, "Henslowe's Diary and the Economics of Play Revision for Revival, 1592–1603," *Theatre Research International* 10 (1985): 1–18, who concludes that "revision for the occasion of revival was neither commonplace nor economically necessary" and that "under normal circumstances companies did not pay for revisions of old playbooks."
44. We have no evidence for whether Edmund Tilney (who was Master of the Revels during the period when the canonical enlarged *Hamlet* must have been written) charged for relicensing a revised play. Henry Herbert, early in his tenure as Master of the Revels, on 19 August 1623, licensed Shakespeare's *The Winter's Tale* (an "ould play") without charging a fee, "on Mr. Hemmings his worde that there was nothing profane added or reformed": see N. W. Bawcutt, ed., *The Control and Censorship of Caroline Drama: The Records of Sir Henry Herbert, Master of the Revels 1623–73* (Oxford: Clarendon, 1996), 142. The King's Men thus, in Herbert's time, might at their own peril avoid a licensing fee, by promising that any additions or changes were not "profane." G. E. Bentley shows that Herbert charged half as much for relicensing an old play with significant additions as for licensing a new play (*The Jacobean and Caroline Stage* [Oxford: Clarendon, 1941–68], 3:265).
45. Dulwich MS VII, fol 9. An image of the manuscript is available online at the Henslowe-Alleyn Digitization Project, henslowe-alleyn.org.uk; this passage is transcribed in R. A. Foakes and R. T. Rickert, eds., *Henslowe's Diary*, 2nd ed. (Cambridge: Cambridge University Press, 2002), 21–2. See also Glynne Wickham, Herbert Berry, and William Ingram, eds., *English Professional Theatre, 1530–1600* (Cambridge: Cambridge University Press, 2000), 328 ("the two companies did not now reunite but took turns playing their own plays").
46. The highest takings between 3 and 13 June were for *Bellendon*, the only play marked "ne" (17 shillings). On debates about "ne," see Diana Price, "Henslowe's 'ne' and 'the tyeringe-howsse doore,'" *Research Opportunities in Renaissance Drama* 42 (2003): 62–78; and Rosalyn Knutson, *The Repertory of Shakespeare's Company 1594–1613* (Fayetteville: University of Arkansas Press, 1991), 25.
47. Holger Schott Syme, "The Meaning of Success: Stories of 1594 and Its Aftermath," *Shakespeare Quarterly* 61:4 (Winter 2010): 490–525; Marino, *Owning*, 1–106. Marino's bibliography does not include Syme, and his book was in press when Syme's was published, so each argument is independent of the other.
48. Menzer provides strong evidence for the reliability of "in the City" on play title pages, and of its specificity in designating "the 677 acres...ruled by the lord mayor and Corporation of London" (*Hamlets*, 145–54).

49. See the letter of Lord Hunsdon (the Lord Chamberlain) to the Lord Mayor on 8 October 1594, requesting permission for "my nowe companie of Players... to plaie this winter time within the Citye at the Cross kayes in Gracious street" (E. K. Chambers, *The Elizabethan Stage* [Oxford: Clarendon, 1923], 4:316), and Andrew Gurr, "Henry Carey's Peculiar Letter," *Shakespeare Quarterly* 56 (2005): 51–75.
50. Menzer speculates that the Chamberlain's Men continued to perform within the City after 1595, in order to save his assumption that "Shakespeare's *Hamlet*" (meaning the canonical play) "did play in the City," though he admits that "If so, they played in the face of continued efforts to stop them" (162). Lawrence Manley also observes that "there are certainly some signs... that the suppression of inn playhouses was not final until at least 1600": see "Why Did London Inns Function as Theaters?" *Huntington Library Quarterly* 71 (2008): 181–97, esp. 195.
51. It might be possible to date the printing of the Ling/Simmes quarto by situating it within the sequence of paper and types in the Simmes shop in 1602–4. I have not attempted such a reconstruction of the printer's work-flow.
52. John R. Elliott, Jr., and Alan H. Nelson, Alexandra F. Johnston, and Diana Wyatt, eds., *Records of Early English Drama: Oxford* (Elliott, Jr., and Nelson [University]; Johnston and Wyatt [City]) (London: British Library, 2004), 276, 858.
53. Alan H. Nelson, *Records of Early English Drama: Cambridge*, 2 vols. (Toronto: University of Toronto Press, 1989), 2: 985. For the 1594–5 visit, see 1:355; for the complete absence of visits by the King's Men, 1603–42, see 2:1272–3.
54. Nelson, *Cambridge*, 2:985. The title page specification of "Universities" may be a misunderstanding of the distinction between town and university; that distinction was vital for fiscal records, but may have seemed irrelevant to a London publisher, or even to playing companies, who would have been well aware that even performances in "town" were attended by members of the university, who dominated the town economically and demographically. If the Chamberlain's Men performed at inns in either town, there might be no record of their performances.
55. Honigmann, *Impact,* Chapter 6; Peter Thomson, *Shakespeare's Professional Career* (Cambridge: Cambridge University Press, 1992), 30–48; Gurr, *The Shakespearian Playing Companies* (Oxford: Clarendon, 1996), 262 ("very likely that Shakespeare was one of the players in Strange's Men up to the time when Pembroke's was formed").
56. Gurr, *Playing Companies*, 259. Gurr's conjecture is endorsed by Lawrence Manley and Sally-Beth MacLean, *Lord Strange's Men and Their Plays* (New Haven, CT: Yale University Press, 2013), 62, 69, 280–320. Leicester died on 4 September 1588, and Manley and MacLean argue (32–5) that members of his company had joined Strange's company by Christmas 1588.
57. Boas, "'*Hamlet*' at Oxford: New Facts and Suggestions," *Fortnightly Review* 94 (1913): 245–53, esp. 252.

58. *REED Oxford*, 233; *REED Cambridge,* 338.
59. Manley and MacLean, *Strange's Men,* 41.
60. *REED Oxford*, 323; *REED Cambridge,* 1586-7 (205), 1587-8 (206), 1589-90 (211), 1590-91 (214), 1594-5 (237), 1595-6 (240).
61. Scott McMillin and Sally-Beth MacLean, *The Queen's Men and Their Plays* (Cambridge: Cambridge University Press, 1998), 160-66.
62. *REED Oxford*, 1588-9 (209, 211), 1589-90 (211), 1590-1 (214), 1592-3 (233), 1594-5 (238), 1594-5 (237, entertainers), 1595-6 (240), 1596-7 (243), 1598-9 (253); *REED Cambridge,* 1586-7 (319), 1590-1 (332, debarred), 1591-2 (338 debarred, 340-3 complaints), 1596-7 (369).
63. Helen Ostovich, Holger Schott Syme, and Andrew Griffin, eds., *Locating the Queen's Men, 1583–1603: Material Practices and Conditions of Playing* (Farnham: Ashgate, 2009).
64. McMillin, *The Elizabethan Theatre and The Book of Sir Thomas More* (Ithaca, NY: Cornell University Press, 1987), 62. The "1018" lines for *Spanish Tragedy* include the additions printed in 1602.
65. Syme notes that the "Jeronimo" performed by the Admiral's Men may not be *The Spanish Tragedy,* elsewhere associated with Burbage and the Chamberlain/King's Men ("Success"). But in either case, McMillin's argument stands: the role was played by Alleyn, Burbage, or both.
66. My line counts are based on *Hamlet 1603,* ed. Thompson and Taylor.
67. Manley and MacLean, *Strange's Men,* 5-6. Accepting the traditional Malone narrative, they do not consider the 1589 *Hamlet* as a possible part of the company's repertoire.
68. See, for instance, Bart Van Es, *Shakespeare in Company* (Oxford: Oxford University Press, 2013), which devotes an entire chapter (163-94) to Shakespeare's relationship with Armin, beginning with *As You Like It,* but says nothing whatever about the "Clown" in *Hamlet.*
69. G. Sjogren, "Thomas Bull and other 'English instrumentalists' in Denmark in the 1580s," *Shakespeare Survey* 22 (1969): 119-24.
70. Q1 has "Rossencraft" consistently, and "Gilderstone" nine times (to one "Guilderstone"); Q2 has "Rosencraus" and "Guyldensterne" consistently; F1 prefers "Rosincrance" (but also has "Rosincrane" and "Rosincran"). These variants may be attempts at the unfamiliar Danish proper names, transmitted aurally from actors who visited Denmark to other actors (including Shakespeare) back in London, then complicated by compositorial and scribal misreading.
71. Manley and MacLean, *Strange's Men,* 40.
72. Lukas Erne, *Beyond "The Spanish Tragedy": A Study of the Works of Thomas Kyd* (Manchester: Manchester University Press, 2001), 154-5; Geoffrey Bullough, *Narrative and Dramatic Sources of Shakespeare,* 8 vols. (London: Athlone, 1957-75), VII: 19.
73. *OED* principal, *adj.* 1b.
74. Mary C. Erler, ed., *Records of Early English Drama: Ecclesiastical London* (Toronto: University of Toronto Press, 2008), xxi.

75. Taylor, "Canon and Chronology," 112–13.
76. Erne, *Beyond*, 147.
77. Francis Meres, *Palladis Tamia: Wits Treasury* (1598) fol. 281v–282.
78. Taylor, "Canon and Chronology," 109–12. The most recent chronology also places all four plays in the period before the closing of the theatres in summer 1592: Martin Wiggins, in association with Catherine Richardson, *British Drama 1533–1642: A Catalogue*, Vol. 3, *1590–1597* (Oxford: Oxford University Press, 2013).
79. See R. B. McKerrow, ed., *The Works of Thomas Nashe*, rev. F. P. Wilson, 5 vols (Oxford: Blackwell, 1958), 3:300–325. However, McKerrow's edition is based on the 1610 reprint.
80. Robertus Greene, *Menaphon* (1589), sig. **3r–3v.
81. Malone, "Attempt" (1778), 295–6; Malone, "Attempt" (1790), 305. Malone's word "before" unnecessarily pushes the date back to 1588 or earlier, and therefore, from his perspective, makes it even more unlikely chronologically. A more cautious statement would be "by spring or summer 1589."
82. van Es, *Shakespeare in Company*, 6.
83. McKerrow, *The Works of Thomas Nashe*, 4:450.
84. Meres, *Palladis Tamia*, fol. 282.
85. Madeleine Doran, *Endeavours of Art: A Study of Form in Elizabethan Drama* (Madison: University of Wisconsin Press, 1954), 16.
86. Geoffrey Bullough, "Sénèque, Greville et le jeune Shakespeare," in *Les Tragédies de Sénèque et le Théâtre de la Renaissance,* ed. Jean Jacquot and Marcel Oddon (Paris: Editions du Centre National de la Recherche Scientfique, 1964), 189–20: "Il ne fait pas de doute" of Seneca's influence during the period when Shakespeare wrote *Henry VI, Richard III*, and *Titus Andronicus* (196).
87. Robert S. Miola, *Shakespeare and Classical Tragedy: The Influence of Seneca* (Oxford: Clarendon Press, 1992), esp. 1–71.
88. Miola, *Seneca*, 37–46. Miola takes for granted the existence of an Ur-*Hamlet,* and for *Hamlet* cites the old Jenkins/Arden edition of the traditional conflated text, which does not even collate Q1 variants. I have personally checked all Miola's examples of Senecan influence against *Hamlet* (1603), ed. Thompson and Taylor: see 2.61, 4.54, 7.115–36, 7.340–75, 7.404–35, 10.14–31, 16.145–6.
89. Miola, *Seneca*, 49–52. Studley's *Agammemnon*, first published in 1566, was reprinted in the 1581 collection of *Seneca his tenne tragedies, translated into Englysh.*
90. See, for instance, Gordon Braden, *Renaissance Tragedy and the Senecan Tradition: Anger's Privilege* (New Haven, CT: Yale University Press, 1985).
91. Thomas Kyd, *The Spanish Tragedy,* ed. Clara Calvo and Jesús Tronch, Arden Early Modern Drama (London: Bloomsbury, 2013), 3.13–35. See also the Latin of 1.2.12–14, 1.2.55–6, 2.5.67–80.

92. David Riggs, *The World of Christopher Marlowe* (New York: Henry Holt, 2005), 228. Riggs, unfortunately, assumes that Kyd was Nashe's target, but the only evidence he gives is "Noverint" and the fact that Kyd "had just translated two works into Italian" (*sic*).
93. McKerrow, *Nashe*, 4:449–50 (his italics), excerpted from his full discussion of this passage (448–52). I have modernized the spelling of his quotations from Nashe.
94. Greg's December 1936 letter to McKerrow is quoted, with Greg's permission, in F. P. Wilson's "A Supplement to McKerrow's Edition of Nashe" (1957) in McKerrow, *Nashe*, p. 68 (separately paginated after the Index in volume 5). Greg's continuing skepticism postdated John Dover Wilson's 1934 efforts to revive the Kyd hypothesis.
95. Frederick S. Boas, ed., *The Works of Thomas Kyd* (Oxford: Clarendon, 1901), xx–xxix; Arthur Freeman, *Thomas Kyd: Facts and Problems* (Oxford: Clarendon, 1967); Philip Edwards, ed., *The Spanish Tragedy*, Revels Plays (London: Methuen, 1959); Calvo and Tronch, eds., *The Spanish Tragedy*, 10–11; Michael Neill, ed., *The Spanish Tragedy*, Norton Critical Editions (New York: W. W. Norton, 2014), xii–xiii. The recent editions of *Spanish Tragedy*, typically, do not analyze the Nashe passage, but simply take for granted Malone's hypothesis, despite the many objections to it made by other scholars.
96. STC 23702.5, 23703. Neither Erne's discussion of *Hamlet* (*Beyond*, 146–56), nor his discussion of *Householder's Philosophy* (*Beyond*, 217–20), note the exact size and probable price of the latter.
97. In *The Business of Playing: The Beginnings of the Adult Professional Theatre in Elizabethan London* (Ithaca, NY: Cornell University Press, 1992), William Ingram calculates that, that for the period 1576–1586, the commercial playing companies would have needed one hundred new plays a year (239–42); but only a handful of plays from the commercial theatres were published before 1590.
98. McKerrow, *Nashe*, 4: 451.
99. Chambers, *Shakespeare*, 1:424.
100. George Ian Duthie, *The "Bad" Quarto of Hamlet: A Critical Study* (Cambridge: Cambridge University Press, 1941), 71.
101. E. A. J. Honigmann, "Shakespeare's Lost Source-Plays," *Modern Language Review* 49 (1954): 293–307.
102. Eric Sams, "Taboo or not Taboo? The Text, Dating and Authorship of *Hamlet*, 1589–1623," *Hamlet Studies* 10 (1998): 12–46; and *The Real Shakespeare: Retrieving the Early Years, 1564–1594* (New Haven, CT: Yale University Press, 1995), 121–35.
103. On Shakespeare's direct use of French and Italian, see Robert S. Miola, *Shakespeare's Reading* (Oxford: Oxford University Press, 2000),168. Miola's cautious "perhaps...Belleforest" is based on the traditional idea that all the elements of Belleforest present in Shakespeare's *Hamlet* might

have been taken over from the lost play by someone else. But the 1589 *Hamlet* must be based on Belleforest.
104. The famously collaborative Middleton's first extant play is the single-authored *Phoenix*; his first documentary appearance as a playwright records his work on one collaborative play for Henslowe beginning in May 1602, followed by a single-authored play in October and November 1602 (Thomas Middleton, *The Collected Works*, ed. Gary Taylor and John Lavagnino [Oxford: Clarendon, 2007], 328).
105. Jenkins, ed., *Hamlet*, 544.
106. Edgar I. Fripp, *Shakespeare: Man and Artist* (London: Oxford University Press, 1964), 146. Fripp also speculates that the young Shakespeare "was probably in Rogers's office" when the inquest was held. (Henry Rogers was the Stratford town clerk and steward from 1570 to 1586, and Fripp assumes that Shakespeare worked as a legal scribe in the 1580s.)
107. Fripp, *Shakespeare*, 147.
108. Fripp notes that if a suspicious death was deemed to be a suicide the "verdict would have been somewhat in these terms, that the deceased 'regardless of the salvation of her soul, and led astray by the instigation of the Devil,' threw herself into the water and 'wilfully drowned herself.' Whereby she would sacrifice her claim to Christian burial; her body would not be reinterred in the churchyard, but cast into a hole at a crossway or on a refuse heap.... Wilfully... she would have murdered herself... then guilty, that is, of breach of the sixth commandment, and forfeited her right to sleep in consecrated ground" (*Shakespeare*, 147).
109. Jenkins, ed., *Hamlet*, 544.
110. "On the Festival of the Purification, Tuesday, 2 February 1585, the Shakespeares had their newborn twins christened Hamnet and Judith, no doubt in deference to their friends Hamnet and Judith Sadler. The boy's name was interchangeable with 'Hamlet'—in Shakespeare's will, in a legal hand, his friend would appear as 'Hamlet Sadler'—and among abundant local variants of the same name were, for example, Amblet, Hamolet, and even Hamletti." See Park Honan, *Shakespeare: A Life* (Oxford: Oxford University Press, 1998), 90. Lots of British people still say "chimley" for "chimney."
111. Sadler's name changed from "Hamnet" to "Hamlet" to "Hamlett" several times in documents, including and other than Shakespeare's will. "Shakespeare's twins were named Hamnet and Judith, and the Sadlers named a son William in 1597." See Mark Eccles, *Shakespeare in Warwickshire* (Madison: University of Wisconsin Press, 1963), 125–6.
112. See, for instance, Mark Alexander's online "Shakespeare Authorship Sourcebook," which has a four-part blog on "Polonius as Lord Burghley." The earliest link that he cites between Corambis and Burghley's motto is an article by J. Shera Atkinson in *The Shakespeare Fellowship News-Letter* of April 1950, reprinted in Ruth Loyd Miller, ed., *Hidden Allusions*

in Shakespeare's Plays, 3rd ed. (Port Washington, NY: Kennikat, 1974), 668–70.
113. It was printed, with Burghley's coat of arms, as a frontispiece to Gabriel Harvey's *Gratulationes Valdinenses* (1578).
114. George Russell French, *Shakespeareana Genealogica* (London: 1869), 301; Chambers, *Shakespeare*, 1:418; Lilian Winstanley, *Hamlet and the Scottish Succession* (Cambridge: Cambridge University Press, 1921), 109–28; John Dover Wilson, *The Essential Shakespeare* (Cambridge: Cambridge University Press, 1937), 104; A. L. Rowse, *William Shakespeare: A Biography* (New York: HarperCollins, 1963), 323.
115. Looney, *Shakespeare Identified* (New York: Stokes, 1920), 400–407.
116. On Walsingham, see, most recently, John Cooper, *The Queen's Agent: Francis Walsingham at the Court of Elizabeth I* (London: Faber, 2011), 178–80 (Marlowe), 325 (Watson). For more on Watson's links to the Burghley/Walsingham spy network, see A. Chatterley, *Thomas Watson: Italian madrigals Englished* (London: Stainer and Bell for the Musica Britannica Trust, 1999), xxviii–xxxiv.
117. Marcus, *Unediting the Renaissance*, 135.
118. David Scott Kastan, *Shakespeare and the Book* (Cambridge: Cambridge University Press, 2001), 30.
119. Gunmar Sjörgen, "Producing the First Quarto *Hamlet*," *Hamlet Studies* 1 (1979): 35–44, esp. 44. More generally, see the surveys of productions in Irace, *First Quarto,* and Thompson and Taylor, *Hamlet 1603*. This issue is also related to the First Quarto's demonstrable theatrical appeal to young audiences, discussed in chapter 4: young people are not always unsophisticated, but in our time they certainly know less about Elizabethan theatrical conventions than Globe audiences in 1600–3. The same pattern explains the success of the twenty-first century Globe touring production, taking *Hamlet* to audiences around the world with little experience of Shakespeare or Renaissance drama.
120. "Uniquely" in Q1, not Q2 or F. The only other occurrence of "whilom" is in *Merry Wives,* when Evans sings an old ballad that contains it. Shakespeare used "whenas" elsewhere only in early plays (*3 Henry VI* 1.2, 5.7, *Titus* 4.4, *Errors* 4.4), in what seems to be an early sonnet (49), and in quoting an ancient prophesy in *Cymbeline* 5.5, 5.6.
121. The phrase "flaming fire," which Shakespeare does not use elsewhere, occurs in sixteenth century English translations of Psalm 104, in Lyly's *Euphues and his England* (1579), three times in Spenser's deliberately archaic *Faerie Queene,* and three times in Harington's 1591 *Orlando Furioso.*
122. Taylor, "Canon and Chronology," Table 9, columns 23, 24, 25, 26 (pp. 104–5).
123. Taylor apparently does not count these, but see also the similarly old-fashioned trisyllabic "entrance" (3.33) and "business" (7.57).

124. See Philip W. Timberlake, *The Feminine Ending in English Blank Verse* (Menasha, WI: Printed by George Banta, 1931).
125. Thompson and Taylor, *Hamlet [1604]*, 258; Jenkins, *Hamlet*, 254 ("not of course the jester, who is mentioned next"). Chapman's 1597 play may be the "comedy of humours" which was the most successful play of 1597 in Henslowe's records.
126. *The true tragedie of Richard the third* (1594), sig. H1v. Like other editors I have emended "heads" to "herds."
127. Thompson and Taylor, *Hamlet [1604]*, 303; *The True Tragedy of Richard III*, ed. W. W. Greg, Malone Society Reprint (Oxford, 1929).
128. McMillin and Maclean, *Queen's Men*, 95.
129. Brian Walsh, *Shakespeare, the Queen's Men, and the Elizabethan Performance of History* (Cambridge: Cambridge University Press, 2009), 76. Wiggins and Richardson (*British Drama* #839, 2:487–91) give a date range of 1588–91, and a "best guess" of 1589, but give no reason for their best guess and no discussion of dating; they do not cite McMillin and Maclean, or Walsh, and assume the 1594 text was "memorially reconstructed," without reference to Maguire's verdict "Not Memorial Reconstruction" (*Suspect Texts*, 325).
130. Ibid, 37, 156.
131. Two of the examples in this passage are recorded in *Tartleton's Jests* (1613); see Marcus, *Unediting*, 173–4; and David Wiles, *Shakespeare's Clown: Actor and Text in the Elizabethan Playhouse* (Cambridge: Cambridge University Press, 1987).
132. By the turn of the century, Hamlet's specific condemnation of Tarlton's "one suit of jests" had become irrelevant, or in bad taste, and its absence from the "enlarged" 1604 and 1623 texts is not surprising. In those later texts, Yorick becomes "the King's jester" (5.1.171); in Q1 he has no such specific court function, but is simply a memorable comedian.
133. Diana Whaley, "Voices from the Past: A Note on Termagant and Herod," in *Shakespearean Continuities*, ed. John Batchelor, Tom Cain, and Claire Lamont (New York: St. Martin's, 1997), 23–39.
134. Q1 and F agree on "your"; Q2 has "our," which could easily be a compositorial or scribal error, and is emended by most editors; it seems inappropriate in any circumstances.
135. Marino, *Owning*, 100; S. P. Cerasano, "Edward Alleyn, the New Model Actor, and the Rise of the Celebrity in the 1590s," *Medieval and Renaissance Drama in England* (2005): 47–58.
136. Dekker, *The Wonderful Year* (1603), 31; *The Black Book* (early 1604), in Middleton, *Works*, lines 415–18.
137. Q1 has "*Enter Clowne and an other*" (16.0.1); Q2 and F substitute "*Enter two Clowns*" (5.1.0.1).
138. Jenkins, *Hamlet*, 548–50.
139. Kyd, *Spanish Tragedy*, 4.1.188. Their edition preserves the spelling "And if," found in the early quartos of both plays; I have modernized both to

"An if," as do Thompson and Taylor. Because Kyd's play was first printed in 1592, a 1589 *Hamlet* would have been quoting from memory; hence, perhaps, the insignificant change from "this" to "the."
140. Wickham et al., *English Professional Theatre*, 360.

6 Revising *Hamlet*?

1. Gary Taylor, "Canon and Chronology of Shakespeare's Plays," in Stanley Wells et al., *William Shakespeare: A Textual Companion* (Oxford: Clarendon, 1987), 122. Taylor changed his mind as a result of reading an earlier version of this book.
2. Taylor, "Canon," 122–3.
3. David Daniell, ed., *Julius Caesar* (London: Arden Shakespeare, 1998), 6–23, gives a full account of evidence for the date, but reaches the same conclusion as almost all modern scholars.
4. For a survey of recent examples, see Ann Thompson and Neil Taylor, eds., *Hamlet [1604]* (London: Arden, 2006), 36–44.
5. The 1623 Folio collection of Shakespeare's *Comedies, Histories, and Tragedies* contains at least two texts that seem to have been adapted after Shakespeare's death. The 2007 Oxford edition of Middleton's *Collected Works*, drawing on centuries of Shakespeare scholarship, identified passages written by Middleton in both *Macbeth* and *Measure for Measure*. For new evidence supporting this consensus, see Gary Taylor, "Middleton and *Macbeth*," in *Macbeth*, ed. Robert Miola, 2nd ed. (New York: W. W. Norton, 2014), 296–305; and Terri Bourus and Gary Taylor, "*Measure for Measure*(s): Performance-Testing the Adaptation Hypothesis," *Shakespeare* 10.2 (2014) (available online, forthcoming in print). By contrast, nothing in the 1623 *Hamlet* seems to have been written by Middleton, or anyone else. Just as the text of *Hamlet* first printed in 1603 apparently derives, at one or more removes, from a manuscript written by Shakespeare 14 or 15 years earlier, the text printed in 1623 might derive, at one or more removes, from a manuscript written by Shakespeare two decades earlier. The 1623 edition contains texts of plays written three or more decades earlier (*The Two Gentlemen of Verona, 1 Henry VI*, etc.), so there would be nothing abnormal about this assumption.
6. The Children of the Chapel were dissolved, and vacated the Blackfriars playhouse, in the summer of 1608, so the passage could hardly have been written after that date. Moreover, once they moved into the Blackfriars, the King's Men began systematically dividing their plays into five acts, with musical intervals in between, and F1 *Hamlet* is not systematically divided into five acts: see Gary Taylor, "The Structure of Performance," in Gary Taylor and John Jowett, *Shakespeare Reshaped: 1606–1623* (Oxford: Clarendon, 1993), 3–50.
7. These conclusions are summarized in Taylor, "Canon," 122–3; notice the anomalous position of *Hamlet* in his own graph on p. 99, and the prose

statistics in Table 8 (p. 96). For Oras, see *Pause Patterns in Elizabethan and Jacobean Drama: An Experiment in Prosody*, University of Florida Monographs, Humanities, 3 (Gainesville: University of Florida Press, 1960), 46–9, where the A-graphs and B-graphs both place it after both *Troilus* and *Othello*, and the C-graphs between them; for Eliot Slater, *The Problem of "The Reign of King Edward III": A Statistical Approach* (Cambridge: Cambridge University Press, 1988), 181; for Brainerd, "The Chronology of Shakespeare's Plays: A Statistical Study," *Computers and the Humanities* 14 (1980): 221–30, esp. 229. (Taylor notes that Brainerd "also predicts a late date," but does not say how much later.) Brainerd's evidence also pointed to a later date for *All's Well that Ends Well* (1607), a change accepted in the 2005 revised edition of the Oxford *Complete Works*; his anomalies also supported claims (unconventional in 1980, but now widely accepted) that *Henry VI, Titus, Pericles, Henry VIII*, and *Two Noble Kinsmen* were written in collaboration. In Taylor's summary, the only evidence that *Hamlet* might precede *Troilus* is "the metrical tests," but he acknowledges serious weaknesses in that data (106–7).
8. Malone, "Attempt" (1821), 370. This interpretation has been supported by many scholars, including E. A. J. Honigmann, "The Date of *Hamlet*," *Shakespeare Survey* 9 (1956): 24–34.
9. See the excellent Long Note by Jenkins (ed.) (*Hamlet*, 470–2). Jenkins acknowledges the possibility of an allusion to the Essex rebellion, but (given his commitment to the theory of bad quartos, and his assumption that Shakespeare did not write the 1589 *Hamlet*) he did not even consider the death of Elizabeth.
10. Thompson and Taylor, eds., *Hamlet [1604]*, 59.
11. Among the many arguments for a relationship between *Hamlet* and Essex, see Karen S. Coddon, "'Such strange desyns': Madness, Subjectivity and Treason in *Hamlet* and Elizabethan Culture," *Renaissance Drama* 20 (1989): 51–75; and James Shapiro, *1599: A Year in the Life of William Shakespeare* (London: Faber, 2005), 283–317.
12. James Bednarz, *Shakespeare and the Poets' War* (New York: Columbia University Press, 2001), 248.
13. Taylor, "Hamlet," *Textual Companion*, 398–9.
14. In both the later versions, the anonymous braggart of Q1 is given a name, Osric (F) or Ostrick (Q2). Marino sees "Osric" as an allusion to the title character of a play staged at the Rose in 1597, which was significantly adapted beginning in September 1602 and performed there in November 1602; the title character's new costume cost 26 shillings (James J. Marino, *Owning William Shakespeare: The King's Men and Their Intellectual Property* [Philadelphia: University of Pennsylvania Press, 2011], 99). If true, this would push the date of the manuscripts behind Q2 and F to the very end of 1602.
15. Paul Werstine, "The Textual Mystery of *Hamlet*," *Shakespeare Quarterly* 39 (1988): 1–26.

16. Taylor, *Textual Companion*, 400.
17. Tiffany Stern, *Making Shakespeare: From Stage to Page* (London: Routledge, 2004), 135–6.
18. Paul Werstine, *Early Modern Playhouse Manuscripts and the Editing of Shakespeare* (Cambridge: Cambridge University Press, 2013), 232–3.
19. Taylor and Lavagnino, ed., *Textual Companion*, 874–991.
20. Jenkins, ed., *Hamlet*, 256; Bednarz, *Poets' War*, 255–6, 275–6.
21. Gabriele Bernhard Jackson, ed., *Poetaster*, in *The Cambridge Edition of the Works of Ben Jonson*, gen. eds. David Bevington, Martin Butler, and Ian Donaldson, 7 vols. (Cambridge: Cambridge University Press, 2012), 2:6–8.
22. The introduction to *Satiromastix* in Cyrus Hoy's *Introductions, Notes and Commentaries to texts in "The Dramatic Works of Thomas Dekker,"* 4 vols. (Cambridge: Cambridge University Press, 1980), 1:179–97, predates the new scholarship on the date of *Poetaster*, but in other respects remains authoritative.
23. David M. Bevington, ed., *Troilus and Cressida* (London: Arden, 2001), 6–18.
24. *3H6* 1.4 and 2.5, *Titus* 3.1, *R3* 4 times (1.2, then 3 times in 2.2, speaking to children), *LLL* 5.2, *R2* 1.2, *AWW* 1.1 (Helena). I have not counted the example in *1H6* 2.5, because there is a strong consensus among attribution experts that Shakespeare did not write the scene. The three occurrences in *R3* 2.2 all refer to the father of children (the young daughter and son of Clarence).
25. Park Honan, *Shakespeare: A Life* (Oxford: Oxford University Press, 1998), 25–42, esp. 38–40.
26. See the discussion and illustration of mourning in Roland Mushat Frye, *The Renaissance Hamlet: Issues and Responses in 1600* (Princeton, NJ: Princeton University Press, 1984), 83–102.
27. Margreta de Grazia, *"Hamlet" without Hamlet* (Cambridge: Cambridge University Press, 2007).
28. Honan, *Shakespeare*, 290–92.
29. His maternal and paternal grandfathers both died before he was born; his father's brother Henry died in 1596; his mother was one of eight daughters, so he had no maternal uncles.
30. For a skeptical survey of the evidence, see Thomas Postlewait, "The Criteria for Evidence: Anecdotes in Shakespearean Biography, 1709–2000," in *Theorizing Practice: Redefining Theatre History*, ed. W. B. Worthen and Peter Holland (New York: Palgrave, 2003), 47–9. Postlewait assumes that Betterton got the information "on a trip to Stratford-upon-Avon," which he certainly took, but that trip was presumably in search of evidence about Shakespeare's life in Warwickshire; the London theatre community was a better, and nearer, source of information about Shakespeare's acting. See Andrew Gurr, "Joseph Taylor," *Oxford Dictionary of National Biography* (*ODNB*).

31. Stephen Greenblatt, *Hamlet and Purgatory* (Princeton, NJ: Princeton University Press, 2001), 248–9.
32. Terri Bourus, "Counterfeiting Faith: Thomas Middleton's Re-formation of *Measure for Measure*," in *Stages of Engagement: Drama and Religion in Post-Reformation England*, ed. Katherine McPherson and James Mardock (Pittsburgh, PA: Duquesne University Press, 2014), 195–216. On the Warwickshire background, see Patrick Collinson, "William Shakespeare's Religious Inheritance," in his *Elizabethan Essays* (London: Bloomsbury, 1994). On a sympathy for Catholicism in Shakespeare's work, my position is closest to Gary Taylor's in three essays: "The Fortunes of Oldcastle," *Shakespeare Survey* 38 (1985): 85–100; "Forms of Opposition: Shakespeare and Middleton," *English Literary Renaissance* 24 (1994): 283–314; "Divine [ ]sences," *Shakespeare Survey* 54 (2001): 13–30. None of this is dependent on whether Shakespeare is the "William Shakeshafte" of Lancashire.
33. Stephen Greenblatt, "The Death of Hamnet and the Making of *Hamlet*," *New York Review of Books* 51.16 (21 October 2004): 42–7.
34. Greenblatt, *Purgatory*, 51–4. (Greenblatt does not mention any of the textual variants.)
35. For the East India corporation, see James Shapiro, *1599: A Year in the Life of William Shakespeare* (London: Faber, 2005), 302–8. Shapiro, understandably given his project, accepts the earliest possible date for the canonical *Hamlet* (late 1599).
36. E. A. J. Honigmann, "Shakespeare Suppressed: The Unfortunate History of *Troilus and Cressida*," in *Myriad-Minded Shakespeare* (New York: St. Martin's, 1989), 112–29.

Epilogue: Conclusions and Rebeginnings

1. Leah S. Marcus, *Unediting the Renaissance: Shakespeare, Marlowe, Milton* (London: Routledge, 1996), 107; William Hazlitt, *Characters of Shakespeare's Plays* (London: Printed by C. H. Reynell, for R. Hunter, 1817), 107.
2. Johann Wolfgang von Goethe, *Wilhelm Meister's Apprenticeship*, Book IV, chapter 13; Book VIII, chapter 5.
3. "First Edition of *Hamlet*" (1827), reviewing "*The First Edition of the tragedy of Hamlet*, by William Shakespeare, London, 1603" (Leipzig: Fleisher, 1825), in Johann Wolfgang von Goethe, *Goethe's Literary Essays: A Selection in English*, ed. J. E. Spingarn (Oxford: Oxford University Press, 1921), 190–194.

Works Cited

Albright, Evelyn May. *Dramatic Publication in England, 1580–1640*. London: Oxford UP, 1927. Print.

Alexander, Mark. Shakespeare Authorship Sourcebook. Web.

Alexander, Peter. *Shakespeare's Henry VI and Richard III*. Cambridge: Cambridge UP, 1929. Print.

Andrews, Robert. "Video Nasties Gallery: Fifteen Years of Anti-Piracy Warnings." *The Guardian* 8 Apr. 2009. Web. Feb. 2014.

Arber, Edward. *A Transcript of the Registers of the Company of Stationers of London 1554–1640, A.D.* Vol. 3. London: Priv. Print., 1875–1894. Print.

Baldwin, Thomas Whitfield. *Shakespeare's Love's Labor's Won: New Evidence from the Account Books of an Elizabethan Bookseller*. Carbondale: Southern Illinois UP, 1957. Print.

Barnard, John, and Maureen Bell. "The Inventory of Henry Bynneman (1583): A Preliminary Survey." *Publishing History* 29 (1991): 5–46. Print.

Barroll, J. Leeds. *Politics, Plague, and Shakespeare's Theater: The Stuart Years*. Ithaca, NY: Cornell UP, 1991. Print.

Batchelor, John, T. G. S. Cain, and Claire Lamont, eds. *Shakespearean Continuities: Essays in Honour of E. A. J. Honigmann*. New York: St. Martin's, 1997. Print.

Bawcutt, N. W., ed. *The Control and Censorship of Caroline Drama: The Records of Sir Henry Herbert, Master of the Revels, 1623–73*. Oxford: Clarendon, 1996. Print.

Bednarz, James P. "Canonizing Shakespeare: *The Passionate Pilgrim*, *England's Helicon* and the Question of Authenticity." *Shakespeare Survey* 60 (2007): 252–67. Print.

Bednarz, James P. *Shakespeare & the Poets' War*. New York: Columbia UP, 2001. Print.

Bell, Maureen, and John Barnard. "The English Provinces." *The Cambridge History of the Book in Britain*. Vol. IV. *1557–1695*. Ed. John Barnard and D. F. McKenzie. Cambridge: Cambridge UP, 2002. 665–86. Print.

Bentley, Gerald Eades. *The Jacobean and Caroline Stage*. 7 vols. Oxford: Clarendon, 1941–68. Print.

Berry, Ralph. "Hamlet's Doubles." *Shakespeare Quarterly* 37.2 (1986): 204–12. Print.

Bevington, David M., ed. *Troilus and Cressida*. London: Arden Shakespeare, 2001. Print.

Billington, Michael. "Hamlet, Old Vic." *Guardian*. Guardian News and Media, 28 Apr. 2004. Web. Dec. 2013.

Bird, Alan. "Hamlet at the Old Vic." LondonTheatre.co.uk. 28 Apr. 2004. Web. Dec. 2013.

Blayney, Peter W. M. "The Alleged Popularity of Playbooks." *Shakespeare Quarterly* 56.1 (2005): 33–50. Print.

Blayney, Peter W. M. *The Bookshops in Paul's Cross Churchyard*. London: Bibliographical Society, 1990. Print.

Blayney, Peter W. M. *The First Folio of Shakespeare*. Washington, DC: Folger Library Publications, 1991. Print.

Blayney, Peter W. M. "The Publication of Playbooks." *A New History of Early English Drama*. Ed. John D. Cox and David Scott Kastan. New York: Columbia UP, 1997. 383–422. Print.

Blayney, Peter W. M. *The Stationers' Company and the Printers of London: 1501–1557*. Cambridge: Cambridge UP, 2013. Print.

Boas, Frederick S. "'Hamlet' at Oxford: New Facts and Suggestions." *Fortnightly Review* 94 (1913): 245–53. Print.

Bourus, Terri. "Counterfeiting Faith: Thomas Middleton's Re-formation of *Measure for Measure*." *Stages of Engagement: Drama and Religion in Post-Reformation England*. Ed. Katherine McPherson and James Mardock. Pittsburgh, PA: Duquesne University Press, 2014. 195–216. Print.

Bourus, Terri. "The First Quarto of *Hamlet* in Film: The Revenge Tragedies of Tony Richardson and Franco Zeffirelli." *EnterText* 1.2 (August 2001). Web.

Bourus, Terri. "'May I Be Metamorphosed': Cardenio by Stages." *The Quest for Cardenio: Shakespeare, Fletcher, Cervantes, and the Lost Play*. Ed. David Carnegie and Gary Taylor. Oxford: Oxford UP, 2012. 387–403. Print.

Bourus, Terri. "Poner in Escena *The History of Cardenio*." *The Creation and Re-creation of Cardenio: Performing Shakespeare, Transforming Cervantes*. Ed. Terri Bourus and Gary Taylor. New York: Palgrave Macmillan, 2013. 297–318. Print.

Bourus, Terri. "Shakespeare and the London Publishing Environment: The Publisher and Printers of Q1 and Q2 *Hamlet*." *Analytical and Enumerative Bibliography* 12 (2001): 206–28. Print.

Bourus, Terri. "'With thouwsand mothers blessings': Gertred's Motivations and the Commonwealth of Denmark." Blackfriars Scholars Conference. Staunton, VA, 2005.

Bourus, Terri, and Gary Taylor, "*Measure for Measure*(s): Performance-testing the adaptation hypothesis." *Shakespeare* 10.2 (2014). Web.

Bowers, Fredson. *On Editing Shakespeare and the Elizabethan Dramatists*. London: Oxford UP, 1955. Print.

Braden, Gordon. *Renaissance Tragedy and the Senecan Tradition: Anger's Privilege*. New Haven, CT: Yale UP, 1985. Print.

Brainerd, Barron "The Chronology of Shakespeare's Plays: A Statistical Study." *Computers and the Humanities* 14.4 (1980): 221–30. Print.

Brathwaite, Richard. *Whimzies: Or, a New Cast of Characters*. London: Printed by F K and Are to Be Sold by Ambrose Rithirdon at the Signe of the Bulls-head in Pauls Church-yard, 1631. Print.

Brinsley, John. *Ludus Literarius: Or, The Grammar Schoole*. London: Printed for Thomas Man, 1612. Print.
British Book Trade Index. Birmingham, UK: University of Birmingham. Web.
Brown, Griselda Murray. "Hamlet, Shakespeare's Globe, London." *Financial Times*. 5 May 2011. Web. Feb. 2014.
Brown, John Russell. "The Compositors of *Hamlet* Q2 and *The Merchant of Venice*." *Studies in Bibliography* 7 (1955): 17–40. Print.
Bullough, Geoffrey. *Narrative and Dramatic Sources of Shakespeare*. 7 vols. London: Routledge and Paul, 1957–1975. Print.
Bullough, Geoffrey. "Sénèque, Greville et le jeune Shakespeare." *Les Tragédies de Sénèque et le Théâtre de la Renaissance*. Ed. Jean Jacquot and Marcel Oddon. Paris: Editions du Centre National de la Recherche Scientfique, 1964: 189–20. Print.
Bunbury, Henry, ed. *The Correspondence of Sir Thomas Hanmer, Bart., Speaker of the House of Commons: With a Memoir of His Life; To Which Are Added, Other Relicks of a Gentleman's Family*. London: E. Moxon, 1838. Print.
Burton, William. *A Sermon Preached in the Cathedral Church of Norwich, 1589*. 1591. Print.
Carroll, William C., ed. *Love's Labour's Lost*. Cambridge: Cambridge UP, 2009. Print.
Cerasano, S. P. "Edward Alleyn, the New Model Actor, and the Rise of the Celebrity in the 1590s." *Medieval and Renaissance Drama in England* 18 (2005): 47–58. Print.
Chambers, E. K. *The Elizabethan Stage*. 4 vols. Oxford: Clarendon, 1923. Print.
Chambers, E. K. *Shakespeare*. 2 vols. Oxford: Clarendon, 1930. Print.
Chambers, Edmund, Frederick James Furnivall, Clement Mansfield Ingleby, et al. *The Shakespeare Allusion-Book: A Collection of Allusions to Shakespeare from 1591 to 1700*. 2 vols. London: Oxford UP, 1932. Print.
Cheney, Patrick. *Shakespeare's Literary Authorship*. Cambridge: Cambridge UP, 2008. Print.
Christian, Margaret. "*Zepheria* (1595; STC 26124): A Critical Edition." *Studies in Philology* 100.2 (2003): 177–243. Print.
Clair, William St. *The Reading Nation in the Romantic Period*. Cambridge: Cambridge UP, 2004. Print.
Clark, Eva Turner. *Hidden Allusions in Shakespeare's Plays: A Study of the Early Court Revels and Personalities of the times*. Port Washington, NY: Kennikat, 1974. Print.
Coddon, Karen S. "'Such strange desyns': Madness, Subjectivity and Treason in *Hamlet* and Elizabethan Culture." *Renaissance Drama* 20 (1989): 51–75. Print.
Coleridge, Samuel Taylor. *Coleridge on Shakespeare: The Text of the Lectures of 1811–12*. Ed. R. A. Foakes. Charlottesville: Published for the Folger Shakespeare Library by the University Press of Virginia, 1971. Print.
Collier, J. Payne. "The Edition of 'Hamlet' in 1603." *Athenaeum* 1510 (Oct. 1856): 1220–21. Print.
Collier, J. Payne. ed. *The Works of William Shakespeare: The Text Formed from an Entirely New Collation of the Old Editions*. Vol. VII. London: Whittaker (1843). 189–93. Print.

Collinson, Patrick. *Elizabethan Essays*. London: Bloomsbury, 1994. Print.
Cooper, J. P. D. *The Queen's Agent: Francis Walsingham at the Court of Elizabeth I*. London: Faber and Faber, 2011. Print.
Craig, D. H., and Arthur F. Kinney. *Shakespeare, Computers, and the Mystery of Authorship*. Cambridge: Cambridge UP, 2009. Print.
Craven, Alan E. "Proofreading in the Shop of Valentine Simmes." *Papers of the Bibliographical Society of America* 68 (1974): 361–72. Print.
Craven, Alan E. "The Reliability of Simmes's Compositor A." *Studies in Bibliography* 32 (1979): 186–97. Print.
Craven, Alan E. "Simmes' Compositor A and Five Shakespeare Quartos." *Studies in Bibliography* 26 (1973): 37–60. Print.
Daniell, David., ed. *Julius Caesar*. London: Arden Shakespeare, 1998. Print.
Darnton, Robert. *The Kiss of Lamourette: Reflections in Cultural History*. New York: Norton, 1990. 107–35. Print.
Davis, William. "Now, Gods, Stand Up For Bastards: The 1603 Good Quarto?" *Textual Cultures: Text, Contexts, Interpretation* 1.2 (2006): 60–89. Print.
Dekker, Thomas, and John Webster. *West-Ward Hoe as It Hath Beene Diuers times Acted by the Children of Paules*. London: 1607. Print.
Dekker, Thomas. *Satiro-mastix*. London: 1602. Print.
Dessen, Alan C., and Leslie Thomson. *A Dictionary of Stage Directions in English Drama: 1580–1642*. Cambridge: Cambridge UP, 1999. Print.
Doran, Madeleine. *Endeavours of Art: A Study of Form in Elizabethan Drama*. Madison: University of Wisconsin Press, 1954. Print.
Duthie, George Ian. *The "Bad" Quarto of Hamlet: A Critical Study*. Cambridge: Cambridge UP, 1941. Print.
Duthie, George Ian. *Elizabethan Shorthand and the First Quarto of King Lear*. Oxford: Blackwell, 1949. Print.
Duthie, George Ian, ed. *Shakespeare's King Lear: A Critical Edition*. Oxford: Blackwell, 1949. Print.
Eccles, Mark. "Bynneman's Books." *Library* V, 12 (1957): 81–92. Print.
Eccles, Mark. *Shakespeare in Warwickshire*. Madison: U of Wisconsin Press, 1961. Print.
Edmondson, Paul M. "'A sad story tolde': Playing Horatio in Q1 *Hamlet*." *Hamlet Studies* 22 (2000): 26–39. Print.
EEBO: Early English Books Online. Web.
Egan, Gabriel. "Shakespeare: Editions and Textual Matters." *The Year's Work in English Studies, vol. 91: Covering Work Published in 2010*. Oxford: Oxford UP, 2012: 328–410. Print.
Egan, Gabriel. *The Struggle for Shakespeare's Text: Twentieth-century Editorial Theory and Practice*. Cambridge: Cambridge UP, 2010. Print.
Egan, Gabriel. "The Theatre in Shoreditch 1576–1599." *The Oxford Handbook of Early Modern Theatre*. Ed. Richard Dutton. Oxford: Oxford UP, 2009. 168–85. Print.
Elliott, John R., Jr., Alan H. Nelson, Alexandra F. Johnston, and Diana Wyatt, eds. *Records of Early English Drama: Oxford*. London: British Library, 2004. Print.

Erler, Mary Carpenter. *Records of Early English Drama: Ecclesiastical London*. Toronto: U of Toronto P, 2008. Print.

Erne, Lukas. *Beyond "The Spanish Tragedy": A Study of the Works of Thomas Kyd*. Manchester: Manchester UP, 2001. Print.

Erne, Lukas. *Shakespeare and the Book Trade*. Cambridge: Cambridge UP, 2013. Print.

Erne, Lukas. *Shakespeare as Literary Dramatist*. Revised ed. Cambridge: Cambridge UP, 2013. Print.

Es, Bart Van. *Shakespeare in Company*. Oxford: Oxford UP, 2013. Print.

ESTC: *English Short Title Catalogue*. London: British Library. Web.

Farmer, Alan B., and Zachary Lesser, eds. *DEEP: Database of Early English Playbooks*. Philadelphia: University of Pennsylvania. Web.

Farmer, Alan B., and Zachary Lesser. "The Popularity of Playbooks Revisited." *Shakespeare Quarterly* 56.1 (2005): 1–32. Print.

Farmer, Alan B., and Zachary Lesser. "Structures of Popularity in the Early Modern Book Trade." *Shakespeare Quarterly* 56.2 (2005): 206–13. Print.

Ferguson, W. Craig. *Pica Roman Type in Elizabethan England*. Aldershot: Scolar, 1989. Print.

Ferguson, W. Craig. "Valentine Simmes." *Dictionary of Literary Biography*. Ed. James K. Bracken and Joel Silver. Vol. 170. Detroit, MI: Gale, 1996. 244. Print.

Ferguson, W. Craig. *Valentine Simmes: Printer to Drayton, Shakespeare, Chapman, Greene, Dekker, Middleton, Daniel, Jonson, Marlowe, Marston, Heywood, and Other Elizabethans*. Charlottesville: Bibliographical Society of the U of Virginia, 1968. Print.

Fisher, Philip. ""Hamlet, Old Vic (2004)." British Theatre Guide. Web. Dec. 2013.

Foakes, R. A., and R. T. Rickert, ed., *Henslowe's Diary*. 2nd ed. Cambridge: Cambridge UP, 2002.

Forgeng, Jeffrey L. *Daily Life in Elizabethan England*. Westport, CT: Greenwood, 2009. Print.

Freeman, Arthur, and J. I. Freeman. "Did Halliwell Steal and Mutilate the First Quarto of Hamlet?" *Library* 2.4 (2001): 349–63. Print.

Freeman, Arthur, and Janet Ing Freeman. *John Payne Collier: Scholarship and Forgery in the Nineteenth Century*. New Haven, CT: Yale UP, 2004. Print.

Freeman, Arthur, and Paul Grinke. "Four New Shakespeare Quartos?" *TLS* 5 Apr. 2002: 17–18. Print.

Freeman, Arthur. *Thomas Kyd: Facts and Problems*. Oxford: Clarendon, 1967. Print.

French, George Russell. *Shakespeareana Genealogica*. London: 1869. Print.

Fripp, Edgar I. *Shakespeare, Man and Artist*. London: Oxford UP, 1964. Print.

Frye, Roland Mushat. *The Renaissance Hamlet: Issues and Responses in 1600*. Princeton, NJ: Princeton UP, 1984. Print.

Gardner, Lyn. "Hamlet—Review: Shakespeare's Globe." *Guardian*. 5 May 2011. Web. Feb. 2014.

Goethe, Johann Wolfgang von. *Goethe's Literary Essays: A Selection in English*. Ed. Joel Elias Spingarn. Oxford: Oxford UP, 1921. Print.

Goethe, Johann Wolfgang von. *Wilhelm Meister's Apprenticeship*. Trans. Thomas Carlyle. Edinburgh: Oliver & Boyd, 1824. Print.

Gollancz, Israel. *The Sources of Hamlet*. London: Oxford UP, 1926. Print.
Greenblatt, Stephen. "The Death of Hamnet and the Making of *Hamlet*." *New York Review of Books* 51.16 (21 Oct. 2004): 42–47. Print.
Greenblatt, Stephen. *Hamlet in Purgatory*. Princeton, NJ: Princeton UP, 2001. Print.
Greg, W. W. *A Bibliography of the English Printed Drama to the Restoration*. 4 vols. London: Printed for the Bibliographical Society by Oxford UP, 1939–1949. Print.
Greg, W. W. "Introduction." *The Merry Wives of Windsor 1602*. Shakespeare Quartos. Oxford: Clarendon, 1910. Print.
Griffiths, Paul. *Youth and Authority: Formative Experience in England, 1560–1640*. Oxford: Clarendon, 1996. Print.
Guilpin, Edward, ed. D. Allen Carroll. *Skialetheia: Or, A Shadowe of Truth, in Certaine Epigrams and Satyres*. Chapel Hill: U of North Carolina P, 1974. Print.
Gunthio, Ambrose. "A Running Commentary on the Hamlet of 1603." *European Magazine*, n.s. 1:4 (December 1825): 339–47. Print.
Gurr, Andrew. "Henry Carey's Peculiar Letter." *Shakespeare Quarterly* 56.1 (2005): 51–75. Print.
Gurr, Andrew. "Maximal and Minimal Texts: Shakespeare v. the Globe" *Shakespeare Survey* 52 (1999): 68–87. Print.
Gurr, Andrew., ed. *The First Quarto of King Henry V*. Cambridge: Cambridge UP, 2000. Print.
Gurr, Andrew. *The Shakespeare Company, 1594–1642*. Cambridge: Cambridge UP, 2004. Print.
Gurr, Andrew. *The Shakespearian Playing Companies*. Oxford: Clarendon, 1996. Print.
Hailey, R. Carter. "The Dating Game: New Evidence for the Dates of Q4 *Romeo and Juliet* and Q4 *Hamlet*." *Shakespeare Quarterly* 58.3 (2007): 367–87. Print.
Harington, Sir John. "An Apologie of Poetrie." *Orlando Furioso in English Heroical Verse* (1591). Print.
Harvey, Jay. "'Young Hamlet' Features a Less Philosophical Hero." *Indianapolis Star* 13 Feb. 2011. Web. Dec. 2013.
Hazlitt, William. *Characters of Shakespear's Plays*. London: Printed by C. H. Reynell, for R. Hunter, 1817. Print.
Hebel, William J. "Nicholas Ling and *England's Hellicon*." *Library* IV, 5 (1924). Print.
Helgerson, Richard. *Forms of Nationhood: The Elizabethan Writing of England*. Chicago: U of Chicago P, 1992. Print.
Hellinga, Lotte, and Joseph Burney Trapp, eds. *The Cambridge History of the Book in Britain*. Vol. 3. *1400–1557*. Cambridge: Cambridge UP, 1999. Print.
Henslowe-Alleyn Digitization Project. Web.
Heywood, Thomas. *If You Know Not Me*. London, 1639. Print.
Heywood, Thomas. *The Rape of Lucrece*. London, 1608. Print.
Hirrel, Michael J. "Duration of Performances and Lengths of Plays: How Shall We Beguile the Lazy Time?" *Shakespeare Quarterly* 61.2 (2010): 159–82. Print.

Hirrell, Michael James. "The Roberts Memorandum: A Solution." *Review of English Studies* 71 (2010): 711–728. Print.
Honan, Park. *Shakespeare: A Life*. Oxford: Oxford UP, 1998. Print.
Honigmann, E. A. J. "The Date of *Hamlet*." *Shakespeare Survey* 9 (1956): 24–34. Print.
Honigmann, E. A. J. *John Weever: A Biography of a Literary Associate of Shakespeare and Jonson, Together with a Photographic Facsimile of Weever's Epigrammes (1599)*. Manchester: Manchester UP, 1987. Print.
Honigmann, E. A. J. *Myriad-minded Shakespeare: Essays, Chiefly on the Tragedies and Problem Comedies*. New York: St. Martin's, 1989. Print.
Honigmann, E. A. J. *Shakespeare's Impact on His Contemporaries*. London: Macmillan, 1982. Print.
Honigmann, E. A. J. "Shakespeare's Lost Source-Plays." *Modern Language Review* 49.3 (1954): 293–307. Print.
Hoy, Cyrus. *Introductions, Notes, and Commentaries to Texts in The Dramatic Works of Thomas Dekker*. 4 vols. Cambridge: Cambridge UP, 1980. Print.
Hume, Robert D., and Harold Love, eds. *Plays, Poems, and Miscellaneous Writings Associated with George Villiers, Second Duke of Buckingham*. 2 vols. Oxford: Oxford UP, 2007. Print.
Ingram, William. *The Business of Playing: The Beginnings of the Adult Professional Theater in Elizabethan London*. Ithaca, NY: Cornell UP, 1992. Print.
Irace, Kathleen. "Origins and Agents of Q1 *Hamlet*." *The Hamlet First Published (Q1, 1603): Origins, Form, Intertextualities*. Ed. Thomas Clayton. Newark: U of Delaware P, 1992. 90–122. Print.
Irace, Kathleen O. *Reforming the "Bad" Quartos: Performance and Provenance of Six Shakespearean First Editions*. Newark: U of Delaware P, 1994. Print.
Irace, Kathleen O., ed. *The First Quarto of Hamlet*. Cambridge: Cambridge UP, 1998. Print.
Jack, Adolphus Alfred. *Young Hamlet*. Aberdeen: Aberdeen UP, 1950. Print.
Jackson, MacDonald P. *Studies in Attribution: Middleton and Shakespeare*. Vol. 79. Salzburg: Institut für Anglistik und Amerikanistik, Universität Salzburg, 1979. Print.
Jackson, Shannon. *Professing Performance: Theatre in the Academy from Philology to Performativity*. New York: Cambridge UP, 2004. Print.
Jenkins, Harold. "Playhouse Interpolations in the Folio Text of *Hamlet*." *Studies in Bibliography* 13 (1960): 31–47. Print.
Johns, Adrian. *The Nature of the Book: Print and Knowledge in the Making*. Chicago: U of Chicago P, 1998. Print.
Johns, Adrian. *Piracy: The Intellectual Property Wars from Gutenberg to Gates*. Chicago: U of Chicago P, 2009. Print.
Johnson, Francis R. "Notes on English Retail Book-prices, 1550–1640." *Library* V, 2 (1950): 83–112. Print.
Johnson, Gerald D. "John Busby and the Stationers' Trade, 1590–1612." *Library* VI,7 (1985): 1–15. Print.
Johnson, Gerald D. "John Trundle and the Book-Trade 1603–1626." *Studies in Bibliography* 39 (1986): 177–99. Print.

Johnson, Gerald D. "Nicholas Ling, Publisher 1580–1607." *Studies in Bibliography* 38 (1985): 203–14. Print.
Johnson, Samuel. *Johnson on Shakespeare*. Ed. Arthur Sherbo and Bertrand Harris Bronson. New Haven, CT: Yale UP, 1968. Print.
Jolly, Margrethe. "*Hamlet* and the French Connection: The Relationship of Q1 and Q2 *Hamlet* and the Evidence of Belleforest's *Histoires Tragiques*." *Parergon* 29.1 (2012): 83–105. Print.
Jones, G. P. "A Burbage Ballad and John Payne Collier." *Review of English Studies* 40.159 (1989): 393–97. Print.
Jonson, Ben. *Poetaster*. Ed. Gabriele Bernhard Jackson. *The Cambridge Edition of the Works of Ben Jonson*. Ed. David M. Bevington, Martin Butler, and Ian Donaldson. 7 vols. Cambridge: Cambridge UP, 2012. Print.
Kahneman, Daniel. *Thinking, Fast and Slow*. New York: Farrar, Straus and Giroux, 2011. Print.
Kastan, David Scott. *A Companion to Shakespeare*. Oxford: Blackwell, 1999. Print.
Kastan, David Scott. *Shakespeare and the Book*. Cambridge: Cambridge UP, 2001. Print.
Kehler, Dorothea. "The First Quarto of *Hamlet*: Reforming Widow Gertred." *Shakespeare Quarterly* 46 (1995): 398–413. Print.
Kelly, Charles Adams. *The Evidence Matrix for the 1st Quarto of Shakespeare's Hamlet*. Ann Arbor, MI: Howland Research, 2008. Rev. ed. 2014. Print.
Kenny, Thomas. *The Life and Genius of Shakespeare*. London: Longman, 1864. Print.
Kirschbaum, Leo. *Shakespeare and the Stationers*. Columbus: Ohio State UP, 1955. Print.
Knight, Charles. *Studies of Shakspere*. London: Routledge, 1849. Print.
Knighton, C. S. "Burton, Thomas (c.1545–1616)." *Oxford Dictionary of National Biography*. Oxford: Oxford UP, 2004. Web.
Knowles, Richard. "Shakespeare and Shorthand Once Again." *PBSA* 194 (2010): 141–80. Print.
Knutson, Roslyn L. "Henslowe's Diary and the Economics of Play Revision for Revival, 1592–1603." *Theatre Research International* 10.1 (1985): 1–18. Print.
Knutson, Roslyn L. *The Repertory of Shakespeare's Company: 1594–1613*. Fayetteville: U of Arkansas P, 1991. Print.
Kyd, Thomas. *The Spanish Tragedy*. Ed. Clara Calvo and Jesús Tronch. London: Arden Shakespeare, 2013. Print.
Kyd, Thomas. *The Spanish Tragedy*. Ed. Michael Neill. New York: Norton, 2014. Print.
Kyd, Thomas. *The Spanish Tragedy*. Ed. Philip Edwards. London: Methuen, 1959. Print.
Kyd, Thomas. *The Works of Thomas Kyd*. Ed. Frederick S. Boas. Oxford: Clarendon, 1901. Print.
Kyle, Chris R. *Theater of State: Parliament and Political Culture in Early Stuart England*. Stanford: Stanford UP, 2012. Print.

Lamb, Charles, and Mary Lamb. *Tales from Shakespear Designed for the Use of Young Persons*. London: Thomas Hodgkins, 1807. Print.

Lander, Jesse M. *Inventing Polemic: Religion, Print, and Literary Culture in Early Modern England*. Cambridge: Cambridge UP, 2006. Print.

Lesser, Zachary, and Peter Stallybrass. "The First Literary *Hamlet* and the Commonplacing of Professional Plays." *Shakespeare Quarterly* 59.4 (2008): 371–420. Print.

Lesser, Zachary. *Renaissance Drama and the Politics of Publication: Readings in the English Book Trade*. Cambridge: Cambridge UP, 2004. Print.

Lloyd, W. "Scribal Copy for Q1 *Richard II*?" *Notes and Queries* 51.3 (2004): 280–83. Print.

Lodge, Thomas. *VVits Miserie, and the VVorlds Madnesse Discouering the Deuils Incarnat of This Age*. London, 1596. Print.

Looney, John Thomas. *Shakespeare Identified*. New York: Stokes, 1920. Print.

Lost Plays Database. Eds. Roslyn L. Knutson and David McInnis. Melbourne: University of Melbourne. Web.

Loughrey, Brian. "Q1 in Recent Performance: An Interview." *The Hamlet First Published*. Ed. Thomas Clayton. Newark: U of Delaware P, 1992. 123–36. Print.

Lundstrom, Rinda F. *William Poel's Hamlets: The Director as Critic*. Ann Arbor, MI: UMI Research, 1984. Print.

Lynn, Raphael. "Thomas Churchyard." *Oxford Dictionary of National Biography*. Oxford: Oxford UP, 2004. Web.

Maguire, Laurie E. *Shakespearean Suspect Texts: The "Bad" Quartos and Their Contexts*. Cambridge: Cambridge UP, 1996. Print.

Malone, Edmond. *The Life of William Shakspeare*. Ed. James Boswell. London: Privately printed, 1821. Print.

Manley, Lawrence, and Sally-Beth MacLean. *Lord Strange's Men and Their Plays*. New Haven, CT: Yale UP, 2013. Print.

Manley, Lawrence. "Why Did London Inns Function as Theaters?" *Huntington Library Quarterly* 71.1 (2008): 181–97. Print.

Marcus, Leah S. *Unediting the Renaissance: Shakespeare, Marlowe, Milton*. London: Routledge, 1996. Print.

Marino, James J. *Owning William Shakespeare: The King's Men and Their Intellectual Property*. Philadelphia: U of Pennsylvania P, 2011. Print.

Matthews, William. "Shorthand and the Bad Shakespeare Quartos." *Modern Language Review* 27.3 (1932): 243–62. Print.

Matthews, William. "Shakespeare and the Reporters." *Library* XV: 4 (1935): 481–500. Print.

May, Steven W. "George Puttenham's Lewd and Illicit Career." *Texas Studies in Literature and Language* 50.2 (2008): 143–76. Print.

McGuire, Philip C. "Which Fortinbras, Which *Hamlet*?" *The Hamlet First Published*. Ed. Thomas Clayton. Newark: U of Delaware P, 1992. 151–78.

McKerrow, Ronald Brunlees. *Printers' & Publishers' Devices in England & Scotland, 1485–1640*. London: Bibliographical Society, 1949. Print.

McKerrow, Ronald Brunlees. *A Dictionary of Printers and Booksellers in England, Scotland and Ireland, and of Foreign Printers of English Books 1557–1640*. London: Bibliographical Society, 1968. Print.

McKitterick, David. *A History of Cambridge University Press*. Vol. I. Cambridge: Cambridge UP, 1992. Print.

McLeod, Randall. "*Gon*. No More, the Text Is Foolish." *The Division of the Kingdoms: Shakespeare's Two Versions of King Lear*. Ed. Gary Taylor and Michael Warren. Oxford: Clarendon, 1983. Print.

McMillin, Scott. *The Elizabethan Theatre and The Book of Sir Thomas More*. Ithaca, NY: Cornell UP, 1987. Print.

McMillin, Scott, and Sally-Beth MacLean. *The Queen's Men and Their Plays*. Cambridge: Cambridge UP, 1998. Print.

Melnikoff, Kirk. "Nicolas Ling's Republican *Hamlet* (1603)." *Shakespeare's Stationers: Studies in Cultural Bibliography*. Ed. Marta Straznicky. Philadelphia: U of Pennsylvania P, 2012. 95–111. Print.

Melnikoff, Kirk, and Edward Gieskes, eds. *Writing Robert Greene: Essays on England's First Notorious Professional Writer*. Aldershot: Ashgate, 2008. Print.

Mendle, Michael. "News and the Pamphlet Culture of Mid-seventeenth-century England." *The Politics of Information in Early Modern Europe*. Ed. Brendan Maurice Dooley and Sabrina A. Baron. London: Routledge, 2001. 57–79. Print.

Mentz, Steve. *Romance for Sale in Early Modern England: The Rise of Prose Fiction*. Aldershot: Ashgate, 2006. Print.

Menzer, Paul. *The Hamlets: Cues, Qs, and Remembered Texts*. Newark: U of Delaware P, 2008. Print.

Middleton, Thomas. *The Collected Works*. Ed. Gary Taylor and John Lavagnino. Oxford: Clarendon, 2007. Print.

Mikhail, E. H. *Goldsmith: Interviews and Recollections*. Houndmills, Basingstoke: Macmillan, 1993. Print.

Millican, Percy. *The Register of the Freemen of Norwich, 1548–1713: A Transcript, with an Introduction, an Appendix to Those Freemen Whose Apprenticeship Indentures are Enrolled in the City Records, and Indexes of Names and Places*. Norwich: Jarrold & Sons, 1934. Print.

Miola, Robert S. *Shakespeare and Classical Tragedy: The Influence of Seneca*. Oxford: Clarendon, 1992. Print.

Miola, Robert S. *Shakespeare's Reading*. Oxford: Oxford UP, 2000. Print.

Mitchell, C. Ainsworth. "Pencil Markings in the Bodleian Library." *Nature* 109.2738 (1922): 516–17. Print.

Mommsen, Tycho. "*Hamlet*, 1603; and *Romeo and Juliet*, 1597." *Athenaeum*. 7 Feb. 1857: 182. Print.

Morgan, Jude. *The Secret Life of William Shakespeare*. New York: St. Martin's, 2014. Print.

Munday, Anthony. *A Critical Edition of Fedele and Fortunio*. Ed. Richard Hosley. New York: Garland, 1981. Print.

Munkelt, Marga. "Traditions of Emendation in *Hamlet*: The Handling of the First Quarto." *The Hamlet First Published*. Ed. Thomas Clayton. Newark: U of Delaware P, 1992. 211–40. Print.

Murphy, Andrew. *Shakespeare in Print: A History and Chronology of Shakespeare Publishing*. Cambridge: Cambridge UP, 2003. Print.

Nadel, Ira. *Double Act: A Life of Tom Stoppard*. London: Methuen, 2004. Print.

Nashe, Thomas. *The Works of Thomas Nashe*. Ed. R. B. McKerrow. Rev. F. P. Wilson. 5 vols. Oxford: Blackwell, 1958. Print.

Neill, Heather. "Dominic Dromgoole on His Touring Hamlet." TheatreVOICE. com. 11 May 2011. Web. Feb. 2014.

Nelson, Alan H., ed. *Records of Early English Drama: Cambridge*. Toronto: U of Toronto P, 1989. Print.

Nelson, Alan H. *Monstrous Adversary: The Life of Edward De Vere, 17th Earl of Oxford*. Liverpool: Liverpool UP, 2003. Print.

Newcomb, Lori Humphrey. *Reading Popular Romance in Early Modern England*. New York: Columbia UP, 2002. Print.

Oras, Ants. *Pause Patterns in Elizabethan and Jacobean Drama: An Experiment in Prosody*. Gainesville: U of Florida P, 1960. Print.

Ostovich, Helen, Holger Schott Syme, and Andrew Griffin, eds. *Locating the Queen's Men, 1583–1603: Material Practices and Conditions of Playing*. Farnham: Ashgate, 2009. Print.

Oxford Dictionary of National Biography: In Association with the British Academy; From the Earliest Times to the Year 2000. Ed. H. C. G. Matthew and Brian Harrison. Oxford: Oxford UP, 2004. Web.

Palfrey, Simon, and Tiffany Stern. *Shakespeare in Parts*. Oxford: Oxford UP, 2007. Print.

Paul, Henry N. "Mr. Hughs' Edition of Hamlet." *Modern Language Notes* 49.7 (1934): 438–43. Print.

Pechter, Edward. *Shakespeare Studies Today: Romanticism Lost*. New York: Palgrave, 2011. Print.

Peele, George. *The Troublesome Reign of John, King of England*. Ed. Charles R. Forker. Manchester: Manchester UP, 2011. Print.

Petersen, Lene B. *Shakespeare's Errant Texts: Textual Form and Linguistic Style in Shakespearean "Bad" Quartos and Co-authored Plays*. Cambridge: Cambridge UP, 2010. Print.

Petroski, Henry. *The Pencil: A History of Design and Circumstance*. New York: Knopf, 1990. Print.

Plomer, H. R. "The Eliot's Court Printing House, 1584–1674." *Library* IV, 2.3 (1921): 175–84. Print.

Pollard, Alfred W. *Shakespeare Folios and Quartos: A Study in the Bibliography of Shakespeare's Plays 1594–1685*. London: Methuen, 1909. Print.

Pollard, Alfred W. *Shakespeare's Fight with the Pirates and the Problems of the Transmission of His Text*. London: Moring, 1917. Print.

Pollard, Alfred W., G. R. Redgrave, William A. Jackson, F. S. Ferguson, and Katharine F. Pantzer. *A Short-title Catalogue of Books Printed in England,*

Scotland, & Ireland and of English Books Printed Abroad, 1475–1640. 3 vols. London: Bibliographical Society, 1976–1991. Print.
Postlewait, Thomas. "The Criteria for Evidence: Anecdotes in Shakespearean Biography, 1709–2000." *Theorizing Practice: Redefining Theatre History*. Ed. William B. Worthen and Peter Holland. New York: Palgrave, 2003. Print.
Pound, John Frederick. *The Norwich Census of the Poor, 1570*. London: Norfolk Record Society, 1971. Print.
Pound, John. *Tudor and Stuart Norwich*. Chichester: Phillimore, 1988. Print.
Price, Diana. "Henslowe's 'ne' and 'the tyeringe-howsse doore.'" *Research Opportunities in Renaissance Drama* 42 (2003): 62–78. Print.
Price, Hereward Thimbleby. *The Text of "Henry V."* Newcastle-under-Lyme: Mandley & Unett, 1920. Print.
The Prince of Jutland. Dir. Gabriel Axel. 1994. Film.
Prynne, William. *Histrio-mastix, the Players Scourge, Or, Actors Tragedie*. London: 1633. Print.
Rawcliffe, Carole, Richard Wilson, and Christine Clark. *Norwich since 1550*. London: Hambledon, 2004. Print.
REED: *Records of Early English Drama*. Toronto: University of Toronto. Web.
Reynolds, Matthew. *Godly Reformers and Their Opponents in Early Modern England: Religion in Norwich, c.1560–1643*. Woodbridge: Boydell, 2005. Print.
Riggs, David. *The World of Christopher Marlowe*. New York: Henry Holt, 2005. Print.
Rodger, Alexander. "Roger Ward's Shrewsbury Stock: An Inventory of 1585." *Library* V, 13 (1958): 247–68. Print.
Rollins, H. E., ed. *England's Helicon*. Oxford: Clarendon, 1935. Print.
Rowse, A. L. *William Shakespeare: A Biography*. New York: HarperCollins, 1963. Print.
Sams, Eric. *The Real Shakespeare: Retrieving the Early Years, 1564–1594*. New Haven, CT: Yale UP, 1995. Print.
Sams, Eric. "Taboo or not Taboo? The Text, Dating and Authorship of Hamlet, 1589–1623." *Hamlet Studies* 10 (1998): 12–46. Print.
Saunders, H. W. *A History of the Norwich Grammar School*. Norwich: Jarrold & Sons, 1932. Print.
Schlegel, August Wilhelm von. *A Course of Lectures on Dramatic Art and Literature*. Trans. John Black. London: Baldwin, Cradock, and Joy, 1815. Print.
Schoenbaum, S. *William Shakespeare: A Compact Documentary Life*. New York: Oxford UP, 1977. Print.
Schoenbaum, S. *William Shakespeare: A Documentary Life*. New York: Oxford UP, 1975. Print.
Schoenbaum, S. *William Shakespeare: Records and Images*. New York: Oxford UP, 1981. Print.
Semler, Liam E. *Teaching Shakespeare and Marlowe: Learning versus the System*. London: Bloomsbury, 2013. Print.
Shaaber, M. A. "The Meaning of the Imprint in Early Printed Books." *Library* IV, 24.3–4 (1944): 120–41. Print.
Shakespeare, William. *Complete Works*. Ed. Jonathan Bate and Eric Rasmussen. Basingstoke: Macmillan, 2007. Print.

Shakespeare, William. *Hamlet*. Ed. Terri Bourus. Naperville, IL: Sourcebooks, 2006. Print.
Shakespeare, William. *Hamlet*. Ed. Harold Jenkins. London: Methuen, 1982. Print.
Shakespeare, William. *Hamlet*. Ed. Ann Thompson and Neil Taylor. London: Arden Shakespeare, 2006. Print.
Shakespeare, William. *Hamlet: First Quarto, 1603*. Ed. W. W. Greg. Oxford: Clarendon, 1965. Print.
Shakespeare, William. *Hamlet, the First Quarto, 1603*. Ed. Albert B. Weiner. Great Neck, NY: Barron's Educational, 1962. Print.
Shakespeare, William. *Hamlet: The Texts of 1603 and 1623*. Ed. Ann Thompson and Neil Taylor. London: Arden Shakespeare, 2006. Print.
Shakespeare, William. *The Complete Works*. Ed. Stanley Wells and Gary Taylor. 2nd ed. Oxford: Clarendon, 2005. Print.
Shakespeare, William. *The Plays and Poems of William Shakspeare*. Ed. Edmond Malone. London: 1790. Print.
Shakespeare, William. *The Plays and Poems of William Shakspeare*. Ed. Edmond Malone and James Boswell. London: 1821. Print.
Shakespeare, William. *The Plays of William Shakespeare*. Ed. Samuel Johnson and George Steevens. London: 1778. Print.
Shakespeare, William. *The Tragedy of King Richard III*. Ed. John Jowett. Oxford: Oxford UP, 2000. Print.
Shakespeare, William. *The True Tragedy of Richard the Third*. Ed. W. W. Greg. Oxford: Malone Society, 1929. Print.
Shand, G. B. "Gertred, Captive Queen of the First Quarto." *Shakespearean Illuminations: Essays in Honor of Marvin Rosenberg*. Ed. Jay L. Halio and Hugh Richmond. Newark: University of Delaware Press, 1998: 33–49. Print.
Shapiro, James S. *1599: A Year in the Life of William Shakespeare*. London: Faber, 2005. Print.
Sidney, Philip. *Miscellaneous Prose*. Ed. Katherine Duncan-Jones and J. A. Van Dorsten. Oxford: Clarendon, 1973. Print.
Sjörgen, Gunnar. "Producing the First Quarto *Hamlet*." *Hamlet Studies* 1 (1979): 35–44. Print.
Sjörgen, Gunnar. "Thomas Bull and Other 'English instrumentalists' in Denmark in the 1580s." *Shakespeare Survey* 22 (1969): 119–24. Print.
Slack, Paul. *The Impact of Plague in Tudor and Stuart England*. London: Routledge, 1985. Print.
Slater, Eliot. *The Problem of* The Reign of King Edward III*: A Statistical Approach*. Cambridge: Cambridge UP, 1988. Print.
Smith, Henry. *A Fruitful Sermon upon Part of the 5: Chapter of the First Epistle of Saint Paul to the Thessalonians*. Ed. Hereward T. Price. Halle (Salle): M. Niemeyer, 1922. Print.
Spencer, Charles. "Hamlet, Shakespeare's Globe, Review." *Daily Telegraph*. 6 May 2011. Web. Dec. 2013.
Spencer, Charles. "An Unforgettable and Most Lovable Hamlet." *Telegraph*. 28 Apr. 2004. Web. Dec. 2013.

Spevack, Marvin. *A Complete and Systematic Concordance to the Works of Shakespeare*. 9 vols. Hildesheim: Georg Olms, 1968–80. Print.

Stallybrass, Peter, Roger Chartier, John Franklin Mowery, and Heather Wolfe. "Hamlet's Tables and the Technologies of Writing in Renaissance England." *Shakespeare Quarterly* 55.4 (2004): 379–419. Print.

STC: see Pollard et al.

Stern, Tiffany. *Documents of Performance in Early Modern England*. Cambridge: Cambridge UP, 2009. Print.

Stern, Tiffany. "'If I Could See the Puppets Dallying': *Der Bestrafte Brudermord* and Hamlet's Encounters with the Puppets." *Shakespeare Bulletin* 31.3 (2013): 337–52. Print.

Stern, Tiffany. *Making Shakespeare: From Stage to Page*. London: Routledge, 2004. Print.

Stern, Tiffany. "'On Each Wall and Corner Poast': Playbills, Title-pages, and Advertising in Early Modern London." *English Literary Renaissance* 36.1 (2006): 57–89. Print.

Stern, Tiffany. *Rehearsal from Shakespeare to Sheridan*. Oxford: Oxford UP, 2000. Print.

Stern, Tiffany. "Sermons, Plays and Note-takers: *Hamlet* Q1 as a 'Noted' Text." *Shakespeare Survey* 66 (2013): 1–23. Print.

Stern, Tiffany. "Watching as Reading: The Audience and Written Text in the Early Modern Playhouse." *How to Do Things with Shakespeare: New Approaches, New Essays*. Ed. Laurie E. Maguire. Oxford: Blackwell, 2008. 136–59. Print.

Stern, Virginia F. *Gabriel Harvey: His Life, Marginalia and Library*. Oxford: Clarendon, 1980. Print.

Stevenson, Warren. *Shakespeare's Additions to Thomas Kyd's* The Spanish Tragedy*: A Fresh Look at the Evidence regarding the 1602 Additions*. Lewiston: Edwin Mellen, 2008. Print.

Stoker, David. "Anthony De Solempne: Attributions to His Press." *Library* VI, 3 (1981): 17–32. Print.

Stoker, David. *A History of the Norwich Book Trades from 1560 to 1760*. London: Library Association Thesis, 1975. Print.

Stoker, David. "'To All Booksellers, Country Chapmen, Hawkers and Others': How the Population of East Anglia Obtained Its Printed Materials." *Fairs, Markets and the Itinerant Book Trade*. Ed. Robin Myers, Michael Harris, and Giles Mandelbrote. London: British Library, 2007. 107–36. Print.

Straznicky, Marta, ed. *Shakespeare's Stationers: Studies in Cultural Bibliography*. Philadelphia: U of Pennsylvania P, 2013. Print.

Stubbs, Imogen. "Gertrude." *Performing Shakespeare's Tragedies Today: An Actor's Perspective*. Ed. Michael Dobson. Cambridge: Cambridge UP, 2006: 29–40. Print.

Syme, Holger Schott. "The Meaning of Success: Stories of 1594 and Its Aftermath." *Shakespeare Quarterly* 61.4 (2010): 490–525. Print.

Taylor, Gary. "Divine [ ]sences." *Shakespeare Survey* 54 (2001): 13–30. Print.

Taylor, Gary. "Feeling Bodies." *Shakespeare and the Twentieth Century: The Selected Proceedings of the International Shakespeare Association World Congress,*

Los Angeles, 1996. Ed. Jonathan Bate, Jill Levenson, Dieter Mehl. University of Delaware Press, 1998. 258–79. Print.

Taylor, Gary. "Forms of Opposition: Shakespeare and Middleton." *English Literary Renaissance* 24 (1994): 283–314. Print.

Taylor, Gary. "Making Meaning Marketing Shakespeare 1623." *From Performance to Print in Shakespeare's England*. Ed. Peter Holland and Stephen Orgel. Basingstoke: Palgrave, 2006. 55–72. Print.

Taylor, Gary. "Middleton and Macbeth." *Macbeth*. By William Shakespeare. Ed. Robert S. Miola. New York: Norton, 2014. 296–305. Print.

Taylor, Gary. "Sleight of Mind: Cognitive Illusions and Shakespearian Desire." *The Creation and Re-creation of Cardenio: Performing Shakespeare, Transforming Cervantes*. Ed. Terri Bourus and Gary Taylor. New York: Palgrave, 2013. 125–69. Print.

Taylor, Gary. "The Fortunes of Oldcastle." *Shakespeare Survey* 38 (1985): 85–100. Print.

Taylor, Gary, and John Jowett. *Shakespeare Reshaped: 1606–1623*. Oxford: Clarendon, 1993. Print.

Taylor, Gary, and John Lavagnino, eds. *Thomas Middleton and Early Modern Textual Culture: A Companion to the Collected Works*. Oxford: Clarendon, 2007. Print.

Taylor, Gary, and Michael Warren. *The Division of the Kingdoms: Shakespeare's Two Versions of King Lear*. Oxford: Clarendon, 1983. Print.

Taylor, Paul. "Hamlet, Shakespeare's Globe, London." *Independent*. 6 May 2011. Web. Feb. 2014.

Thomson, Peter. *Shakespeare's Professional Career*. Cambridge: Cambridge UP, 1992. Print.

Timberlake, Philip Wolcott. *The Feminine Ending in English Blank Verse*. Menasha, WI: Printed by George Banta, 1931. Print.

Tversky, Amos, and Daniel Kahneman. "Extensional versus Intuitive Reasoning: The Conjunction Fallacy in Probability Judgment." *Psychological Review* 90.4 (1983): 293–315. Print.

Vadnais, Matthew W. "'According to the scrippe': Speeches, Speech Order, and Performance in Shakespeare's Early Printed Play Texts." PhD diss, Ohio State University, 2012. Web. April 2014.

Van Dam, B. A. P. *The Text of Shakespeare's Hamlet*. London: John Lane, 1924. Print.

Vickers, Brian. "*Hamlet by Dogberry*: A Perverse Reading of the Bad Quarto." *TLS*. 14. Dec. 1993. Print.

Vickers, Brian. "Identifying Shakespeare's Additions to *The Spanish Tragedy* (1602): A New(er) Approach." *Shakespeare* 8.1 (2012): 13–43. Print.

Walsh, Brian. *Shakespeare, the Queen's Men, and the Elizabethan Performance of History*. Cambridge: Cambridge UP, 2009. Print.

Watson, Thomas. *Thomas Watson: Italian Madrigals Englished (1590)*. Ed. Albert Chatterley. London: Stainer and Bell for the Musica Britannica Trust, 1999. Print.

Webbe, William. *A Discourse of English Poetrie*. Ed. Edward Arber. London: Arber, 1870. Print.

Wells, Stanley, and Gary Taylor. *William Shakespeare: A Textual Companion*. Oxford: Clarendon, 1987. Print.

Werstine, Paul. "A Century of 'Bad' Shakespeare Quartos." *Shakespeare Quarterly* 50.3 (1999): 310–33. Print.

Werstine, Paul. *Early Modern Playhouse Manuscripts and the Editing of Shakespeare.* Cambridge: Cambridge UP, 2013. Print.

Werstine, Paul. "Narratives about Printed Shakespeare Texts: 'Foul Papers' and 'Bad' Quartos." *Shakespeare Quarterly* 41.1 (1990): 65–86. Print.

Werstine, Paul. "The Textual Mystery of Hamlet." *Shakespeare Quarterly* 39.1 (1988): 1–26. Print.

Wickham, Glynne, Herbert Berry, and William Ingram, eds. *English Professional Theatre: 1530–1660.* Cambridge: Cambridge UP, 2000. Print.

Wiggins, Martin, with Catherine Richardson. *British Drama, 1533–1642: A Catalogue.* Vols. 2–3. Oxford: Oxford UP, 2013. Print.

Wiles, David. *Shakespeare's Clown: Actor and Text in the Elizabethan Playhouse.* Cambridge: Cambridge UP, 1987. Print.

Williams, Joe. "Review: 'Young Hamlet' at IndyFringe." *NUVO.* 8 Feb. 2011. Web. Dec. 2013.

Wilson, F. P. *Marlowe and the Early Shakespeare.* Oxford: Clarendon, 1953. Print.

Wilson, F. P. "Shakespeare and the New Bibliography." *The Bibliographical Society, 1892–1942: Studies in Retrospect.* London: Bibliographical Society, 1945. Print.

Wilson, John Dover. *The Essential Shakespeare.* Cambridge: Cambridge UP, 1937. Print.

Winstanley, Lilian. *Hamlet and the Scottish Succession.* Cambridge: Cambridge UP, 1921. Print.

Woudhuysen, H. R. "Writing-Tables and Table Books." *British Library Journal* (2004): 1–11. Print.

Wright, George Thaddeus. *Shakespeare's Metrical Art.* Berkeley: U of California P, 1988. Print.

Ziegler, Georgianna, ed. *Shakespeare Study Today.* New York: AMS, 1986. Print.

Index

acting companies, 1, 4–5, 12, 20, 32–3, 44–6, 73, 79, 85, 91–3, 96, 102–4, 109, 142, 155, 175–6, 183, 195–7, 206, 209–10
 See also Admiral's Men
 See also Chamberlain's Men
 See also King's Men
 See also Leicester's Men
 See also Pembroke's Men
 See also Queen's Men
 See also Strange's Men
Admiral's Men, 151–6, 178
adolescence, 106, 109, 116–17, 123, 127–30, 134, 203, 209
Albright, May, 38
Alexander, Peter, 144
Alexander, William, 27
Allde, John, 142
Alleyn, Edward (actor), 154–6, 176, 178
Allott, Robert. *See* stationers
American Shakespeare Center, 2
amphitheatres, 93, 158, 170, 176
Andrewes, Lancelot, 20
Anouka, Jade (actor), 127–8
Arden Shakespeare, 3, 7, 38, 40–1, 49, 64, 94, 115, 197, 213
 See also Jenkins, Harold, *and* Thompson, Anne
Armin, Robert, 156–7, 251, 254
Arthur, Prince of Wales, 113
Astaire, Fred (actor), 49
Athenaeum, 74

attribution, 1, 24, 29, 67, 71, 84–6, 101, 163, 168, 178, 199
Axel, Gabriel (director), 134, 247–8

bad quarto, 25, 29, 37–8, 41, 46–8, 56, 59, 73, 83–6, 95–8, 131, 165, 170, 190
 See also memorial reconstruction
Bale, Christian (actor), 134
Beaufort, Margaret (Countess of Richmond and Derby), 114
Beaumont, Francis, 97
Bednarz, James P., 42, 185, 197
Belleforest, François de, 4, 99–100, 108–9, 134, 145, 157, 161–3, 167–8, 203
Berry, Ralph, 43
Betterton, Thomas, 35, 62, 203–4, 262
Billington, Michael, 118, 134
Blackfriars playhouse (London), 158, 185, 197, 260
Blackfriars Theatre (Virginia), 124
blackmail, 84–6
Bland, Mark, 84
Blayney, Peter W. M., 24, 30, 97–9
Blount, Edward. *See* stationers
Boas, Frederick S., 155, 165
Bodleian Library, 77
Bogart, Humphrey (actor), 146
bookselling, 5–6, 8, 11–17, 22–5, 28, 33–7, 44, 84–5, 102, 141, 154, 163, 168
Boswell, James, 137

Bourus, Terri (actor), 125, 129–30
Bowers, Fredson, 226
boy actors, 94, 109
Brathwaite, Richard, 79
Breton, Nicholas, 19
British Library, 62
British Museum, 29, 36–7, 77
Bryan, George (actor), 157
Buc, Sir George, 89–90
Bullough, Geoffrey, 157, 161
Bunbury, Sir Henry Edward, 36
Burbage, Richard (actor), 12, 93, 104–5, 109–10, 134, 145, 154–8, 179, 206–9, 242
Burby, Cuthbert. *See* stationers
Burton, William, 17
Busby, John. *See* stationers
Butter, Nathaniel. *See* stationers
Bynneman, Henry. *See* stationers

Cambridge University Press, 69, 94
Cambridge, 12, 32, 42, 56, 69, 94, 115, 138–9, 143, 152–5, 158, 179
Camden, William, 15
Cardwell, Thomas (actor), 125, 129–30
Casablanca (1942 film), 146
Catherine de Medici, Queen of France, 123
Catholicism, 31, 158, 169
censorship, 31, 83, 90, 150–1, 197
Cervantes, Miguel de, 19, 90
Chamberlain's Men, 17, 27, 30, 32–3, 44–5, 92–3, 139–40, 145–6, 149–58, 181–2, 196–7, 207
Chambers, E. K., 30, 76, 138, 143–4, 165, 169
Chartier, Roger, 77
Chaucer, Geoffrey, 18, 138, 140
Cheney, Patrick, 2
Christian IV, King of Denmark and Norway, 109
Churchyard, Thomas, 18
clown, 17, 62, 104, 156, 173–5, 177–8
Coke, Edward, 15, 17, 218, 220
Coleridge, Samuel Taylor, 133

collaboration, 30, 105, 156–66
Collier, John Payne, 71–6, 79, 84, 234
Condell, Henry (actor), 74
confirmation bias, 71
conspiracy, 67, 81, 95, 111, 123–4, 126
copyright, 11, 13, 17, 19, 23, 29–30, 32–3, 196, 219
See also intellectual property *and* piracy
Craig, Hardin, 59
Craig, Hugh, 2
Cross Keys Inn (playhouse), 152–3, 155, 176
Cues, 21, 39, 44–6, 65, 93–4, 111, 240

Daniel, Samuel, 148
Danter, John. *See* stationers
Darnton, Robert, 213
Davenant, William, 62, 203
Davidson, Adele, 238
Davies, Sir John, 19
De Vere, Edward (Earl of Oxford), 142
Decker, Tim (actor), 131
Dekker, Thomas, 19, 78–9, 149, 170, 176, 197
Satiromastix, 149–50, 197
Denmark (ambassador, 1580s), 60, 157
Dickens, Charles, 122
Dirty Harry (1971 film), 146
Donne, John, 20
Douglas, Michael (actor), 146
dramatis personae, 72
Drayton, Michael, 15, 19–21, 27, 30, 148–9, 170
Dromgoole, Dominic (director), 127–9, 131
Dryden, John, 35
Dublin, 36–7, 62
Duthie, George Ian, 39–40, 165

Eastwood, Clint (actor), 146
Edmondson, Paul, 103
Edmund Ironside, 165
Edward VI, King of England, 16, 108, 142

Index • 283

Edwards, Richard, 141–2
Egan, Gabriel, 56, 231
Einstein, Albert, 43
Eliot's Court Press. *See* stationers
Elizabeth I, Queen of England, 13, 18, 31–3, 90–2, 103, 114, 121–5, 143, 183–4, 195
Empire Strikes Back, The (1980 film), 146
England's Parnassus (1600), 20
Erne, Lukas, 12, 20, 24, 32, 38, 60, 94–9, 110, 157, 164–5, 170, 195, 220, 228, 238, 240
Essex, Earl of, 139, 185

Fair Em, 165
Fairfax, Edward, 138
Farmer, Alan B., 24
Ferrers, George, 142
Field, Richard. *See* stationers
First Part of the Contention. *See* Shakespeare: 2 Henry VI
Fleet Street, 14, 22
Fletcher, John, 97
forgery, 71, 74
Fortune (playhouse), 138
Frederick II, King of Denmark and Norway, 109, 157
Fuller, Ivan (director), 245

Gardner, Lyn, 128
Garnier, Robert, 20, 163
Garrick, David (actor), 35, 83
Gascoigne, George, 141
gender, 8–9, 46, 113–26, 158, 167, 173, 203, 205
Gentry, John (photographer), 125, 129–30
Globe (playhouse), 77, 138–9, 150, 248
Globe Theatre (Reconstruction), 127, 131
Goethe, Johann Wolfgang von, 210–12
Goldsmith, Oliver, 37
good quartos, 46, 85, 98, 101, 194
Graduate, The (1967 film), 146

Grammaticus, Saxo, 134, 161, 203
graphite pencils, 76–7
Greenblatt, Stephen, 41, 204
Greene, Robert, 18–21, 143, 148, 154, 159–60, 166, 170, 205, 220–1
Greg, W. W., 37–8, 76, 96, 164, 229
Guilpin, Edward, 19
Guinness, Peter (actor), 131, 134
Gunthio, Ambrose, 69–71, 73–4, 83, 107, 122–3, 234
Gurr, Andrew, 98–9, 154
Gutenberg, Johannes, 101

Hakluyt, Richard, 15
Hamlet, characters/roles
  Corambis(Polonius), 45–6, 62, 66, 70–2, 104, 107–8, 111–15, 124, 129, 169–70, 179, 220, 231
  Fortinbras, 8, 60, 62, 104, 106, 112, 162, 192–3, 199
  Gertrude (Gertrad), 8, 62, 70, 105, 117–27, 157, 199–200, 245
  Ghost, 46, 60, 82, 122, 131–2, 145–50, 157, 169, 192, 203–4, 251
  Gravedigger (clown), 57, 62, 104, 108, 157, 162, 175, 177, 179, 231, 254
  Hamlet (age), 1, 8, 10, 104–35, 168, 203, 209
  Horatio, 43, 58–62, 66–7, 87–8, 104, 107, 124, 131, 162, 172, 177, 188–90, 199, 204
  King (Claudius), 62, 66, 107, 117, 121–3, 134, 157, 191, 199
  Laertes (Leartes), 8, 64–9, 104, 111–13, 115, 117, 120, 126, 188–91, 194, 199
  Lucianus, 42, 44, 60–2, 93, 111–12, 151, 162, 174
  Marcellus, 42–5, 60–2, 93, 107–8, 111–12, 172, 232
  Montano (Reynaldo), 72, 112, 169–70
  Ophelia (Ofelia), 8, 46, 62, 65–7, 70, 104, 107–8, 110–20, 128, 162, 167, 171, 177–9, 199, 204

Hamlet, characters/roles—*Continued*
  Osric (Ostricke, Braggart Gentleman), 8, 62, 112, 189–90, 261
  Polonius. *See* Corambis (above)
  Prologue, 44
  Rosencrantz and Guildenstern (Rosencraft and Gilderstone), 11, 157, 254
  Voltemand (Voltemar), 42–5, 60–2, 70, 87, 93, 111–12, 151
Hamlet, costumes, props, stage directions
  armor, 204, 246
  beards, 107, 111, 160, 204, 243
  cloak (black), 145, 200–1
  costumes (teenage), 116, 118, 126–30
  grave/trapdoor (for leaping into), 104, 179
  hair (wig), 46, 111, 117
  lute, 46
  make-up (ghost), 145, 147
  nightgown, 46, 122, 246
  paper (letter), 64, 234
  skull (Yorick's), 106, 135, 175, 177
  songs, 57, 117, 177–8
  tables (notebook), 69, 78–9, 82
Hamlet, dates of composition
  Folio (1602), 181–207, 210
  Q1 (1588–89), 135–79, 209
  Q2 (1603–4), 182–96, 210
Hamlet, productions
  Hamlet (1882 London), 115
  Hamlet (1948 film), 134
  Hamlet (1968 Swedish), 130
  Hamlet (1985 Orange Tree), 130
  Hamlet (1992 Fort Worth), 131
  Hamlet (1999 Loyola), 131
  Hamlet (1999–2000 Red Shift), 131
  Hamlet (2004 Old Vic), 116–17, 121, 126, 129, 245
  Hamlet (2005, Blackfriars), 124
  Hamlet (2011 Shakespeare's Globe), 129, 258
  Hamlet (2012 Taffety Punk), 134

Young Hamlet (2011 Hoosier Bard), 116–21, 124–5, 129–30, 134, 234, 245
Hamlett, Katherine, 9, 167
Harrington, Sir John, 141–3
Harvey, Gabriel, 138–40, 144, 166, 182, 184, 249
Hathaway, Anne (Anne Shakespeare), 103
Hazlitt, William, 63, 133, 182
Helgerson, Richard, 15
Heminge, John (actor), 74
Henry VII, King of England, 113–14
Henry VIII, King of England, 113
Henslowe, Philip, 151–2
"ne," 152, 159
hexameter, 55, 160
Heywood, Thomas, 88–92
Hiliard, Nicholas, 77
Hirrel, Michael J., 98
Hoffman, Dustin (actor), 146
Holinshed, Raphael, 161
Holland, Peter, 102, 131
Honigmann, E. A. J., 144, 165, 205, 250
Hooker, Richard, 15
Hostmyer, Tracy (actor), 124
Howard, Henry, Earl of Surrey, 18
Huntington, Henry, 36

iambic pentameter, 48, 56, 70
intellectual property, 7, 14, 30, 33, 85, 196, 210
  See also piracy *and* copyright
interpolation, 46–7, 55–6, 65, 251
Irace, Kathleen O., 41–9, 54–8, 60, 88, 96, 115

Jack, A. A., 105, 242
Jackson, MacDonald P., 43, 229
Jaggard, William. *See* stationers
James I, King of England, 12, 78, 81, 103, 185
James, Henry, 57
Jenkins, Harold, 39, 48, 54–5, 167, 189, 197, 242

Johns, Adrian, 7, 33, 90
Johnson, Gerald D., 30
Johnson, Samuel, 70
Jolly, Margrethe, 99–100, 108–9
Jongh, Nicholas de, 126
Jonson, Ben, 19–20, 72, 144, 149–50, 170, 173, 195, 197–8, 205–7
  Bartholomew Fair, 144
  Every Man in his Humour, 72, 173, 205
  Every Man Out of his Humour, 20–1, 173, 198
Jowett, John, 40–1

Kean, Edmund (actor), 35
Kelly, Charles Adams, 56–7, 232
Kemble, Charles (actor), 35
Kemp, Will (actor), 17, 21–2, 156–8, 231
King's Men, 30, 32, 153, 194–6, 203
  See also Chamberlain's Men
Kirschbaum, Leo, 30
Knowles, Richard, 82
Kyd, Thomas, 19–21, 26, 144, 148, 155, 163–6, 168, 178–9, 205
  Cornelia, 20–1
  Householder's Philosophy, The, 164
  Spanish Tragedy, The, 26, 155, 163, 170, 178, 203
Kyle, Chris R., 80–1

Lamb, Charles, 63
Langland, William, 18
Leicester's Men, 154
Lesser, Zachary, 2, 18, 21, 24–5, 94–5, 216, 222
Ling, Nicholas. *See* stationers
Locrine, 165
Lodge, Thomas, 19–21, 144–52, 155, 159, 170, 221, 251
  Euphues Shadow, 19
  Glaucus and Scilla, 148
  Robert, Duke of Normandy, 19
  Rosalynde, 19
  Wit's Misery, 144–52, 155, 166, 182, 205

Lyly, John, 148–9, 170, 178, 205
Lyng, John, 16, 17, 217

MacLean, Sally-Beth, 156, 174
madness, 46, 70, 115–17, 128, 145, 156, 161, 178, 192, 199
Maguire, Laurie E., 38–41, 43, 46–7, 95–6, 229–30
Malone, Edmond, 35, 137–45, 148, 151, 153–4, 159–61, 163–6, 168–9, 182–4, 203
Manley, Lawrence, 156
Marcus, Leah, 38, 58, 102, 170
Marino, James J., 36, 45–6, 152
Markham, Gervase, 19
Marlowe, Christopher, 123, 144, 148, 155–6, 169, 173–4, 177–9, 205–6
  Edward II, 123
  Jew of Malta, 156, 223
  Tamburlaine, 155, 170, 174–6
marriage, 105–6, 113–14, 117, 122–3, 128, 134, 147, 157, 168, 178, 184
Mary I, Queen of England, 11, 178
Mary, Queen of Scots, 157–8
Master of the Revels, 90, 98, 151
May, Steven W., 142
McGuire, Joshua (actor), 127–9
McGuire, Philip, 103
McKerrow, Ronald B., 161, 163–5
McLeod, Randall, 38, 63
McMillin, Scott, 155–6, 174
Melnikoff, Kirk, 30–1, 103, 215, 222
memorial reconstruction, 8, 37–69, 73, 86, 92–6, 99, 108, 132, 138, 146, 151, 165, 170–2, 178, 182, 186, 189, 200
memory, 5–6, 9, 37–40, 44, 49, 55–7, 63–8, 72–3, 82, 87, 144–6, 163
Mendle, Michael, 74, 79
Menzer, Paul, 2, 38, 45–6, 231
Meres, Francis, 159, 182
Mickey Mouse, 130
Middleton, Christopher, 19
Middleton, Thomas, 6, 41, 176, 257
  Game at Chess, A, 59, 83, 87–8, 195

286 • Index

Miola, Robert S., 161–2
Mirren, Helen (actor), 134
Mirror for Magistrates, The, 18, 142
Mitchell, C. Ainsworth, 77
Mommsen, Tycho, 37, 44
monarchy, 12, 31, 81, 158, 169, 185
Montaigne, Michel de, 19
Montgomery, William, 41
Moorhead, Fiona (photographer), 127
Morgan, Jude, 134
Moseley, Humphrey. *See* stationers
Muir, Alastair (Photographer), 117–18, 126
Muller, Michael, 131
Munday, Anthony, 18, 20–1, 141–2, 148, 165–6, 168, 170
Murphy, Andrew, 2

Nashe, Thomas, 18–21, 139–40, 144, 148–9, 154–5, 159–66, 172, 178–9, 205–6, 210
Nero, Emperor of Rome, 111, 162
New Bibliography, 37
New Cambridge Shakespeare, 40, 42
  See also Philips, Edward
New Historicism, 41, 202, 220
New Jersey Shakespeare Festival, 116
Newington Butts (playhouse), 151–2
Norton Shakespeare, 41
Norwich, 15–16, 19, 22, 108, 219–20
note-taking, 69–100, 108–9, 132, 170, 200, 231
Nunn, Trevor (director), 115–18, 126, 245

Old Vic (theatre), 11, 115–16, 129
Olivier, Laurence (actor), 134
Orange Tree (theatre), 130
Ovid, 20, 148
Oxford English Dictionary, 77–8, 236
Oxford Shakespeare, 3, 40–1, 76, 241
Oxford University, 3, 69

Palfrey, Simon, 44
Parliament, 74, 77, 79–82, 86

Pasfield, Zachariah, 31, 150
Pasqualigo, Luigi, 142
Pavier, Thomas. *See* stationers
Payne & Foss (publishing firm), 36
Peele, George, 19–21, 148
Pembroke's Men, 154, 156
pencil, 76–8, 236
Perkins, William, 84
Petersen, Lene B., 56–8
Philip II, King of Spain, 26
Philips, Edward, 82. *See also* New Cambridge Shakespeare
piracy, 7–8, 28–30, 33, 38, 40–3, 49, 56, 59–61, 66–9, 73–7, 80–1, 84, 88–92, 99–104, 109, 138, 170, 181, 186, 194, 197, 209
plague, 19, 22–4, 26, 32
Playfere, Thomas, 84
playhouses, 81–2, 153, 184
Plutarch, 161, 182, 206
Poel, William (director), 115
Pollard, Alfred W., 29, 37–8, 59, 98
Ponsonby, William. *See* stationers
Pope, Alexander, 35
Pope, Thomas (actor), 157
Pound, John, 17
Prince of Jutland, The (1993 film), 134
Printing. *See also* stationers
  binding, 12, 36, 78
  broadsheets, 23, 26
  compositors, 5, 49, 52, 54–5, 86–8, 188, 194, 232, 243, 245, 251, 254, 259
  duodecimo format, 233
  folio format, 12, 14, 22, 28, 217
  pamphlets, 17, 23, 36, 149, 159–60, 164–5
  paper, 9, 12, 25, 27–8, 36, 75–6, 78–9, 165, 215, 228, 253
  parchment, 217
  playbills, 5, 24, 31, 150, 227–8
  publisher, 216
  quarto format, 49
  quarto playbooks, 12, 14, 27, 36
  quotation marks, 37, 41, 94–5

tablebooks, 76–80
title pages, 12–14, 17, 20, 23–9, 33, 36, 85, 90–1, 100–1, 152–4, 158, 195–6, 215, 224, 226, 229, 238, 252–3
typesetting errors, 91
Privy Council, 153, 184
Pullin, Nicholas (actor), 131
Puttenham, George, 141–2

Queen's Men, 155, 174–9

Ramel, Henrik, 157
rape, 116
reconstruction. *See* memorial reconstruction
Records of Early English Drama (REED), 153
Reported text, reporters. *See* note-taking
revenge, 61, 64–7, 124–7, 132–4, 145–51, 157, 161, 174, 177–8, 204, 209
revision, 8, 45, 57, 66–7, 70–4, 92, 97–9, 100, 109, 112, 123, 132, 135, 150–1, 182, 185, 193, 198, 203, 209–10
revisionism (textual), 41–2
Rich, Sir Nathaniel, 77
Richard Duke of York. *See* Shakespeare: *3 Henry VI*
Riggs, David, 163
Riverside Shakespeare, 49, 231
Roberts, James. *See* stationers
Rogers, Ginger (actor), 49
Rose (playhouse), 154
Rowe, Nicholas, 35
Rowlands, Samuel, 149
Royal Academy of Dramatic Art, 126
RSC (Royal Shakespeare Company), 3, 245

Sackville, Thomas - 1st Earl of Dorset, 141, 142
Sams, Eric, 40, 58, 165
Schlegel, A. W. von, 133–4
Schoen, Eric (actor), 124
Scott, Robert. *See* stationers
Scott, Steve (director), 131
Scull, Stephen (actor), 129
Semler, Liam E., 4
Seneca, 132, 159–64, 206
sermons, 17, 20, 77–86, 89–92
sexuality, 117, 121–2, 191–2
Shakespeare Survey, 69
Shakespeare, Hamlet (Hamnet), 167–8, 182, 203, 257
Shakespeare, John, 9, 198–205
Shakespeare, William
 1 Henry IV, 13, 35, 65, 88
 2 Henry IV, 24, 88
 2 Henry VI, 41, 70
 3 Henry VI, 35, 41, 70, 123
 Antony and Cleopatra, 21, 207
 As You Like It, 19, 156, 182
 attribution to, 5, 29, 42, 70, 85, 104, 135, 140
 Cardenio/Double Falsehood, 237
 collaboration, 140
 Comedy of Errors, 133
 Coriolanus, 21, 65, 207, 242
 Edward III, 229
 Hamlet. *See* main entries
 Henry V, 24, 29, 41, 85, 95–7, 105, 170, 182, 185
 Henry VI (1, 2 & 3), 140, 159
 King John, 61
 King Lear, 3, 13, 21, 40–1, 97, 102, 105, 183, 207
 Love's Labour's Lost, 13, 35, 78, 163, 175, 238
 Loves Labour's Won, 35
 Macbeth, 21, 105, 207
 Measure for Measure, 105, 141, 183
 Merchant of Venice, 24
 Merry Wives of Windsor, 24, 29, 37, 41, 85
 Midsummer Night's Dream, 24, 163, 170, 175
 Much Ado About Nothing, 24, 65, 113, 170, 182

Shakespeare, William—*Continued*
  Othello, 21, 97, 102, 105, 183–4, 207
  Passionate Pilgrim, 35
  Pericles, 29, 215
  "Phoenix and the Turtle, The," 102
  Rape of Lucrece, 13, 20, 88, 90,
    138–9, 168, 185
  Richard II, 13, 88, 170
  Richard III, 13, 41, 85, 88, 143, 156,
    170, 174
  Romeo and Juliet, 29, 41, 85–6,
    95–8, 114, 170, 206
  Sonnets, 13, 67, 103, 178, 222
  Taming of the Shrew, 74, 113, 159,
    163, 175
  Tempest, 133, 163, 175
  Titus Andronicus, 35, 71, 140, 144,
    152, 161, 182
  Troilus and Cressida, 13, 65, 102,
    183–4, 197–8, 205–7
  Twelfth Night, 102, 105, 156, 172
  Two Noble Kinsmen, 163
  Venus and Adonis, 13, 20, 35, 138–41,
    148, 168, 185
Shatner, William (actor), 147
shorthand, 71–5, 79–83, 86–92, 170,
  238
Shrimpton, Nicholas, 130
Sidney, Sir Philip, 19–20, 141, 170,
  177
Simmes, Valentine. *See* stationers
Sjögren, Gunnar, 130
Smethwicke, John. *See* stationers
Smith, Henry, 20, 84–6, 238
Souza, Maria (actor), 116–17
Spanish Armada, 90
speech prefixes, 45, 242
Spencer, Charles, 127–8
Spenser, Edmund, 15, 20, 148
St. Dunstan's in the West, 14–15
St. Paul's (playhouse), 158
St. Paul's Cathedral, 12–14, 22, 163
stage directions, 1, 21, 44–6, 64, 67,
  115, 194, 242, 246
Stallybrass, Peter, 21, 25, 77, 94–5

Star Trek: The Voyage Home (1987
  film), 146
stationers, 4, 11, 14–17, 22–3, 26–7,
  30–3, 38, 59, 73, 84–6, 90–1,
  141, 168, 181, 196, 207
  Allott, Robert, 20
  Blount, Edward, 19, 27
  Burby, Cuthbert, 85
  Busby, John, 21, 219, 224
  Butter, Nathaniel, 89–92
  Bynneman, Henry, 16, 18, 22, 25, 218
  Charlewood, John, 227
  Danter, John, 85
  Eliot's Court Press, 22
  Field, Richard, 168
  Jaggard, William, 12
  Ling, Nicholas, 8, 14–36, 44–5, 57,
    71, 84–8, 91–2, 99–102, 137,
    142–3, 146–8, 153–9, 162, 170,
    182–4, 194–6, 205, 207, 209,
    211–12, 218–20, 222, 238
  Moseby, Humphrey, 97–8
  Pavier, Thomas, 29
  Ponsonby, William, 19
  Roberts, James, 14, 25, 29–33, 88,
    150, 183, 194–5, 207, 228
  Scott, Robert, 16
  Simmes, Valentine, 14, 25, 31–3, 71,
    87–8
  Smethwicke, John, 14–15, 27–30, 210
  Sutton, Henry, 223
  Trundle, John, 14, 23–5, 29–33, 36,
    84, 223
  Vautrollier, Thomas, 168
  Ward, Robert, 218
  Wise, Andrew, 221
Stationers' Company, 11–12, 15–18,
  27–9, 91
Stationers' Register, 19, 29–33, 90–1,
  150, 159, 183, 197, 207
Steevens, George, 35
Stern, Tiffany, 30, 44, 68–100
Stern, Victoria F., 139
Stoppard, Tom, 11
Strange's Men, 154–6

Stratford-upon-Avon, 142, 167–8, 176, 198, 202–3
Stuart, Henry (1st Duke of Albany), 157
Stubbs, Imogen (actor), 117–18
Studley, John, 162
Swan (playhouse), 149
Syme, Holger, 152

Tarlton, Richard (actor), 18, 174–5, 259
Tarzan, the Ape Man (1932 film), 146
Tasso, Torquato, 138, 164
Taylor, Gary, 40–1, 43, 104, 138, 159, 171, 173–4, 182, 184–6, 189–90, 194, 203–4, 214, 229
Taylor, Neil, 38–9, 43, 46, 49, 55, 115, 130, 184
Taylor, Paul, 127
Theobald, Lewis, 35, 62, 190
Thomas Lord Cromwell (1602), 24
Thompson, Ann, 38–9, 43, 46, 49, 55, 115, 130, 184
Trinity College (Dublin), 37
Trundle, John. *See* stationers

Urbino, Duke of, 242
Ur-Hamlet (1589), 145, 149, 165, 210, 251, 255
Urkowitz, Steven, 38, 103

Vadnais, Matthew, 45, 46, 231
van Dam, Bastiaan Adriaan Pieter, 65–8

Van Es, Bart, 105, 161
Vaux, Lord Thomas, 57
Vickers, Brian, 40, 170, 229
virginity, 113–14, 123

Wall Street (1987 film), 146
Walsh, Brian, 2
Walsingham, Sir Francis, 143, 169, 250
Warren, Michael, 40
Watson, Thomas, 148
Webbe, William, 140–1
Webster, John, 26, 149, 150
Weever, John, 19
Weiner, Albert B., 59
Weismuller, Johnny (actor), 146
Wells, Stanley, 40–1, 102
Werstine, Paul, 21, 38, 59, 73, 95–8, 189–90, 194
Whetstone, George, 141
Whishaw, Ben (actor), 117–18, 126–9, 134
Whittaker, Samantha (actor), 116
Wiggins, Martin, 250–1, 259
Wilkes, Robert (actor), 62
Wilson, F. P., 30, 144
Worshipful Company of Stationers. *See* Stationers' Company
Wright, George T., 48

Zepheria (1594), 19